2006 | LITTLE GREEN DATA BOOK

W0082796

THE WORLD BANK

ISBN 0-8213-6476-6

The Little Green Data Book 2006 is a product of the Development Economics
Data Group and the Environment Department of the World Bank.

Editing, design, and layout by Communications Development Incorporated,
Washington, D.C.
Cover design by Grundy & Northedge, London, UK.

Contents

Acknowledgments

The Little Green Data Book 2006 is based on World Development Indicators 2006 and its accompanying CD-ROM. Defining, gathering, and disseminating international statistics is a collective effort of many people and organizations. The indicators in World Development Indicators are the fruit of decades of work at many levels, from the field workers who administer censuses and household surveys to the committees and working parties of the national and international statistical agencies that develop the nomenclature, classifications, and standards fundamental to the international statistical system. Nongovernmental organizations have also made important contributions. We are indebted to the network of World Development Indicators' partners, as detailed in World Development Indicators 2006. The financial assistance of the Government of Sweden is also gratefully acknowledged.

The Little Green Data Book is the result of close collaboration between the staff of the Environment Department and the Development Economics Data Group. Mehdi Akhlaghi, Richard Fix, Kirk Hamilton, Beat Hintermann, Gonca Okur, M. H. Saeed Ordoubadi, Suzette Pedroso-Galinato, Giovanni Ruta, and Alexandra Sears contributed to its preparation. Communications Development Incorporated provided design, editing, and layout, led by Meta de Coquereaumont with the assistance of Christopher Trott. The production team also included Jodi Baxter, Brendon Boyle, and Michael Diavolikis. Staff from External Affairs oversaw publication and dissemination of the book.

foreword

The 2006 edition of *The Little Green Data Book* coincides with a wave of renewed attention to the energy sector coming out of the Group of Eight Summit at Gleneagles, Scotland. While energy demand is rising along with GDP in the developing world, many poor countries still lack the basic infrastructure that sustains everyday needs. Electric power consumption per capita is 25 times lower in low-income countries than in high-income countries. The poorest people in the world depend heavily on natural resources to meet their energy needs. In Sub-Saharan Africa nearly 60 percent of the energy used comes from combustible renewables and waste.

Development and poverty alleviation—the World Bank's mission—call for a long-term vision. Besides meeting increasing energy needs through clean means, important steps toward poverty reduction include enhancing environmental quality, improving natural resources management, and maintaining global ecosystems. Better environmental management can improve people's livelihoods, health, and security today and in the future.

To achieve these lasting results, we need to start from a sound base of information that helps us set priorities and measure progress toward environmental sustainability goals. *The Little Green Data Book* is a step in this direction, with key indicators of the environment and its relationship to people for more than 200 countries. This year's edition includes recently updated data on carbon dioxide emissions and on particulate matter concentrations in urban areas, as well as the new GEF benefits index for biodiversity. While there are gaps and shortcomings in the data, we hope that this book will inspire decisionmakers at all levels to use this information and to seek to fill the gaps for their own countries.

The Little Green Data Book represents a succinct collection of information from *World Development Indicators 2006* and its accompanying CD-ROM. It is a collaboration between the Development Data Group and the Environment Department of the World Bank. We welcome your suggestions for how to improve future editions and make them more useful.

Shaida Badiee
Director,
Development Data Group

James Warren Evans
Director,
Environment Department

03/12007

Data notes

The data in this book are for the most recent year available; for details, see the glossary. Regional aggregates include data for low- and middle-income economies only. Aggregates for regions and income groups are shown only if data are available for 66 percent of the economies in that group.

Symbols used:

..	indicates that data are not available or that aggregates cannot be calculated because of missing data.
0 or 0.0	indicates zero or less than half the unit shown.
$	indicates current U.S. dollars.

Data are shown for economies with populations greater than 30,000 or for smaller economies if they are members of the World Bank. The word *country* (used interchangeably with *economy*) does not imply political independence or official recognition by the World Bank but refers to any economy for which the authorities report separate social or economic statistics.

In keeping with *World Development Indicators 2006*, this edition of *The Little Green Data Book* uses terminology in line with the 1993 System of National Accounts. In particular, gross national product (GNP) is replaced by gross national income (GNI).

The selection of indicators in these pages includes some that are being used to monitor progress toward the Millennium Development Goals. For more information about the eight goals—halving poverty and increasing well-being by 2015—please visit our Web site www.developmentgoals.org or see the other books in the *World Development Indicators 2006* series.

Regional tables

The country composition of regions is based on the World Bank's analytical regions and may differ from common geographic usage.

East Asia and Pacific

American Samoa, Cambodia, China, Fiji, Indonesia, Kiribati, Korea, Dem. Rep., Lao PDR, Malaysia, Marshall Islands, Micronesia, Fed. Sts., Mongolia, Myanmar, Northern Mariana Islands, Palau, Papua New Guinea, Philippines, Samoa, Solomon Islands, Thailand, Timor-Leste, Tonga, Vanuatu, Vietnam

Europe and Central Asia

Albania, Armenia, Azerbaijan, Belarus, Bosnia and Herzegovina, Bulgaria, Croatia, Czech Republic, Estonia, Georgia, Hungary, Kazakhstan, Kyrgyz Republic, Latvia, Lithuania, Macedonia, FYR, Moldova, Poland, Romania, Russian Federation, Serbia and Montenegro, Slovak Republic, Tajikistan, Turkey, Turkmenistan, Ukraine, Uzbekistan

Latin America and Caribbean

Antigua and Barbuda, Argentina, Barbados, Belize, Bolivia, Brazil, Chile, Colombia, Costa Rica, Cuba, Dominica, Dominican Republic, Ecuador, El Salvador, Grenada, Guatemala, Guyana, Haiti, Honduras, Jamaica, Mexico, Nicaragua, Panama, Paraguay, Peru, St. Kitts and Nevis, St. Lucia, St. Vincent and the Grenadines, Suriname, Trinidad and Tobago, Uruguay, Venezuela, RB

Middle East and North Africa

Algeria, Djibouti, Egypt, Arab Rep., Iran, Islamic Rep., Iraq, Jordan, Lebanon, Libya, Morocco, Oman, Saudi Arabia, Syrian Arab Republic, Tunisia, West Bank and Gaza, Yemen, Rep.

South Asia

Afghanistan, Bangladesh, Bhutan, India, Maldives, Nepal, Pakistan, Sri Lanka

Sub-Saharan Africa

Angola, Benin, Botswana, Burkina Faso, Burundi, Cameroon, Cape Verde, Central African Republic, Chad, Comoros, Congo, Dem. Rep., Congo, Rep., Côte d'Ivoire, Equatorial Guinea, Eritrea, Ethiopia, Gabon, The Gambia, Ghana, Guinea, Guinea-Bissau, Kenya, Lesotho, Liberia, Madagascar, Malawi, Mali, Mauritania, Mauritius, Mayotte Mozambique, Namibia, Niger, Nigeria, Rwanda, São Tomé and Principe, Senegal, Seychelles, Sierra Leone, Somalia, South Africa, Sudan, Swaziland, Tanzania, Togo, Uganda, Zambia, Zimbabwe

World

Population (millions)	6,365.0
Urban population (% of total)	48.8
GDP ($ billions)	41,290.4
GNI per capita, *World Bank Atlas* method ($)	6,329

Agriculture

Land area (1,000 sq. km)	129,663
Agricultural land (% of land area)	38
Irrigated land (% of cropland)	18.0
Fertilizer consumption (100 grams/ha of arable land)	1,009
Population density, rural (people/sq. km of arable land)	492

Forests and biodiversity

Forest area (% of land area)	30.5
Annual deforestation (% change, 1990–2005)	0.1
Nationally protected areas (% of total land area)	10.7
Mammal species, total known	
Mammal species, threatened	
Bird species, total known	
Bird species, threatened	
GEF benefits index for biodiversity (0–100)	

Energy

GDP per unit of energy use (2000 PPP $/kg oil equiv)	4.7
Energy use per capita (kg oil equiv)	1,734
Energy from combustible renewables & waste (% of tot.)	10.4
Energy imports, net (% of energy use)	−1
Electric power consumption per capita (kWh)	2,456
Electricity generated by coal (% of total)	40.1

Emissions and pollution

CO_2 emissions per unit of GDP (kg/2000 PPP $ of GDP)	0.5
CO_2 emissions per capita (metric tons)	3.9
Particulate matter (urban-pop.-weighted avg., µg/cu. m)	60
Passenger cars (per 1,000 people)	100

Water and sanitation

Internal freshwater resources per capita (cu. m)	6,872
Freshwater withdrawal	
Total (% of internal resources)	9.0
Agriculture (% of total freshwater withdrawal)	70
Access to improved water source (% of total population)	82
Rural (% of rural population)	71
Urban (% of urban population)	94
Access to improved sanitation (% of total population)	54
Rural (% of rural population)	35
Urban (% of urban population)	79

Environment and health

ARI prevalence (% of children under age 5)	
Diarrhea prevalence (% of children under age 5)	
Under-five mortality rate (per 1,000 live births)	79

National accounting aggregates, 2004

Gross savings (% of GNI)	20.8
Consumption of fixed capital (% of GNI)	12.7
Education expenditure (% of GNI)	4.4
Energy depletion (% of GNI)	2.8
Mineral depletion (% of GNI)	0.1
Net forest depletion (% of GNI)	0.0
CO_2 damage (% of GNI)	0.4
Particulate emission damage (% of GNI)	0.5
Adjusted net savings (% of GNI)	8.7

East Asia & Pacific

Population (millions)	1,869.5
Urban population (% of total)	40.6
GDP ($ billions)	2,650.9
GNI per capita, *World Bank Atlas* method ($)	1,416

Agriculture
Land area (1,000 sq. km)	15,885
Agricultural land (% of land area)	51
Irrigated land (% of cropland)	..
Fertilizer consumption (100 grams/ha of arable land)	2,296
Population density, rural (people/sq. km of arable land)	559

Forests and biodiversity
Forest area (% of land area)	28.4
Annual deforestation (% change, 1990–2005)	–0.2
Nationally protected areas (% of total land area)	..
Mammal species, total known	
Mammal species, threatened	
Bird species, total known	
Bird species, threatened	
GEF benefits index for biodiversity (0–100)	

Energy
GDP per unit of energy use (2000 PPP $/kg oil equiv)	4.6
Energy use per capita (kg oil equiv)	1,007
Energy from combustible renewables & waste (% of tot.)	17.7
Energy imports, net (% of energy use)	–2
Electric power consumption per capita (kWh)	1,184
Electricity generated by coal (% of total)	69.4

Emissions and pollution
CO_2 emissions per unit of GDP (kg/2000 PPP $ of GDP)	0.5
CO_2 emissions per capita (metric tons)	2.4
Particulate matter (urban-pop.-weighted avg., µg/cu. m)	80
Passenger cars (per 1,000 people)	12

Water and sanitation
Internal freshwater resources per capita (cu. m)	5,062
Freshwater withdrawal	
Total (% of internal resources)	10.2
Agriculture (% of total freshwater withdrawal)	74
Access to improved water source (% of total population)	78
Rural (% of rural population)	69
Urban (% of urban population)	92
Access to improved sanitation (% of total population)	49
Rural (% of rural population)	35
Urban (% of urban population)	72

Environment and health
ARI prevalence (% of children under age 5)	
Diarrhea prevalence (% of children under age 5)	
Under-five mortality rate (per 1,000 live births)	37

National accounting aggregates, 2004
Gross savings (% of GNI)	39.1
Consumption of fixed capital (% of GNI)	10.5
Education expenditure (% of GNI)	2.3
Energy depletion (% of GNI)	4.1
Mineral depletion (% of GNI)	0.4
Net forest depletion (% of GNI)	0.0
CO_2 damage (% of GNI)	1.2
Particulate emission damage (% of GNI)	1.2
Adjusted net savings (% of GNI)	23.9

Europe & Central Asia

Population (millions)	472.5
Urban population (% of total)	63.6
GDP ($ billions)	1,769.7
GNI per capita, *World Bank Atlas* method ($)	3,295

Agriculture

Land area (1,000 sq. km)	23,371
Agricultural land (% of land area)	29
Irrigated land (% of cropland)	11.1
Fertilizer consumption (100 grams/ha of arable land)	347
Population density, rural (people/sq. km of arable land)	126

Forests and biodiversity

Forest area (% of land area)	38.3
Annual deforestation (% change, 1990–2005)	0.0
Nationally protected areas (% of total land area)	6.9
Mammal species, total known	
Mammal species, threatened	
Bird species, total known	
Bird species, threatened	
GEF benefits index for biodiversity (0–100)	

Energy

GDP per unit of energy use (2000 PPP $/kg oil equiv)	2.7
Energy use per capita (kg oil equiv)	2,794
Energy from combustible renewables & waste (% of tot.)	2.4
Energy imports, net (% of energy use)	−26
Electric power consumption per capita (kWh)	3,531
Electricity generated by coal (% of total)	29.8

Emissions and pollution

CO_2 emissions per unit of GDP (kg/2000 PPP $ of GDP)	1.0
CO_2 emissions per capita (metric tons)	6.7
Particulate matter (urban-pop.-weighted avg., µg/cu. m)	35
Passenger cars (per 1,000 people)	142

Water and sanitation

Internal freshwater resources per capita (cu. m)	11,123
Freshwater withdrawal	
Total (% of internal resources)	7.5
Agriculture (% of total freshwater withdrawal)	59
Access to improved water source (% of total population)	91
Rural (% of rural population)	80
Urban (% of urban population)	98
Access to improved sanitation (% of total population)	82
Rural (% of rural population)	63
Urban (% of urban population)	93

Environment and health

ARI prevalence (% of children under age 5)	
Diarrhea prevalence (% of children under age 5)	
Under-five mortality rate (per 1,000 live births)	34

National accounting aggregates, 2004

Gross savings (% of GNI)	23.4
Consumption of fixed capital (% of GNI)	10.7
Education expenditure (% of GNI)	4.1
Energy depletion (% of GNI)	12.0
Mineral depletion (% of GNI)	0.3
Net forest depletion (% of GNI)	0.0
CO_2 damage (% of GNI)	1.4
Particulate emission damage (% of GNI)	0.7
Adjusted net savings (% of GNI)	2.3

Latin America & Caribbean

Population (millions)	545.9
Urban population (% of total)	77.1
GDP ($ billions)	2,022.0
GNI per capita, *World Bank Atlas* method ($)	3,576

Agriculture

Land area (1,000 sq. km)	20,057
Agricultural land (% of land area)	36
Irrigated land (% of cropland)	11.4
Fertilizer consumption (100 grams/ha of arable land)	923
Population density, rural (people/sq. km of arable land)	212

Forests and biodiversity

Forest area (% of land area)	45.6
Annual deforestation (% change, 1990–2005)	0.4
Nationally protected areas (% of total land area)	11.1
Mammal species, total known	
Mammal species, threatened	
Bird species, total known	
Bird species, threatened	
GEF benefits index for biodiversity (0–100)	

Energy

GDP per unit of energy use (2000 PPP $/kg oil equiv)	6.2
Energy use per capita (kg oil equiv)	1,148
Energy from combustible renewables & waste (% of tot.)	15.0
Energy imports, net (% of energy use)	−40
Electric power consumption per capita (kWh)	1,615
Electricity generated by coal (% of total)	5.4

Emissions and pollution

CO_2 emissions per unit of GDP (kg/2000 PPP $ of GDP)	0.3
CO_2 emissions per capita (metric tons)	2.4
Particulate matter (urban-pop.-weighted avg., µg/cu. m)	43
Passenger cars (per 1,000 people)	108

Water and sanitation

Internal freshwater resources per capita (cu. m)	24,619
Freshwater withdrawal	
Total (% of internal resources)	2.0
Agriculture (% of total freshwater withdrawal)	71
Access to improved water source (% of total population)	89
Rural (% of rural population)	69
Urban (% of urban population)	96
Access to improved sanitation (% of total population)	75
Rural (% of rural population)	44
Urban (% of urban population)	84

Environment and health

ARI prevalence (% of children under age 5)	
Diarrhea prevalence (% of children under age 5)	
Under-five mortality rate (per 1,000 live births)	31

National accounting aggregates, 2004

Gross savings (% of GNI)	22.7
Consumption of fixed capital (% of GNI)	12.1
Education expenditure (% of GNI)	4.4
Energy depletion (% of GNI)	7.2
Mineral depletion (% of GNI)	1.1
Net forest depletion (% of GNI)	0.0
CO_2 damage (% of GNI)	0.5
Particulate emission damage (% of GNI)	0.6
Adjusted net savings (% of GNI)	5.6

Middle East & North Africa

Population (millions)	300.3
Urban population (% of total)	56.3
GDP ($ billions)	547.5
GNI per capita, *World Bank Atlas* method ($)	1,972

Agriculture	
Land area (1,000 sq. km)	8,955
Agricultural land (% of land area)	23
Irrigated land (% of cropland)	32.5
Fertilizer consumption (100 grams/ha of arable land)	842
Population density, rural (people/sq. km of arable land)	670

Forests and biodiversity	
Forest area (% of land area)	2.4
Annual deforestation (% change, 1990–2005)	–0.5
Nationally protected areas (% of total land area)	4.2
Mammal species, total known	
Mammal species, threatened	
Bird species, total known	
Bird species, threatened	
GEF benefits index for biodiversity (0–100)	

Energy	
GDP per unit of energy use (2000 PPP $/kg oil equiv)	4.2
Energy use per capita (kg oil equiv)	1,144
Energy from combustible renewables & waste (% of tot.)	1.3
Energy imports, net (% of energy use)	–129
Electric power consumption per capita (kWh)	1,212
Electricity generated by coal (% of total)	3.0

Emissions and pollution	
CO_2 emissions per unit of GDP (kg/2000 PPP $ of GDP)	0.7
CO_2 emissions per capita (metric tons)	3.2
Particulate matter (urban-pop.-weighted avg., µg/cu. m)	90
Passenger cars (per 1,000 people)	..

Water and sanitation	
Internal freshwater resources per capita (cu. m)	761
Freshwater withdrawal	
Total (% of internal resources)	105.0
Agriculture (% of total freshwater withdrawal)	89
Access to improved water source (% of total population)	88
Rural (% of rural population)	79
Urban (% of urban population)	95
Access to improved sanitation (% of total population)	75
Rural (% of rural population)	56
Urban (% of urban population)	89

Environment and health	
ARI prevalence (% of children under age 5)	
Diarrhea prevalence (% of children under age 5)	
Under-five mortality rate (per 1,000 live births)	55

National accounting aggregates, 2004	
Gross savings (% of GNI)	30.0
Consumption of fixed capital (% of GNI)	11.2
Education expenditure (% of GNI)	4.5
Energy depletion (% of GNI)	27.3
Mineral depletion (% of GNI)	0.1
Net forest depletion (% of GNI)	0.1
CO_2 damage (% of GNI)	1.2
Particulate emission damage (% of GNI)	0.9
Adjusted net savings (% of GNI)	–6.2

South Asia

Population (millions)	1,446.8
Urban population (% of total)	28.3
GDP ($ billions)	880.2
GNI per capita, *World Bank Atlas* method ($)	594

Agriculture

Land area (1,000 sq. km)	4,781
Agricultural land (% of land area)	54
Irrigated land (% of cropland)	39.6
Fertilizer consumption (100 grams/ha of arable land)	1,040
Population density, rural (people/sq. km of arable land)	586

Forests and biodiversity

Forest area (% of land area)	16.8
Annual deforestation (% change, 1990–2005)	−0.2
Nationally protected areas (% of total land area)	4.8
Mammal species, total known	
Mammal species, threatened	
Bird species, total known	
Bird species, threatened	
GEF benefits index for biodiversity (0–100)	

Energy

GDP per unit of energy use (2000 PPP $/kg oil equiv)	5.3
Energy use per capita (kg oil equiv)	474
Energy from combustible renewables & waste (% of tot.)	38.8
Energy imports, net (% of energy use)	19
Electric power consumption per capita (kWh)	394
Electricity generated by coal (% of total)	58.2

Emissions and pollution

CO_2 emissions per unit of GDP (kg/2000 PPP $ of GDP)	0.4
CO_2 emissions per capita (metric tons)	1.0
Particulate matter (urban-pop.-weighted avg., μg/cu. m)	99
Passenger cars (per 1,000 people)	6

Water and sanitation

Internal freshwater resources per capita (cu. m)	1,255
Freshwater withdrawal	
Total (% of internal resources)	51.8
Agriculture (% of total freshwater withdrawal)	90
Access to improved water source (% of total population)	84
Rural (% of rural population)	80
Urban (% of urban population)	94
Access to improved sanitation (% of total population)	35
Rural (% of rural population)	23
Urban (% of urban population)	64

Environment and health

ARI prevalence (% of children under age 5)	
Diarrhea prevalence (% of children under age 5)	
Under-five mortality rate (per 1,000 live births)	92

National accounting aggregates, 2004

Gross savings (% of GNI)	23.6
Consumption of fixed capital (% of GNI)	9.1
Education expenditure (% of GNI)	3.6
Energy depletion (% of GNI)	2.7
Mineral depletion (% of GNI)	0.3
Net forest depletion (% of GNI)	0.7
CO_2 damage (% of GNI)	1.2
Particulate emission damage (% of GNI)	0.8
Adjusted net savings (% of GNI)	12.4

Sub-Saharan Africa

Population (millions)	725.8
Urban population (% of total)	36.4
GDP ($ billions)	523.3
GNI per capita, *World Bank Atlas* method ($)	601

Agriculture
Land area (1,000 sq. km)	23,596
Agricultural land (% of land area)	44
Irrigated land (% of cropland)	3.6
Fertilizer consumption (100 grams/ha of arable land)	136
Population density, rural (people/sq. km of arable land)	355

Forests and biodiversity
Forest area (% of land area)	26.5
Annual deforestation (% change, 1990–2005)	0.6
Nationally protected areas (% of total land area)	8.7
Mammal species, total known	
Mammal species, threatened	
Bird species, total known	
Bird species, threatened	
GEF benefits index for biodiversity (0–100)	

Energy
GDP per unit of energy use (2000 PPP $/kg oil equiv)	2.8
Energy use per capita (kg oil equiv)	681
Energy from combustible renewables & waste (% of tot.)	57.4
Energy imports, net (% of energy use)	−59
Electric power consumption per capita (kWh)	513
Electricity generated by coal (% of total)	68.0

Emissions and pollution
CO_2 emissions per unit of GDP (kg/2000 PPP $ of GDP)	0.4
CO_2 emissions per capita (metric tons)	0.7
Particulate matter (urban-pop.-weighted avg., µg/cu. m)	73
Passenger cars (per 1,000 people)	..

Water and sanitation
Internal freshwater resources per capita (cu. m)	5,353
Freshwater withdrawal	
Total (% of internal resources)	3.1
Agriculture (% of total freshwater withdrawal)	87
Access to improved water source (% of total population)	58
Rural (% of rural population)	45
Urban (% of urban population)	82
Access to improved sanitation (% of total population)	36
Rural (% of rural population)	26
Urban (% of urban population)	55

Environment and health
ARI prevalence (% of children under age 5)	
Diarrhea prevalence (% of children under age 5)	
Under-five mortality rate (per 1,000 live births)	168

National accounting aggregates, 2004
Gross savings (% of GNI)	17.1
Consumption of fixed capital (% of GNI)	10.9
Education expenditure (% of GNI)	3.9
Energy depletion (% of GNI)	9.8
Mineral depletion (% of GNI)	0.4
Net forest depletion (% of GNI)	0.6
CO_2 damage (% of GNI)	0.7
Particulate emission damage (% of GNI)	0.5
Adjusted net savings (% of GNI)	−1.9

Income group tables

For operational and analytical purposes the World Bank's main criterion for classifying economies is gross national income (GNI) per capita. Every economy is classified as low income, middle income (subdivided into lower middle and upper middle), or high income. Low-and middle-income economies are sometimes referred to as developing economies. The use of the term is convenient; it is not intended to imply that all economies in the group are experiencing similar development or that other economies have reached a preferred or final stage of development. Classification by income does not necessarily reflect development status.

Low-income economies are those with a GNI per capita of $825 or less in 2004.

Middle-income economies are those with a GNI per capita of more than $825 but less than $10,066. **Lower-middle-income** and **upper-middle-income** economies are separated at a GNI per capita of $3,255.

High-income economies are those with a GNI per capita of $10,066 or more.

The 12 participating member countries of the **European Monetary Union (EMU)** are Austria, Belgium, Finland, France, Germany, Greece, Ireland, Italy, Luxembourg, Netherlands, Portugal, and Spain.

Low income

Population (millions)	2,343.0
Urban population (% of total)	30.6
GDP ($ billions)	1,239.2
GNI per capita, *World Bank Atlas* method ($)	507

Agriculture

Land area (1,000 sq. km)	29,192
Agricultural land (% of land area)	45
Irrigated land (% of cropland)	23.9
Fertilizer consumption (100 grams/ha of arable land)	646
Population density, rural (people/sq. km of arable land)	524

Forests and biodiversity

Forest area (% of land area)	24.8
Annual deforestation (% change, 1990–2005)	0.5
Nationally protected areas (% of total land area)	7.7
Mammal species, total known	
Mammal species, threatened	
Bird species, total known	
Bird species, threatened	
GEF benefits index for biodiversity (0–100)	

Energy

GDP per unit of energy use (2000 PPP $/kg oil equiv)	4.2
Energy use per capita (kg oil equiv)	501
Energy from combustible renewables & waste (% of tot.)	48.9
Energy imports, net (% of energy use)	–4
Electric power consumption per capita (kWh)	358
Electricity generated by coal (% of total)	46.3

Emissions and pollution

CO_2 emissions per unit of GDP (kg/2000 PPP $ of GDP)	0.4
CO_2 emissions per capita (metric tons)	0.8
Particulate matter (urban-pop.-weighted avg., µg/cu. m)	89
Passenger cars (per 1,000 people)	6

Water and sanitation

Internal freshwater resources per capita (cu. m)	3,456
Freshwater withdrawal	
Total (% of internal resources)	15.5
Agriculture (% of total freshwater withdrawal)	88
Access to improved water source (% of total population)	75
Rural (% of rural population)	69
Urban (% of urban population)	89
Access to improved sanitation (% of total population)	36
Rural (% of rural population)	24
Urban (% of urban population)	61

Environment and health

ARI prevalence (% of children under age 5)	
Diarrhea prevalence (% of children under age 5)	
Under-five mortality rate (per 1,000 live births)	122

National accounting aggregates, 2004

Gross savings (% of GNI)	22.7
Consumption of fixed capital (% of GNI)	9.2
Education expenditure (% of GNI)	3.4
Energy depletion (% of GNI)	6.7
Mineral depletion (% of GNI)	0.4
Net forest depletion (% of GNI)	0.7
CO_2 damage (% of GNI)	1.1
Particulate emission damage (% of GNI)	0.8
Adjusted net savings (% of GNI)	7.3

Middle income

Population (millions)	3,017.8
Urban population (% of total)	53.2
GDP ($ billions)	7,156.8
GNI per capita, *World Bank Atlas* method ($)	2,274

Agriculture

Land area (1,000 sq. km)	67,453
Agricultural land (% of land area)	36
Irrigated land (% of cropland)	17.8
Fertilizer consumption (100 grams/ha of arable land)	1,119
Population density, rural (people/sq. km of arable land)	480

Forests and biodiversity

Forest area (% of land area)	33.6
Annual deforestation (% change, 1990–2005)	0.1
Nationally protected areas (% of total land area)	8.5
Mammal species, total known	
Mammal species, threatened	
Bird species, total known	
Bird species, threatened	
GEF benefits index for biodiversity (0–100)	

Energy

GDP per unit of energy use (2000 PPP $/kg oil equiv)	4.2
Energy use per capita (kg oil equiv)	1,373
Energy from combustible renewables & waste (% of tot.)	10.8
Energy imports, net (% of energy use)	−27
Electric power consumption per capita (kWh)	1,720
Electricity generated by coal (% of total)	42.4

Emissions and pollution

CO_2 emissions per unit of GDP (kg/2000 PPP $ of GDP)	0.6
CO_2 emissions per capita (metric tons)	3.3
Particulate matter (urban-pop.-weighted avg., µg/cu. m)	62
Passenger cars (per 1,000 people)	51

Water and sanitation

Internal freshwater resources per capita (cu. m)	8,611
Freshwater withdrawal	
Total (% of internal resources)	6.4
Agriculture (% of total freshwater withdrawal)	71
Access to improved water source (% of total population)	83
Rural (% of rural population)	71
Urban (% of urban population)	94
Access to improved sanitation (% of total population)	61
Rural (% of rural population)	41
Urban (% of urban population)	81

Environment and health

ARI prevalence (% of children under age 5)	
Diarrhea prevalence (% of children under age 5)	
Under-five mortality rate (per 1,000 live births)	37

National accounting aggregates, 2004

Gross savings (% of GNI)	28.3
Consumption of fixed capital (% of GNI)	11.1
Education expenditure (% of GNI)	3.6
Energy depletion (% of GNI)	8.4
Mineral depletion (% of GNI)	0.5
Net forest depletion (% of GNI)	0.0
CO_2 damage (% of GNI)	1.0
Particulate emission damage (% of GNI)	0.9
Adjusted net savings (% of GNI)	9.8

Lower middle income

Population (millions)	2,441.6
Urban population (% of total)	48.7
GDP ($ billions)	4,165.3
GNI per capita, *World Bank Atlas* method ($)	1,686

Agriculture

Land area (1,000 sq. km)	38,470
Agricultural land (% of land area)	43
Irrigated land (% of cropland)	23.1
Fertilizer consumption (100 grams/ha of arable land)	1,530
Population density, rural (people/sq. km of arable land)	523

Forests and biodiversity

Forest area (% of land area)	30.7
Annual deforestation (% change, 1990–2005)	0.1
Nationally protected areas (% of total land area)	7.7
Mammal species, total known	
Mammal species, threatened	
Bird species, total known	
Bird species, threatened	
GEF benefits index for biodiversity (0–100)	

Energy

GDP per unit of energy use (2000 PPP $/kg oil equiv)	4.6
Energy use per capita (kg oil equiv)	1,090
Energy from combustible renewables & waste (% of tot.)	14.6
Energy imports, net (% of energy use)	−14
Electric power consumption per capita (kWh)	1,329
Electricity generated by coal (% of total)	49.4

Emissions and pollution

CO_2 emissions per unit of GDP (kg/2000 PPP $ of GDP)	0.5
CO_2 emissions per capita (metric tons)	2.6
Particulate matter (urban-pop.-weighted avg., µg/cu. m)	70
Passenger cars (per 1,000 people)	29

Water and sanitation

Internal freshwater resources per capita (cu. m)	7,295
Freshwater withdrawal	
Total (% of internal resources)	7.7
Agriculture (% of total freshwater withdrawal)	75
Access to improved water source (% of total population)	81
Rural (% of rural population)	70
Urban (% of urban population)	93
Access to improved sanitation (% of total population)	57
Rural (% of rural population)	39
Urban (% of urban population)	78

Environment and health

ARI prevalence (% of children under age 5)	
Diarrhea prevalence (% of children under age 5)	
Under-five mortality rate (per 1,000 live births)	40

National accounting aggregates, 2004

Gross savings (% of GNI)	32.1
Consumption of fixed capital (% of GNI)	10.8
Education expenditure (% of GNI)	2.9
Energy depletion (% of GNI)	6.5
Mineral depletion (% of GNI)	0.5
Net forest depletion (% of GNI)	0.0
CO_2 damage (% of GNI)	1.1
Particulate emission damage (% of GNI)	1.0
Adjusted net savings (% of GNI)	15.1

Upper middle income

Population (millions)	576.2
Urban population (% of total)	72.3
GDP ($ billions)	2,991.5
GNI per capita, *World Bank Atlas* method ($)	4,769
Agriculture	
Land area (1,000 sq. km)	28,983
Agricultural land (% of land area)	26
Irrigated land (% of cropland)	8.7
Fertilizer consumption (100 grams/ha of arable land)	469
Population density, rural (people/sq. km of arable land)	131
Forests and biodiversity	
Forest area (% of land area)	37.3
Annual deforestation (% change, 1990–2005)	0.1
Nationally protected areas (% of total land area)	..
Mammal species, total known	
Mammal species, threatened	
Bird species, total known	
Bird species, threatened	
GEF benefits index for biodiversity (0–100)	
Energy	
GDP per unit of energy use (2000 PPP $/kg oil equiv)	3.5
Energy use per capita (kg oil equiv)	2,574
Energy from combustible renewables & waste (% of tot.)	3.9
Energy imports, net (% of energy use)	−51
Electric power consumption per capita (kWh)	3,378
Electricity generated by coal (% of total)	31.0
Emissions and pollution	
CO_2 emissions per unit of GDP (kg/2000 PPP $ of GDP)	0.7
CO_2 emissions per capita (metric tons)	6.2
Particulate matter (urban-pop.-weighted avg., µg/cu. m)	40
Passenger cars (per 1,000 people)	143
Water and sanitation	
Internal freshwater resources per capita (cu. m)	14,190
Freshwater withdrawal	
Total (% of internal resources)	3.8
Agriculture (% of total freshwater withdrawal)	53
Access to improved water source (% of total population)	93
Rural (% of rural population)	82
Urban (% of urban population)	97
Access to improved sanitation (% of total population)	81
Rural (% of rural population)	61
Urban (% of urban population)	91
Environment and health	
ARI prevalence (% of children under age 5)	
Diarrhea prevalence (% of children under age 5)	
Under-five mortality rate (per 1,000 live births)	28
National accounting aggregates, 2004	
Gross savings (% of GNI)	23.1
Consumption of fixed capital (% of GNI)	11.5
Education expenditure (% of GNI)	4.5
Energy depletion (% of GNI)	11.2
Mineral depletion (% of GNI)	0.6
Net forest depletion (% of GNI)	0.0
CO_2 damage (% of GNI)	0.9
Particulate emission damage (% of GNI)	0.7
Adjusted net savings (% of GNI)	2.6

Low & middle income

Population (millions)	5,360.8
Urban population (% of total)	43.3
GDP ($ billions)	8,395.2
GNI per capita, *World Bank Atlas* method ($)	1,502

Agriculture

Land area (1,000 sq. km)	96,645
Agricultural land (% of land area)	38
Irrigated land (% of cropland)	20.0
Fertilizer consumption (100 grams/ha of arable land)	942
Population density, rural (people/sq. km of arable land)	503

Forests and biodiversity

Forest area (% of land area)	30.9
Annual deforestation (% change, 1990–2005)	0.2
Nationally protected areas (% of total land area)	8.3
Mammal species, total known	
Mammal species, threatened	
Bird species, total known	
Bird species, threatened	
GEF benefits index for biodiversity (0–100)	

Energy

GDP per unit of energy use (2000 PPP $/kg oil equiv)	4.2
Energy use per capita (kg oil equiv)	1,014
Energy from combustible renewables & waste (% of tot.)	18.2
Energy imports, net (% of energy use)	–22
Electric power consumption per capita (kWh)	1,159
Electricity generated by coal (% of total)	42.9

Emissions and pollution

CO_2 emissions per unit of GDP (kg/2000 PPP $ of GDP)	0.6
CO_2 emissions per capita (metric tons)	2.2
Particulate matter (urban-pop.-weighted avg., µg/cu. m)	70
Passenger cars (per 1,000 people)	35

Water and sanitation

Internal freshwater resources per capita (cu. m)	6,358
Freshwater withdrawal	
Total (% of internal resources)	8.6
Agriculture (% of total freshwater withdrawal)	78
Access to improved water source (% of total population)	79
Rural (% of rural population)	70
Urban (% of urban population)	93
Access to improved sanitation (% of total population)	50
Rural (% of rural population)	32
Urban (% of urban population)	74

Environment and health

ARI prevalence (% of children under age 5)	
Diarrhea prevalence (% of children under age 5)	
Under-five mortality rate (per 1,000 live births)	86

National accounting aggregates, 2004

Gross savings (% of GNI)	27.5
Consumption of fixed capital (% of GNI)	10.8
Education expenditure (% of GNI)	3.5
Energy depletion (% of GNI)	8.2
Mineral depletion (% of GNI)	0.5
Net forest depletion (% of GNI)	0.1
CO_2 damage (% of GNI)	1.0
Particulate emission damage (% of GNI)	0.9
Adjusted net savings (% of GNI)	9.4

Population (millions)	309.3
Urban population (% of total)	76.1
GDP ($ billions)	9,500.9
GNI per capita, *World Bank Atlas* method ($)	27,921

Agriculture

Land area (1,000 sq. km)	2,435
Agricultural land (% of land area)	48
Irrigated land (% of cropland)	17.0
Fertilizer consumption (100 grams/ha of arable land)	1,977
Population density, rural (people/sq. km of arable land)	182

Forests and biodiversity

Forest area (% of land area)	37.0
Annual deforestation (% change, 1990–2005)	–0.8
Nationally protected areas (% of total land area)	13.5
Mammal species, total known	
Mammal species, threatened	
Bird species, total known	
Bird species, threatened	
GEF benefits index for biodiversity (0–100)	

Energy

GDP per unit of energy use (2000 PPP $/kg oil equiv)	6.4
Energy use per capita (kg oil equiv)	3,964
Energy from combustible renewables & waste (% of tot.)	3.9
Energy imports, net (% of energy use)	64
Electric power consumption per capita (kWh)	6,506
Electricity generated by coal (% of total)	27.7

Emissions and pollution

CO_2 emissions per unit of GDP (kg/2000 PPP $ of GDP)	0.3
CO_2 emissions per capita (metric tons)	8.3
Particulate matter (urban-pop.-weighted avg., µg/cu. m)	27
Passenger cars (per 1,000 people)	476

Water and sanitation

Internal freshwater resources per capita (cu. m)	2,942
Freshwater withdrawal	
Total (% of internal resources)	22.3
Agriculture (% of total freshwater withdrawal)	38
Access to improved water source (% of total population)	..
Rural (% of rural population)	..
Urban (% of urban population)	100
Access to improved sanitation (% of total population)	..
Rural (% of rural population)	..
Urban (% of urban population)	..

Environment and health

ARI prevalence (% of children under age 5)	
Diarrhea prevalence (% of children under age 5)	
Under-five mortality rate (per 1,000 live births)	5

National accounting aggregates, 2004

Gross savings (% of GNI)	20.8
Consumption of fixed capital (% of GNI)	14.2
Education expenditure (% of GNI)	4.6
Energy depletion (% of GNI)	0.1
Mineral depletion (% of GNI)	0.0
Net forest depletion (% of GNI)	0.0
CO_2 damage (% of GNI)	0.2
Particulate emission damage (% of GNI)	0.3
Adjusted net savings (% of GNI)	10.6

High income

Population (millions)	1,004.2
Urban population (% of total)	78.5
GDP ($ billions)	32,900.1
GNI per capita, *World Bank Atlas* method ($)	32,112

Agriculture

Land area (1,000 sq. km)	33,018
Agricultural land (% of land area)	38
Irrigated land (% of cropland)	11.9
Fertilizer consumption (100 grams/ha of arable land)	1,205
Population density, rural (people/sq. km of arable land)	331

Forests and biodiversity

Forest area (% of land area)	29.3
Annual deforestation (% change, 1990–2005)	–0.1
Nationally protected areas (% of total land area)	..
Mammal species, total known	
Mammal species, threatened	
Bird species, total known	
Bird species, threatened	
GEF benefits index for biodiversity (0–100)	

Energy

GDP per unit of energy use (2000 PPP $/kg oil equiv)	5.2
Energy use per capita (kg oil equiv)	5,410
Energy from combustible renewables & waste (% of tot.)	3.0
Energy imports, net (% of energy use)	19
Electric power consumption per capita (kWh)	9,503
Electricity generated by coal (% of total)	38.2

Emissions and pollution

CO_2 emissions per unit of GDP (kg/2000 PPP $ of GDP)	0.5
CO_2 emissions per capita (metric tons)	12.8
Particulate matter (urban-pop.-weighted avg., µg/cu. m)	29
Passenger cars (per 1,000 people)	433

Water and sanitation

Internal freshwater resources per capita (cu. m)	9,703
Freshwater withdrawal	
Total (% of internal resources)	10.4
Agriculture (% of total freshwater withdrawal)	42
Access to improved water source (% of total population)	99
Rural (% of rural population)	98
Urban (% of urban population)	100
Access to improved sanitation (% of total population)	..
Rural (% of rural population)	..
Urban (% of urban population)	..

Environment and health

ARI prevalence (% of children under age 5)	
Diarrhea prevalence (% of children under age 5)	
Under-five mortality rate (per 1,000 live births)	7

National accounting aggregates, 2004

Gross savings (% of GNI)	19.4
Consumption of fixed capital (% of GNI)	13.2
Education expenditure (% of GNI)	4.6
Energy depletion (% of GNI)	1.4
Mineral depletion (% of GNI)	0.0
Net forest depletion (% of GNI)	0.0
CO_2 damage (% of GNI)	0.3
Particulate emission damage (% of GNI)	0.4
Adjusted net savings (% of GNI)	8.7

Country tables

China

Unless otherwise noted, data for China do not include data for Hong Kong, China; Macao, China; or Taiwan, China.

Timor-Leste

Data for Indonesia include Timor-Leste through 1999 unless otherwise noted.

Afghanistan

Environmental strategy/action plan prepared in ..

	Country data	Group data South Asia	Low income
Population (millions)	28.6	1,447	2,343
Urban population (% of total)	23.8	28.3	30.6
GDP ($ billions)	5.8	880	1,239
GNI per capita, *World Bank Atlas* method ($)	190	594	507
Agriculture			
Land area (1,000 sq. km)	652	4,781	29,192
Agricultural land (% of land area)	58	54	45
Irrigated land (% of cropland)	33.8	39.6	23.9
Fertilizer consumption (100 grams/ha of arable land)	26	1,040	646
Population density, rural (people/sq. km of arable land)	264	586	524
Forests and biodiversity			
Forest area (% of land area)	1.3	16.8	24.8
Annual deforestation (% change, 1990–2005)	2.3	–0.2	0.5
Nationally protected areas (% of total land area)	0.3	4.8	7.7
Mammal species, total known	144		
Mammal species, threatened	12		
Bird species, total known	434		
Bird species, threatened	17		
GEF benefits index for biodiversity (0–100)	3.6		
Energy			
GDP per unit of energy use (2000 PPP $/kg oil equiv)	..	5.3	4.2
Energy use per capita (kg oil equiv)	..	474	501
Energy from combustible renewables & waste (% of tot.)	..	38.8	48.9
Energy imports, net (% of energy use)	..	19	–4
Electric power consumption per capita (kWh)	..	394	358
Electricity generated by coal (% of total)	..	58.2	46.3
Emissions and pollution			
CO_2 emissions per unit of GDP (kg/2000 PPP $ of GDP)	..	0.4	0.4
CO_2 emissions per capita (metric tons)	0.0	1.0	0.8
Particulate matter (urban-pop.-weighted avg., μg/cu. m)	27	99	89
Passenger cars (per 1,000 people)	..	6	6
Water and sanitation			
Internal freshwater resources per capita (cu. m)	1,925	1,255	3,456
Freshwater withdrawal			
Total (% of internal resources)	42.3	51.8	15.5
Agriculture (% of total freshwater withdrawal)	98	90	88
Access to improved water source (% of total population)	13	84	75
Rural (% of rural population)	11	80	69
Urban (% of urban population)	19	94	89
Access to improved sanitation (% of total population)	8	35	36
Rural (% of rural population)	5	23	24
Urban (% of urban population)	16	64	61
Environment and health			
ARI prevalence (% of children under age 5)	..		
Diarrhea prevalence (% of children under age 5)	..		
Under-five mortality rate (per 1,000 live births)	257	92	122
National accounting aggregates, 2004			
Gross savings (% of GNI)	..	23.6	22.7
Consumption of fixed capital (% of GNI)	7.7	9.1	9.2
Education expenditure (% of GNI)	..	3.6	3.4
Energy depletion (% of GNI)	0.0	2.7	6.7
Mineral depletion (% of GNI)	..	0.3	0.4
Net forest depletion (% of GNI)	1.3	0.7	0.7
CO_2 damage (% of GNI)	0.1	1.2	1.1
Particulate emission damage (% of GNI)	0.1	0.8	0.8
Adjusted net savings (% of GNI)	..	12.4	7.3

Albania

Environmental strategy/action plan prepared in **1993**

	Country data	Europe & Central Asia	Lower middle income
		Group data	
Population (millions)	3.1	472	2,442
Urban population (% of total)	44.4	63.6	48.7
GDP ($ billions)	7.6	1,770	4,165
GNI per capita, *World Bank Atlas* method ($)	2,120	3,295	1,686
Agriculture			
Land area (1,000 sq. km)	27	23,371	38,470
Agricultural land (% of land area)	41	29	43
Irrigated land (% of cropland)	50.5	11.1	23.1
Fertilizer consumption (100 grams/ha of arable land)	612	347	1,530
Population density, rural (people/sq. km of arable land)	301	126	523
Forests and biodiversity			
Forest area (% of land area)	29.0	38.3	30.7
Annual deforestation (% change, 1990–2005)	0.0	0.0	0.1
Nationally protected areas (% of total land area)	3.8	6.9	7.7
Mammal species, total known	73		
Mammal species, threatened	1		
Bird species, total known	303		
Bird species, threatened	9		
GEF benefits index for biodiversity (0–100)	0.2		
Energy			
GDP per unit of energy use (2000 PPP $/kg oil equiv)	6.4	2.7	4.6
Energy use per capita (kg oil equiv)	674	2,794	1,090
Energy from combustible renewables & waste (% of tot.)	6.8	2.4	14.6
Energy imports, net (% of energy use)	57	−26	−14
Electric power consumption per capita (kWh)	1,311	3,531	1,329
Electricity generated by coal (% of total)	..	29.8	49.4
Emissions and pollution			
CO_2 emissions per unit of GDP (kg/2000 PPP $ of GDP)	0.2	1.0	0.5
CO_2 emissions per capita (metric tons)	0.8	6.7	2.6
Particulate matter (urban-pop.-weighted avg., µg/cu. m)	58	35	70
Passenger cars (per 1,000 people)	47	142	29
Water and sanitation			
Internal freshwater resources per capita (cu. m)	8,645	11,123	7,295
Freshwater withdrawal			
Total (% of internal resources)	6.4	7.5	7.7
Agriculture (% of total freshwater withdrawal)	62	59	75
Access to improved water source (% of total population)	97	91	81
Rural (% of rural population)	95	80	70
Urban (% of urban population)	99	98	93
Access to improved sanitation (% of total population)	89	82	57
Rural (% of rural population)	81	63	39
Urban (% of urban population)	99	93	78
Environment and health			
ARI prevalence (% of children under age 5)	1.4		
Diarrhea prevalence (% of children under age 5)	7.3		
Under-five mortality rate (per 1,000 live births)	19	34	40
National accounting aggregates, 2004			
Gross savings (% of GNI)	17.1	23.4	32.1
Consumption of fixed capital (% of GNI)	10.8	10.7	10.8
Education expenditure (% of GNI)	2.8	4.1	2.9
Energy depletion (% of GNI)	1.2	12.0	6.5
Mineral depletion (% of GNI)	0.0	0.3	0.5
Net forest depletion (% of GNI)	0.0	0.0	0.0
CO_2 damage (% of GNI)	0.2	1.4	1.1
Particulate emission damage (% of GNI)	0.3	0.7	1.0
Adjusted net savings (% of GNI)	7.4	2.3	15.1

Algeria

Environmental strategy/action plan prepared in **1993**

	Country data	Middle East & North Africa	Lower middle income
		Group data	
Population (millions)	32.4	300	2,442
Urban population (% of total)	59.4	56.3	48.7
GDP ($ billions)	84.6	547	4,165
GNI per capita, *World Bank Atlas* method ($)	2,270	1,972	1,686
Agriculture			
Land area (1,000 sq. km)	2,382	8,955	38,470
Agricultural land (% of land area)	17	23	43
Irrigated land (% of cropland)	6.9	32.5	23.1
Fertilizer consumption (100 grams/ha of arable land)	130	842	1,530
Population density, rural (people/sq. km of arable land)	174	670	523
Forests and biodiversity			
Forest area (% of land area)	1.0	2.4	30.7
Annual deforestation (% change, 1990–2005)	–1.8	–0.5	0.1
Nationally protected areas (% of total land area)	5.0	4.2	7.7
Mammal species, total known	100		
Mammal species, threatened	12		
Bird species, total known	372		
Bird species, threatened	11		
GEF benefits index for biodiversity (0–100)	3.0		
Energy			
GDP per unit of energy use (2000 PPP $/kg oil equiv)	5.6	4.2	4.6
Energy use per capita (kg oil equiv)	1,036	1,144	1,090
Energy from combustible renewables & waste (% of tot.)	0.2	1.3	14.6
Energy imports, net (% of energy use)	–395	–129	–14
Electric power consumption per capita (kWh)	796	1,212	1,329
Electricity generated by coal (% of total)	..	3.0	49.4
Emissions and pollution			
CO_2 emissions per unit of GDP (kg/2000 PPP $ of GDP)	0.5	0.7	0.5
CO_2 emissions per capita (metric tons)	2.9	3.2	2.6
Particulate matter (urban-pop.-weighted avg., µg/cu. m)	65	90	70
Passenger cars (per 1,000 people)	..	..	29
Water and sanitation			
Internal freshwater resources per capita (cu. m)	348	761	7,295
Freshwater withdrawal			
Total (% of internal resources)	54.0	105.0	7.7
Agriculture (% of total freshwater withdrawal)	65	89	75
Access to improved water source (% of total population)	87	88	81
Rural (% of rural population)	80	79	70
Urban (% of urban population)	92	95	93
Access to improved sanitation (% of total population)	92	75	57
Rural (% of rural population)	82	56	39
Urban (% of urban population)	99	89	78
Environment and health			
ARI prevalence (% of children under age 5)	9.0		
Diarrhea prevalence (% of children under age 5)	19.8		
Under-five mortality rate (per 1,000 live births)	40	55	40
National accounting aggregates, 2004			
Gross savings (% of GNI)	47.6	30.0	32.1
Consumption of fixed capital (% of GNI)	11.6	11.2	10.8
Education expenditure (% of GNI)	4.5	4.5	2.9
Energy depletion (% of GNI)	35.2	27.3	6.5
Mineral depletion (% of GNI)	0.0	0.1	0.5
Net forest depletion (% of GNI)	0.1	0.1	0.0
CO_2 damage (% of GNI)	0.8	1.2	1.1
Particulate emission damage (% of GNI)	0.7	0.9	1.0
Adjusted net savings (% of GNI)	3.6	–6.2	15.1

American Samoa

Environmental strategy/action plan prepared in **2001**

	Country data	East Asia & Pacific	Upper middle income
		Group data	
Population (millions)	0.1	1,870	576
Urban population (% of total)	90.7	40.6	72.3
GDP ($ billions)	..	2,651	2,992
GNI per capita, *World Bank Atlas* method ($)	..	1,416	4,769
Agriculture			
Land area (1,000 sq. km)	0	15,885	28,983
Agricultural land (% of land area)	25	51	26
Irrigated land (% of cropland)	..	..	8.7
Fertilizer consumption (100 grams/ha of arable land)	..	2,296	469
Population density, rural (people/sq. km of arable land)	280	559	131
Forests and biodiversity			
Forest area (% of land area)	90.0	28.4	37.3
Annual deforestation (% change, 1990–2005)	0.0	−0.2	0.1
Nationally protected areas (% of total land area)	..	..	..
Mammal species, total known	10		
Mammal species, threatened	3		
Bird species, total known	36		
Bird species, threatened	9		
GEF benefits index for biodiversity (0–100)	0.4		
Energy			
GDP per unit of energy use (2000 PPP $/kg oil equiv)	..	4.6	3.5
Energy use per capita (kg oil equiv)	..	1,007	2,574
Energy from combustible renewables & waste (% of tot.)	..	17.7	3.9
Energy imports, net (% of energy use)	..	−2	−51
Electric power consumption per capita (kWh)	..	1,184	3,378
Electricity generated by coal (% of total)	..	69.4	31.0
Emissions and pollution			
CO_2 emissions per unit of GDP (kg/2000 PPP $ of GDP)	..	0.5	0.7
CO_2 emissions per capita (metric tons)	..	2.4	6.2
Particulate matter (urban-pop.-weighted avg., µg/cu. m)	..	80	40
Passenger cars (per 1,000 people)	..	12	143
Water and sanitation			
Internal freshwater resources per capita (cu. m)	..	5,062	14,190
Freshwater withdrawal			
Total (% of internal resources)	..	10.2	3.8
Agriculture (% of total freshwater withdrawal)	..	74	53
Access to improved water source (% of total population)	..	78	93
Rural (% of rural population)	..	69	82
Urban (% of urban population)	..	92	97
Access to improved sanitation (% of total population)	..	49	81
Rural (% of rural population)	..	35	61
Urban (% of urban population)	..	72	91
Environment and health			
ARI prevalence (% of children under age 5)	..		
Diarrhea prevalence (% of children under age 5)	..		
Under-five mortality rate (per 1,000 live births)	..	37	28
National accounting aggregates, 2004			
Gross savings (% of GNI)	..	39.1	23.1
Consumption of fixed capital (% of GNI)	..	10.5	11.5
Education expenditure (% of GNI)	..	2.3	4.5
Energy depletion (% of GNI)	..	4.1	11.2
Mineral depletion (% of GNI)	..	0.4	0.6
Net forest depletion (% of GNI)	..	0.0	0.0
CO_2 damage (% of GNI)	..	1.2	0.9
Particulate emission damage (% of GNI)	..	1.2	0.7
Adjusted net savings (% of GNI)	..	23.9	2.6

Andorra

Environmental strategy/action plan prepared in ..

	Country data	Group data — High income
Population (millions)	0.1	1,004
Urban population (% of total)	91.5	78.5
GDP ($ billions)	..	32,900
GNI per capita, *World Bank Atlas* method ($)	..	32,112
Agriculture		
Land area (1,000 sq. km)	0	33,018
Agricultural land (% of land area)	55	38
Irrigated land (% of cropland)	..	11.9
Fertilizer consumption (100 grams/ha of arable land)	..	1,205
Population density, rural (people/sq. km of arable land)	545	331
Forests and biodiversity		
Forest area (% of land area)	34.0	29.3
Annual deforestation (% change, 1990–2005)	0.0	–0.1
Nationally protected areas (% of total land area)	..	..
Mammal species, total known	..	
Mammal species, threatened	..	
Bird species, total known	..	
Bird species, threatened	..	
GEF benefits index for biodiversity (0–100)	0.0	
Energy		
GDP per unit of energy use (2000 PPP $/kg oil equiv)	..	5.2
Energy use per capita (kg oil equiv)	..	5,410
Energy from combustible renewables & waste (% of tot.)	..	3.0
Energy imports, net (% of energy use)	..	19
Electric power consumption per capita (kWh)	..	9,503
Electricity generated by coal (% of total)	..	38.2
Emissions and pollution		
CO_2 emissions per unit of GDP (kg/2000 PPP $ of GDP)	..	0.5
CO_2 emissions per capita (metric tons)	..	12.8
Particulate matter (urban-pop.-weighted avg., µg/cu. m)	41	29
Passenger cars (per 1,000 people)	..	433
Water and sanitation		
Internal freshwater resources per capita (cu. m)	..	9,703
Freshwater withdrawal		
Total (% of internal resources)	..	10.4
Agriculture (% of total freshwater withdrawal)	..	42
Access to improved water source (% of total population)	100	99
Rural (% of rural population)	100	98
Urban (% of urban population)	100	100
Access to improved sanitation (% of total population)	100	..
Rural (% of rural population)	100	..
Urban (% of urban population)	100	..
Environment and health		
ARI prevalence (% of children under age 5)	..	
Diarrhea prevalence (% of children under age 5)	..	
Under-five mortality rate (per 1,000 live births)	7	7
National accounting aggregates, 2004		
Gross savings (% of GNI)	..	19.4
Consumption of fixed capital (% of GNI)	..	13.2
Education expenditure (% of GNI)	..	4.6
Energy depletion (% of GNI)	..	1.4
Mineral depletion (% of GNI)	..	0.0
Net forest depletion (% of GNI)	..	0.0
CO_2 damage (% of GNI)	..	0.3
Particulate emission damage (% of GNI)	..	0.4
Adjusted net savings (% of GNI)	..	8.7

Angola

Environmental strategy/action plan prepared in ..

	Country data	Group data Sub-Saharan Africa	Group data Lower middle income
Population (millions)	15.5	726	2,442
Urban population (% of total)	36.5	36.4	48.7
GDP ($ billions)	19.5	523	4,165
GNI per capita, *World Bank Atlas* method ($)	930	601	1,686

Agriculture
Land area (1,000 sq. km)	1,247	23,596	38,470
Agricultural land (% of land area)	46	44	43
Irrigated land (% of cropland)	2.2	3.6	23.1
Fertilizer consumption (100 grams/ha of arable land)	0	136	1,530
Population density, rural (people/sq. km of arable land)	293	355	523

Forests and biodiversity
Forest area (% of land area)	47.4	26.5	30.7
Annual deforestation (% change, 1990–2005)	0.2	0.6	0.1
Nationally protected areas (% of total land area)	6.6	8.7	7.7
Mammal species, total known	296		
Mammal species, threatened	11		
Bird species, total known	930		
Bird species, threatened	20		
GEF benefits index for biodiversity (0–100)	9.6		

Energy
GDP per unit of energy use (2000 PPP $/kg oil equiv)	3.1	2.8	4.6
Energy use per capita (kg oil equiv)	606	681	1,090
Energy from combustible renewables & waste (% of tot.)	66.4	57.4	14.6
Energy imports, net (% of energy use)	–457	–59	–14
Electric power consumption per capita (kWh)	113	513	1,329
Electricity generated by coal (% of total)	..	68.0	49.4

Emissions and pollution
CO_2 emissions per unit of GDP (kg/2000 PPP $ of GDP)	0.3	0.4	0.5
CO_2 emissions per capita (metric tons)	0.5	0.7	2.6
Particulate matter (urban-pop.-weighted avg., µg/cu. m)	113	73	70
Passenger cars (per 1,000 people)	..	..	29

Water and sanitation
Internal freshwater resources per capita (cu. m)	9,555	5,353	7,295
Freshwater withdrawal			
Total (% of internal resources)	0.2	3.1	7.7
Agriculture (% of total freshwater withdrawal)	60	87	75
Access to improved water source (% of total population)	50	58	81
Rural (% of rural population)	40	45	70
Urban (% of urban population)	70	82	93
Access to improved sanitation (% of total population)	30	36	57
Rural (% of rural population)	16	26	39
Urban (% of urban population)	56	55	78

Environment and health
ARI prevalence (% of children under age 5)	8.0		
Diarrhea prevalence (% of children under age 5)	..		
Under–five mortality rate (per 1,000 live births)	260	168	40

National accounting aggregates, 2004
Gross savings (% of GNI)	18.4	17.1	32.1
Consumption of fixed capital (% of GNI)	11.5	10.9	10.8
Education expenditure (% of GNI)	3.1	3.9	2.9
Energy depletion (% of GNI)	45.0	9.8	6.5
Mineral depletion (% of GNI)	0.0	0.4	0.5
Net forest depletion (% of GNI)	0.0	0.6	0.0
CO_2 damage (% of GNI)	0.3	0.7	1.1
Particulate emission damage (% of GNI)	1.1	0.5	1.0
Adjusted net savings (% of GNI)	–36.3	–1.9	15.1

Antigua and Barbuda

Environmental strategy/action plan prepared in ..

	Country data	Group data Latin America & Caribbean	Upper middle income
Population (millions)	0.1	546	576
Urban population (% of total)	38.1	77.1	72.3
GDP ($ billions)	0.9	2,022	2,992
GNI per capita, *World Bank Atlas* method ($)	9,480	3,576	4,769
Agriculture			
Land area (1,000 sq. km)	0	20,057	28,983
Agricultural land (% of land area)	32	36	26
Irrigated land (% of cropland)	..	11.4	8.7
Fertilizer consumption (100 grams/ha of arable land)	..	923	469
Population density, rural (people/sq. km of arable land)	616	212	131
Forests and biodiversity			
Forest area (% of land area)	20.5	45.6	37.3
Annual deforestation (% change, 1990–2005)	0.0	0.4	0.1
Nationally protected areas (% of total land area)	..	11.1	..
Mammal species, total known	8		
Mammal species, threatened	0		
Bird species, total known	178		
Bird species, threatened	2		
GEF benefits index for biodiversity (0–100)	0.5		
Energy			
GDP per unit of energy use (2000 PPP $/kg oil equiv)	..	6.2	3.5
Energy use per capita (kg oil equiv)	..	1,148	2,574
Energy from combustible renewables & waste (% of tot.)	..	15.0	3.9
Energy imports, net (% of energy use)	..	–40	–51
Electric power consumption per capita (kWh)	..	1,615	3,378
Electricity generated by coal (% of total)	..	5.4	31.0
Emissions and pollution			
CO_2 emissions per unit of GDP (kg/2000 PPP $ of GDP)	0.5	0.3	0.7
CO_2 emissions per capita (metric tons)	4.7	2.4	6.2
Particulate matter (urban-pop.-weighted avg., µg/cu. m)	26	43	40
Passenger cars (per 1,000 people)	..	108	143
Water and sanitation			
Internal freshwater resources per capita (cu. m)	649	24,619	14,190
Freshwater withdrawal			
Total (% of internal resources)	..	2.0	3.8
Agriculture (% of total freshwater withdrawal)	..	71	53
Access to improved water source (% of total population)	91	89	93
Rural (% of rural population)	89	69	82
Urban (% of urban population)	95	96	97
Access to improved sanitation (% of total population)	95	75	81
Rural (% of rural population)	94	44	61
Urban (% of urban population)	98	84	91
Environment and health			
ARI prevalence (% of children under age 5)	..		
Diarrhea prevalence (% of children under age 5)	..		
Under-five mortality rate (per 1,000 live births)	12	31	28
National accounting aggregates, 2004			
Gross savings (% of GNI)	..	22.7	23.1
Consumption of fixed capital (% of GNI)	14.8	12.1	11.5
Education expenditure (% of GNI)	3.9	4.4	4.5
Energy depletion (% of GNI)	0.0	7.2	11.2
Mineral depletion (% of GNI)	0.0	1.1	0.6
Net forest depletion (% of GNI)	..	0.0	0.0
CO_2 damage (% of GNI)	0.3	0.5	0.9
Particulate emission damage (% of GNI)	..	0.6	0.7
Adjusted net savings (% of GNI)	..	5.6	2.6

Argentina

Environmental strategy/action plan prepared in **1992**

	Country data	Latin America & Caribbean	Upper middle income
		Group data	
Population (millions)	38.4	546	576
Urban population (% of total)	90.3	77.1	72.3
GDP ($ billions)	153.0	2,022	2,992
GNI per capita, *World Bank Atlas* method ($)	3,580	3,576	4,769
Agriculture			
Land area (1,000 sq. km)	2,737	20,057	28,983
Agricultural land (% of land area)	47	36	26
Irrigated land (% of cropland)	5.4	11.4	8.7
Fertilizer consumption (100 grams/ha of arable land)	265	923	469
Population density, rural (people/sq. km of arable land)	13	212	131
Forests and biodiversity			
Forest area (% of land area)	12.1	45.6	37.3
Annual deforestation (% change, 1990–2005)	0.4	0.4	0.1
Nationally protected areas (% of total land area)	6.6	11.1	..
Mammal species, total known	375		
Mammal species, threatened	32		
Bird species, total known	1,038		
Bird species, threatened	55		
GEF benefits index for biodiversity (0–100)	18.5		
Energy			
GDP per unit of energy use (2000 PPP $/kg oil equiv)	7.2	6.2	3.5
Energy use per capita (kg oil equiv)	1,575	1,148	2,574
Energy from combustible renewables & waste (% of tot.)	5.3	15.0	3.9
Energy imports, net (% of energy use)	–41	–40	–51
Electric power consumption per capita (kWh)	2,185	1,615	3,378
Electricity generated by coal (% of total)	1.0	5.4	31.0
Emissions and pollution			
CO_2 emissions per unit of GDP (kg/2000 PPP $ of GDP)	0.3	0.3	0.7
CO_2 emissions per capita (metric tons)	3.5	2.4	6.2
Particulate matter (urban-pop.-weighted avg., µg/cu. m)	78	43	40
Passenger cars (per 1,000 people)	140	108	143
Water and sanitation			
Internal freshwater resources per capita (cu. m)	7,193	24,619	14,190
Freshwater withdrawal			
Total (% of internal resources)	10.6	2.0	3.8
Agriculture (% of total freshwater withdrawal)	74	71	53
Access to improved water source (% of total population)	..	89	93
Rural (% of rural population)	..	69	82
Urban (% of urban population)	97	96	97
Access to improved sanitation (% of total population)	..	75	81
Rural (% of rural population)	..	44	61
Urban (% of urban population)	..	84	91
Environment and health			
ARI prevalence (% of children under age 5)	..		
Diarrhea prevalence (% of children under age 5)	..		
Under-five mortality rate (per 1,000 live births)	18	31	28
National accounting aggregates, 2004			
Gross savings (% of GNI)	22.2	22.7	23.1
Consumption of fixed capital (% of GNI)	12.4	12.1	11.5
Education expenditure (% of GNI)	4.3	4.4	4.5
Energy depletion (% of GNI)	8.2	7.2	11.2
Mineral depletion (% of GNI)	0.3	1.1	0.6
Net forest depletion (% of GNI)	0.0	0.0	0.0
CO_2 damage (% of GNI)	0.6	0.5	0.9
Particulate emission damage (% of GNI)	2.3	0.6	0.7
Adjusted net savings (% of GNI)	2.7	5.6	2.6

Armenia

Environmental strategy/action plan prepared in ..

	Country data	Group data	
		Europe & Central Asia	Lower middle income
Population (millions)	3.0	472	2,442
Urban population (% of total)	64.3	63.6	48.7
GDP ($ billions)	3.1	1,770	4,165
GNI per capita, *World Bank Atlas* method ($)	1,060	3,295	1,686

Agriculture

Land area (1,000 sq. km)	28	23,371	38,470
Agricultural land (% of land area)	49	29	43
Irrigated land (% of cropland)	51.1	11.1	23.1
Fertilizer consumption (100 grams/ha of arable land)	228	347	1,530
Population density, rural (people/sq. km of arable land)	216	126	523

Forests and biodiversity

Forest area (% of land area)	10.0	38.3	30.7
Annual deforestation (% change, 1990–2005)	1.2	0.0	0.1
Nationally protected areas (% of total land area)	7.6	6.9	7.7
Mammal species, total known	78		
Mammal species, threatened	9		
Bird species, total known	302		
Bird species, threatened	12		
GEF benefits index for biodiversity (0–100)	0.3		

Energy

GDP per unit of energy use (2000 PPP $/kg oil equiv)	5.2	2.7	4.6
Energy use per capita (kg oil equiv)	660	2,794	1,090
Energy from combustible renewables & waste (% of tot.)	0.0	2.4	14.6
Energy imports, net (% of energy use)	65	−26	−14
Electric power consumption per capita (kWh)	1,312	3,531	1,329
Electricity generated by coal (% of total)	..	29.8	49.4

Emissions and pollution

CO_2 emissions per unit of GDP (kg/2000 PPP $ of GDP)	0.5	1.0	0.5
CO_2 emissions per capita (metric tons)	1.0	6.7	2.6
Particulate matter (urban-pop.-weighted avg., µg/cu. m)	84	35	70
Passenger cars (per 1,000 people)	..	142	29

Water and sanitation

Internal freshwater resources per capita (cu. m)	2,998	11,123	7,295
Freshwater withdrawal			
Total (% of internal resources)	32.5	7.5	7.7
Agriculture (% of total freshwater withdrawal)	66	59	75
Access to improved water source (% of total population)	92	91	81
Rural (% of rural population)	80	80	70
Urban (% of urban population)	99	98	93
Access to improved sanitation (% of total population)	84	82	57
Rural (% of rural population)	61	63	39
Urban (% of urban population)	96	93	78

Environment and health

ARI prevalence (% of children under age 5)	16.5		
Diarrhea prevalence (% of children under age 5)	7.8		
Under-five mortality rate (per 1,000 live births)	32	34	40

National accounting aggregates, 2004

Gross savings (% of GNI)	13.7	23.4	32.1
Consumption of fixed capital (% of GNI)	9.8	10.7	10.8
Education expenditure (% of GNI)	3.0	4.1	2.9
Energy depletion (% of GNI)	0.0	12.0	6.5
Mineral depletion (% of GNI)	0.7	0.3	0.5
Net forest depletion (% of GNI)	0.0	0.0	0.0
CO_2 damage (% of GNI)	0.9	1.4	1.1
Particulate emission damage (% of GNI)	3.0	0.7	1.0
Adjusted net savings (% of GNI)	2.4	2.3	15.1

Aruba

Environmental strategy/action plan prepared in **1992**

	Country data	Group data — High income
Population (millions)	0.1	1,004
Urban population (% of total)	45.1	78.5
GDP ($ billions)	..	32,900
GNI per capita, *World Bank Atlas* method ($)	..	32,112

Agriculture

Land area (1,000 sq. km)	0	33,018
Agricultural land (% of land area)	11	38
Irrigated land (% of cropland)	..	11.9
Fertilizer consumption (100 grams/ha of arable land)	..	1,205
Population density, rural (people/sq. km of arable land)	2,699	331

Forests and biodiversity

Forest area (% of land area)	..	29.3
Annual deforestation (% change, 1990–2005)	..	–0.1
Nationally protected areas (% of total land area)	..	..
Mammal species, total known	4	
Mammal species, threatened	1	
Bird species, total known	88	
Bird species, threatened	1	
GEF benefits index for biodiversity (0–100)	0.4	

Energy

GDP per unit of energy use (2000 PPP $/kg oil equiv)	..	5.2
Energy use per capita (kg oil equiv)	..	5,410
Energy from combustible renewables & waste (% of tot.)	..	3.0
Energy imports, net (% of energy use)	..	19
Electric power consumption per capita (kWh)	..	9,503
Electricity generated by coal (% of total)	..	38.2

Emissions and pollution

CO_2 emissions per unit of GDP (kg/2000 PPP $ of GDP)	..	0.5
CO_2 emissions per capita (metric tons)	..	12.8
Particulate matter (urban-pop.-weighted avg., µg/cu. m)	..	29
Passenger cars (per 1,000 people)	..	433

Water and sanitation

Internal freshwater resources per capita (cu. m)	..	9,703
Freshwater withdrawal		
Total (% of internal resources)	..	10.4
Agriculture (% of total freshwater withdrawal)	..	42
Access to improved water source (% of total population)	100	99
Rural (% of rural population)	100	98
Urban (% of urban population)	100	100
Access to improved sanitation (% of total population)	..	..
Rural (% of rural population)	..	..
Urban (% of urban population)	..	..

Environment and health

ARI prevalence (% of children under age 5)	..	
Diarrhea prevalence (% of children under age 5)	..	
Under-five mortality rate (per 1,000 live births)	..	7

National accounting aggregates, 2004

Gross savings (% of GNI)	..	19.4
Consumption of fixed capital (% of GNI)	..	13.2
Education expenditure (% of GNI)	..	4.6
Energy depletion (% of GNI)	..	1.4
Mineral depletion (% of GNI)	..	0.0
Net forest depletion (% of GNI)	..	0.0
CO_2 damage (% of GNI)	..	0.3
Particulate emission damage (% of GNI)	..	0.4
Adjusted net savings (% of GNI)	..	8.7

Australia

Environmental strategy/action plan prepared in **1992**

	Country data	High income
		Group data
Population (millions)	20.1	1,004
Urban population (% of total)	92.3	78.5
GDP ($ billions)	637.3	32,900
GNI per capita, *World Bank Atlas* method ($)	27,070	32,112
Agriculture		
Land area (1,000 sq. km)	7,682	33,018
Agricultural land (% of land area)	57	38
Irrigated land (% of cropland)	5.3	11.9
Fertilizer consumption (100 grams/ha of arable land)	472	1,205
Population density, rural (people/sq. km of arable land)	3	331
Forests and biodiversity		
Forest area (% of land area)	21.3	29.3
Annual deforestation (% change, 1990–2005)	0.2	–0.1
Nationally protected areas (% of total land area)	13.4	..
Mammal species, total known	376	
Mammal species, threatened	63	
Bird species, total known	851	
Bird species, threatened	60	
GEF benefits index for biodiversity (0–100)	95.8	
Energy		
GDP per unit of energy use (2000 PPP $/kg oil equiv)	4.8	5.2
Energy use per capita (kg oil equiv)	5,668	5,410
Energy from combustible renewables & waste (% of tot.)	4.4	3.0
Energy imports, net (% of energy use)	–125	19
Electric power consumption per capita (kWh)	10,713	9,503
Electricity generated by coal (% of total)	77.2	38.2
Emissions and pollution		
CO_2 emissions per unit of GDP (kg/2000 PPP $ of GDP)	0.7	0.5
CO_2 emissions per capita (metric tons)	18.1	12.8
Particulate matter (urban-pop.-weighted avg., µg/cu. m)	18	29
Passenger cars (per 1,000 people)	..	433
Water and sanitation		
Internal freshwater resources per capita (cu. m)	24,464	9,703
Freshwater withdrawal		
Total (% of internal resources)	4.9	10.4
Agriculture (% of total freshwater withdrawal)	75	42
Access to improved water source (% of total population)	100	99
Rural (% of rural population)	100	98
Urban (% of urban population)	100	100
Access to improved sanitation (% of total population)	100	..
Rural (% of rural population)	100	..
Urban (% of urban population)	100	..
Environment and health		
ARI prevalence (% of children under age 5)	..	
Diarrhea prevalence (% of children under age 5)	..	
Under-five mortality rate (per 1,000 live births)	6	7
National accounting aggregates, 2004		
Gross savings (% of GNI)	19.5	19.4
Consumption of fixed capital (% of GNI)	15.0	13.2
Education expenditure (% of GNI)	4.8	4.6
Energy depletion (% of GNI)	1.5	1.4
Mineral depletion (% of GNI)	1.3	0.0
Net forest depletion (% of GNI)	0.0	0.0
CO_2 damage (% of GNI)	0.4	0.3
Particulate emission damage (% of GNI)	0.1	0.4
Adjusted net savings (% of GNI)	6.0	8.7

Austria

Environmental strategy/action plan prepared in ..

	Country data	Group data High income
Population (millions)	8.2	1,004
Urban population (% of total)	65.8	78.5
GDP ($ billions)	292.3	32,900
GNI per capita, *World Bank Atlas* method ($)	32,280	32,112
Agriculture		
Land area (1,000 sq. km)	82	33,018
Agricultural land (% of land area)	41	38
Irrigated land (% of cropland)	0.3	11.9
Fertilizer consumption (100 grams/ha of arable land)	1,497	1,205
Population density, rural (people/sq. km of arable land)	200	331
Forests and biodiversity		
Forest area (% of land area)	46.8	29.3
Annual deforestation (% change, 1990–2005)	−0.2	−0.1
Nationally protected areas (% of total land area)	33.1	..
Mammal species, total known	101	
Mammal species, threatened	5	
Bird species, total known	412	
Bird species, threatened	8	
GEF benefits index for biodiversity (0–100)	0.3	
Energy		
GDP per unit of energy use (2000 PPP $/kg oil equiv)	7.2	5.2
Energy use per capita (kg oil equiv)	4,086	5,410
Energy from combustible renewables & waste (% of tot.)	11.0	3.0
Energy imports, net (% of energy use)	70	19
Electric power consumption per capita (kWh)	8,104	9,503
Electricity generated by coal (% of total)	15.4	38.2
Emissions and pollution		
CO_2 emissions per unit of GDP (kg/2000 PPP $ of GDP)	0.3	0.5
CO_2 emissions per capita (metric tons)	7.9	12.8
Particulate matter (urban-pop.-weighted avg., μg/cu. m)	37	29
Passenger cars (per 1,000 people)	494	433
Water and sanitation		
Internal freshwater resources per capita (cu. m)	6,729	9,703
Freshwater withdrawal		
Total (% of internal resources)	3.8	10.4
Agriculture (% of total freshwater withdrawal)	1	42
Access to improved water source (% of total population)	100	99
Rural (% of rural population)	100	98
Urban (% of urban population)	100	100
Access to improved sanitation (% of total population)	100	..
Rural (% of rural population)	100	..
Urban (% of urban population)	100	..
Environment and health		
ARI prevalence (% of children under age 5)	..	
Diarrhea prevalence (% of children under age 5)	..	
Under-five mortality rate (per 1,000 live births)	5	7
National accounting aggregates, 2004		
Gross savings (% of GNI)	24.3	19.4
Consumption of fixed capital (% of GNI)	14.4	13.2
Education expenditure (% of GNI)	5.6	4.6
Energy depletion (% of GNI)	0.1	1.4
Mineral depletion (% of GNI)	0.0	0.0
Net forest depletion (% of GNI)	0.0	0.0
CO_2 damage (% of GNI)	0.1	0.3
Particulate emission damage (% of GNI)	0.5	0.4
Adjusted net savings (% of GNI)	14.7	8.7

Azerbaijan

Environmental strategy/action plan prepared in **1998**

	Country data	Europe & Central Asia	Lower middle income
		Group data	
Population (millions)	8.3	472	2,442
Urban population (% of total)	50.0	63.6	48.7
GDP ($ billions)	8.5	1,770	4,165
GNI per capita, *World Bank Atlas* method ($)	940	3,295	1,686
Agriculture			
Land area (1,000 sq. km)	83	23,371	38,470
Agricultural land (% of land area)	57	29	43
Irrigated land (% of cropland)	72.3	11.1	23.1
Fertilizer consumption (100 grams/ha of arable land)	99	347	1,530
Population density, rural (people/sq. km of arable land)	230	126	523
Forests and biodiversity			
Forest area (% of land area)	11.3	38.3	30.7
Annual deforestation (% change, 1990–2005)	0.0	0.0	0.1
Nationally protected areas (% of total land area)	6.4	6.9	7.7
Mammal species, total known	82		
Mammal species, threatened	11		
Bird species, total known	364		
Bird species, threatened	11		
GEF benefits index for biodiversity (0–100)	0.9		
Energy			
GDP per unit of energy use (2000 PPP $/kg oil equiv)	2.3	2.7	4.6
Energy use per capita (kg oil equiv)	1,493	2,794	1,090
Energy from combustible renewables & waste (% of tot.)	0.0	2.4	14.6
Energy imports, net (% of energy use)	–61	–26	–14
Electric power consumption per capita (kWh)	2,355	3,531	1,329
Electricity generated by coal (% of total)	..	29.8	49.4
Emissions and pollution			
CO_2 emissions per unit of GDP (kg/2000 PPP $ of GDP)	1.4	1.0	0.5
CO_2 emissions per capita (metric tons)	3.4	6.7	2.6
Particulate matter (urban-pop.-weighted avg., µg/cu. m)	64	35	70
Passenger cars (per 1,000 people)	43	142	29
Water and sanitation			
Internal freshwater resources per capita (cu. m)	977	11,123	7,295
Freshwater withdrawal			
Total (% of internal resources)	212.6	7.5	7.7
Agriculture (% of total freshwater withdrawal)	68	59	75
Access to improved water source (% of total population)	77	91	81
Rural (% of rural population)	59	80	70
Urban (% of urban population)	95	98	93
Access to improved sanitation (% of total population)	55	82	57
Rural (% of rural population)	36	63	39
Urban (% of urban population)	73	93	78
Environment and health			
ARI prevalence (% of children under age 5)	3.1		
Diarrhea prevalence (% of children under age 5)	21.7		
Under-five mortality rate (per 1,000 live births)	90	34	40
National accounting aggregates, 2004			
Gross savings (% of GNI)	26.3	23.4	32.1
Consumption of fixed capital (% of GNI)	10.8	10.7	10.8
Education expenditure (% of GNI)	3.3	4.1	2.9
Energy depletion (% of GNI)	54.6	12.0	6.5
Mineral depletion (% of GNI)	0.0	0.3	0.5
Net forest depletion (% of GNI)	0.0	0.0	0.0
CO_2 damage (% of GNI)	3.4	1.4	1.1
Particulate emission damage (% of GNI)	0.7	0.7	1.0
Adjusted net savings (% of GNI)	–40.0	2.3	15.1

Bahamas, The

Environmental strategy/action plan prepared in ..

	Country data	Group data High income
Population (millions)	0.3	1,004
Urban population (% of total)	89.7	78.5
GDP ($ billions)	5.3	32,900
GNI per capita, *World Bank Atlas* method ($)	..	32,112
Agriculture		
Land area (1,000 sq. km)	10	33,018
Agricultural land (% of land area)	1	38
Irrigated land (% of cropland)	8.3	11.9
Fertilizer consumption (100 grams/ha of arable land)	1,000	1,205
Population density, rural (people/sq. km of arable land)	416	331
Forests and biodiversity		
Forest area (% of land area)	51.4	29.3
Annual deforestation (% change, 1990–2005)	0.0	–0.1
Nationally protected areas (% of total land area)	..	..
Mammal species, total known	31	
Mammal species, threatened	5	
Bird species, total known	316	
Bird species, threatened	10	
GEF benefits index for biodiversity (0–100)	4.3	
Energy		
GDP per unit of energy use (2000 PPP $/kg oil equiv)	..	5.2
Energy use per capita (kg oil equiv)	..	5,410
Energy from combustible renewables & waste (% of tot.)	..	3.0
Energy imports, net (% of energy use)	..	19
Electric power consumption per capita (kWh)	..	9,503
Electricity generated by coal (% of total)	..	38.2
Emissions and pollution		
CO_2 emissions per unit of GDP (kg/2000 PPP $ of GDP)	0.4	0.5
CO_2 emissions per capita (metric tons)	6.7	12.8
Particulate matter (urban-pop.-weighted avg., µg/cu. m)	18	29
Passenger cars (per 1,000 people)	..	433
Water and sanitation		
Internal freshwater resources per capita (cu. m)	63	9,703
Freshwater withdrawal		
Total (% of internal resources)	..	10.4
Agriculture (% of total freshwater withdrawal)	..	42
Access to improved water source (% of total population)	97	99
Rural (% of rural population)	86	98
Urban (% of urban population)	98	100
Access to improved sanitation (% of total population)	100	..
Rural (% of rural population)	100	..
Urban (% of urban population)	100	..
Environment and health		
ARI prevalence (% of children under age 5)	..	
Diarrhea prevalence (% of children under age 5)	..	
Under-five mortality rate (per 1,000 live births)	13	7
National accounting aggregates, 2004		
Gross savings (% of GNI)	..	19.4
Consumption of fixed capital (% of GNI)	..	13.2
Education expenditure (% of GNI)	3.8	4.6
Energy depletion (% of GNI)	..	1.4
Mineral depletion (% of GNI)	..	0.0
Net forest depletion (% of GNI)	..	0.0
CO_2 damage (% of GNI)	..	0.3
Particulate emission damage (% of GNI)	0.1	0.4
Adjusted net savings (% of GNI)	..	8.7

Bahrain

Environmental strategy/action plan prepared in ..

	Country data	Group data High income
Population (millions)	0.7	1,004
Urban population (% of total)	90.1	78.5
GDP ($ billions)	11.0	32,900
GNI per capita, *World Bank Atlas* method ($)	14,370	32,112
Agriculture		
Land area (1,000 sq. km)	1	33,018
Agricultural land (% of land area)	14	38
Irrigated land (% of cropland)	66.7	11.9
Fertilizer consumption (100 grams/ha of arable land)	500	1,205
Population density, rural (people/sq. km of arable land)	3,533	331
Forests and biodiversity		
Forest area (% of land area)	..	29.3
Annual deforestation (% change, 1990–2005)	..	–0.1
Nationally protected areas (% of total land area)	..	..
Mammal species, total known	14	
Mammal species, threatened	1	
Bird species, total known	196	
Bird species, threatened	7	
GEF benefits index for biodiversity (0–100)	0.0	
Energy		
GDP per unit of energy use (2000 PPP $/kg oil equiv)	1.8	5.2
Energy use per capita (kg oil equiv)	10,253	5,410
Energy from combustible renewables & waste (% of tot.)	..	3.0
Energy imports, net (% of energy use)	–116	19
Electric power consumption per capita (kWh)	10,576	9,503
Electricity generated by coal (% of total)	..	38.2
Emissions and pollution		
CO_2 emissions per unit of GDP (kg/2000 PPP $ of GDP)	1.7	0.5
CO_2 emissions per capita (metric tons)	30.6	12.8
Particulate matter (urban-pop.-weighted avg., µg/cu. m)	65	29
Passenger cars (per 1,000 people)	320	433
Water and sanitation		
Internal freshwater resources per capita (cu. m)	6	9,703
Freshwater withdrawal		
Total (% of internal resources)	..	10.4
Agriculture (% of total freshwater withdrawal)	57	42
Access to improved water source (% of total population)	..	99
Rural (% of rural population)	..	98
Urban (% of urban population)	100	100
Access to improved sanitation (% of total population)	..	..
Rural (% of rural population)	..	..
Urban (% of urban population)	100	..
Environment and health		
ARI prevalence (% of children under age 5)	..	
Diarrhea prevalence (% of children under age 5)	..	
Under-five mortality rate (per 1,000 live births)	11	7
National accounting aggregates, 2004		
Gross savings (% of GNI)	37.7	19.4
Consumption of fixed capital (% of GNI)	14.2	13.2
Education expenditure (% of GNI)	4.4	4.6
Energy depletion (% of GNI)	35.7	1.4
Mineral depletion (% of GNI)	0.0	0.0
Net forest depletion (% of GNI)	0.0	0.0
CO_2 damage (% of GNI)	1.4	0.3
Particulate emission damage (% of GNI)	0.6	0.4
Adjusted net savings (% of GNI)	–9.9	8.7

Bangladesh

Environmental strategy/action plan prepared in **1991**

	Country data	South Asia	Low income
		Group data	
Population (millions)	139.2	1,447	2,343
Urban population (% of total)	24.6	28.3	30.6
GDP ($ billions)	56.6	880	1,239
GNI per capita, *World Bank Atlas* method ($)	440	594	507
Agriculture			
Land area (1,000 sq. km)	130	4,781	29,192
Agricultural land (% of land area)	69	54	45
Irrigated land (% of cropland)	56.1	39.6	23.9
Fertilizer consumption (100 grams/ha of arable land)	1,780	1,040	646
Population density, rural (people/sq. km of arable land)	1,297	586	524
Forests and biodiversity			
Forest area (% of land area)	6.7	16.8	24.8
Annual deforestation (% change, 1990–2005)	0.1	−0.2	0.5
Nationally protected areas (% of total land area)	0.8	4.8	7.7
Mammal species, total known	131		
Mammal species, threatened	22		
Bird species, total known	604		
Bird species, threatened	23		
GEF benefits index for biodiversity (0–100)	1.6		
Energy			
GDP per unit of energy use (2000 PPP $/kg oil equiv)	10.4	5.3	4.2
Energy use per capita (kg oil equiv)	159	474	501
Energy from combustible renewables & waste (% of tot.)	36.9	38.8	48.9
Energy imports, net (% of energy use)	19	19	−4
Electric power consumption per capita (kWh)	128	394	358
Electricity generated by coal (% of total)	..	58.2	46.3
Emissions and pollution			
CO_2 emissions per unit of GDP (kg/2000 PPP $ of GDP)	0.2	0.4	0.4
CO_2 emissions per capita (metric tons)	0.3	1.0	0.8
Particulate matter (urban-pop.-weighted avg., µg/cu. m)	157	99	89
Passenger cars (per 1,000 people)	0	6	6
Water and sanitation			
Internal freshwater resources per capita (cu. m)	754	1,255	3,456
Freshwater withdrawal			
Total (% of internal resources)	75.6	51.8	15.5
Agriculture (% of total freshwater withdrawal)	96	90	88
Access to improved water source (% of total population)	75	84	75
Rural (% of rural population)	72	80	69
Urban (% of urban population)	82	94	89
Access to improved sanitation (% of total population)	48	35	36
Rural (% of rural population)	39	23	24
Urban (% of urban population)	75	64	61
Environment and health			
ARI prevalence (% of children under age 5)	21.0		
Diarrhea prevalence (% of children under age 5)	6.1		
Under-five mortality rate (per 1,000 live births)	77	92	122
National accounting aggregates, 2004			
Gross savings (% of GNI)	29.0	23.6	22.7
Consumption of fixed capital (% of GNI)	8.2	9.1	9.2
Education expenditure (% of GNI)	1.9	3.6	3.4
Energy depletion (% of GNI)	2.4	2.7	6.7
Mineral depletion (% of GNI)	0.0	0.3	0.4
Net forest depletion (% of GNI)	0.7	0.7	0.7
CO_2 damage (% of GNI)	0.4	1.2	1.1
Particulate emission damage (% of GNI)	0.5	0.8	0.8
Adjusted net savings (% of GNI)	18.7	12.4	7.3

Barbados

Environmental strategy/action plan prepared in ..

	Country data	Group data Latin America & Caribbean	Group data Upper middle income
Population (millions)	0.3	546	576
Urban population (% of total)	52.3	77.1	72.3
GDP ($ billions)	2.8	2,022	2,992
GNI per capita, *World Bank Atlas* method ($)	..	3,576	4,769
Agriculture			
Land area (1,000 sq. km)	0	20,057	28,983
Agricultural land (% of land area)	44	36	26
Irrigated land (% of cropland)	29.4	11.4	8.7
Fertilizer consumption (100 grams/ha of arable land)	507	923	469
Population density, rural (people/sq. km of arable land)	809	212	131
Forests and biodiversity			
Forest area (% of land area)	4.7	45.6	37.3
Annual deforestation (% change, 1990–2005)	0.0	0.4	0.1
Nationally protected areas (% of total land area)	..	11.1	..
Mammal species, total known	13		
Mammal species, threatened	0		
Bird species, total known	223		
Bird species, threatened	3		
GEF benefits index for biodiversity (0–100)	0.3		
Energy			
GDP per unit of energy use (2000 PPP $/kg oil equiv)	..	6.2	3.5
Energy use per capita (kg oil equiv)	..	1,148	2,574
Energy from combustible renewables & waste (% of tot.)	..	15.0	3.9
Energy imports, net (% of energy use)	..	–40	–51
Electric power consumption per capita (kWh)	..	1,615	3,378
Electricity generated by coal (% of total)	..	5.4	31.0
Emissions and pollution			
CO_2 emissions per unit of GDP (kg/2000 PPP $ of GDP)	..	0.3	0.7
CO_2 emissions per capita (metric tons)	4.6	2.4	6.2
Particulate matter (urban-pop.-weighted avg., µg/cu. m)	95	43	40
Passenger cars (per 1,000 people)	303	108	143
Water and sanitation			
Internal freshwater resources per capita (cu. m)	298	24,619	14,190
Freshwater withdrawal			
Total (% of internal resources)	112.5	2.0	3.8
Agriculture (% of total freshwater withdrawal)	22	71	53
Access to improved water source (% of total population)	100	89	93
Rural (% of rural population)	100	69	82
Urban (% of urban population)	100	96	97
Access to improved sanitation (% of total population)	99	75	81
Rural (% of rural population)	100	44	61
Urban (% of urban population)	99	84	91
Environment and health			
ARI prevalence (% of children under age 5)	..		
Diarrhea prevalence (% of children under age 5)	..		
Under-five mortality rate (per 1,000 live births)	12	31	28
National accounting aggregates, 2004			
Gross savings (% of GNI)	..	22.7	23.1
Consumption of fixed capital (% of GNI)	13.5	12.1	11.5
Education expenditure (% of GNI)	7.1	4.4	4.5
Energy depletion (% of GNI)	0.1	7.2	11.2
Mineral depletion (% of GNI)	0.0	1.1	0.6
Net forest depletion (% of GNI)	..	0.0	0.0
CO_2 damage (% of GNI)	0.3	0.5	0.9
Particulate emission damage (% of GNI)	0.2	0.6	0.7
Adjusted net savings (% of GNI)	..	5.6	2.6

Belarus

Environmental strategy/action plan prepared in ..

	Country data	Group data Europe & Central Asia	Lower middle income
Population (millions)	9.8	472	2,442
Urban population (% of total)	71.3	63.6	48.7
GDP ($ billions)	22.9	1,770	4,165
GNI per capita, *World Bank Atlas* method ($)	2,140	3,295	1,686

Agriculture
Land area (1,000 sq. km)	207	23,371	38,470
Agricultural land (% of land area)	43	29	43
Irrigated land (% of cropland)	2.3	11.1	23.1
Fertilizer consumption (100 grams/ha of arable land)	1,334	347	1,530
Population density, rural (people/sq. km of arable land)	52	126	523

Forests and biodiversity
Forest area (% of land area)	38.0	38.3	30.7
Annual deforestation (% change, 1990–2005)	−0.5	0.0	0.1
Nationally protected areas (% of total land area)	6.3	6.9	7.7
Mammal species, total known	71		
Mammal species, threatened	6		
Bird species, total known	226		
Bird species, threatened	4		
GEF benefits index for biodiversity (0–100)	0.0		

Energy
GDP per unit of energy use (2000 PPP $/kg oil equiv)	2.2	2.7	4.6
Energy use per capita (kg oil equiv)	2,613	2,794	1,090
Energy from combustible renewables & waste (% of tot.)	4.2	2.4	14.6
Energy imports, net (% of energy use)	86	−26	−14
Electric power consumption per capita (kWh)	3,039	3,531	1,329
Electricity generated by coal (% of total)	0.0	29.8	49.4

Emissions and pollution
CO_2 emissions per unit of GDP (kg/2000 PPP $ of GDP)	1.2	1.0	0.5
CO_2 emissions per capita (metric tons)	6.0	6.7	2.6
Particulate matter (urban-pop.-weighted avg., µg/cu. m)	9	35	70
Passenger cars (per 1,000 people)	156	142	29

Water and sanitation
Internal freshwater resources per capita (cu. m)	3,786	11,123	7,295
Freshwater withdrawal			
Total (% of internal resources)	7.5	7.5	7.7
Agriculture (% of total freshwater withdrawal)	30	59	75
Access to improved water source (% of total population)	100	91	81
Rural (% of rural population)	100	80	70
Urban (% of urban population)	100	98	93
Access to improved sanitation (% of total population)	..	82	57
Rural (% of rural population)	..	63	39
Urban (% of urban population)	..	93	78

Environment and health
ARI prevalence (% of children under age 5)	..		
Diarrhea prevalence (% of children under age 5)	..		
Under-five mortality rate (per 1,000 live births)	11	34	40

National accounting aggregates, 2004
Gross savings (% of GNI)	23.6	23.4	32.1
Consumption of fixed capital (% of GNI)	11.0	10.7	10.8
Education expenditure (% of GNI)	5.4	4.1	2.9
Energy depletion (% of GNI)	2.1	12.0	6.5
Mineral depletion (% of GNI)	0.0	0.3	0.5
Net forest depletion (% of GNI)	0.0	0.0	0.0
CO_2 damage (% of GNI)	2.1	1.4	1.1
Particulate emission damage (% of GNI)	..	0.7	1.0
Adjusted net savings (% of GNI)	13.8	2.3	15.1

Belgium

Environmental strategy/action plan prepared in ..

	Country data	Group data High income
Population (millions)	10.4	1,004
Urban population (% of total)	97.2	78.5
GDP ($ billions)	352.3	32,900
GNI per capita, *World Bank Atlas* method ($)	31,280	32,112

Agriculture		
Land area (1,000 sq. km)	33	33,018
Agricultural land (% of land area)	46	38
Irrigated land (% of cropland)	4.5	11.9
Fertilizer consumption (100 grams/ha of arable land)	3,310	1,205
Population density, rural (people/sq. km of arable land)	33	331

Forests and biodiversity		
Forest area (% of land area)	20.3	29.3
Annual deforestation (% change, 1990–2005)	0.1	–0.1
Nationally protected areas (% of total land area)	..	..
Mammal species, total known	92	
Mammal species, threatened	9	
Bird species, total known	427	
Bird species, threatened	10	
GEF benefits index for biodiversity (0–100)	0.0	

Energy		
GDP per unit of energy use (2000 PPP $/kg oil equiv)	4.9	5.2
Energy use per capita (kg oil equiv)	5,701	5,410
Energy from combustible renewables & waste (% of tot.)	2.0	3.0
Energy imports, net (% of energy use)	77	19
Electric power consumption per capita (kWh)	8,412	9,503
Electricity generated by coal (% of total)	13.9	38.2

Emissions and pollution		
CO_2 emissions per unit of GDP (kg/2000 PPP $ of GDP)	0.4	0.5
CO_2 emissions per capita (metric tons)	8.9	12.8
Particulate matter (urban-pop.-weighted avg., µg/cu. m)	28	29
Passenger cars (per 1,000 people)	467	433

Water and sanitation		
Internal freshwater resources per capita (cu. m)	1,152	9,703
Freshwater withdrawal		
Total (% of internal resources)	..	10.4
Agriculture (% of total freshwater withdrawal)	..	42
Access to improved water source (% of total population)	..	99
Rural (% of rural population)	..	98
Urban (% of urban population)	100	100
Access to improved sanitation (% of total population)	..	..
Rural (% of rural population)	..	..
Urban (% of urban population)	..	..

Environment and health		
ARI prevalence (% of children under age 5)	..	
Diarrhea prevalence (% of children under age 5)	..	
Under-five mortality rate (per 1,000 live births)	5	7

National accounting aggregates, 2004		
Gross savings (% of GNI)	23.2	19.4
Consumption of fixed capital (% of GNI)	15.6	13.2
Education expenditure (% of GNI)	3.0	4.6
Energy depletion (% of GNI)	0.0	1.4
Mineral depletion (% of GNI)	0.0	0.0
Net forest depletion (% of GNI)	0.0	0.0
CO_2 damage (% of GNI)	0.2	0.3
Particulate emission damage (% of GNI)	0.3	0.4
Adjusted net savings (% of GNI)	10.1	8.7

Belize

Environmental strategy/action plan prepared in ..

	Country data	Group data Latin America & Caribbean	Group data Upper middle income
Population (millions)	0.3	546	576
Urban population (% of total)	48.5	77.1	72.3
GDP ($ billions)	1.1	2,022	2,992
GNI per capita, World Bank Atlas method ($)	3,940	3,576	4,769
Agriculture			
Land area (1,000 sq. km)	23	20,057	28,983
Agricultural land (% of land area)	7	36	26
Irrigated land (% of cropland)	2.9	11.4	8.7
Fertilizer consumption (100 grams/ha of arable land)	671	923	469
Population density, rural (people/sq. km of arable land)	202	212	131
Forests and biodiversity			
Forest area (% of land area)	72.5	45.6	37.3
Annual deforestation (% change, 1990–2005)	0.0	0.4	0.1
Nationally protected areas (% of total land area)	..	11.1	..
Mammal species, total known	147		
Mammal species, threatened	5		
Bird species, total known	544		
Bird species, threatened	3		
GEF benefits index for biodiversity (0–100)	1.9		
Energy			
GDP per unit of energy use (2000 PPP $/kg oil equiv)	..	6.2	3.5
Energy use per capita (kg oil equiv)	..	1,148	2,574
Energy from combustible renewables & waste (% of tot.)	..	15.0	3.9
Energy imports, net (% of energy use)	..	−40	−51
Electric power consumption per capita (kWh)	..	1,615	3,378
Electricity generated by coal (% of total)	..	5.4	31.0
Emissions and pollution			
CO_2 emissions per unit of GDP (kg/2000 PPP $ of GDP)	0.5	0.3	0.7
CO_2 emissions per capita (metric tons)	3.0	2.4	6.2
Particulate matter (urban-pop.-weighted avg., µg/cu. m)	12	43	40
Passenger cars (per 1,000 people)	42	108	143
Water and sanitation			
Internal freshwater resources per capita (cu. m)	56,617	24,619	14,190
Freshwater withdrawal			
Total (% of internal resources)	0.9	2.0	3.8
Agriculture (% of total freshwater withdrawal)	20	71	53
Access to improved water source (% of total population)	91	89	93
Rural (% of rural population)	82	69	82
Urban (% of urban population)	100	96	97
Access to improved sanitation (% of total population)	47	75	81
Rural (% of rural population)	25	44	61
Urban (% of urban population)	71	84	91
Environment and health			
ARI prevalence (% of children under age 5)	..		
Diarrhea prevalence (% of children under age 5)	..		
Under-five mortality rate (per 1,000 live births)	39	31	28
National accounting aggregates, 2004			
Gross savings (% of GNI)	..	22.7	23.1
Consumption of fixed capital (% of GNI)	12.0	12.1	11.5
Education expenditure (% of GNI)	5.2	4.4	4.5
Energy depletion (% of GNI)	0.0	7.2	11.2
Mineral depletion (% of GNI)	0.0	1.1	0.6
Net forest depletion (% of GNI)	0.0	0.0	0.0
CO_2 damage (% of GNI)	0.5	0.5	0.9
Particulate emission damage (% of GNI)	..	0.6	0.7
Adjusted net savings (% of GNI)	..	5.6	2.6

Benin

Environmental strategy/action plan prepared in **1993**

	Country data	Group data Sub-Saharan Africa	Low income
Population (millions)	8.2	726	2,343
Urban population (% of total)	45.3	36.4	30.6
GDP ($ billions)	4.1	523	1,239
GNI per capita, *World Bank Atlas* method ($)	450	601	507

Agriculture

Land area (1,000 sq. km)	111	23,596	29,192
Agricultural land (% of land area)	31	44	45
Irrigated land (% of cropland)	0.4	3.6	23.9
Fertilizer consumption (100 grams/ha of arable land)	188	136	646
Population density, rural (people/sq. km of arable land)	166	355	524

Forests and biodiversity

Forest area (% of land area)	21.3	26.5	24.8
Annual deforestation (% change, 1990–2005)	1.9	0.6	0.5
Nationally protected areas (% of total land area)	11.4	8.7	7.7
Mammal species, total known	159		
Mammal species, threatened	6		
Bird species, total known	485		
Bird species, threatened	2		
GEF benefits index for biodiversity (0–100)	0.2		

Energy

GDP per unit of energy use (2000 PPP $/kg oil equiv)	3.5	2.8	4.2
Energy use per capita (kg oil equiv)	292	681	501
Energy from combustible renewables & waste (% of tot.)	68.6	57.4	48.9
Energy imports, net (% of energy use)	31	–59	–4
Electric power consumption per capita (kWh)	61	513	358
Electricity generated by coal (% of total)	..	68.0	46.3

Emissions and pollution

CO_2 emissions per unit of GDP (kg/2000 PPP $ of GDP)	0.2	0.4	0.4
CO_2 emissions per capita (metric tons)	0.3	0.7	0.8
Particulate matter (urban-pop.-weighted avg., µg/cu. m)	51	73	89
Passenger cars (per 1,000 people)	..	..	6

Water and sanitation

Internal freshwater resources per capita (cu. m)	1,260	5,353	3,456
Freshwater withdrawal			
Total (% of internal resources)	1.3	3.1	15.5
Agriculture (% of total freshwater withdrawal)	45	87	88
Access to improved water source (% of total population)	68	58	75
Rural (% of rural population)	60	45	69
Urban (% of urban population)	79	82	89
Access to improved sanitation (% of total population)	32	36	36
Rural (% of rural population)	12	26	24
Urban (% of urban population)	58	55	61

Environment and health

ARI prevalence (% of children under age 5)	41.2		
Diarrhea prevalence (% of children under age 5)	13.4		
Under-five mortality rate (per 1,000 live births)	152	168	122

National accounting aggregates, 2004

Gross savings (% of GNI)	12.5	17.1	22.7
Consumption of fixed capital (% of GNI)	9.0	10.9	9.2
Education expenditure (% of GNI)	2.4	3.9	3.4
Energy depletion (% of GNI)	0.1	9.8	6.7
Mineral depletion (% of GNI)	0.0	0.4	0.4
Net forest depletion (% of GNI)	0.0	0.6	0.7
CO_2 damage (% of GNI)	0.3	0.7	1.1
Particulate emission damage (% of GNI)	0.5	0.5	0.8
Adjusted net savings (% of GNI)	5.1	–1.9	7.3

Bermuda

Environmental strategy/action plan prepared in ..

	Country data	Group data High income
Population (millions)	0.1	1,004
Urban population (% of total)	100.0	78.5
GDP ($ billions)	..	32,900
GNI per capita, *World Bank Atlas* method ($)	..	32,112

Agriculture
Land area (1,000 sq. km)	0	33,018
Agricultural land (% of land area)	20	38
Irrigated land (% of cropland)	..	11.9
Fertilizer consumption (100 grams/ha of arable land)	1,000	1,205
Population density, rural (people/sq. km of arable land)	0	331

Forests and biodiversity
Forest area (% of land area)	20.0	29.3
Annual deforestation (% change, 1990–2005)	0.0	–0.1
Nationally protected areas (% of total land area)	..	..
Mammal species, total known	8	
Mammal species, threatened	2	
Bird species, total known	235	
Bird species, threatened	3	
GEF benefits index for biodiversity (0–100)	1.5	

Energy
GDP per unit of energy use (2000 PPP $/kg oil equiv)	..	5.2
Energy use per capita (kg oil equiv)	..	5,410
Energy from combustible renewables & waste (% of tot.)	..	3.0
Energy imports, net (% of energy use)	..	19
Electric power consumption per capita (kWh)	..	9,503
Electricity generated by coal (% of total)	..	38.2

Emissions and pollution
CO_2 emissions per unit of GDP (kg/2000 PPP $ of GDP)	..	0.5
CO_2 emissions per capita (metric tons)	7.7	12.8
Particulate matter (urban-pop.-weighted avg., µg/cu. m)	..	29
Passenger cars (per 1,000 people)	..	433

Water and sanitation
Internal freshwater resources per capita (cu. m)	..	9,703
Freshwater withdrawal		
Total (% of internal resources)	..	10.4
Agriculture (% of total freshwater withdrawal)	..	42
Access to improved water source (% of total population)	..	99
Rural (% of rural population)	..	98
Urban (% of urban population)	..	100
Access to improved sanitation (% of total population)	..	..
Rural (% of rural population)	..	..
Urban (% of urban population)	..	..

Environment and health
ARI prevalence (% of children under age 5)	..	
Diarrhea prevalence (% of children under age 5)	..	
Under-five mortality rate (per 1,000 live births)	..	7

National accounting aggregates, 2004
Gross savings (% of GNI)	..	19.4
Consumption of fixed capital (% of GNI)	..	13.2
Education expenditure (% of GNI)	3.3	4.6
Energy depletion (% of GNI)	..	1.4
Mineral depletion (% of GNI)	..	0.0
Net forest depletion (% of GNI)	..	0.0
CO_2 damage (% of GNI)	..	0.3
Particulate emission damage (% of GNI)	..	0.4
Adjusted net savings (% of GNI)	..	8.7

Bhutan

Environmental strategy/action plan prepared in ..

	Country data	South Asia	Low income
		Group data	
Population (millions)	0.9	1,447	2,343
Urban population (% of total)	8.8	28.3	30.6
GDP ($ billions)	0.7	880	1,239
GNI per capita, *World Bank Atlas* method ($)	760	594	507
Agriculture			
Land area (1,000 sq. km)	47	4,781	29,192
Agricultural land (% of land area)	12	54	45
Irrigated land (% of cropland)	31.3	39.6	23.9
Fertilizer consumption (100 grams/ha of arable land)	0	1,040	646
Population density, rural (people/sq. km of arable land)	740	586	524
Forests and biodiversity			
Forest area (% of land area)	68.0	16.8	24.8
Annual deforestation (% change, 1990–2005)	–0.4	–0.2	0.5
Nationally protected areas (% of total land area)	25.1	4.8	7.7
Mammal species, total known	92		
Mammal species, threatened	21		
Bird species, total known	625		
Bird species, threatened	18		
GEF benefits index for biodiversity (0–100)	1.1		
Energy			
GDP per unit of energy use (2000 PPP $/kg oil equiv)	..	5.3	4.2
Energy use per capita (kg oil equiv)	..	474	501
Energy from combustible renewables & waste (% of tot.)	..	38.8	48.9
Energy imports, net (% of energy use)	..	19	–4
Electric power consumption per capita (kWh)	..	394	358
Electricity generated by coal (% of total)	..	58.2	46.3
Emissions and pollution			
CO_2 emissions per unit of GDP (kg/2000 PPP $ of GDP)	..	0.4	0.4
CO_2 emissions per capita (metric tons)	0.5	1.0	0.8
Particulate matter (urban-pop.-weighted avg., µg/cu. m)	13	99	89
Passenger cars (per 1,000 people)	12	6	6
Water and sanitation			
Internal freshwater resources per capita (cu. m)	106,026	1,255	3,456
Freshwater withdrawal			
Total (% of internal resources)	0.4	51.8	15.5
Agriculture (% of total freshwater withdrawal)	94	90	88
Access to improved water source (% of total population)	62	84	75
Rural (% of rural population)	60	80	69
Urban (% of urban population)	86	94	89
Access to improved sanitation (% of total population)	70	35	36
Rural (% of rural population)	70	23	24
Urban (% of urban population)	65	64	61
Environment and health			
ARI prevalence (% of children under age 5)	..		
Diarrhea prevalence (% of children under age 5)	..		
Under-five mortality rate (per 1,000 live births)	80	92	122
National accounting aggregates, 2004			
Gross savings (% of GNI)	..	23.6	22.7
Consumption of fixed capital (% of GNI)	9.7	9.1	9.2
Education expenditure (% of GNI)	4.0	3.6	3.4
Energy depletion (% of GNI)	0.0	2.7	6.7
Mineral depletion (% of GNI)	0.0	0.3	0.4
Net forest depletion (% of GNI)	4.2	0.7	0.7
CO_2 damage (% of GNI)	0.5	1.2	1.1
Particulate emission damage (% of GNI)	..	0.8	0.8
Adjusted net savings (% of GNI)	..	12.4	7.3

Bolivia

Environmental strategy/action plan prepared in **1994**

	Country data	Latin America & Caribbean	Lower middle income
		Group data	
Population (m llions)	9.0	546	2,442
Urban population (% of total)	63.9	77.1	48.7
GDP ($ billions)	8.8	2,022	4,165
GNI per capita, *World Bank Atlas* method ($)	960	3,576	1,686

Agriculture

Land area (1,000 sq. km)	1,084	20,057	38,470
Agricultural land (% of land area)	34	36	43
Irrigated land (% of cropland)	4.1	11.4	23.1
Fertilizer consumption (100 grams/ha of arable land)	45	923	1,530
Population density, rural (people/sq. km of arable land)	106	212	523

Forests and biodiversity

Forest area (% of land area)	54.2	45.6	30.7
Annual deforestation (% change, 1990–2005)	0.4	0.4	0.1
Nationally protected areas (% of total land area)	13.4	11.1	7.7
Mammal species, total known	361		
Mammal species, threatened	26		
Bird species, tctal known	1,414		
Bird species, threatened	30		
GEF benefits index for biodiversity (0–100)	13.8		

Energy

GDP per unit of energy use (2000 PPP $/kg oil equiv)	4.9	6.2	4.6
Energy use per capita (kg oil equiv)	504	1,148	1,090
Energy from combustible renewables & waste (% of tot.)	16.2	15.0	14.6
Energy imports, net (% of energy use)	−74	−40	−14
Electric power consumption per capita (kWh)	422	1,615	1,329
Electricity generated by coal (% of total)	..	5.4	49.4

Emissions and pollution

CO_2 emissions per unit of GDP (kg/2000 PPP $ of GDP)	0.4	0.3	0.5
CO_2 emissions per capita (metric tons)	1.2	2.4	2.6
Particulate matter (urban-pop.-weighted avg., μg/cu. m)	92	43	70
Passenger cars (per 1,000 people)	3	108	29

Water and sanitation

Internal freshwater resources per capita (cu. m)	33,692	24,619	7,295
Freshwater withdrawal			
Total (% of inte·nal resources)	0.5	2.0	7.7
Agriculture (% of total freshwater withdrawal)	81	71	75
Access to improved water source (% of total population)	85	89	81
Rural (% of rural population)	68	69	70
Urban (% of urban population)	95	96	93
Access to improved sanitation (% of total population)	45	75	57
Rural (% of rural population)	23	44	39
Urban (% of urban population)	58	84	78

Environment and health

ARI prevalence (% of children under age 5)	22.0		
Diarrhea prevalence (% of children under age 5)	24.8		
Under-five mortali:y rate (per 1,000 live births)	69	31	40

National accounting aggregates, 2004

Gross savings (% of GNI)	18.2	22.7	32.1
Consumption of fixed capital (% of GNI)	10.3	12.1	10.8
Education expenditure (% of GNI)	6.3	4.4	2.9
Energy depletion (% of GNI)	15.4	7.2	6.5
Mineral depletion (% of GNI)	1.0	1.1	0.5
Net forest depletion (% of GNI)	0.0	0.0	0.0
CO_2 damage (% of GNI)	0.7	0.5	1.1
Particulate emission damage (% of GNI)	1.0	0.6	1.0
Adjusted net savings (% of GNI)	−3.9	5.6	15.1

Bosnia and Herzegovina

Environmental strategy/action plan prepared in ..

	Country data	Group data — Europe & Central Asia	Group data — Lower middle income
Population (millions)	3.9	472	2,442
Urban population (% of total)	44.9	63.6	48.7
GDP ($ billions)	8.5	1,770	4,165
GNI per capita, *World Bank Atlas* method ($)	2,040	3,295	1,686
Agriculture			
Land area (1,000 sq. km)	51	23,371	38,470
Agricultural land (% of land area)	42	29	43
Irrigated land (% of cropland)	0.3	11.1	23.1
Fertilizer consumption (100 grams/ha of arable land)	327	347	1,530
Population density, rural (people/sq. km of arable land)	217	126	523
Forests and biodiversity			
Forest area (% of land area)	42.7	38.3	30.7
Annual deforestation (% change, 1990–2005)	0.1	0.0	0.1
Nationally protected areas (% of total land area)	0.5	6.9	7.7
Mammal species, total known	78		
Mammal species, threatened	8		
Bird species, total known	312		
Bird species, threatened	8		
GEF benefits index for biodiversity (0–100)	0.4		
Energy			
GDP per unit of energy use (2000 PPP $/kg oil equiv)	5.3	2.7	4.6
Energy use per capita (kg oil equiv)	1,136	2,794	1,090
Energy from combustible renewables & waste (% of tot.)	4.2	2.4	14.6
Energy imports, net (% of energy use)	30	−26	−14
Electric power consumption per capita (kWh)	2,096	3,531	1,329
Electricity generated by coal (% of total)	50.9	29.8	49.4
Emissions and pollution			
CO_2 emissions per unit of GDP (kg/2000 PPP $ of GDP)	0.9	1.0	0.5
CO_2 emissions per capita (metric tons)	4.7	6.7	2.6
Particulate matter (urban-pop.-weighted avg., µg/cu. m)	22	35	70
Passenger cars (per 1,000 people)	..	142	29
Water and sanitation			
Internal freshwater resources per capita (cu. m)	9,080	11,123	7,295
Freshwater withdrawal			
Total (% of internal resources)	..	7.5	7.7
Agriculture (% of total freshwater withdrawal)	..	59	75
Access to improved water source (% of total population)	98	91	81
Rural (% of rural population)	96	80	70
Urban (% of urban population)	100	98	93
Access to improved sanitation (% of total population)	93	82	57
Rural (% of rural population)	88	63	39
Urban (% of urban population)	99	93	78
Environment and health			
ARI prevalence (% of children under age 5)	1.5		
Diarrhea prevalence (% of children under age 5)	8.9		
Under-five mortality rate (per 1,000 live births)	15	34	40
National accounting aggregates, 2004			
Gross savings (% of GNI)	3.9	23.4	32.1
Consumption of fixed capital (% of GNI)	10.6	10.7	10.8
Education expenditure (% of GNI)	..	4.1	2.9
Energy depletion (% of GNI)	0.1	12.0	6.5
Mineral depletion (% of GNI)	0.0	0.3	0.5
Net forest depletion (% of GNI)	..	0.0	0.0
CO_2 damage (% of GNI)	1.6	1.4	1.1
Particulate emission damage (% of GNI)	0.2	0.7	1.0
Adjusted net savings (% of GNI)	..	2.3	15.1

Botswana

Environmental strategy/action plan prepared in **1990**

	Country data	Group data Sub-Saharan Africa	Group data Upper middle income
Population (millions)	1.8	726	576
Urban population (% of total)	52.1	36.4	72.3
GDP ($ billions)	9.0	523	2,992
GNI per capita, *World Bank Atlas* method ($)	4,360	601	4,769

Agriculture

Land area (1,000 sq. km)	567	23,596	28,983
Agricultural land (% of land area)	46	44	26
Irrigated land (% of cropland)	0.3	3.6	8.7
Fertilizer consumption (100 grams/ha of arable land)	122	136	469
Population density, rural (people/sq. km of arable land)	228	355	131

Forests and biodiversity

Forest area (% of land area)	21.1	26.5	37.3
Annual deforestation (% change, 1990–2005)	0.9	0.6	0.1
Nationally protected areas (% of total land area)	18.5	8.7	..
Mammal species, total known	169		
Mammal species, threatened	6		
Bird species, total known	570		
Bird species, threatened	9		
GEF benefits index for biodiversity (0–100)	1.5		

Energy

GDP per unit of energy use (2000 PPP $/kg oil equiv)	..	2.8	3.5
Energy use per capita (kg oil equiv)	..	681	2,574
Energy from combustible renewables & waste (% of tot.)	..	57.4	3.9
Energy imports, net (% of energy use)	..	−59	−51
Electric power consumption per capita (kWh)	..	513	3,378
Electricity generated by coal (% of total)	..	68.0	31.0

Emissions and pollution

CO_2 emissions per unit of GDP (kg/2000 PPP $ of GDP)	0.3	0.4	0.7
CO_2 emissions per capita (metric tons)	2.3	0.7	6.2
Particulate matter (urban-pop.-weighted avg., µg/cu. m)	25	73	40
Passenger cars (per 1,000 people)	35	..	143

Water and sanitation

Internal freshwater resources per capita (cu. m)	1,357	5,353	14,190
Freshwater withdrawal			
Total (% of internal resources)	8.1	3.1	3.8
Agriculture (% of total freshwater withdrawal)	41	87	53
Access to improved water source (% of total population)	95	58	93
Rural (% of rural population)	90	45	82
Urban (% of urban population)	100	82	97
Access to improved sanitation (% of total population)	41	36	81
Rural (% of rural population)	25	26	61
Urban (% of urban population)	57	55	91

Environment and health

ARI prevalence (% of children under age 5)	40.0		
Diarrhea prevalence (% of children under age 5)	6.5		
Under-five mortality rate (per 1,000 live births)	116	168	28

National accounting aggregates, 2004

Gross savings (% of GNI)	40.0	17.1	23.1
Consumption of fixed capital (% of GNI)	12.5	10.9	11.5
Education expenditure (% of GNI)	5.6	3.9	4.5
Energy depletion (% of GNI)	0.0	9.8	11.2
Mineral depletion (% of GNI)	2.0	0.4	0.6
Net forest depletion (% of GNI)	0.0	0.6	0.0
CO_2 damage (% of GNI)	0.4	0.7	0.9
Particulate emission damage (% of GNI)	..	0.5	0.7
Adjusted net savings (% of GNI)	30.8	−1.9	2.6

Brazil

Environmental strategy/action plan prepared in ..

	Country data	Latin America & Caribbean	Lower middle income
		Group data	
Population (millions)	183.9	546	2,442
Urban population (% of total)	83.6	77.1	48.7
GDP ($ billions)	604.0	2,022	4,165
GNI per capita, World Bank Atlas method ($)	3,000	3,576	1,686
Agriculture			
Land area (1,000 sq. km)	8,459	20,057	38,470
Agricultural land (% of land area)	31	36	43
Irrigated land (% of cropland)	4.4	11.4	23.1
Fertilizer consumption (100 grams/ha of arable land)	1,302	923	1,530
Population density, rural (people/sq. km of arable land)	52	212	523
Forests and biodiversity			
Forest area (% of land area)	56.5	45.6	30.7
Annual deforestation (% change, 1990–2005)	0.5	0.4	0.1
Nationally protected areas (% of total land area)	6.7	11.1	7.7
Mammal species, total known	578		
Mammal species, threatened	74		
Bird species, total known	1,712		
Bird species, threatened	120		
GEF benefits index for biodiversity (0–100)	100.0		
Energy			
GDP per unit of energy use (2000 PPP $/kg oil equiv)	6.9	6.2	4.6
Energy use per capita (kg oil equiv)	1,065	1,148	1,090
Energy from combustible renewables & waste (% of tot.)	25.9	15.0	14.6
Energy imports, net (% of energy use)	11	–40	–14
Electric power consumption per capita (kWh)	1,883	1,615	1,329
Electricity generated by coal (% of total)	2.4	5.4	49.4
Emissions and pollution			
CO_2 emissions per unit of GDP (kg/2000 PPP $ of GDP)	0.2	0.3	0.5
CO_2 emissions per capita (metric tons)	1.8	2.4	2.6
Particulate matter (urban-pop.-weighted avg., µg/cu. m)	35	43	70
Passenger cars (per 1,000 people)	137	108	29
Water and sanitation			
Internal freshwater resources per capita (cu. m)	29,460	24,619	7,295
Freshwater withdrawal			
Total (% of internal resources)	1.1	2.0	7.7
Agriculture (% of total freshwater withdrawal)	62	71	75
Access to improved water source (% of total population)	89	89	81
Rural (% of rural population)	58	69	70
Urban (% of urban population)	96	96	93
Access to improved sanitation (% of total population)	75	75	57
Rural (% of rural population)	35	44	39
Urban (% of urban population)	83	84	78
Environment and health			
ARI prevalence (% of children under age 5)	..		
Diarrhea prevalence (% of children under age 5)	..		
Under-five mortality rate (per 1,000 live births)	34	31	40
National accounting aggregates, 2004			
Gross savings (% of GNI)	24.0	22.7	32.1
Consumption of fixed capital (% of GNI)	11.8	12.1	10.8
Education expenditure (% of GNI)	4.1	4.4	2.9
Energy depletion (% of GNI)	3.7	7.2	6.5
Mineral depletion (% of GNI)	1.1	1.1	0.5
Net forest depletion (% of GNI)	0.0	0.0	0.0
CO_2 damage (% of GNI)	0.4	0.5	1.1
Particulate emission damage (% of GNI)	0.4	0.6	1.0
Adjusted net savings (% of GNI)	10.7	5.6	15.1

Brunei Darussalam

Environmental strategy/action plan prepared in ..

	Country data	Group data — High income
Population (millions)	0.4	1,004
Urban population (% of total)	76.9	78.5
GDP ($ billions)	..	32,900
GNI per capita, *World Bank Atlas* method ($)	..	32,112

Agriculture
Land area (1,000 sq. km)	5	33,018
Agricultural land (% of land area)	4	38
Irrigated land (% of cropland)	5.9	11.9
Fertilizer consumption (100 grams/ha of arable land)	0	1,205
Population density, rural (people/sq. km of arable land)	712	331

Forests and biodiversity
Forest area (% of land area)	52.8	29.3
Annual deforestation (% change, 1990–2005)	0.7	–0.1
Nationally protected areas (% of total land area)	..	..
Mammal species, total known	112	
Mammal species, threatened	11	
Bird species, total known	455	
Bird species, threatened	25	
GEF benefits index for biodiversity (0–100)	0.1	

Energy
GDP per unit of energy use (2000 PPP $/kg oil equiv)	..	5.2
Energy use per capita (kg oil equiv)	7,495	5,410
Energy from combustible renewables & waste (% of tot.)	0.7	3.0
Energy imports, net (% of energy use)	–692	19
Electric power consumption per capita (kWh)	7,515	9,503
Electricity generated by coal (% of total)	..	38.2

Emissions and pollution
CO_2 emissions per unit of GDP (kg/2000 PPP $ of GDP)	..	0.5
CO_2 emissions per capita (metric tons)	17.7	12.8
Particulate matter (urban-pop.-weighted avg., μg/cu. m)	48	29
Passenger cars (per 1,000 people)	329	433

Water and sanitation
Internal freshwater resources per capita (cu. m)	23,244	9,703
Freshwater withdrawal		
Total (% of internal resources)	..	10.4
Agriculture (% of total freshwater withdrawal)	..	42
Access to improved water source (% of total population)	..	99
Rural (% of rural population)	..	98
Urban (% of urban population)	..	100
Access to improved sanitation (% of total population)	..	..
Rural (% of rural population)	..	..
Urban (% of urban population)	..	..

Environment and health
ARI prevalence (% of children under age 5)	..	
Diarrhea prevalence (% of children under age 5)	..	
Under-five mortality rate (per 1,000 live births)	9	7

National accounting aggregates, 2004
Gross savings (% of GNI)	..	19.4
Consumption of fixed capital (% of GNI)	..	13.2
Education expenditure (% of GNI)	2.8	4.6
Energy depletion (% of GNI)	..	1.4
Mineral depletion (% of GNI)	..	0.0
Net forest depletion (% of GNI)	..	0.0
CO_2 damage (% of GNI)	..	0.3
Particulate emission damage (% of GNI)	0.2	0.4
Adjusted net savings (% of GNI)	..	8.7

Bulgaria

Environmental strategy/action plan prepared in ..

	Country data	Group data	
		Europe & Central Asia	Lower middle income
Population (millions)	7.8	472	2,442
Urban population (% of total)	70.2	63.6	48.7
GDP ($ billions)	24.1	1,770	4,165
GNI per capita, *World Bank Atlas* method ($)	2,750	3,295	1,686
Agriculture			
Land area (1,000 sq. km)	111	23,371	38,470
Agricultural land (% of land area)	48	29	43
Irrigated land (% of cropland)	16.6	11.1	23.1
Fertilizer consumption (100 grams/ha of arable land)	495	347	1,530
Population density, rural (people/sq. km of arable land)	71	126	523
Forests and biodiversity			
Forest area (% of land area)	32.8	38.3	30.7
Annual deforestation (% change, 1990–2005)	–0.6	0.0	0.1
Nationally protected areas (% of total land area)	4.5	6.9	7.7
Mammal species, total known	106		
Mammal species, threatened	12		
Bird species, total known	379		
Bird species, threatened	11		
GEF benefits index for biodiversity (0–100)	0.9		
Energy			
GDP per unit of energy use (2000 PPP $/kg oil equiv)	2.8	2.7	4.6
Energy use per capita (kg oil equiv)	2,494	2,794	1,090
Energy from combustible renewables & waste (% of tot.)	3.6	2.4	14.6
Energy imports, net (% of energy use)	48	–26	–14
Electric power consumption per capita (kWh)	3,965	3,531	1,329
Electricity generated by coal (% of total)	46.1	29.8	49.4
Emissions and pollution			
CO_2 emissions per unit of GDP (kg/2000 PPP $ of GDP)	0.9	1.0	0.5
CO_2 emissions per capita (metric tons)	5.3	6.7	2.6
Particulate matter (urban-pop.-weighted avg., μg/cu. m)	69	35	70
Passenger cars (per 1,000 people)	286	142	29
Water and sanitation			
Internal freshwater resources per capita (cu. m)	2,706	11,123	7,295
Freshwater withdrawal			
Total (% of internal resources)	50.0	7.5	7.7
Agriculture (% of total freshwater withdrawal)	19	59	75
Access to improved water source (% of total population)	100	91	81
Rural (% of rural population)	100	80	70
Urban (% of urban population)	100	98	93
Access to improved sanitation (% of total population)	100	82	57
Rural (% of rural population)	100	63	39
Urban (% of urban population)	100	93	78
Environment and health			
ARI prevalence (% of children under age 5)	..		
Diarrhea prevalence (% of children under age 5)	..		
Under-five mortality rate (per 1,000 live births)	15	34	40
National accounting aggregates, 2004			
Gross savings (% of GNI)	16.3	23.4	32.1
Consumption of fixed capital (% of GNI)	11.6	10.7	10.8
Education expenditure (% of GNI)	3.5	4.1	2.9
Energy depletion (% of GNI)	0.2	12.0	6.5
Mineral depletion (% of GNI)	0.7	0.3	0.5
Net forest depletion (% of GNI)	0.0	0.0	0.0
CO_2 damage (% of GNI)	1.4	1.4	1.1
Particulate emission damage (% of GNI)	2.4	0.7	1.0
Adjusted net savings (% of GNI)	3.5	2.3	15.1

Burkina Faso

Environmental strategy/action plan prepared in **1993**

	Country data	Group data	
		Sub-Saharan Africa	Low income
Population (millions)	12.8	726	2,343
Urban population (% of total)	18.2	36.4	30.6
GDP ($ billions)	4.8	523	1,239
GNI per capita, *World Bank Atlas* method ($)	350	601	507
Agriculture			
Land area (1,000 sq. km)	274	23,596	29,192
Agricultural land (% of land area)	40	44	45
Irrigated land (% of cropland)	0.5	3.6	23.9
Fertilizer consumption (100 grams/ha of arable land)	4	136	646
Population density, rural (people/sq. km of arable land)	211	355	524
Forests and biodiversity			
Forest area (% of land area)	24.8	26.5	24.8
Annual deforestation (% change, 1990–2005)	0.3	0.6	0.5
Nationally protected areas (% of total land area)	11.5	8.7	7.7
Mammal species, total known	129		
Mammal species, threatened	6		
Bird species, total known	452		
Bird species, threatened	2		
GEF benefits index for biodiversity (0–100)	0.3		
Energy			
GDP per unit of energy use (2000 PPP $/kg oil equiv)	..	2.8	4.2
Energy use per capita (kg oil equiv)	..	681	501
Energy from combustible renewables & waste (% of tot.)	..	57.4	48.9
Energy imports, net (% of energy use)	..	−59	−4
Electric power consumption per capita (kWh)	..	513	358
Electricity generated by coal (% of total)	..	68.0	46.3
Emissions and pollution			
CO_2 emissions per unit of GDP (kg/2000 PPP $ of GDP)	0.1	0.4	0.4
CO_2 emissions per capita (metric tons)	0.1	0.7	0.8
Particulate matter (urban-pop.-weighted avg., µg/cu. m)	97	73	89
Passenger cars (per 1,000 people)	..	..	6
Water and sanitation			
Internal freshwater resources per capita (cu. m)	975	5,353	3,456
Freshwater withdrawal			
Total (% of internal resources)	6.4	3.1	15.5
Agriculture (% of total freshwater withdrawal)	86	87	88
Access to improved water source (% of total population)	51	58	75
Rural (% of rural population)	44	45	69
Urban (% of urban population)	82	82	89
Access to improved sanitation (% of total population)	12	36	36
Rural (% of rural population)	5	26	24
Urban (% of urban population)	45	55	61
Environment and health			
ARI prevalence (% of children under age 5)	9.0		
Diarrhea prevalence (% of children under age 5)	..		
Under-five mortality rate (per 1,000 live births)	192	168	122
National accounting aggregates, 2004			
Gross savings (% of GNI)	..	17.1	22.7
Consumption of fixed capital (% of GNI)	8.6	10.9	9.2
Education expenditure (% of GNI)	2.4	3.9	3.4
Energy depletion (% of GNI)	0.0	9.8	6.7
Mineral depletion (% of GNI)	0.0	0.4	0.4
Net forest depletion (% of GNI)	1.2	0.6	0.7
CO_2 damage (% of GNI)	0.2	0.7	1.1
Particulate emission damage (% of GNI)	0.5	0.5	0.8
Adjusted net savings (% of GNI)	..	−1.9	7.3

Burundi

Environmental strategy/action plan prepared in **1994**

	Country data	Group data Sub-Saharan Africa	Low income
Population (millions)	7.3	726	2,343
Urban population (% of total)	10.3	36.4	30.6
GDP ($ billions)	0.7	523	1,239
GNI per capita, *World Bank Atlas* method ($)	90	601	507
Agriculture			
Land area (1,000 sq. km)	26	23,596	29,192
Agricultural land (% of land area)	91	44	45
Irrigated land (% of cropland)	1.5	3.6	23.9
Fertilizer consumption (100 grams/ha of arable land)	26	136	646
Population density, rural (people/sq. km of arable land)	640	355	524
Forests and biodiversity			
Forest area (% of land area)	5.9	26.5	24.8
Annual deforestation (% change, 1990–2005)	3.2	0.6	0.5
Nationally protected areas (% of total land area)	5.7	8.7	7.7
Mammal species, total known	116		
Mammal species, threatened	7		
Bird species, total known	597		
Bird species, threatened	9		
GEF benefits index for biodiversity (0–100)	0.5		
Energy			
GDP per unit of energy use (2000 PPP $/kg oil equiv)	..	2.8	4.2
Energy use per capita (kg oil equiv)	..	681	501
Energy from combustible renewables & waste (% of tot.)	..	57.4	48.9
Energy imports, net (% of energy use)	..	−59	−4
Electric power consumption per capita (kWh)	..	513	358
Electricity generated by coal (% of total)	..	68.0	46.3
Emissions and pollution			
CO_2 emissions per unit of GDP (kg/2000 PPP $ of GDP)	0.1	0.4	0.4
CO_2 emissions per capita (metric tons)	0.0	0.7	0.8
Particulate matter (urban-pop.-weighted avg., μg/cu. m)	99	73	89
Passenger cars (per 1,000 people)	..	..	6
Water and sanitation			
Internal freshwater resources per capita (cu. m)	1,382	5,353	3,456
Freshwater withdrawal			
Total (% of internal resources)	2.9	3.1	15.5
Agriculture (% of total freshwater withdrawal)	77	87	88
Access to improved water source (% of total population)	79	58	75
Rural (% of rural population)	78	45	69
Urban (% of urban population)	90	82	89
Access to improved sanitation (% of total population)	36	36	36
Rural (% of rural population)	35	26	24
Urban (% of urban population)	47	55	61
Environment and health			
ARI prevalence (% of children under age 5)	..		
Diarrhea prevalence (% of children under age 5)	..		
Under-five mortality rate (per 1,000 live births)	190	168	122
National accounting aggregates, 2004			
Gross savings (% of GNI)	15.5	17.1	22.7
Consumption of fixed capital (% of GNI)	6.8	10.9	9.2
Education expenditure (% of GNI)	3.7	3.9	3.4
Energy depletion (% of GNI)	0.0	9.8	6.7
Mineral depletion (% of GNI)	0.0	0.4	0.4
Net forest depletion (% of GNI)	14.6	0.6	0.7
CO_2 damage (% of GNI)	0.3	0.7	1.1
Particulate emission damage (% of GNI)	0.3	0.5	0.8
Adjusted net savings (% of GNI)	−2.9	−1.9	7.3

Cambodia

Environmental strategy/action plan prepared in **1999**

	Country data	Group data East Asia & Pacific	Low income
Population (millions)	13.8	1,870	2,343
Urban population (% of total)	19.2	40.6	30.6
GDP ($ billions)	4.9	2,651	1,239
GNI per capita, *World Bank Atlas* method ($)	350	1,416	507

Agriculture
Land area (1,000 sq. km)	177	15,885	29,192
Agricultural land (% of land area)	30	51	45
Irrigated land (% of cropland)	7.1	..	23.9
Fertilizer consumption (100 grams/ha of arable land)	0	2,296	646
Population density, rural (people/sq. km of arable land)	298	559	524

Forests and biodiversity
Forest area (% of land area)	59.2	28.4	24.8
Annual deforestation (% change, 1990–2005)	1.3	−0.2	0.5
Nationally protected areas (% of total land area)	18.5	..	7.7
Mammal species, total known	127		
Mammal species, threatened	23		
Bird species, total known	521		
Bird species, threatened	24		
GEF benefits index for biodiversity (0–100)	3.9		

Energy
GDP per unit of energy use (2000 PPP $/kg oil equiv)	..	4.6	4.2
Energy use per capita (kg oil equiv)	..	1,007	501
Energy from combustible renewables & waste (% of tot.)	..	17.7	48.9
Energy imports, net (% of energy use)	..	−2	−4
Electric power consumption per capita (kWh)	..	1,184	358
Electricity generated by coal (% of total)	..	69.4	46.3

Emissions and pollution
CO_2 emissions per unit of GDP (kg/2000 PPP $ of GDP)	0.0	0.5	0.4
CO_2 emissions per capita (metric tons)	0.0	2.4	0.8
Particulate matter (urban-pop.-weighted avg., µg/cu. m)	51	80	89
Passenger cars (per 1,000 people)	25	12	6

Water and sanitation
Internal freshwater resources per capita (cu. m)	8,738	5,062	3,456
Freshwater withdrawal			
Total (% of internal resources)	3.4	10.2	15.5
Agriculture (% of total freshwater withdrawal)	98	74	88
Access to improved water source (% of total population)	34	78	75
Rural (% of rural population)	29	69	69
Urban (% of urban population)	58	92	89
Access to improved sanitation (% of total population)	16	49	36
Rural (% of rural population)	8	35	24
Urban (% of urban population)	53	72	61

Environment and health
ARI prevalence (% of children under age 5)	..		
Diarrhea prevalence (% of children under age 5)	18.9		
Under-five mortality rate (per 1,000 live births)	141	37	122

National accounting aggregates, 2004
Gross savings (% of GNI)	19.6	39.1	22.7
Consumption of fixed capital (% of GNI)	8.9	10.5	9.2
Education expenditure (% of GNI)	1.8	2.3	3.4
Energy depletion (% of GNI)	0.0	4.1	6.7
Mineral depletion (% of GNI)	0.0	0.4	0.4
Net forest depletion (% of GNI)	0.8	0.0	0.7
CO_2 damage (% of GNI)	0.1	1.2	1.1
Particulate emission damage (% of GNI)	0.1	1.2	0.8
Adjusted net savings (% of GNI)	11.6	23.9	7.3

Cameroon

Environmental strategy/action plan prepared in ..

	Country data	Sub-Saharan Africa	Low income
		Group data	
Population (millions)	16.0	726	2,343
Urban population (% of total)	52.2	36.4	30.6
GDP ($ billions)	14.4	523	1,239
GNI per capita, *World Bank Atlas* method ($)	810	601	507
Agriculture			
Land area (1,000 sq. km)	465	23,596	29,192
Agricultural land (% of land area)	20	44	45
Irrigated land (% of cropland)	0.4	3.6	23.9
Fertilizer consumption (100 grams/ha of arable land)	59	136	646
Population density, rural (people/sq. km of arable land)	129	355	524
Forests and biodiversity			
Forest area (% of land area)	45.6	26.5	24.8
Annual deforestation (% change, 1990–2005)	0.9	0.6	0.5
Nationally protected areas (% of total land area)	4.5	8.7	7.7
Mammal species, total known	322		
Mammal species, threatened	42		
Bird species, total known	936		
Bird species, threatened	18		
GEF benefits index for biodiversity (0–100)	13.3		
Energy			
GDP per unit of energy use (2000 PPP $/kg oil equiv)	4.6	2.8	4.2
Energy use per capita (kg oil equiv)	429	681	501
Energy from combustible renewables & waste (% of tot.)	78.8	57.4	48.9
Energy imports, net (% of energy use)	–80	–59	–4
Electric power consumption per capita (kWh)	178	513	358
Electricity generated by coal (% of total)	..	68.0	46.3
Emissions and pollution			
CO_2 emissions per unit of GDP (kg/2000 PPP $ of GDP)	0.1	0.4	0.4
CO_2 emissions per capita (metric tons)	0.2	0.7	0.8
Particulate matter (urban-pop.-weighted avg., µg/cu. m)	86	73	89
Passenger cars (per 1,000 people)	..	..	6
Water and sanitation			
Internal freshwater resources per capita (cu. m)	17,022	5,353	3,456
Freshwater withdrawal			
Total (% of internal resources)	0.4	3.1	15.5
Agriculture (% of total freshwater withdrawal)	74	87	88
Access to improved water source (% of total population)	63	58	75
Rural (% of rural population)	41	45	69
Urban (% of urban population)	84	82	89
Access to improved sanitation (% of total population)	48	36	36
Rural (% of rural population)	33	26	24
Urban (% of urban population)	63	55	61
Environment and health			
ARI prevalence (% of children under age 5)	11.0		
Diarrhea prevalence (% of children under age 5)	18.9		
Under-five mortality rate (per 1,000 live births)	149	168	122
National accounting aggregates, 2004			
Gross savings (% of GNI)	15.4	17.1	22.7
Consumption of fixed capital (% of GNI)	10.0	10.9	9.2
Education expenditure (% of GNI)	3.5	3.9	3.4
Energy depletion (% of GNI)	10.8	9.8	6.7
Mineral depletion (% of GNI)	0.0	0.4	0.4
Net forest depletion (% of GNI)	0.0	0.6	0.7
CO_2 damage (% of GNI)	0.2	0.7	1.1
Particulate emission damage (% of GNI)	0.9	0.5	0.8
Adjusted net savings (% of GNI)	–3.0	–1.9	7.3

Canada

Environmental strategy/action plan prepared in **1990**

	Country data	High income
		Group data
Population (millions)	32.0	1,004
Urban population (% of total)	80.8	78.5
GDP ($ billions)	978.0	32,900
GNI per capita, *World Bank Atlas* method ($)	28,310	32,112
Agriculture		
Land area (1,000 sq. km)	9,094	33,018
Agricultural land (% of land area)	7	38
Irrigated land (% of cropland)	1.5	11.9
Fertilizer consumption (100 grams/ha of arable land)	572	1,205
Population density, rural (people/sq. km of arable land)	14	331
Forests and biodiversity		
Forest area (% of land area)	34.1	29.3
Annual deforestation (% change, 1990–2005)	0.0	−0.1
Nationally protected areas (% of total land area)	11.3	..
Mammal species, total known	211	
Mammal species, threatened	16	
Bird species, total known	472	
Bird species, threatened	19	
GEF benefits index for biodiversity (0–100)	22.2	
Energy		
GDP per unit of energy use (2000 PPP $/kg oil equiv)	3.4	5.2
Energy use per capita (kg oil equiv)	8,240	5,410
Energy from combustible renewables & waste (% of tot.)	4.5	3.0
Energy imports, net (% of energy use)	−48	19
Electric power consumption per capita (kWh)	17,290	9,503
Electricity generated by coal (% of total)	19.3	38.2
Emissions and pollution		
CO_2 emissions per unit of GDP (kg/2000 PPP $ of GDP)	0.6	0.5
CO_2 emissions per capita (metric tons)	16.5	12.8
Particulate matter (urban-pop.-weighted avg., μg/cu. m)	21	29
Passenger cars (per 1,000 people)	559	433
Water and sanitation		
Internal freshwater resources per capita (cu. m)	89,134	9,703
Freshwater withdrawal		
Total (% of internal resources)	1.6	10.4
Agriculture (% of total freshwater withdrawal)	12	42
Access to improved water source (% of total population)	100	99
Rural (% of rural population)	99	98
Urban (% of urban population)	100	100
Access to improved sanitation (% of total population)	100	..
Rural (% of rural population)	99	..
Urban (% of urban population)	100	..
Environment and health		
ARI prevalence (% of children under age 5)	..	
Diarrhea prevalence (% of children under age 5)	..	
Under-five mortality rate (per 1,000 live births)	6	7
National accounting aggregates, 2004		
Gross savings (% of GNI)	20.7	19.4
Consumption of fixed capital (% of GNI)	14.7	13.2
Education expenditure (% of GNI)	5.2	4.6
Energy depletion (% of GNI)	5.1	1.4
Mineral depletion (% of GNI)	0.3	0.0
Net forest depletion (% of GNI)	0.0	0.0
CO_2 damage (% of GNI)	0.4	0.3
Particulate emission damage (% of GNI)	0.3	0.4
Adjusted net savings (% of GNI)	5.2	8.7

Cape Verde

Environmental strategy/action plan prepared in ..

	Country data	Group data Sub-Saharan Africa	Group data Lower middle income
Population (millions)	0.5	726	2,442
Urban population (% of total)	56.7	36.4	48.7
GDP ($ billions)	0.9	523	4,165
GNI per capita, *World Bank Atlas* method ($)	1,720	601	1,686

Agriculture

Land area (1,000 sq. km)	4	23,596	38,470
Agricultural land (% of land area)	18	44	43
Irrigated land (% of cropland)	6.1	3.6	23.1
Fertilizer consumption (100 grams/ha of arable land)	48	136	1,530
Population density, rural (people/sq. km of arable land)	464	355	523

Forests and biodiversity

Forest area (% of land area)	20.8	26.5	30.7
Annual deforestation (% change, 1990–2005)	-3.0	0.6	0.1
Nationally protected areas (% of total land area)	..	8.7	7.7
Mammal species, total known	26		
Mammal species, threatened	3		
Bird species, total known	160		
Bird species, threatened	4		
GEF benefits index for biodiversity (0–100)	3.2		

Energy

GDP per unit of energy use (2000 PPP $/kg oil equiv)	..	2.8	4.6
Energy use per capita (kg oil equiv)	..	681	1,090
Energy from combustible renewables & waste (% of tot.)	..	57.4	14.6
Energy imports, net (% of energy use)	..	-59	-14
Electric power consumption per capita (kWh)	..	513	1,329
Electricity generated by coal (% of total)	..	68.0	49.4

Emissions and pollution

CO_2 emissions per unit of GDP (kg/2000 PPP $ of GDP)	0.1	0.4	0.5
CO_2 emissions per capita (metric tons)	0.3	0.7	2.6
Particulate matter (urban-pop.-weighted avg., µg/cu. m)	..	73	70
Passenger cars (per 1,000 people)	..	..	29

Water and sanitation

Internal freshwater resources per capita (cu. m)	606	5,353	7,295
Freshwater withdrawal			
Total (% of internal resources)	7.3	3.1	7.7
Agriculture (% of total freshwater withdrawal)	91	87	75
Access to improved water source (% of total population)	80	58	81
Rural (% of rural population)	73	45	70
Urban (% of urban population)	86	82	93
Access to improved sanitation (% of total population)	42	36	57
Rural (% of rural population)	19	26	39
Urban (% of urban population)	61	55	78

Environment and health

ARI prevalence (% of children under age 5)	..		
Diarrhea prevalence (% of children under age 5)	..		
Under-five mortality rate (per 1,000 live births)	36	168	40

National accounting aggregates, 2004

Gross savings (% of GNI)	13.3	17.1	32.1
Consumption of fixed capital (% of GNI)	10.9	10.9	10.8
Education expenditure (% of GNI)	5.0	3.9	2.9
Energy depletion (% of GNI)	0.0	9.8	6.5
Mineral depletion (% of GNI)	0.0	0.4	0.5
Net forest depletion (% of GNI)	0.0	0.6	0.0
CO_2 damage (% of GNI)	0.1	0.7	1.1
Particulate emission damage (% of GNI)	..	0.5	1.0
Adjusted net savings (% of GNI)	7.3	-1.9	15.1

Cayman Islands

Environmental strategy/action plan prepared in **1990**

	Country data	Group data: High income
Population (millions)	0.0	1,004
Urban population (% of total)	100.0	78.5
GDP ($ billions)	..	32,900
GNI per capita, *World Bank Atlas* method ($)	..	32,112
Agriculture		
Land area (1,000 sq. km)	0	33,018
Agricultural land (% of land area)	12	38
Irrigated land (% of cropland)	..	11.9
Fertilizer consumption (100 grams/ha of arable land)	..	1,205
Population density, rural (people/sq. km of arable land)	0	331
Forests and biodiversity		
Forest area (% of land area)	46.2	29.3
Annual deforestation (% change, 1990–2005)	0.0	–0.1
Nationally protected areas (% of total land area)	..	..
Mammal species, total known	12	
Mammal species, threatened	0	
Bird species, total known	209	
Bird species, threatened	3	
GEF benefits index for biodiversity (0–100)	0.7	
Energy		
GDP per unit of energy use (2000 PPP $/kg oil equiv)	..	5.2
Energy use per capita (kg oil equiv)	..	5,410
Energy from combustible renewables & waste (% of tot.)	..	3.0
Energy imports, net (% of energy use)	..	19
Electric power consumption per capita (kWh)	..	9,503
Electricity generated by coal (% of total)	..	38.2
Emissions and pollution		
CO_2 emissions per unit of GDP (kg/2000 PPP $ of GDP)	..	0.5
CO_2 emissions per capita (metric tons)	..	12.8
Particulate matter (urban-pop.-weighted avg., µg/cu. m)	25	29
Passenger cars (per 1,000 people)	..	433
Water and sanitation		
Internal freshwater resources per capita (cu. m)	..	9,703
Freshwater withdrawal		
Total (% of internal resources)	..	10.4
Agriculture (% of total freshwater withdrawal)	..	42
Access to improved water source (% of total population)	..	99
Rural (% of rural population)	..	98
Urban (% of urban population)	..	100
Access to improved sanitation (% of total population)	..	..
Rural (% of rural population)	..	..
Urban (% of urban population)	..	..
Environment and health		
ARI prevalence (% of children under age 5)	..	
Diarrhea prevalence (% of children under age 5)	..	
Under-five mortality rate (per 1,000 live births)	..	7
National accounting aggregates, 2004		
Gross savings (% of GNI)	..	19.4
Consumption of fixed capital (% of GNI)	..	13.2
Education expenditure (% of GNI)	..	4.6
Energy depletion (% of GNI)	..	1.4
Mineral depletion (% of GNI)	..	0.0
Net forest depletion (% of GNI)	..	0.0
CO_2 damage (% of GNI)	..	0.3
Particulate emission damage (% of GNI)	..	0.4
Adjusted net savings (% of GNI)	..	8.7

Central African Republic

Environmental strategy/action plan prepared in ..

	Country data	Group data Sub-Saharan Africa	Group data Low income
Population (millions)	4.0	726	2,343
Urban population (% of total)	43.3	36.4	30.6
GDP ($ billions)	1.3	523	1,239
GNI per capita, *World Bank Atlas* method ($)	310	601	507
Agriculture			
Land area (1,000 sq. km)	623	23,596	29,192
Agricultural land (% of land area)	8	44	45
Irrigated land (% of cropland)	0.1	3.6	23.9
Fertilizer consumption (100 grams/ha of arable land)	3	136	646
Population density, rural (people/sq. km of arable land)	117	355	524
Forests and biodiversity			
Forest area (% of land area)	36.5	26.5	24.8
Annual deforestation (% change, 1990–2005)	0.1	0.6	0.5
Nationally protected areas (% of total land area)	8.7	8.7	7.7
Mammal species, total known	187		
Mammal species, threatened	11		
Bird species, total known	663		
Bird species, threatened	3		
GEF benefits index for biodiversity (0–100)	1.7		
Energy			
GDP per unit of energy use (2000 PPP $/kg oil equiv)	..	2.8	4.2
Energy use per capita (kg oil equiv)	..	681	501
Energy from combustible renewables & waste (% of tot.)	..	57.4	48.9
Energy imports, net (% of energy use)	..	–59	–4
Electric power consumption per capita (kWh)	..	513	358
Electricity generated by coal (% of total)	..	68.0	46.3
Emissions and pollution			
CO_2 emissions per unit of GDP (kg/2000 PPP $ of GDP)	0.1	0.4	0.4
CO_2 emissions per capita (metric tons)	0.1	0.7	0.8
Particulate matter (urban-pop.-weighted avg., µg/cu. m)	24	73	89
Passenger cars (per 1,000 people)	..	..	6
Water and sanitation			
Internal freshwater resources per capita (cu. m)	35,374	5,353	3,456
Freshwater withdrawal			
Total (% of internal resources)	0.0	3.1	15.5
Agriculture (% of total freshwater withdrawal)	4	87	88
Access to improved water source (% of total population)	75	58	75
Rural (% of rural population)	61	45	69
Urban (% of urban population)	93	82	89
Access to improved sanitation (% of total population)	27	36	36
Rural (% of rural population)	12	26	24
Urban (% of urban population)	47	55	61
Environment and health			
ARI prevalence (% of children under age 5)	..		
Diarrhea prevalence (% of children under age 5)	..		
Under-five mortality rate (per 1,000 live births)	193	168	122
National accounting aggregates, 2004			
Gross savings (% of GNI)	14.1	17.1	22.7
Consumption of fixed capital (% of GNI)	8.3	10.9	9.2
Education expenditure (% of GNI)	1.6	3.9	3.4
Energy depletion (% of GNI)	0.0	9.8	6.7
Mineral depletion (% of GNI)	0.0	0.4	0.4
Net forest depletion (% of GNI)	0.0	0.6	0.7
CO_2 damage (% of GNI)	0.1	0.7	1.1
Particulate emission damage (% of GNI)	0.1	0.5	0.8
Adjusted net savings (% of GNI)	7.2	–1.9	7.3

Chad

Environmental strategy/action plan prepared in **1990**

	Country data	Sub-Saharan Africa	Low income
		Group data	
Population (millions)	9.4	726	2,343
Urban population (% of total)	25.4	36.4	30.6
GDP ($ billions)	4.2	523	1,239
GNI per capita, *World Bank Atlas* method ($)	250	601	507
Agriculture			
Land area (1,000 sq. km)	1,259	23,596	29,192
Agricultural land (% of land area)	39	44	45
Irrigated land (% of cropland)	0.8	3.6	23.9
Fertilizer consumption (100 grams/ha of arable land)	49	136	646
Population density, rural (people/sq. km of arable land)	190	355	524
Forests and biodiversity			
Forest area (% of land area)	9.5	26.5	24.8
Annual deforestation (% change, 1990–2005)	0.6	0.6	0.5
Nationally protected areas (% of total land area)	9.1	8.7	7.7
Mammal species, total known	104		
Mammal species, threatened	12		
Bird species, total known	531		
Bird species, threatened	5		
GEF benefits index for biodiversity (0–100)	2.1		
Energy			
GDP per unit of energy use (2000 PPP $/kg oil equiv)	..	2.8	4.2
Energy use per capita (kg oil equiv)	..	681	501
Energy from combustible renewables & waste (% of tot.)	..	57.4	48.9
Energy imports, net (% of energy use)	..	−59	−4
Electric power consumption per capita (kWh)	..	513	358
Electricity generated by coal (% of total)	..	68.0	46.3
Emissions and pollution			
CO_2 emissions per unit of GDP (kg/2000 PPP $ of GDP)	0.0	0.4	0.4
CO_2 emissions per capita (metric tons)	0.0	0.7	0.8
Particulate matter (urban-pop.-weighted avg., μg/cu. m)	73	73	89
Passenger cars (per 1,000 people)	..	..	6
Water and sanitation			
Internal freshwater resources per capita (cu. m)	1,588	5,353	3,456
Freshwater withdrawal			
Total (% of internal resources)	1.5	3.1	15.5
Agriculture (% of total freshwater withdrawal)	83	87	88
Access to improved water source (% of total population)	34	58	75
Rural (% of rural population)	32	45	69
Urban (% of urban population)	40	82	89
Access to improved sanitation (% of total population)	8	36	36
Rural (% of rural population)	0	26	24
Urban (% of urban population)	30	55	61
Environment and health			
ARI prevalence (% of children under age 5)	12.5		
Diarrhea prevalence (% of children under age 5)	31.2		
Under-five mortality rate (per 1,000 live births)	200	168	122
National accounting aggregates, 2004			
Gross savings (% of GNI)	10.0	17.1	22.7
Consumption of fixed capital (% of GNI)	13.7	10.9	9.2
Education expenditure (% of GNI)	1.4	3.9	3.4
Energy depletion (% of GNI)	79.1	9.8	6.7
Mineral depletion (% of GNI)	0.0	0.4	0.4
Net forest depletion (% of GNI)	0.0	0.6	0.7
CO_2 damage (% of GNI)	0.0	0.7	1.1
Particulate emission damage (% of GNI)	0.7	0.5	0.8
Adjusted net savings (% of GNI)	−82.2	−1.9	7.3

Channel Islands

Environmental strategy/action plan prepared in ..

	Country data	Group data High income
Population (millions)	0.1	1,004
Urban population (% of total)	30.5	78.5
GDP ($ billions)	..	32,900
GNI per capita, *World Bank Atlas* method ($)	..	32,112

Agriculture
Land area (1,000 sq. km)	..	33,018
Agricultural land (% of land area)	..	38
Irrigated land (% of cropland)	..	11.9
Fertilizer consumption (100 grams/ha of arable land)	..	1,205
Population density, rural (people/sq. km of arable land)	..	331

Forests and biodiversity
Forest area (% of land area)	..	29.3
Annual deforestation (% change, 1990–2005)	0.0	–0.1
Nationally protected areas (% of total land area)	..	..
Mammal species, total known	..	
Mammal species, threatened	..	
Bird species, total known	..	
Bird species, threatened	..	
GEF benefits index for biodiversity (0–100)	0.0	

Energy
GDP per unit of energy use (2000 PPP $/kg oil equiv)	..	5.2
Energy use per capita (kg oil equiv)	..	5,410
Energy from combustible renewables & waste (% of tot.)	..	3.0
Energy imports, net (% of energy use)	..	19
Electric power consumption per capita (kWh)	..	9,503
Electricity generated by coal (% of total)	..	38.2

Emissions and pollution
CO_2 emissions per unit of GDP (kg/2000 PPP $ of GDP)	..	0.5
CO_2 emissions per capita (metric tons)	..	12.8
Particulate matter (urban-pop.-weighted avg., µg/cu. m)	..	29
Passenger cars (per 1,000 people)	..	433

Water and sanitation
Internal freshwater resources per capita (cu. m)	..	9,703
Freshwater withdrawal		
Total (% of internal resources)	..	10.4
Agriculture (% of total freshwater withdrawal)	..	42
Access to improved water source (% of total population)	..	99
Rural (% of rural population)	..	98
Urban (% of urban population)	..	100
Access to improved sanitation (% of total population)	..	..
Rural (% of rural population)	..	..
Urban (% of urban population)	..	..

Environment and health
ARI prevalence (% of children under age 5)	..	
Diarrhea prevalence (% of children under age 5)	..	
Under-five mortality rate (per 1,000 live births)	..	7

National accounting aggregates, 2004
Gross savings (% of GNI)	..	19.4
Consumption of fixed capital (% of GNI)	..	13.2
Education expenditure (% of GNI)	..	4.6
Energy depletion (% of GNI)	..	1.4
Mineral depletion (% of GNI)	..	0.0
Net forest depletion (% of GNI)	..	0.0
CO_2 damage (% of GNI)	..	0.3
Particulate emission damage (% of GNI)	..	0.4
Adjusted net savings (% of GNI)	..	8.7

Chile

Environmental strategy/action plan prepared in ..

	Country data	Latin America & Caribbean	Upper middle income
		Group data	
Population (millions)	16.1	546	576
Urban population (% of total)	87.3	77.1	72.3
GDP ($ billions)	94.1	2,022	2,992
GNI per capita, *World Bank Atlas* method ($)	5,220	3,576	4,769
Agriculture			
Land area (1,000 sq. km)	749	20,057	28,983
Agricultural land (% of land area)	20	36	26
Irrigated land (% of cropland)	82.4	11.4	8.7
Fertilizer consumption (100 grams/ha of arable land)	2,296	923	469
Population density, rural (people/sq. km of arable land)	105	212	131
Forests and biodiversity			
Forest area (% of land area)	21.5	45.6	37.3
Annual deforestation (% change, 1990–2005)	–0.4	0.4	0.1
Nationally protected areas (% of total land area)	18.9	11.1	..
Mammal species, total known	159		
Mammal species, threatened	22		
Bird species, total known	445		
Bird species, threatened	32		
GEF benefits index for biodiversity (0–100)	16.2		
Energy			
GDP per unit of energy use (2000 PPP $/kg oil equiv)	5.9	6.2	3.5
Energy use per capita (kg oil equiv)	1,647	1,148	2,574
Energy from combustible renewables & waste (% of tot.)	15.4	15.0	3.9
Energy imports, net (% of energy use)	68	–40	–51
Electric power consumption per capita (kWh)	2,880	1,615	3,378
Electricity generated by coal (% of total)	13.5	5.4	31.0
Emissions and pollution			
CO_2 emissions per unit of GDP (kg/2000 PPP $ of GDP)	0.4	0.3	0.7
CO_2 emissions per capita (metric tons)	3.6	2.4	6.2
Particulate matter (urban-pop.-weighted avg., µg/cu. m)	56	43	40
Passenger cars (per 1,000 people)	88	108	143
Water and sanitation			
Internal freshwater resources per capita (cu. m)	54,826	24,619	14,190
Freshwater withdrawal			
Total (% of internal resources)	1.4	2.0	3.8
Agriculture (% of total freshwater withdrawal)	64	71	53
Access to improved water source (% of total population)	95	89	93
Rural (% of rural population)	59	69	82
Urban (% of urban population)	100	96	97
Access to improved sanitation (% of total population)	92	75	81
Rural (% of rural population)	64	44	61
Urban (% of urban population)	96	84	91
Environment and health			
ARI prevalence (% of children under age 5)	..		
Diarrhea prevalence (% of children under age 5)	..		
Under-five mortality rate (per 1,000 live births)	8	31	28
National accounting aggregates, 2004			
Gross savings (% of GNI)	22.7	22.7	23.1
Consumption of fixed capital (% of GNI)	12.5	12.1	11.5
Education expenditure (% of GNI)	3.9	4.4	4.5
Energy depletion (% of GNI)	0.2	7.2	11.2
Mineral depletion (% of GNI)	10.8	1.1	0.6
Net forest depletion (% of GNI)	0.0	0.0	0.0
CO_2 damage (% of GNI)	0.5	0.5	0.9
Particulate emission damage (% of GNI)	1.2	0.6	0.7
Adjusted net savings (% of GNI)	1.5	5.6	2.6

China

Environmental strategy/action plan prepared in **1994**

	Country data	East Asia & Pacific	Lower middle income
		Group data	
Population (millions)	1,296.2	1,870	2,442
Urban population (% of total)	39.6	40.6	48.7
GDP ($ billions)	1,931.7	2,651	4,165
GNI per capita, *World Bank Atlas* method ($)	1,500	1,416	1,686

Agriculture
Land area (1,000 sq. km)	9,327	15,885	38,470
Agricultural land (% of land area)	59	51	43
Irrigated land (% of cropland)	35.3	..	23.1
Fertilizer consumption (100 grams/ha of arable land)	2,777	2,296	1,530
Population density, rural (people/sq. km of arable land)	554	559	523

Forests and biodiversity
Forest area (% of land area)	21.2	28.4	30.7
Annual deforestation (% change, 1990–2005)	–1.7	–0.2	0.1
Nationally protected areas (% of total land area)	7.8	..	7.7
Mammal species, total known	502		
Mammal species, threatened	80		
Bird species, total known	1,221		
Bird species, threatened	82		
GEF benefits index for biodiversity (0–100)	64.8		

Energy
GDP per unit of energy use (2000 PPP $/kg oil equiv)	4.5	4.6	4.6
Energy use per capita (kg oil equiv)	1,094	1,007	1,090
Energy from combustible renewables & waste (% of tot.)	15.5	17.7	14.6
Energy imports, net (% of energy use)	2	–2	–14
Electric power consumption per capita (kWh)	1,379	1,184	1,329
Electricity generated by coal (% of total)	79.4	69.4	49.4

Emissions and pollution
CO_2 emissions per unit of GDP (kg/2000 PPP $ of GDP)	0.6	0.5	0.5
CO_2 emissions per capita (metric tons)	2.7	2.4	2.6
Particulate matter (urban-pop.-weighted avg., µg/cu. m)	80	80	70
Passenger cars (per 1,000 people)	8	12	29

Water and sanitation
Internal freshwater resources per capita (cu. m)	2,170	5,062	7,295
Freshwater withdrawal			
Total (% of internal resources)	22.4	10.2	7.7
Agriculture (% of total freshwater withdrawal)	68	74	75
Access to improved water source (% of total population)	77	78	81
Rural (% of rural population)	68	69	70
Urban (% of urban population)	92	92	93
Access to improved sanitation (% of total population)	44	49	57
Rural (% of rural population)	29	35	39
Urban (% of urban population)	69	72	78

Environment and health
ARI prevalence (% of children under age 5)	..		
Diarrhea prevalence (% of children under age 5)	..		
Under-five mortality rate (per 1,000 live births)	31	37	40

National accounting aggregates, 2004
Gross savings (% of GNI)	42.3	39.1	32.1
Consumption of fixed capital (% of GNI)	10.4	10.5	10.8
Education expenditure (% of GNI)	2.0	2.3	2.9
Energy depletion (% of GNI)	3.0	4.1	6.5
Mineral depletion (% of GNI)	0.2	0.4	0.5
Net forest depletion (% of GNI)	0.0	0.0	0.0
CO_2 damage (% of GNI)	1.4	1.2	1.1
Particulate emission damage (% of GNI)	1.5	1.2	1.0
Adjusted net savings (% of GNI)	27.8	23.9	15.1

Colombia

Environmental strategy/action plan prepared in **1998**

	Country data	Latin America & Caribbean	Lower middle income
		Group data	
Population (millions)	44.9	546	2,442
Urban population (% of total)	76.9	77.1	48.7
GDP ($ billions)	97.7	2,022	4,165
GNI per capita, *World Bank Atlas* method ($)	2,020	3,576	1,686

Agriculture

Land area (1,000 sq. km)	1,039	20,057	38,470
Agricultural land (% of land area)	44	36	43
Irrigated land (% of cropland)	23.4	11.4	23.1
Fertilizer consumption (100 grams/ha of arable land)	3,016	923	1,530
Population density, rural (people/sq. km of arable land)	455	212	523

Forests and biodiversity

Forest area (% of land area)	58.5	45.6	30.7
Annual deforestation (% change, 1990–2005)	0.1	0.4	0.1
Nationally protected areas (% of total land area)	10.2	11.1	7.7
Mammal species, total known	467		
Mammal species, threatened	39		
Bird species, total known	1,821		
Bird species, threatened	86		
GEF benefits index for biodiversity (0–100)	57.3		

Energy

GDP per unit of energy use (2000 PPP $/kg oil equiv)	10.1	6.2	4.6
Energy use per capita (kg oil equiv)	642	1,148	1,090
Energy from combustible renewables & waste (% of tot.)	17.4	15.0	14.6
Energy imports, net (% of energy use)	−162	−40	−14
Electric power consumption per capita (kWh)	834	1,615	1,329
Electricity generated by coal (% of total)	8.1	5.4	49.4

Emissions and pollution

CO_2 emissions per unit of GDP (kg/2000 PPP $ of GDP)	0.2	0.3	0.5
CO_2 emissions per capita (metric tons)	1.3	2.4	2.6
Particulate matter (urban-pop.-weighted avg., μg/cu. m)	24	43	70
Passenger cars (per 1,000 people)	43	108	29

Water and sanitation

Internal freshwater resources per capita (cu. m)	47,022	24,619	7,295
Freshwater withdrawal			
Total (% of internal resources)	0.5	2.0	7.7
Agriculture (% of total freshwater withdrawal)	46	71	75
Access to improved water source (% of total population)	92	89	81
Rural (% of rural population)	71	69	70
Urban (% of urban population)	99	96	93
Access to improved sanitation (% of total population)	86	75	57
Rural (% of rural population)	54	44	39
Urban (% of urban population)	96	84	78

Environment and health

ARI prevalence (% of children under age 5)	12.6		
Diarrhea prevalence (% of children under age 5)	13.9		
Under-five mortality rate (per 1,000 live births)	21	31	40

National accounting aggregates, 2004

Gross savings (% of GNI)	17.6	22.7	32.1
Consumption of fixed capital (% of GNI)	11.4	12.1	10.8
Education expenditure (% of GNI)	5.0	4.4	2.9
Energy depletion (% of GNI)	7.2	7.2	6.5
Mineral depletion (% of GNI)	0.8	1.1	0.5
Net forest depletion (% of GNI)	0.0	0.0	0.0
CO_2 damage (% of GNI)	0.4	0.5	1.1
Particulate emission damage (% of GNI)	0.1	0.6	1.0
Adjusted net savings (% of GNI)	2.6	5.6	15.1

Comoros

Environmental strategy/action plan prepared in ..

	Country data	Group data	
		Sub-Saharan Africa	Low income
Population (millions)	0.6	726	2,343
Urban population (% of total)	35.7	36.4	30.6
GDP ($ billions)	0.4	523	1,239
GNI per capita, *World Bank Atlas* method ($)	560	601	507
Agriculture			
Land area (1,000 sq. km)	2	23,596	29,192
Agricultural land (% of land area)	66	44	45
Irrigated land (% of cropland)	..	3.6	23.9
Fertilizer consumption (100 grams/ha of arable land)	38	136	646
Population density, rural (people/sq. km of arable land)	467	355	524
Forests and biodiversity			
Forest area (% of land area)	2.2	26.5	24.8
Annual deforestation (% change, 1990–2005)	3.9	0.6	0.5
Nationally protected areas (% of total land area)	..	8.7	7.7
Mammal species, total known	15		
Mammal species, threatened	2		
Bird species, total known	138		
Bird species, threatened	10		
GEF benefits index for biodiversity (0–100)	2.2		
Energy			
GDP per unit of energy use (2000 PPP $/kg oil equiv)	..	2.8	4.2
Energy use per capita (kg oil equiv)	..	681	501
Energy from combustible renewables & waste (% of tot.)	..	57.4	48.9
Energy imports, net (% of energy use)	..	−59	−4
Electric power consumption per capita (kWh)	..	513	358
Electricity generated by coal (% of total)	..	68.0	46.3
Emissions and pollution			
CO_2 emissions per unit of GDP (kg/2000 PPP $ of GDP)	0.1	0.4	0.4
CO_2 emissions per capita (metric tons)	0.1	0.7	0.8
Particulate matter (urban-pop.-weighted avg., μg/cu. m)	125	73	89
Passenger cars (per 1,000 people)	..	..	6
Water and sanitation			
Internal freshwater resources per capita (cu. m)	2,041	5,353	3,456
Freshwater withdrawal			
Total (% of internal resources)	0.8	3.1	15.5
Agriculture (% of total freshwater withdrawal)	47	87	88
Access to improved water source (% of total population)	94	58	75
Rural (% of rural population)	96	45	69
Urban (% of urban population)	90	82	89
Access to improved sanitation (% of total population)	23	36	36
Rural (% of rural population)	15	26	24
Urban (% of urban population)	38	55	61
Environment and health			
ARI prevalence (% of children under age 5)	10.1		
Diarrhea prevalence (% of children under age 5)	18.3		
Under-five mortality rate (per 1,000 live births)	70	168	122
National accounting aggregates, 2004			
Gross savings (% of GNI)	7.0	17.1	22.7
Consumption of fixed capital (% of GNI)	9.3	10.9	9.2
Education expenditure (% of GNI)	4.2	3.9	3.4
Energy depletion (% of GNI)	0.0	9.8	6.7
Mineral depletion (% of GNI)	0.0	0.4	0.4
Net forest depletion (% of GNI)	0.1	0.6	0.7
CO_2 damage (% of GNI)	0.2	0.7	1.1
Particulate emission damage (% of GNI)	0.4	0.5	0.8
Adjusted net savings (% of GNI)	1.2	−1.9	7.3

Congo, Dem. Rep.

Environmental strategy/action plan prepared in ..

	Country data	Group data Sub-Saharan Africa	Low income
Population (millions)	55.9	726	2,343
Urban population (% of total)	32.3	36.4	30.6
GDP ($ billions)	6.6	523	1,239
GNI per capita, World Bank Atlas method ($)	110	601	507

Agriculture

Land area (1,000 sq. km)	2,267	23,596	29,192
Agricultural land (% of land area)	10	44	45
Irrigated land (% of cropland)	0.1	3.6	23.9
Fertilizer consumption (100 grams/ha of arable land)	16	136	646
Population density, rural (people/sq. km of arable land)	552	355	524

Forests and biodiversity

Forest area (% of land area)	58.9	26.5	24.8
Annual deforestation (% change, 1990–2005)	0.3	0.6	0.5
Nationally protected areas (% of total land area)	5.0	8.7	7.7
Mammal species, total known	430		
Mammal species, threatened	29		
Bird species, total known	1,148		
Bird species, threatened	30		
GEF benefits index for biodiversity (0–100)	17.0		

Energy

GDP per unit of energy use (2000 PPP $/kg oil equiv)	2.1	2.8	4.2
Energy use per capita (kg oil equiv)	293	681	501
Energy from combustible renewables & waste (% of tot.)	93.5	57.4	48.9
Energy imports, net (% of energy use)	−4	−59	−4
Electric power consumption per capita (kWh)	87	513	358
Electricity generated by coal (% of total)	..	68.0	46.3

Emissions and pollution

CO_2 emissions per unit of GDP (kg/2000 PPP $ of GDP)	0.1	0.4	0.4
CO_2 emissions per capita (metric tons)	0.0	0.7	0.8
Particulate matter (urban-pop.-weighted avg., µg/cu. m)	57	73	89
Passenger cars (per 1,000 people)	..	..	6

Water and sanitation

Internal freshwater resources per capita (cu. m)	16,114	5,353	3,456
Freshwater withdrawal			
Total (% of internal resources)	0.0	3.1	15.5
Agriculture (% of total freshwater withdrawal)	31	87	88
Access to improved water source (% of total population)	46	58	75
Rural (% of rural population)	29	45	69
Urban (% of urban population)	83	82	89
Access to improved sanitation (% of total population)	29	36	36
Rural (% of rural population)	23	26	24
Urban (% of urban population)	43	55	61

Environment and health

ARI prevalence (% of children under age 5)	..		
Diarrhea prevalence (% of children under age 5)	..		
Under-five mortality rate (per 1,000 live births)	205	168	122

National accounting aggregates, 2004

Gross savings (% of GNI)	7.6	17.1	22.7
Consumption of fixed capital (% of GNI)	7.3	10.9	9.2
Education expenditure (% of GNI)	0.9	3.9	3.4
Energy depletion (% of GNI)	2.8	9.8	6.7
Mineral depletion (% of GNI)	0.9	0.4	0.4
Net forest depletion (% of GNI)	0.0	0.6	0.7
CO_2 damage (% of GNI)	0.3	0.7	1.1
Particulate emission damage (% of GNI)	0.6	0.5	0.8
Adjusted net savings (% of GNI)	−3.3	−1.9	7.3

Congo, Rep.

Environmental strategy/action plan prepared in ..

	Country data	Group data	
		Sub-Saharan Africa	Low income
Population (millions)	3.9	726	2,343
Urban population (% of total)	54.0	36.4	30.6
GDP ($ billions)	4.3	523	1,239
GNI per capita, *World Bank Atlas* method ($)	760	601	507
Agriculture			
Land area (1,000 sq. km)	342	23,596	29,192
Agricultural land (% of land area)	31	44	45
Irrigated land (% of cropland)	0.4	3.6	23.9
Fertilizer consumption (100 grams/ha of arable land)	5	136	646
Population density, rural (people/sq. km of arable land)	354	355	524
Forests and biodiversity			
Forest area (% of land area)	65.8	26.5	24.8
Annual deforestation (% change, 1990–2005)	0.1	0.6	0.5
Nationally protected areas (% of total land area)	6.5	8.7	7.7
Mammal species, total known	166		
Mammal species, threatened	14		
Bird species, total known	597		
Bird species, threatened	4		
GEF benefits index for biodiversity (0–100)	3.4		
Energy			
GDP per unit of energy use (2000 PPP $/kg oil equiv)	3.3	2.8	4.2
Energy use per capita (kg oil equiv)	273	681	501
Energy from combustible renewables & waste (% of tot.)	62.1	57.4	48.9
Energy imports, net (% of energy use)	–1,078	–59	–4
Electric power consumption per capita (kWh)	122	513	358
Electricity generated by coal (% of total)	..	68.0	46.3
Emissions and pollution			
CO_2 emissions per unit of GDP (kg/2000 PPP $ of GDP)	0.0	0.4	0.4
CO_2 emissions per capita (metric tons)	0.6	0.7	0.8
Particulate matter (urban-pop.-weighted avg., μg/cu. m)	74	73	89
Passenger cars (per 1,000 people)	..	..	6
Water and sanitation			
Internal freshwater resources per capita (cu. m)	57,173	5,353	3,456
Freshwater withdrawal			
Total (% of internal resources)	0.0	3.1	15.5
Agriculture (% of total freshwater withdrawal)	9	87	88
Access to improved water source (% of total population)	46	58	75
Rural (% of rural population)	17	45	69
Urban (% of urban population)	72	82	89
Access to improved sanitation (% of total population)	9	36	36
Rural (% of rural population)	2	26	24
Urban (% of urban population)	14	55	61
Environment and health			
ARI prevalence (% of children under age 5)	..		
Diarrhea prevalence (% of children under age 5)	..		
Under-five mortality rate (per 1,000 live births)	108	168	122
National accounting aggregates, 2004			
Gross savings (% of GNI)	36.0	17.1	22.7
Consumption of fixed capital (% of GNI)	13.3	10.9	9.2
Education expenditure (% of GNI)	3.8	3.9	3.4
Energy depletion (% of GNI)	54.1	9.8	6.7
Mineral depletion (% of GNI)	0.0	0.4	0.4
Net forest depletion (% of GNI)	0.0	0.6	0.7
CO_2 damage (% of GNI)	0.2	0.7	1.1
Particulate emission damage (% of GNI)	..	0.5	0.8
Adjusted net savings (% of GNI)	–27.8	–1.9	7.3

Costa Rica

Environmental strategy/action plan prepared in **1990**

	Country data	Latin America & Caribbean	Upper middle income
		Group data	
Population (millions)	4.3	546	576
Urban population (% of total)	61.2	77.1	72.3
GDP ($ billions)	18.5	2,022	2,992
GNI per capita, *World Bank Atlas* method ($)	4,470	3,576	4,769
Agriculture			
Land area (1,000 sq. km)	51	20,057	28,983
Agricultural land (% of land area)	56	36	26
Irrigated land (% of cropland)	20.6	11.4	8.7
Fertilizer consumption (100 grams/ha of arable land)	6,736	923	469
Population density, rural (people/sq. km of arable land)	731	212	131
Forests and biodiversity			
Forest area (% of land area)	46.8	45.6	37.3
Annual deforestation (% change, 1990–2005)	0.4	0.4	0.1
Nationally protected areas (% of total land area)	23.0	11.1	..
Mammal species, total known	232		
Mammal species, threatened	13		
Bird species, total known	838		
Bird species, threatened	18		
GEF benefits index for biodiversity (0–100)	11.1		
Energy			
GDP per unit of energy use (2000 PPP $/kg oil equiv)	9.9	6.2	3.5
Energy use per capita (kg oil equiv)	880	1,148	2,574
Energy from combustible renewables & waste (% of tot.)	8.2	15.0	3.9
Energy imports, net (% of energy use)	56	−40	−51
Electric power consumption per capita (kWh)	1,666	1,615	3,378
Electricity generated by coal (% of total)	..	5.4	31.0
Emissions and pollution			
CO_2 emissions per unit of GDP (kg/2000 PPP $ of GDP)	0.2	0.3	0.7
CO_2 emissions per capita (metric tons)	1.4	2.4	6.2
Particulate matter (urban-pop.-weighted avg., µg/cu. m)	40	43	40
Passenger cars (per 1,000 people)	93	108	143
Water and sanitation			
Internal freshwater resources per capita (cu. m)	26,428	24,619	14,190
Freshwater withdrawal			
Total (% of internal resources)	2.4	2.0	3.8
Agriculture (% of total freshwater withdrawal)	53	71	53
Access to improved water source (% of total population)	97	89	93
Rural (% of rural population)	92	69	82
Urban (% of urban population)	100	96	97
Access to improved sanitation (% of total population)	92	75	81
Rural (% of rural population)	97	44	61
Urban (% of urban population)	89	84	91
Environment and health			
ARI prevalence (% of children under age 5)	..		
Diarrhea prevalence (% of children under age 5)	..		
Under-five mortality rate (per 1,000 live births)	13	31	28
National accounting aggregates, 2004			
Gross savings (% of GNI)	17.8	22.7	23.1
Consumption of fixed capital (% of GNI)	6.1	12.1	11.5
Education expenditure (% of GNI)	4.2	4.4	4.5
Energy depletion (% of GNI)	0.0	7.2	11.2
Mineral depletion (% of GNI)	0.0	1.1	0.6
Net forest depletion (% of GNI)	0.3	0.0	0.0
CO_2 damage (% of GNI)	0.2	0.5	0.9
Particulate emission damage (% of GNI)	0.5	0.6	0.7
Adjusted net savings (% of GNI)	14.9	5.6	2.6

Côte d'Ivoire

Environmental strategy/action plan prepared in **1994**

	Country data	Group data Sub-Saharan Africa	Low income
Population (millions)	17.9	726	2,343
Urban population (% of total)	45.4	36.4	30.6
GDP ($ billions)	15.5	523	1,239
GNI per capita, *World Bank Atlas* method ($)	760	601	507
Agriculture			
Land area (1,000 sq. km)	318	23,596	29,192
Agricultural land (% of land area)	63	44	45
Irrigated land (% of cropland)	1.1	3.6	23.9
Fertilizer consumption (100 grams/ha of arable land)	330	136	646
Population density, rural (people/sq. km of arable land)	294	355	524
Forests and biodiversity			
Forest area (% of land area)	32.7	26.5	24.8
Annual deforestation (% change, 1990–2005)	–0.1	0.6	0.5
Nationally protected areas (% of total land area)	6.0	8.7	7.7
Mammal species, total known	229		
Mammal species, threatened	23		
Bird species, total known	702		
Bird species, threatened	11		
GEF benefits index for biodiversity (0–100)	3.9		
Energy			
GDP per unit of energy use (2000 PPP $/kg oil equiv)	3.8	2.8	4.2
Energy use per capita (kg oil equiv)	374	681	501
Energy from combustible renewables & waste (% of tot.)	65.7	57.4	48.9
Energy imports, net (% of energy use)	–2	–59	–4
Electric power consumption per capita (kWh)	174	513	358
Electricity generated by coal (% of total)	..	68.0	46.3
Emissions and pollution			
CO_2 emissions per unit of GDP (kg/2000 PPP $ of GDP)	0.3	0.4	0.4
CO_2 emissions per capita (metric tons)	0.4	0.7	0.8
Particulate matter (urban-pop.-weighted avg., µg/cu. m)	38	73	89
Passenger cars (per 1,000 people)	..	..	6
Water and sanitation			
Internal freshwater resources per capita (cu. m)	4,299	5,353	3,456
Freshwater withdrawal			
Total (% of internal resources)	1.2	3.1	15.5
Agriculture (% of total freshwater withdrawal)	65	87	88
Access to improved water source (% of total population)	84	58	75
Rural (% of rural population)	74	45	69
Urban (% of urban population)	98	82	89
Access to improved sanitation (% of total population)	40	36	36
Rural (% of rural population)	23	26	24
Urban (% of urban population)	61	55	61
Environment and health			
ARI prevalence (% of children under age 5)	3.7		
Diarrhea prevalence (% of children under age 5)	20.1		
Under-five mortality rate (per 1,000 live births)	194	168	122
National accounting aggregates, 2004			
Gross savings (% of GNI)	15.5	17.1	22.7
Consumption of fixed capital (% of GNI)	10.2	10.9	9.2
Education expenditure (% of GNI)	4.6	3.9	3.4
Energy depletion (% of GNI)	2.9	9.8	6.7
Mineral depletion (% of GNI)	0.0	0.4	0.4
Net forest depletion (% of GNI)	0.6	0.6	0.7
CO_2 damage (% of GNI)	0.3	0.7	1.1
Particulate emission damage (% of GNI)	0.3	0.5	0.8
Adjusted net savings (% of GNI)	5.7	–1.9	7.3

Croatia

Environmental strategy/action plan prepared in ..

	Country data	Group data Europe & Central Asia	Group data Upper middle income
Population (millions)	4.4	472	576
Urban population (% of total)	59.4	63.6	72.3
GDP ($ billions)	34.3	1,770	2,992
GNI per capita, *World Bank Atlas* method ($)	6,820	3,295	4,769
Agriculture			
Land area (1,000 sq. km)	56	23,371	28,983
Agricultural land (% of land area)	56	29	26
Irrigated land (% of cropland)	0.7	11.1	8.7
Fertilizer consumption (100 grams/ha of arable land)	1,176	347	469
Population density, rural (people/sq. km of arable land)	125	126	131
Forests and biodiversity			
Forest area (% of land area)	38.2	38.3	37.3
Annual deforestation (% change, 1990–2005)	–0.1	0.0	0.1
Nationally protected areas (% of total land area)	7.5	6.9	..
Mammal species, total known	96		
Mammal species, threatened	7		
Bird species, total known	365		
Bird species, threatened	9		
GEF benefits index for biodiversity (0–100)	0.5		
Energy			
GDP per unit of energy use (2000 PPP $/kg oil equiv)	5.6	2.7	3.5
Energy use per capita (kg oil equiv)	1,976	2,794	2,574
Energy from combustible renewables & waste (% of tot.)	4.3	2.4	3.9
Energy imports, net (% of energy use)	57	–26	–51
Electric power consumption per capita (kWh)	3,156	3,531	3,378
Electricity generated by coal (% of total)	19.1	29.8	31.0
Emissions and pollution			
CO_2 emissions per unit of GDP (kg/2000 PPP $ of GDP)	0.5	1.0	0.7
CO_2 emissions per capita (metric tons)	4.7	6.7	6.2
Particulate matter (urban-pop.-weighted avg., µg/cu. m)	35	35	40
Passenger cars (per 1,000 people)	280	142	143
Water and sanitation			
Internal freshwater resources per capita (cu. m)	8,486	11,123	14,190
Freshwater withdrawal			
Total (% of internal resources)	..	7.5	3.8
Agriculture (% of total freshwater withdrawal)	..	59	53
Access to improved water source (% of total population)	..	91	93
Rural (% of rural population)	..	80	82
Urban (% of urban population)	..	98	97
Access to improved sanitation (% of total population)	..	82	81
Rural (% of rural population)	..	63	61
Urban (% of urban population)	..	93	91
Environment and health			
ARI prevalence (% of children under age 5)	..		
Diarrhea prevalence (% of children under age 5)	..		
Under-five mortality rate (per 1,000 live births)	7	34	28
National accounting aggregates, 2004			
Gross savings (% of GNI)	24.6	23.4	23.1
Consumption of fixed capital (% of GNI)	12.9	10.7	11.5
Education expenditure (% of GNI)	4.1	4.1	4.5
Energy depletion (% of GNI)	1.0	12.0	11.2
Mineral depletion (% of GNI)	0.0	0.3	0.6
Net forest depletion (% of GNI)	0.2	0.0	0.0
CO_2 damage (% of GNI)	0.5	1.4	0.9
Particulate emission damage (% of GNI)	0.3	0.7	0.7
Adjusted net savings (% of GNI)	13.8	2.3	2.6

Cuba

Environmental strategy/action plan prepared in ..

	Country data	Latin America & Caribbean	Lower middle income
		Group data	
Population (millions)	11.2	546	2,442
Urban population (% of total)	75.8	77.1	48.7
GDP ($ billions)	..	2,022	4,165
GNI per capita, *World Bank Atlas* method ($)	..	3,576	1,686
Agriculture			
Land area (1,000 sq. km)	110	20,057	38,470
Agricultural land (% of land area)	61	36	43
Irrigated land (% of cropland)	23.0	11.4	23.1
Fertilizer consumption (100 grams/ha of arable land)	398	923	1,530
Population density, rural (people/sq. km of arable land)	89	212	523
Forests and biodiversity			
Forest area (% of land area)	24.7	45.6	30.7
Annual deforestation (% change, 1990–2005)	-2.1	0.4	0.1
Nationally protected areas (% of total land area)	69.1	11.1	7.7
Mammal species, total known	65		
Mammal species, threatened	11		
Bird species, total known	358		
Bird species, threatened	18		
GEF benefits index for biodiversity (0–100)	13.5		
Energy			
GDP per unit of energy use (2000 PPP $/kg oil equiv)	..	6.2	4.6
Energy use per capita (kg oil equiv)	1,000	1,148	1,090
Energy from combustible renewables & waste (% of tot.)	22.3	15.0	14.6
Energy imports, net (% of energy use)	41	-40	-14
Electric power consumption per capita (kWh)	1,200	1,615	1,329
Electricity generated by coal (% of total)	..	5.4	49.4
Emissions and pollution			
CO_2 emissions per unit of GDP (kg/2000 PPP $ of GDP)	..	0.3	0.5
CO_2 emissions per capita (metric tons)	2.1	2.4	2.6
Particulate matter (urban-pop.-weighted avg., µg/cu. m)	25	43	70
Passenger cars (per 1,000 people)	16	108	29
Water and sanitation			
Internal freshwater resources per capita (cu. m)	3,390	24,619	7,295
Freshwater withdrawal			
Total (% of internal resources)	21.5	2.0	7.7
Agriculture (% of total freshwater withdrawal)	69	71	75
Access to improved water source (% of total population)	91	89	81
Rural (% of rural population)	78	69	70
Urban (% of urban population)	95	96	93
Access to improved sanitation (% of total population)	98	75	57
Rural (% of rural population)	95	44	39
Urban (% of urban population)	99	84	78
Environment and health			
ARI prevalence (% of children under age 5)	..		
Diarrhea prevalence (% of children under age 5)	..		
Under-five mortality rate (per 1,000 live births)	7	31	40
National accounting aggregates, 2004			
Gross savings (% of GNI)	..	22.7	32.1
Consumption of fixed capital (% of GNI)	..	12.1	10.8
Education expenditure (% of GNI)	8.1	4.4	2.9
Energy depletion (% of GNI)	..	7.2	6.5
Mineral depletion (% of GNI)	..	1.1	0.5
Net forest depletion (% of GNI)	..	0.0	0.0
CO_2 damage (% of GNI)	..	0.5	1.1
Particulate emission damage (% of GNI)	0.2	0.6	1.0
Adjusted net savings (% of GNI)	..	5.6	15.1

Cyprus

Environmental strategy/action plan prepared in ..

	Country data	High income
		Group data
Population (millions)	0.8	1,004
Urban population (% of total)	69.4	78.5
GDP ($ billions)	15.4	32,900
GNI per capita, World Bank Atlas method ($)	16,510	32,112

Agriculture

Land area (1,000 sq. km)	9	33,018
Agricultural land (% of land area)	16	38
Irrigated land (% of cropland)	28.6	11.9
Fertilizer consumption (100 grams/ha of arable land)	1,541	1,205
Population density, rural (people/sq. km of arable land)	251	331

Forests and biodiversity

Forest area (% of land area)	18.8	29.3
Annual deforestation (% change, 1990–2005)	-0.5	-0.1
Nationally protected areas (% of total land area)	..	..
Mammal species, total known	21	
Mammal species, threatened	3	
Bird species, total known	349	
Bird species, threatened	11	
GEF benefits index for biodiversity (0–100)	0.5	

Energy

GDP per unit of energy use (2000 PPP $/kg oil equiv)	6.3	5.2
Energy use per capita (kg oil equiv)	3,279	5,410
Energy from combustible renewables & waste (% of tot.)	0.3	3.0
Energy imports, net (% of energy use)	98	19
Electric power consumption per capita (kWh)	4,759	9,503
Electricity generated by coal (% of total)	..	38.2

Emissions and pollution

CO_2 emissions per unit of GDP (kg/2000 PPP $ of GDP)	0.4	0.5
CO_2 emissions per capita (metric tons)	8.3	12.8
Particulate matter (urban-pop.-weighted avg., µg/cu. m)	60	29
Passenger cars (per 1,000 people)	376	433

Water and sanitation

Internal freshwater resources per capita (cu. m)	944	9,703
Freshwater withdrawal		
Total (% of internal resources)	30.8	10.4
Agriculture (% of total freshwater withdrawal)	71	42
Access to improved water source (% of total population)	100	99
Rural (% of rural population)	100	98
Urban (% of urban population)	100	100
Access to improved sanitation (% of total population)	100	..
Rural (% of rural population)	100	..
Urban (% of urban population)	100	..

Environment and health

ARI prevalence (% of children under age 5)	..	
Diarrhea prevalence (% of children under age 5)	..	
Under-five mortality rate (per 1,000 live births)	5	7

National accounting aggregates, 2004

Gross savings (% of GNI)	..	19.4
Consumption of fixed capital (% of GNI)	14.1	13.2
Education expenditure (% of GNI)	5.6	4.6
Energy depletion (% of GNI)	0.0	1.4
Mineral depletion (% of GNI)	0.0	0.0
Net forest depletion (% of GNI)	0.0	0.0
CO_2 damage (% of GNI)	0.3	0.3
Particulate emission damage (% of GNI)	..	0.4
Adjusted net savings (% of GNI)	..	8.7

Czech Republic

Environmental strategy/action plan prepared in **1994**

	Country data	Europe & Central Asia	Upper middle income
		Group data	
Population (millions)	10.2	472	576
Urban population (% of total)	74.4	63.6	72.3
GDP ($ billions)	107.0	1,770	2,992
GNI per capita, *World Bank Atlas* method ($)	9,130	3,295	4,769
Agriculture			
Land area (1,000 sq. km)	77	23,371	28,983
Agricultural land (% of land area)	55	29	26
Irrigated land (% of cropland)	0.7	11.1	8.7
Fertilizer consumption (100 grams/ha of arable land)	1,202	347	469
Population density, rural (people/sq. km of arable land)	85	126	131
Forests and biodiversity			
Forest area (% of land area)	34.3	38.3	37.3
Annual deforestation (% change, 1990–2005)	0.0	0.0	0.1
Nationally protected areas (% of total land area)	16.1	6.9	..
Mammal species, total known	88		
Mammal species, threatened	6		
Bird species, total known	386		
Bird species, threatened	9		
GEF benefits index for biodiversity (0–100)	0.1		
Energy			
GDP per unit of energy use (2000 PPP $/kg oil equiv)	3.9	2.7	3.5
Energy use per capita (kg oil equiv)	4,324	2,794	2,574
Energy from combustible renewables & waste (% of tot.)	2.6	2.4	3.9
Energy imports, net (% of energy use)	25	−26	−51
Electric power consumption per capita (kWh)	6,070	3,531	3,378
Electricity generated by coal (% of total)	62.3	29.8	31.0
Emissions and pollution			
CO_2 emissions per unit of GDP (kg/2000 PPP $ of GDP)	0.8	1.0	0.7
CO_2 emissions per capita (metric tons)	11.2	6.7	6.2
Particulate matter (urban-pop.-weighted avg., µg/cu. m)	25	35	40
Passenger cars (per 1,000 people)	358	142	143
Water and sanitation			
Internal freshwater resources per capita (cu. m)	1,287	11,123	14,190
Freshwater withdrawal			
Total (% of internal resources)	19.6	7.5	3.8
Agriculture (% of total freshwater withdrawal)	2	59	53
Access to improved water source (% of total population)	..	91	93
Rural (% of rural population)	..	80	82
Urban (% of urban population)	..	98	97
Access to improved sanitation (% of total population)	..	82	81
Rural (% of rural population)	..	63	61
Urban (% of urban population)	..	93	91
Environment and health			
ARI prevalence (% of children under age 5)	..		
Diarrhea prevalence (% of children under age 5)	..		
Under-five mortality rate (per 1,000 live births)	4	34	28
National accounting aggregates, 2004			
Gross savings (% of GNI)	23.6	23.4	23.1
Consumption of fixed capital (% of GNI)	13.7	10.7	11.5
Education expenditure (% of GNI)	4.2	4.1	4.5
Energy depletion (% of GNI)	0.1	12.0	11.2
Mineral depletion (% of GNI)	0.0	0.3	0.6
Net forest depletion (% of GNI)	0.0	0.0	0.0
CO_2 damage (% of GNI)	0.8	1.4	0.9
Particulate emission damage (% of GNI)	0.1	0.7	0.7
Adjusted net savings (% of GNI)	13.0	2.3	2.6

Denmark

Environmental strategy/action plan prepared in **1994**

	Country data	High income
		Group data
Population (millions)	5.4	1,004
Urban population (% of total)	85.5	78.5
GDP ($ billions)	241.4	32,900
GNI per capita, *World Bank Atlas* method ($)	40,750	32,112
Agriculture		
Land area (1,000 sq. km)	42	33,018
Agricultural land (% of land area)	63	38
Irrigated land (% of cropland)	19.7	11.9
Fertilizer consumption (100 grams/ha of arable land)	1,303	1,205
Population density, rural (people/sq. km of arable land)	35	331
Forests and biodiversity		
Forest area (% of land area)	11.8	29.3
Annual deforestation (% change, 1990–2005)	−0.8	−0.1
Nationally protected areas (% of total land area)	34.0	..
Mammal species, total known	81	
Mammal species, threatened	4	
Bird species, total known	427	
Bird species, threatened	10	
GEF benefits index for biodiversity (0–100)	0.2	
Energy		
GDP per unit of energy use (2000 PPP $/kg oil equiv)	7.5	5.2
Energy use per capita (kg oil equiv)	3,853	5,410
Energy from combustible renewables & waste (% of tot.)	10.7	3.0
Energy imports, net (% of energy use)	−37	19
Electric power consumption per capita (kWh)	6,602	9,503
Electricity generated by coal (% of total)	54.7	38.2
Emissions and pollution		
CO_2 emissions per unit of GDP (kg/2000 PPP $ of GDP)	0.3	0.5
CO_2 emissions per capita (metric tons)	8.8	12.8
Particulate matter (urban-pop.-weighted avg., µg/cu. m)	22	29
Passenger cars (per 1,000 people)	360	433
Water and sanitation		
Internal freshwater resources per capita (cu. m)	1,110	9,703
Freshwater withdrawal		
Total (% of internal resources)	21.2	10.4
Agriculture (% of total freshwater withdrawal)	43	42
Access to improved water source (% of total population)	100	99
Rural (% of rural population)	100	98
Urban (% of urban population)	100	100
Access to improved sanitation (% of total population)	..	..
Rural (% of rural population)	..	..
Urban (% of urban population)	..	..
Environment and health		
ARI prevalence (% of children under age 5)	..	
Diarrhea prevalence (% of children under age 5)	..	
Under-five mortality rate (per 1,000 live births)	5	7
National accounting aggregates, 2004		
Gross savings (% of GNI)	22.7	19.4
Consumption of fixed capital (% of GNI)	15.4	13.2
Education expenditure (% of GNI)	8.1	4.6
Energy depletion (% of GNI)	1.3	1.4
Mineral depletion (% of GNI)	0.0	0.0
Net forest depletion (% of GNI)	0.0	0.0
CO_2 damage (% of GNI)	0.1	0.3
Particulate emission damage (% of GNI)	0.1	0.4
Adjusted net savings (% of GNI)	13.9	8.7

Djibouti

Environmental strategy/action plan prepared in ..

	Country data	Group data Middle East & North Africa	Group data Lower middle income
Population (millions)	0.8	300	2,442
Urban population (% of total)	84.1	56.3	48.7
GDP ($ billions)	0.7	547	4,165
GNI per capita, *World Bank Atlas* method ($)	950	1,972	1,686
Agriculture			
Land area (1,000 sq. km)	23	8,955	38,470
Agricultural land (% of land area)	73	23	43
Irrigated land (% of cropland)	..	32.5	23.1
Fertilizer consumption (100 grams/ha of arable land)	0	842	1,530
Population density, rural (people/sq. km of arable land)	12,513	670	523
Forests and biodiversity			
Forest area (% of land area)	0.3	2.4	30.7
Annual deforestation (% change, 1990–2005)	0.0	–0.5	0.1
Nationally protected areas (% of total land area)	..	4.2	7.7
Mammal species, total known	106		
Mammal species, threatened	4		
Bird species, total known	312		
Bird species, threatened	6		
GEF benefits index for biodiversity (0–100)	0.5		
Energy			
GDP per unit of energy use (2000 PPP $/kg oil equiv)	..	4.2	4.6
Energy use per capita (kg oil equiv)	..	1,144	1,090
Energy from combustible renewables & waste (% of tot.)	..	1.3	14.6
Energy imports, net (% of energy use)	..	–129	–14
Electric power consumption per capita (kWh)	..	1,212	1,329
Electricity generated by coal (% of total)	..	3.0	49.4
Emissions and pollution			
CO_2 emissions per unit of GDP (kg/2000 PPP $ of GDP)	0.3	0.7	0.5
CO_2 emissions per capita (metric tons)	0.5	3.2	2.6
Particulate matter (urban-pop.-weighted avg., μg/cu. m)	68	90	70
Passenger cars (per 1,000 people)	..	..	29
Water and sanitation			
Internal freshwater resources per capita (cu. m)	385	761	7,295
Freshwater withdrawal			
Total (% of internal resources)	6.3	105.0	7.7
Agriculture (% of total freshwater withdrawal)	16	89	75
Access to improved water source (% of total population)	80	88	81
Rural (% of rural population)	67	79	70
Urban (% of urban population)	82	95	93
Access to improved sanitation (% of total population)	50	75	57
Rural (% of rural population)	27	56	39
Urban (% of urban population)	55	89	78
Environment and health			
ARI prevalence (% of children under age 5)	..		
Diarrhea prevalence (% of children under age 5)	..		
Under-five mortality rate (per 1,000 live births)	126	55	40
National accounting aggregates, 2004			
Gross savings (% of GNI)	..	30.0	32.1
Consumption of fixed capital (% of GNI)	8.9	11.2	10.8
Education expenditure (% of GNI)	..	4.5	2.9
Energy depletion (% of GNI)	0.0	27.3	6.5
Mineral depletion (% of GNI)	0.0	0.1	0.5
Net forest depletion (% of GNI)	0.0	0.1	0.0
CO_2 damage (% of GNI)	0.4	1.2	1.1
Particulate emission damage (% of GNI)	..	0.9	1.0
Adjusted net savings (% of GNI)	..	–6.2	15.1

Dominica

Environmental strategy/action plan prepared in ..

	Country data	Group data Latin America & Caribbean	Upper middle income
Population (millions)	0.1	546	576
Urban population (% of total)	72.4	77.1	72.3
GDP ($ billions)	0.3	2,022	2,992
GNI per capita, *World Bank Atlas* method ($)	3,670	3,576	4,769
Agriculture			
Land area (1,000 sq. km)	1	20,057	28,983
Agricultural land (% of land area)	31	36	26
Irrigated land (% of cropland)	..	11.4	8.7
Fertilizer consumption (100 grams/ha of arable land)	1,086	923	469
Population density, rural (people/sq. km of arable land)	398	212	131
Forests and biodiversity			
Forest area (% of land area)	61.3	45.6	37.3
Annual deforestation (% change, 1990–2005)	0.5	0.4	0.1
Nationally protected areas (% of total land area)	..	11.1	..
Mammal species, total known	16		
Mammal species, threatened	1		
Bird species, total known	164		
Bird species, threatened	4		
GEF benefits index for biodiversity (0–100)	1.1		
Energy			
GDP per unit of energy use (2000 PPP $/kg oil equiv)	..	6.2	3.5
Energy use per capita (kg oil equiv)	..	1,148	2,574
Energy from combustible renewables & waste (% of tot.)	..	15.0	3.9
Energy imports, net (% of energy use)	..	−40	−51
Electric power consumption per capita (kWh)	..	1,615	3,378
Electricity generated by coal (% of total)	..	5.4	31.0
Emissions and pollution			
CO_2 emissions per unit of GDP (kg/2000 PPP $ of GDP)	0.2	0.3	0.7
CO_2 emissions per capita (metric tons)	1.7	2.4	6.2
Particulate matter (urban-pop.-weighted avg., µg/cu. m)	34	43	40
Passenger cars (per 1,000 people)	..	108	143
Water and sanitation			
Internal freshwater resources per capita (cu. m)	..	24,619	14,190
Freshwater withdrawal			
Total (% of internal resources)	..	2.0	3.8
Agriculture (% of total freshwater withdrawal)	..	71	53
Access to improved water source (% of total population)	97	89	93
Rural (% of rural population)	90	69	82
Urban (% of urban population)	100	96	97
Access to improved sanitation (% of total population)	83	75	81
Rural (% of rural population)	75	44	61
Urban (% of urban population)	86	84	91
Environment and health			
ARI prevalence (% of children under age 5)	..		
Diarrhea prevalence (% of children under age 5)	..		
Under-five mortality rate (per 1,000 live births)	14	31	28
National accounting aggregates, 2004			
Gross savings (% of GNI)	4.4	22.7	23.1
Consumption of fixed capital (% of GNI)	12.4	12.1	11.5
Education expenditure (% of GNI)	5.0	4.4	4.5
Energy depletion (% of GNI)	0.0	7.2	11.2
Mineral depletion (% of GNI)	0.0	1.1	0.6
Net forest depletion (% of GNI)	..	0.0	0.0
CO_2 damage (% of GNI)	0.3	0.5	0.9
Particulate emission damage (% of GNI)	..	0.6	0.7
Adjusted net savings (% of GNI)	..	5.6	2.6

Dominican Republic

Environmental strategy/action plan prepared in ..

	Country data	Latin America & Caribbean	Lower middle income
		Group data	
Population (millions)	8.8	546	2,442
Urban population (% of total)	59.7	77.1	48.7
GDP ($ billions)	18.7	2,022	4,165
GNI per capita, *World Bank Atlas* method ($)	2,100	3,576	1,686
Agriculture			
Land area (1,000 sq. km)	48	20,057	38,470
Agricultural land (% of land area)	76	36	43
Irrigated land (% of cropland)	17.2	11.4	23.1
Fertilizer consumption (100 grams/ha of arable land)	818	923	1,530
Population density, rural (people/sq. km of arable land)	320	212	523
Forests and biodiversity			
Forest area (% of land area)	28.4	45.6	30.7
Annual deforestation (% change, 1990–2005)	0.0	0.4	0.1
Nationally protected areas (% of total land area)	51.9	11.1	7.7
Mammal species, total known	36		
Mammal species, threatened	5		
Bird species, total known	224		
Bird species, threatened	16		
GEF benefits index for biodiversity (0–100)	6.8		
Energy			
GDP per unit of energy use (2000 PPP $/kg oil equiv)	7.4	6.2	4.6
Energy use per capita (kg oil equiv)	923	1,148	1,090
Energy from combustible renewables & waste (% of tot.)	18.1	15.0	14.6
Energy imports, net (% of energy use)	81	–40	–14
Electric power consumption per capita (kWh)	1,060	1,615	1,329
Electricity generated by coal (% of total)	21.1	5.4	49.4
Emissions and pollution			
CO_2 emissions per unit of GDP (kg/2000 PPP $ of GDP)	0.4	0.3	0.5
CO_2 emissions per capita (metric tons)	2.5	2.4	2.6
Particulate matter (urban-pop.-weighted avg., μg/cu. m)	36	43	70
Passenger cars (per 1,000 people)	..	108	29
Water and sanitation			
Internal freshwater resources per capita (cu. m)	2,395	24,619	7,295
Freshwater withdrawal			
Total (% of internal resources)	16.1	2.0	7.7
Agriculture (% of total freshwater withdrawal)	66	71	75
Access to improved water source (% of total population)	93	89	81
Rural (% of rural population)	85	69	70
Urban (% of urban population)	98	96	93
Access to improved sanitation (% of total population)	57	75	57
Rural (% of rural population)	43	44	39
Urban (% of urban population)	67	84	78
Environment and health			
ARI prevalence (% of children under age 5)	19.1		
Diarrhea prevalence (% of children under age 5)	20.1		
Under-five mortality rate (per 1,000 live births)	32	31	40
National accounting aggregates, 2004			
Gross savings (% of GNI)	29.3	22.7	32.1
Consumption of fixed capital (% of GNI)	11.8	12.1	10.8
Education expenditure (% of GNI)	2.2	4.4	2.9
Energy depletion (% of GNI)	0.0	7.2	6.5
Mineral depletion (% of GNI)	2.2	1.1	0.5
Net forest depletion (% of GNI)	0.0	0.0	0.0
CO_2 damage (% of GNI)	0.9	0.5	1.1
Particulate emission damage (% of GNI)	0.3	0.6	1.0
Adjusted net savings (% of GNI)	16.3	5.6	15.1

Ecuador

Environmental strategy/action plan prepared in **1993**

	Country data	Latin America & Caribbean	Lower middle income
		Group data	
Population (millions)	13.0	546	2,442
Urban population (% of total)	62.3	77.1	48.7
GDP ($ billions)	30.3	2,022	4,165
GNI per capita, *World Bank Atlas* method ($)	2,210	3,576	1,686
Agriculture			
Land area (1,000 sq. km)	277	20,057	38,470
Agricultural land (% of land area)	29	36	43
Irrigated land (% of cropland)	29.0	11.4	23.1
Fertilizer consumption (100 grams/ha of arable land)	1,417	923	1,530
Population density, rural (people/sq. km of arable land)	303	212	523
Forests and biodiversity			
Forest area (% of land area)	39.2	45.6	30.7
Annual deforestation (% change, 1990–2005)	1.4	0.4	0.1
Nationally protected areas (% of total land area)	18.3	11.1	7.7
Mammal species, total known	341		
Mammal species, threatened	34		
Bird species, total known	1,515		
Bird species, threatened	69		
GEF benefits index for biodiversity (0–100)	30.0		
Energy			
GDP per unit of energy use (2000 PPP $/kg oil equiv)	4.9	6.2	4.6
Energy use per capita (kg oil equiv)	708	1,148	1,090
Energy from combustible renewables & waste (% of tot.)	7.1	15.0	14.6
Energy imports, ret (% of energy use)	−159	−40	−14
Electric power consumption per capita (kWh)	677	1,615	1,329
Electricity generated by coal (% of total)	..	5.4	49.4
Emissions and pollution			
CO_2 emissions per unit of GDP (kg/2000 PPP $ of GDP)	0.5	0.3	0.5
CO_2 emissions per capita (metric tons)	2.0	2.4	2.6
Particulate matter (urban-pop.-weighted avg., µg/cu. m)	28	43	70
Passenger cars (per 1,000 people)	41	108	29
Water and sanitation			
Internal freshwater resources per capita (cu. m)	33,129	24,619	7,295
Freshwater withdrawal			
Total (% of internal resources)	3.9	2.0	7.7
Agriculture (% of total freshwater withdrawal)	82	71	75
Access to improved water source (% of total population)	86	89	81
Rural (% of rural population)	77	69	70
Urban (% of urban population)	92	96	93
Access to improved sanitation (% of total population)	72	75	57
Rural (% of rural population)	59	44	39
Urban (% of urban population)	80	84	78
Environment and health			
ARI prevalence (% of children under age 5)	..		
Diarrhea prevalence (% of children under age 5)	19.9		
Under-five mortality rate (per 1,000 live births)	26	31	40
National accounting aggregates, 2004			
Gross savings (% of GNI)	28.4	22.7	32.1
Consumption of fixed capital (% of GNI)	11.6	12.1	10.8
Education expenditure (% of GNI)	1.4	4.4	2.9
Energy depletion (% of GNI)	19.0	7.2	6.5
Mineral depletion (% of GNI)	0.1	1.1	0.5
Net forest depletion (% of GNI)	0.0	0.0	0.0
CO_2 damage (% of GNI)	0.6	0.5	1.1
Particulate emission damage (% of GNI)	0.2	0.6	1.0
Adjusted net savings (% of GNI)	−1.6	5.6	15.1

Egypt, Arab Rep.

Environmental strategy/action plan prepared in **1992**

	Country data	Middle East & North Africa	Lower middle income
		Group data	
Population (millions)	72.6	300	2,442
Urban population (% of total)	42.2	56.3	48.7
GDP ($ billions)	78.8	547	4,165
GNI per capita, *World Bank Atlas* method ($)	1,250	1,972	1,686
Agriculture			
Land area (1,000 sq. km)	995	8,955	38,470
Agricultural land (% of land area)	3	23	43
Irrigated land (% of cropland)	99.9	32.5	23.1
Fertilizer consumption (100 grams/ha of arable land)	4,342	842	1,530
Population density, rural (people/sq. km of arable land)	1,409	670	523
Forests and biodiversity			
Forest area (% of land area)	0.1	2.4	30.7
Annual deforestation (% change, 1990–2005)	–3.5	–0.5	0.1
Nationally protected areas (% of total land area)	9.7	4.2	7.7
Mammal species, total known	118		
Mammal species, threatened	6		
Bird species, total known	481		
Bird species, threatened	17		
GEF benefits index for biodiversity (0–100)	3.2		
Energy			
GDP per unit of energy use (2000 PPP $/kg oil equiv)	5.1	4.2	4.6
Energy use per capita (kg oil equiv)	735	1,144	1,090
Energy from combustible renewables & waste (% of tot.)	2.6	1.3	14.6
Energy imports, net (% of energy use)	–17	–129	–14
Electric power consumption per capita (kWh)	1,127	1,212	1,329
Electricity generated by coal (% of total)	..	3.0	49.4
Emissions and pollution			
CO_2 emissions per unit of GDP (kg/2000 PPP $ of GDP)	0.5	0.7	0.5
CO_2 emissions per capita (metric tons)	2.1	3.2	2.6
Particulate matter (urban-pop.-weighted avg., µg/cu. m)	136	90	70
Passenger cars (per 1,000 people)	..	..	29
Water and sanitation			
Internal freshwater resources per capita (cu. m)	25	761	7,295
Freshwater withdrawal			
Total (% of internal resources)	3,794.4	105.0	7.7
Agriculture (% of total freshwater withdrawal)	86	89	75
Access to improved water source (% of total population)	98	88	81
Rural (% of rural population)	97	79	70
Urban (% of urban population)	100	95	93
Access to improved sanitation (% of total population)	68	75	57
Rural (% of rural population)	56	56	39
Urban (% of urban population)	84	89	78
Environment and health			
ARI prevalence (% of children under age 5)	17.7		
Diarrhea prevalence (% of children under age 5)	7.1		
Under-five mortality rate (per 1,000 live births)	36	55	40
National accounting aggregates, 2004			
Gross savings (% of GNI)	21.1	30.0	32.1
Consumption of fixed capital (% of GNI)	10.0	11.2	10.8
Education expenditure (% of GNI)	4.4	4.5	2.9
Energy depletion (% of GNI)	10.6	27.3	6.5
Mineral depletion (% of GNI)	0.1	0.1	0.5
Net forest depletion (% of GNI)	0.3	0.1	0.0
CO_2 damage (% of GNI)	1.2	1.2	1.1
Particulate emission damage (% of GNI)	1.7	0.9	1.0
Adjusted net savings (% of GNI)	1.6	–6.2	15.1

El Salvador

Environmental strategy/action plan prepared in **1994**

	Country data	Latin America & Caribbean	Lower middle income
		Group data	
Population (millions)	6.8	546	2,442
Urban population (% of total)	59.8	77.1	48.7
GDP ($ billions)	15.8	2,022	4,165
GNI per capita, *World Bank Atlas* method ($)	2,320	3,576	1,686
Agriculture			
Land area (1,000 sq. km)	21	20,057	38,470
Agricultural land (% of land area)	82	36	43
Irrigated land (% of cropland)	4.9	11.4	23.1
Fertilizer consumption (100 grams/ha of arable land)	838	923	1,530
Population density, rural (people/sq. km of arable land)	408	212	523
Forests and biodiversity			
Forest area (% of land area)	14.4	45.6	30.7
Annual deforestation (% change, 1990–2005)	1.4	0.4	0.1
Nationally protected areas (% of total land area)	0.4	11.1	7.7
Mammal species, total known	137		
Mammal species, threatened	2		
Bird species, total known	434		
Bird species, threatened	3		
GEF benefits index for biodiversity (0–100)	0.8		
Energy			
GDP per unit of energy use (2000 PPP $/kg oil equiv)	6.9	6.2	4.6
Energy use per capita (kg oil equiv)	675	1,148	1,090
Energy from combustible renewables & waste (% of tot.)	32.1	15.0	14.6
Energy imports, net (% of energy use)	47	–40	–14
Electric power consumption per capita (kWh)	584	1,615	1,329
Electricity generated by coal (% of total)	..	5.4	49.4
Emissions and pollution			
CO_2 emissions per unit of GDP (kg/2000 PPP $ of GDP)	0.2	0.3	0.5
CO_2 emissions per capita (metric tons)	1.0	2.4	2.6
Particulate matter (urban-pop.-weighted avg., μg/cu. m)	40	43	70
Passenger cars (per 1,000 people)	30	108	29
Water and sanitation			
Internal freshwater resources per capita (cu. m)	2,625	24,619	7,295
Freshwater withdrawal			
Total (% of internal resources)	7.2	2.0	7.7
Agriculture (% of total freshwater withdrawal)	59	71	75
Access to improved water source (% of total population)	82	89	81
Rural (% of rural population)	68	69	70
Urban (% of urban population)	91	96	93
Access to improved sanitation (% of total population)	63	75	57
Rural (% of rural population)	40	44	39
Urban (% of urban population)	78	84	78
Environment and health			
ARI prevalence (% of children under age 5)	..		
Diarrhea prevalence (% of children under age 5)	19.8		
Under-five mortality rate (per 1,000 live births)	28	31	40
National accounting aggregates, 2004			
Gross savings (% of GNI)	9.4	22.7	32.1
Consumption of fixed capital (% of GNI)	11.3	12.1	10.8
Education expenditure (% of GNI)	2.8	4.4	2.9
Energy depletion (% of GNI)	0.0	7.2	6.5
Mineral depletion (% of GNI)	0.0	1.1	0.5
Net forest depletion (% of GNI)	0.6	0.0	0.0
CO_2 damage (% of GNI)	0.3	0.5	1.1
Particulate emission damage (% of GNI)	0.3	0.6	1.0
Adjusted net savings (% of GNI)	–0.2	5.6	15.1

Equatorial Guinea

Environmental strategy/action plan prepared in ..

	Country data	Group data Sub-Saharan Africa	Group data Upper middle income
Population (millions)	0.5	726	576
Urban population (% of total)	49.0	36.4	72.3
GDP ($ billions)	3.2	523	2,992
GNI per capita, *World Bank Atlas* method ($)	..	601	4,769
Agriculture			
Land area (1,000 sq. km)	28	23,596	28,983
Agricultural land (% of land area)	12	44	26
Irrigated land (% of cropland)	..	3.6	8.7
Fertilizer consumption (100 grams/ha of arable land)	0	136	469
Population density, rural (people/sq. km of arable land)	192	355	131
Forests and biodiversity			
Forest area (% of land area)	58.2	26.5	37.3
Annual deforestation (% change, 1990–2005)	0.8	0.6	0.1
Nationally protected areas (% of total land area)	..	8.7	..
Mammal species, total known	153		
Mammal species, threatened	17		
Bird species, total known	418		
Bird species, threatened	6		
GEF benefits index for biodiversity (0–100)	1.7		
Energy			
GDP per unit of energy use (2000 PPP $/kg oil equiv)	..	2.8	3.5
Energy use per capita (kg oil equiv)	..	681	2,574
Energy from combustible renewables & waste (% of tot.)	..	57.4	3.9
Energy imports, net (% of energy use)	..	−59	−51
Electric power consumption per capita (kWh)	..	513	3,378
Electricity generated by coal (% of total)	..	68.0	31.0
Emissions and pollution			
CO_2 emissions per unit of GDP (kg/2000 PPP $ of GDP)	0.0	0.4	0.7
CO_2 emissions per capita (metric tons)	0.4	0.7	6.2
Particulate matter (urban-pop.-weighted avg., µg/cu. m)	12	73	40
Passenger cars (per 1,000 people)	..	..	143
Water and sanitation			
Internal freshwater resources per capita (cu. m)	52,821	5,353	14,190
Freshwater withdrawal			
Total (% of internal resources)	0.4	3.1	3.8
Agriculture (% of total freshwater withdrawal)	1	87	53
Access to improved water source (% of total population)	44	58	93
Rural (% of rural population)	42	45	82
Urban (% of urban population)	45	82	97
Access to improved sanitation (% of total population)	53	36	81
Rural (% of rural population)	46	26	61
Urban (% of urban population)	60	55	91
Environment and health			
ARI prevalence (% of children under age 5)	..		
Diarrhea prevalence (% of children under age 5)	..		
Under-five mortality rate (per 1,000 live births)	204	168	28
National accounting aggregates, 2004			
Gross savings (% of GNI)	..	17.1	23.1
Consumption of fixed capital (% of GNI)	..	10.9	11.5
Education expenditure (% of GNI)	1.5	3.9	4.5
Energy depletion (% of GNI)	..	9.8	11.2
Mineral depletion (% of GNI)	..	0.4	0.6
Net forest depletion (% of GNI)	..	0.6	0.0
CO_2 damage (% of GNI)	..	0.7	0.9
Particulate emission damage (% of GNI)	..	0.5	0.7
Adjusted net savings (% of GNI)	..	−1.9	2.6

Eritrea

Environmental strategy/action plan prepared in **1995**

	Country data	Sub-Saharan Africa	Low Income
		Group data	
Population (millions)	4.2	726	2,343
Urban population (% of total)	20.4	36.4	30.6
GDP ($ billions)	0.9	523	1,239
GNI per capita, *World Bank Atlas* method ($)	190	601	507
Agriculture			
Land area (1,000 sq. km)	101	23,596	29,192
Agricultural land (% of land area)	75	44	45
Irrigated land (% of cropland)	3.7	3.6	23.9
Fertilizer consumption (100 grams/ha of arable land)	65	136	646
Population density, rural (people/sq. km of arable land)	577	355	524
Forests and biodiversity			
Forest area (% of land area)	15.4	26.5	24.8
Annual deforestation (% change, 1990–2005)	0.3	0.6	0.5
Nationally protected areas (% of total land area)	4.3	8.7	7.7
Mammal species, total known	70		
Mammal species, threatened	9		
Bird species, total known	537		
Bird species, threatened	7		
GEF benefits index for biodiversity (0–100)	0.9		
Energy			
GDP per unit of energy use (2000 PPP $/kg oil equiv)	..	2.8	4.2
Energy use per capita (kg oil equiv)	..	681	501
Energy from combustible renewables & waste (% of tot.)	..	57.4	48.9
Energy imports, net (% of energy use)	..	−59	−4
Electric power consumption per capita (kWh)	..	513	358
Electricity generated by coal (% of total)	..	68.0	46.3
Emissions and pollution			
CO_2 emissions per unit of GDP (kg/2000 PPP $ of GDP)	0.2	0.4	0.4
CO_2 emissions per capita (metric tons)	0.2	0.7	0.8
Particulate matter (urban-pop.-weighted avg., μg/cu. m)	109	73	89
Passenger cars (per 1,000 people)	..	..	6
Water and sanitation			
Internal freshwater resources per capita (cu. m)	662	5,353	3,456
Freshwater withdrawal			
Total (% of internal resources)	10.7	3.1	15.5
Agriculture (% of total freshwater withdrawal)	97	87	88
Access to improved water source (% of total population)	57	58	75
Rural (% of rural population)	54	45	69
Urban (% of urban population)	72	82	89
Access to improved sanitation (% of total population)	9	36	36
Rural (% of rural population)	3	26	24
Urban (% of urban population)	34	55	61
Environment and health			
ARI prevalence (% of children under age 5)	..		
Diarrhea prevalence (% of children under age 5)	..		
Under-five mortality rate (per 1,000 live births)	82	168	122
National accounting aggregates, 2004			
Gross savings (% of GNI)	−8.9	17.1	22.7
Consumption of fixed capital (% of GNI)	8.0	10.9	9.2
Education expenditure (% of GNI)	1.6	3.9	3.4
Energy depletion (% of GNI)	0.0	9.8	6.7
Mineral depletion (% of GNI)	0.0	0.4	0.4
Net forest depletion (% of GNI)	1.2	0.6	0.7
CO_2 damage (% of GNI)	0.5	0.7	1.1
Particulate emission damage (% of GNI)	0.6	0.5	0.8
Adjusted net savings (% of GNI)	−17.6	−1.9	7.3

Estonia

Environmental strategy/action plan prepared in **1998**

	Country data	Europe & Central Asia	Upper middle income
Population (millions)	1.3	472	576
Urban population (% of total)	69.6	63.6	72.3
GDP ($ billions)	11.2	1,770	2,992
GNI per capita, *World Bank Atlas* method ($)	7,080	3,295	4,769
Agriculture			
Land area (1,000 sq. km)	42	23,371	28,983
Agricultural land (% of land area)	20	29	26
Irrigated land (% of cropland)	0.7	11.1	8.7
Fertilizer consumption (100 grams/ha of arable land)	441	347	469
Population density, rural (people/sq. km of arable land)	76	126	131
Forests and biodiversity			
Forest area (% of land area)	53.9	38.3	37.3
Annual deforestation (% change, 1990–2005)	–0.4	0.0	0.1
Nationally protected areas (% of total land area)	11.8	6.9	..
Mammal species, total known	67		
Mammal species, threatened	4		
Bird species, total known	267		
Bird species, threatened	3		
GEF benefits index for biodiversity (0–100)	0.0		
Energy			
GDP per unit of energy use (2000 PPP $/kg oil equiv)	3.4	2.7	3.5
Energy use per capita (kg oil equiv)	3,631	2,794	2,574
Energy from combustible renewables & waste (% of tot.)	10.6	2.4	3.9
Energy imports, net (% of energy use)	26	–26	–51
Electric power consumption per capita (kWh)	5,224	3,531	3,378
Electricity generated by coal (% of total)	92.2	29.8	31.0
Emissions and pollution			
CO_2 emissions per unit of GDP (kg/2000 PPP $ of GDP)	1.2	1.0	0.7
CO_2 emissions per capita (metric tons)	11.7	6.7	6.2
Particulate matter (urban-pop.-weighted avg., μg/cu. m)	17	35	40
Passenger cars (per 1,000 people)	295	142	143
Water and sanitation			
Internal freshwater resources per capita (cu. m)	9,423	11,123	14,190
Freshwater withdrawal			
Total (% of internal resources)	1.2	7.5	3.8
Agriculture (% of total freshwater withdrawal)	5	59	53
Access to improved water source (% of total population)	..	91	93
Rural (% of rural population)	..	80	82
Urban (% of urban population)	..	98	97
Access to improved sanitation (% of total population)	..	82	81
Rural (% of rural population)	..	63	61
Urban (% of urban population)	93	93	91
Environment and health			
ARI prevalence (% of children under age 5)	..		
Diarrhea prevalence (% of children under age 5)	..		
Under-five mortality rate (per 1,000 live births)	8	34	28
National accounting aggregates, 2004			
Gross savings (% of GNI)	19.9	23.4	23.1
Consumption of fixed capital (% of GNI)	13.5	10.7	11.5
Education expenditure (% of GNI)	5.1	4.1	4.5
Energy depletion (% of GNI)	0.6	12.0	11.2
Mineral depletion (% of GNI)	0.0	0.3	0.6
Net forest depletion (% of GNI)	1.0	0.0	0.0
CO_2 damage (% of GNI)	1.2	1.4	0.9
Particulate emission damage (% of GNI)	0.1	0.7	0.7
Adjusted net savings (% of GNI)	8.6	2.3	2.6

Ethiopia

Environmental strategy/action plan prepared in **1994**

	Country data	Group data Sub-Saharan Africa	Low income
Population (millions)	70.0	726	2,343
Urban population (% of total)	15.9	36.4	30.6
GDP ($ billions)	8.0	523	1,239
GNI per capita, *World Bank Atlas* method ($)	110	601	507

Agriculture

Land area (1,000 sq. km)	1,000	23,596	29,192
Agricultural land (% of land area)	32	44	45
Irrigated land (% of cropland)	2.5	3.6	23.9
Fertilizer consumption (100 grams/ha of arable land)	151	136	646
Population density, rural (people/sq. km of arable land)	523	355	524

Forests and biodiversity

Forest area (% of land area)	13.0	26.5	24.8
Annual deforestation (% change, 1990–2005)	0.9	0.6	0.5
Nationally protected areas (% of total land area)	16.9	8.7	7.7
Mammal species, total known	288		
Mammal species, threatened	35		
Bird species, total known	839		
Bird species, threatened	20		
GEF benefits index for biodiversity (0–100)	8.5		

Energy

GDP per unit of energy use (2000 PPP $/kg oil equiv)	2.1	2.8	4.2
Energy use per capita (kg oil equiv)	299	681	501
Energy from combustible renewables & waste (% of tot.)	91.2	57.4	48.9
Energy imports, net (% of energy use)	8	−59	−4
Electric power consumption per capita (kWh)	30	513	358
Electricity generated by coal (% of total)	..	68.0	46.3

Emissions and pollution

CO_2 emissions per unit of GDP (kg/2000 PPP $ of GDP)	0.1	0.4	0.4
CO_2 emissions per capita (metric tons)	0.1	0.7	0.8
Particulate matter (urban-pop.-weighted avg., µg/cu. m)	88	73	89
Passenger cars per 1,000 people	1	..	6

Water and sanitation

Internal freshwater resources per capita (cu. m)	1,744	5,353	3,456
Freshwater withdrawal			
Total (% of internal resources)	4.6	3.1	15.5
Agriculture (% of total freshwater withdrawal)	94	87	88
Access to improved water source (% of total population)	22	58	75
Rural (% of rural population)	11	45	69
Urban (% of urban population)	81	82	89
Access to improved sanitation (% of total population)	6	36	36
Rural (% of rural population)	4	26	24
Urban (% of urban population)	19	55	61

Environment and health

ARI prevalence (% of children under age 5)	24.4		
Diarrhea prevalence (% of children under age 5)	23.6		
Under-five mortality rate (per 1,000 live births)	166	168	122

National accounting aggregates, 2004

Gross savings (% of GNI)	13.5	17.1	22.7
Consumption of fixed capital (% of GNI)	6.9	10.9	9.2
Education expenditure (% of GNI)	3.0	3.9	3.4
Energy depletion (% of GNI)	0.0	9.8	6.7
Mineral depletion (% of GNI)	0.0	0.4	0.4
Net forest depletion (% of GNI)	11.9	0.6	0.7
CO_2 damage (% of GNI)	0.5	0.7	1.1
Particulate emission damage (% of GNI)	0.3	0.5	0.8
Adjusted net savings (% of GNI)	−3.2	−1.9	7.3

Faeroe Islands

Environmental strategy/action plan prepared in ..

	Country data	Group data High income
Population (millions)	0.0	1,004
Urban population (% of total)	39.0	78.5
GDP ($ billions)	..	32,900
GNI per capita, *World Bank Atlas* method ($)	..	32,112
Agriculture		
Land area (1,000 sq. km)	1	33,018
Agricultural land (% of land area)	2	38
Irrigated land (% of cropland)	..	11.9
Fertilizer consumption (100 grams/ha of arable land)	..	1,205
Population density, rural (people/sq. km of arable land)	980	331
Forests and biodiversity		
Forest area (% of land area)	..	29.3
Annual deforestation (% change, 1990–2005)	..	–0.1
Nationally protected areas (% of total land area)	..	..
Mammal species, total known	17	
Mammal species, threatened	4	
Bird species, total known	251	
Bird species, threatened	0	
GEF benefits index for biodiversity (0–100)	0.4	
Energy		
GDP per unit of energy use (2000 PPP $/kg oil equiv)	..	5.2
Energy use per capita (kg oil equiv)	..	5,410
Energy from combustible renewables & waste (% of tot.)	..	3.0
Energy imports, net (% of energy use)	..	19
Electric power consumption per capita (kWh)	..	9,503
Electricity generated by coal (% of total)	..	38.2
Emissions and pollution		
CO_2 emissions per unit of GDP (kg/2000 PPP $ of GDP)	..	0.5
CO_2 emissions per capita (metric tons)	..	12.8
Particulate matter (urban-pop.-weighted avg., µg/cu. m)	15	29
Passenger cars (per 1,000 people)	..	433
Water and sanitation		
Internal freshwater resources per capita (cu. m)	..	9,703
Freshwater withdrawal		
Total (% of internal resources)	..	10.4
Agriculture (% of total freshwater withdrawal)	..	42
Access to improved water source (% of total population)	..	99
Rural (% of rural population)	..	98
Urban (% of urban population)	..	100
Access to improved sanitation (% of total population)	..	..
Rural (% of rural population)	..	..
Urban (% of urban population)	..	..
Environment and health		
ARI prevalence (% of children under age 5)	..	
Diarrhea prevalence (% of children under age 5)	..	
Under-five mortality rate (per 1,000 live births)	..	7
National accounting aggregates, 2004		
Gross savings (% of GNI)	..	19.4
Consumption of fixed capital (% of GNI)	..	13.2
Education expenditure (% of GNI)	..	4.6
Energy depletion (% of GNI)	..	1.4
Mineral depletion (% of GNI)	..	0.0
Net forest depletion (% of GNI)	..	0.0
CO_2 damage (% of GNI)	..	0.3
Particulate emission damage (% of GNI)	..	0.4
Adjusted net savings (% of GNI)	..	8.7

Fiji

Environmental strategy/action plan prepared in **1994**

	Country data	East Asia & Pacific	Lower middle income
		Group data	
Population (millions)	0.8	1,870	2,442
Urban population (% of total)	52.5	40.6	48.7
GDP ($ billions)	2.6	2,651	4,165
GNI per capita, *World Bank Atlas* method ($)	2,720	1,416	1,686
Agriculture			
Land area (1,000 sq. km)	18	15,885	38,470
Agricultural land (% of land area)	25	51	43
Irrigated land (% of cropland)	1.1	..	23.1
Fertilizer consumption (100 grams/ha of arable land)	615	2,296	1,530
Population density, rural (people/sq. km of arable land)	201	559	523
Forests and biodiversity			
Forest area (% of land area)	54.7	28.4	30.7
Annual deforestation (% change, 1990–2005)	–0.1	–0.2	0.1
Nationally protected areas (% of total land area)	..	..	7.7
Mammal species, total known	15		
Mammal species, threatened	5		
Bird species, total known	112		
Bird species, threatened	13		
GEF benefits index for biodiversity (0–100)	5.0		
Energy			
GDP per unit of energy use (2000 PPP $/kg oil equiv)	..	4.6	4.6
Energy use per capita (kg oil equiv)	..	1,007	1,090
Energy from combustible renewables & waste (% of tot.)	..	17.7	14.6
Energy imports, net (% of energy use)	..	–2	–14
Electric power consumption per capita (kWh)	..	1,184	1,329
Electricity generated by coal (% of total)	..	69.4	49.4
Emissions and pollution			
CO_2 emissions per unit of GDP (kg/2000 PPP $ of GDP)	0.3	0.5	0.5
CO_2 emissions per capita (metric tons)	1.6	2.4	2.6
Particulate matter (urban-pop.-weighted avg., µg/cu. m)	17	80	70
Passenger cars (per 1,000 people)	..	12	29
Water and sanitation			
Internal freshwater resources per capita (cu. m)	34,015	5,062	7,295
Freshwater withdrawal			
Total (% of internal resources)	..	10.2	7.7
Agriculture (% of total freshwater withdrawal)	60	74	75
Access to improved water source (% of total population)	..	78	81
Rural (% of rural population)	..	69	70
Urban (% of urban population)	..	92	93
Access to improved sanitation (% of total population)	98	49	57
Rural (% of rural population)	98	35	39
Urban (% of urban population)	99	72	78
Environment and health			
ARI prevalence (% of children under age 5)	..		
Diarrhea prevalence (% of children under age 5)	..		
Under-five mortality rate (per 1,000 live births)	20	37	40
National accounting aggregates, 2004			
Gross savings (% of GNI)	..	39.1	32.1
Consumption of fixed capital (% of GNI)	12.0	10.5	10.8
Education expenditure (% of GNI)	4.6	2.3	2.9
Energy depletion (% of GNI)	0.0	4.1	6.5
Mineral depletion (% of GNI)	0.6	0.4	0.5
Net forest depletion (% of GNI)	0.0	0.0	0.0
CO_2 damage (% of GNI)	0.4	1.2	1.1
Particulate emission damage (% of GNI)	0.0	1.2	1.0
Adjusted net savings (% of GNI)	..	23.9	15.1

Finland

Environmental strategy/action plan prepared in **1995**

	Country data	Group data High income
Population (millions)	5.2	1,004
Urban population (% of total)	60.9	78.5
GDP ($ billions)	185.9	32,900
GNI per capita, *World Bank Atlas* method ($)	32,880	32,112
Agriculture		
Land area (1,000 sq. km)	305	33,018
Agricultural land (% of land area)	7	38
Irrigated land (% of cropland)	2.9	11.9
Fertilizer consumption (100 grams/ha of arable land)	1,332	1,205
Population density, rural (people/sq. km of arable land)	92	331
Forests and biodiversity		
Forest area (% of land area)	73.9	29.3
Annual deforestation (% change, 1990–2005)	–0.1	–0.1
Nationally protected areas (% of total land area)	9.3	..
Mammal species, total known	80	
Mammal species, threatened	3	
Bird species, total known	421	
Bird species, threatened	10	
GEF benefits index for biodiversity (0–100)	0.2	
Energy		
GDP per unit of energy use (2000 PPP $/kg oil equiv)	3.7	5.2
Energy use per capita (kg oil equiv)	7,204	5,410
Energy from combustible renewables & waste (% of tot.)	19.5	3.0
Energy imports, net (% of energy use)	57	19
Electric power consumption per capita (kWh)	16,427	9,503
Electricity generated by coal (% of total)	31.8	38.2
Emissions and pollution		
CO_2 emissions per unit of GDP (kg/2000 PPP $ of GDP)	0.4	0.5
CO_2 emissions per capita (metric tons)	12.0	12.8
Particulate matter (urban-pop.-weighted avg., µg/cu. m)	22	29
Passenger cars (per 1,000 people)	419	433
Water and sanitation		
Internal freshwater resources per capita (cu. m)	20,466	9,703
Freshwater withdrawal		
Total (% of internal resources)	2.3	10.4
Agriculture (% of total freshwater withdrawal)	3	42
Access to improved water source (% of total population)	100	99
Rural (% of rural population)	100	98
Urban (% of urban population)	100	100
Access to improved sanitation (% of total population)	100	..
Rural (% of rural population)	100	..
Urban (% of urban population)	100	..
Environment and health		
ARI prevalence (% of children under age 5)	..	
Diarrhea prevalence (% of children under age 5)	..	
Under-five mortality rate (per 1,000 live births)	4	7
National accounting aggregates, 2004		
Gross savings (% of GNI)	23.7	19.4
Consumption of fixed capital (% of GNI)	16.2	13.2
Education expenditure (% of GNI)	5.9	4.6
Energy depletion (% of GNI)	0.0	1.4
Mineral depletion (% of GNI)	0.0	0.0
Net forest depletion (% of GNI)	0.0	0.0
CO_2 damage (% of GNI)	0.2	0.3
Particulate emission damage (% of GNI)	0.1	0.4
Adjusted net savings (% of GNI)	13.1	8.7

France

Environmental strategy/action plan prepared in **1990**

	Country data	Group data: High income
Population (millions)	60.4	1,004
Urban population (% of total)	76.5	78.5
GDP ($ billions)	2,046.6	32,900
GNI per capita, *World Bank Atlas* method ($)	30,370	32,112
Agriculture		
Land area (1,000 sq. km)	550	33,018
Agricultural land (% of land area)	54	38
Irrigated land (% of cropland)	13.3	11.9
Fertilizer consumption (100 grams/ha of arable land)	2,151	1,205
Population density, rural (people/sq. km of arable land)	77	331
Forests and biodiversity		
Forest area (% of land area)	28.3	29.3
Annual deforestation (% change, 1990–2005)	–0.5	–0.1
Nationally protected areas (% of total land area)	13.3	..
Mammal species, total known	148	
Mammal species, threatened	16	
Bird species, total known	517	
Bird species, threatened	15	
GEF benefits index for biodiversity (0–100)	3.9	
Energy		
GDP per unit of energy use (2000 PPP $/kg oil equiv)	5.9	5.2
Energy use per capita (kg oil equiv)	4,519	5,410
Energy from combustible renewables & waste (% of tot.)	4.4	3.0
Energy imports, net (% of energy use)	50	19
Electric power consumption per capita (kWh)	7,816	9,503
Electricity generated by coal (% of total)	5.3	38.2
Emissions and pollution		
CO_2 emissions per unit of GDP (kg/2000 PPP $ of GDP)	0.2	0.5
CO_2 emissions per capita (metric tons)	6.2	12.8
Particulate matter (urban-pop.-weighted avg., µg/cu. m)	15	29
Passenger cars (per 1,000 people)	490	433
Water and sanitation		
Internal freshwater resources per capita (cu. m)	2,956	9,703
Freshwater withdrawal		
Total (% of internal resources)	22.4	10.4
Agriculture (% of total freshwater withdrawal)	10	42
Access to improved water source (% of total population)	..	99
Rural (% of rural population)	..	98
Urban (% of urban population)	100	100
Access to improved sanitation (% of total population)	..	..
Rural (% of rural population)	..	..
Urban (% of urban population)	..	..
Environment and health		
ARI prevalence (% of children under age 5)	..	
Diarrhea prevalence (% of children under age 5)	..	
Under-five mortality rate (per 1,000 live births)	5	7
National accounting aggregates, 2004		
Gross savings (% of GNI)	19.0	19.4
Consumption of fixed capital (% of GNI)	12.6	13.2
Education expenditure (% of GNI)	5.2	4.6
Energy depletion (% of GNI)	0.1	1.4
Mineral depletion (% of GNI)	0.0	0.0
Net forest depletion (% of GNI)	0.0	0.0
CO_2 damage (% of GNI)	0.1	0.3
Particulate emission damage (% of GNI)	0.0	0.4
Adjusted net savings (% of GNI)	11.2	8.7

French Polynesia

Environmental strategy/action plan prepared in ..

	Country data	Group data High income
Population (millions)	0.3	1,004
Urban population (% of total)	52.1	78.5
GDP ($ billions)	..	32,900
GNI per capita, *World Bank Atlas* method ($)	..	32,112

Agriculture

Land area (1,000 sq. km)	4	33,018
Agricultural land (% of land area)	12	38
Irrigated land (% of cropland)	4.0	11.9
Fertilizer consumption (100 grams/ha of arable land)	4,347	1,205
Population density, rural (people/sq. km of arable land)	3,958	331

Forests and biodiversity

Forest area (% of land area)	28.7	29.3
Annual deforestation (% change, 1990–2005)	0.0	–0.1
Nationally protected areas (% of total land area)	..	..
Mammal species, total known	21	
Mammal species, threatened	3	
Bird species, total known	116	
Bird species, threatened	33	
GEF benefits index for biodiversity (0–100)	5.6	

Energy

GDP per unit of energy use (2000 PPP $/kg oil equiv)	..	5.2
Energy use per capita (kg oil equiv)	..	5,410
Energy from combustible renewables & waste (% of tot.)	..	3.0
Energy imports, net (% of energy use)	..	19
Electric power consumption per capita (kWh)	..	9,503
Electricity generated by coal (% of total)	..	38.2

Emissions and pollution

CO_2 emissions per unit of GDP (kg/2000 PPP $ of GDP)	0.1	0.5
CO_2 emissions per capita (metric tons)	2.9	12.8
Particulate matter (urban-pop.-weighted avg., μg/cu. m)	..	29
Passenger cars (per 1,000 people)	..	433

Water and sanitation

Internal freshwater resources per capita (cu. m)	39,574	9,703
Freshwater withdrawal		
Total (% of internal resources)	..	10.4
Agriculture (% of total freshwater withdrawal)	..	42
Access to improved water source (% of total population)	100	99
Rural (% of rural population)	100	98
Urban (% of urban population)	100	100
Access to improved sanitation (% of total population)	98	..
Rural (% of rural population)	97	..
Urban (% of urban population)	99	..

Environment and health

ARI prevalence (% of children under age 5)	..	
Diarrhea prevalence (% of children under age 5)	..	
Under-five mortality rate (per 1,000 live births)	..	7

National accounting aggregates, 2004

Gross savings (% of GNI)	..	19.4
Consumption of fixed capital (% of GNI)	..	13.2
Education expenditure (% of GNI)	..	4.6
Energy depletion (% of GNI)	..	1.4
Mineral depletion (% of GNI)	..	0.0
Net forest depletion (% of GNI)	..	0.0
CO_2 damage (% of GNI)	..	0.3
Particulate emission damage (% of GNI)	..	0.4
Adjusted net savings (% of GNI)	..	8.7

Gabon

Environmental strategy/action plan prepared in ..

	Country data	Group data Sub-Saharan Africa	Group data Upper middle income
Population (millions)	1.4	726	576
Urban population (% of total)	84.4	36.4	72.3
GDP ($ billions)	7.2	523	2,992
GNI per capita, *World Bank Atlas* method ($)	4,080	601	4,769
Agriculture			
Land area (1,000 sq. km)	258	23,596	28,983
Agricultural land (% of land area)	20	44	26
Irrigated land (% of cropland)	1.4	3.6	8.7
Fertilizer consumption (100 grams/ha of arable land)	9	136	469
Population density, rural (people/sq. km of arable land)	67	355	131
Forests and biodiversity			
Forest area (% of land area)	84.5	26.5	37.3
Annual deforestation (% change, 1990–2005)	0.0	0.6	0.1
Nationally protected areas (% of total land area)	0.7	8.7	..
Mammal species, total known	166		
Mammal species, threatened	11		
Bird species, total known	632		
Bird species, threatened	5		
GEF benefits index for biodiversity (0–100)	3.4		
Energy			
GDP per unit of energy use (2000 PPP $/kg oil equiv)	4.9	2.8	3.5
Energy use per capita (kg oil equiv)	1,256	681	2,574
Energy from combustible renewables & waste (% of tot.)	58.8	57.4	3.9
Energy imports, net (% of energy use)	–637	–59	–51
Electric power consumption per capita (kWh)	922	513	3,378
Electricity generated by coal (% of total)	..	68.0	31.0
Emissions and pollution			
CO_2 emissions per unit of GDP (kg/2000 PPP $ of GDP)	0.4	0.4	0.7
CO_2 emissions per capita (metric tons)	2.6	0.7	6.2
Particulate matter (urban-pop.-weighted avg., µg/cu. m)	13	73	40
Passenger cars per 1,000 people	..	..	143
Water and sanitation			
Internal freshwater resources per capita (cu. m)	120,382	5,353	14,190
Freshwater withdrawal			
Total (% of internal resources)	0.1	3.1	3.8
Agriculture (% of total freshwater withdrawal)	42	87	53
Access to improved water source (% of total population)	87	58	93
Rural (% of rural population)	47	45	82
Urban (% of urban population)	95	82	97
Access to improved sanitation (% of total population)	36	36	81
Rural (% of rural population)	30	26	61
Urban (% of urban population)	37	55	91
Environment and health			
ARI prevalence (% of children under age 5)	29.1		
Diarrhea prevalence (% of children under age 5)	15.7		
Under-five mortality rate (per 1,000 live births)	91	168	28
National accounting aggregates, 2004			
Gross savings (% of GNI)	34.6	17.1	23.1
Consumption of fixed capital (% of GNI)	14.0	10.9	11.5
Education expenditure (% of GNI)	3.3	3.9	4.5
Energy depletion (% of GNI)	25.5	9.8	11.2
Mineral depletion (% of GNI)	0.0	0.4	0.6
Net forest depletion (% of GNI)	0.0	0.6	0.0
CO_2 damage (% of GNI)	0.4	0.7	0.9
Particulate emission damage (% of GNI)	..	0.5	0.7
Adjusted net savings (% of GNI)	–2.0	–1.9	2.6

Gambia, The

Environmental strategy/action plan prepared in **1992**

	Country data	Sub-Saharan Africa	Low income
		Group data	
Population (millions)	1.5	726	2,343
Urban population (% of total)	26.2	36.4	30.6
GDP ($ billions)	0.4	523	1,239
GNI per capita, *World Bank Atlas* method ($)	280	601	507
Agriculture			
Land area (1,000 sq. km)	10	23,596	29,192
Agricultural land (% of land area)	78	44	45
Irrigated land (% of cropland)	0.6	3.6	23.9
Fertilizer consumption (100 grams/ha of arable land)	25	136	646
Population density, rural (people/sq. km of arable land)	337	355	524
Forests and biodiversity			
Forest area (% of land area)	47.1	26.5	24.8
Annual deforestation (% change, 1990–2005)	–0.4	0.6	0.5
Nationally protected areas (% of total land area)	2.3	8.7	7.7
Mammal species, total known	133		
Mammal species, threatened	3		
Bird species, total known	535		
Bird species, threatened	2		
GEF benefits index for biodiversity (0–100)	0.1		
Energy			
GDP per unit of energy use (2000 PPP $/kg oil equiv)	..	2.8	4.2
Energy use per capita (kg oil equiv)	..	681	501
Energy from combustible renewables & waste (% of tot.)	..	57.4	48.9
Energy imports, net (% of energy use)	..	–59	–4
Electric power consumption per capita (kWh)	..	513	358
Electricity generated by coal (% of total)	..	68.0	46.3
Emissions and pollution			
CO_2 emissions per unit of GDP (kg/2000 PPP $ of GDP)	0.1	0.4	0.4
CO_2 emissions per capita (metric tons)	0.2	0.7	0.8
Particulate matter (urban-pop.-weighted avg., µg/cu. m)	138	73	89
Passenger cars (per 1,000 people)	6	..	6
Water and sanitation			
Internal freshwater resources per capita (cu. m)	2,030	5,353	3,456
Freshwater withdrawal			
Total (% of internal resources)	1.0	3.1	15.5
Agriculture (% of total freshwater withdrawal)	65	87	88
Access to improved water source (% of total population)	82	58	75
Rural (% of rural population)	77	45	69
Urban (% of urban population)	95	82	89
Access to improved sanitation (% of total population)	53	36	36
Rural (% of rural population)	46	26	24
Urban (% of urban population)	72	55	61
Environment and health			
ARI prevalence (% of children under age 5)	7.7		
Diarrhea prevalence (% of children under age 5)	21.5		
Under-five mortality rate (per 1,000 live births)	122	168	122
National accounting aggregates, 2004			
Gross savings (% of GNI)	19.1	17.1	22.7
Consumption of fixed capital (% of GNI)	8.6	10.9	9.2
Education expenditure (% of GNI)	2.6	3.9	3.4
Energy depletion (% of GNI)	0.0	9.8	6.7
Mineral depletion (% of GNI)	0.0	0.4	0.4
Net forest depletion (% of GNI)	0.6	0.6	0.7
CO_2 damage (% of GNI)	0.5	0.7	1.1
Particulate emission damage (% of GNI)	1.1	0.5	0.8
Adjusted net savings (% of GNI)	10.8	–1.9	7.3

Georgia

Environmental strategy/action plan prepared in ..

	Country data	Group data	
		Europe & Central Asia	Lower middle income
Population (millions)	4.5	472	2,442
Urban population (% of total)	51.7	63.6	48.7
GDP ($ billions)	5.2	1,770	4,165
GNI per capita, *World Bank Atlas* method ($)	1,060	3,295	1,686

Agriculture

Land area (1,000 sq. km)	69	23,371	38,470
Agricultural land (% of land area)	43	29	43
Irrigated land (% of cropland)	44.0	11.1	23.1
Fertilizer consumption (100 grams/ha of arable land)	355	347	1,530
Population density, rural (people/sq. km of arable land)	273	126	523

Forests and biodiversity

Forest area (% of land area)	39.7	38.3	30.7
Annual deforestation (% change, 1990–2005)	0.0	0.0	0.1
Nationally protected areas (% of total land area)	2.3	6.9	7.7
Mammal species, total known	98		
Mammal species, threatened	11		
Bird species, total known	268		
Bird species, threatened	8		
GEF benefits index for biodiversity (0–100)	0.7		

Energy

GDP per unit of energy use (2000 PPP $/kg oil equiv)	4.1	2.7	4.6
Energy use per capita (kg oil equiv)	597	2,794	1,090
Energy from combustible renewables & waste (% of tot.)	23.7	2.4	14.6
Energy imports, net (% of energy use)	50	−26	−14
Electric power consumption per capita (kWh)	1,507	3,531	1,329
Electricity generated by coal (% of total)	..	29.8	49.4

Emissions and pollution

CO_2 emissions per unit of GDP (kg/2000 PPP $ of GDP)	0.7	1.0	0.5
CO_2 emissions per capita (metric tons)	0.7	6.7	2.6
Particulate matter (urban-pop.-weighted avg., µg/cu. m)	46	35	70
Passenger cars (per 1,000 people)	49	142	29

Water and sanitation

Internal freshwater resources per capita (cu. m)	12,866	11,123	7,295
Freshwater withdrawal			
Total (% of internal resources)	6.2	7.5	7.7
Agriculture (% of total freshwater withdrawal)	59	59	75
Access to improved water source (% of total population)	76	91	81
Rural (% of rural population)	61	80	70
Urban (% of urban population)	90	98	93
Access to improved sanitation (% of total population)	83	82	57
Rural (% of rural population)	69	63	39
Urban (% of urban population)	96	93	78

Environment and health

ARI prevalence (% of children under age 5)	3.8		
Diarrhea prevalence (% of children under age 5)	6.0		
Under-five mortality rate (per 1,000 live births)	45	34	40

National accounting aggregates, 2004

Gross savings (% of GNI)	18.0	23.4	32.1
Consumption of fixed capital (% of GNI)	9.9	10.7	10.8
Education expenditure (% of GNI)	4.3	4.1	2.9
Energy depletion (% of GNI)	0.6	12.0	6.5
Mineral depletion (% of GNI)	0.0	0.3	0.5
Net forest depletion (% of GNI)	0.0	0.0	0.0
CO_2 damage (% of GNI)	0.7	1.4	1.1
Particulate emission damage (% of GNI)	1.1	0.7	1.0
Adjusted net savings (% of GNI)	10.0	2.3	15.1

Germany

Environmental strategy/action plan prepared in ..

	Country data	High Income
		Group data
Population (millions)	82.5	1,004
Urban population (% of total)	88.3	78.5
GDP ($ billions)	2,740.6	32,900
GNI per capita, *World Bank Atlas* method ($)	30,690	32,112
Agriculture		
Land area (1,000 sq. km)	349	33,018
Agricultural land (% of land area)	49	38
Irrigated land (% of cropland)	4.0	11.9
Fertilizer consumption (100 grams/ha of arable land)	2,200	1,205
Population density, rural (people/sq. km of arable land)	83	331
Forests and biodiversity		
Forest area (% of land area)	31.7	29.3
Annual deforestation (% change, 1990–2005)	–0.2	–0.1
Nationally protected areas (% of total land area)	32.6	..
Mammal species, total known	126	
Mammal species, threatened	9	
Bird species, total known	487	
Bird species, threatened	14	
GEF benefits index for biodiversity (0–100)	0.7	
Energy		
GDP per unit of energy use (2000 PPP $/kg oil equiv)	6.1	5.2
Energy use per capita (kg oil equiv)	4,205	5,410
Energy from combustible renewables & waste (% of tot.)	2.8	3.0
Energy imports, net (% of energy use)	61	19
Electric power consumption per capita (kWh)	6,896	9,503
Electricity generated by coal (% of total)	52.9	38.2
Emissions and pollution		
CO_2 emissions per unit of GDP (kg/2000 PPP $ of GDP)	0.4	0.5
CO_2 emissions per capita (metric tons)	10.3	12.8
Particulate matter (urban-pop.-weighted avg., µg/cu. m)	22	29
Passenger cars (per 1,000 people)	516	433
Water and sanitation		
Internal freshwater resources per capita (cu. m)	1,297	9,703
Freshwater withdrawal		
Total (% of internal resources)	44.0	10.4
Agriculture (% of total freshwater withdrawal)	20	42
Access to improved water source (% of total population)	100	99
Rural (% of rural population)	100	98
Urban (% of urban population)	100	100
Access to improved sanitation (% of total population)	..	..
Rural (% of rural population)	..	..
Urban (% of urban population)	..	..
Environment and health		
ARI prevalence (% of children under age 5)	..	
Diarrhea prevalence (% of children under age 5)	..	
Under-five mortality rate (per 1,000 live births)	5	7
National accounting aggregates, 2004		
Gross savings (% of GNI)	20.7	19.4
Consumption of fixed capital (% of GNI)	14.9	13.2
Education expenditure (% of GNI)	4.5	4.6
Energy depletion (% of GNI)	0.1	1.4
Mineral depletion (% of GNI)	0.0	0.0
Net forest depletion (% of GNI)	0.0	0.0
CO_2 damage (% of GNI)	0.2	0.3
Particulate emission damage (% of GNI)	0.1	0.4
Adjusted net savings (% of GNI)	9.7	8.7

Ghana

Environmental strategy/action plan prepared in **1992**

	Country data	Group data Sub-Saharan Africa	Low income
Population (millions)	21.7	726	2,343
Urban population (% of total)	45.8	36.4	30.6
GDP ($ billions)	8.9	523	1,239
GNI per capita, *World Bank Atlas* method ($)	380	601	507

Agriculture

Land area (1,000 sq. km)	228	23,596	29,192
Agricultural land (% of land area)	65	44	45
Irrigated land (% of cropland)	0.5	3.6	23.9
Fertilizer consumption (100 grams/ha of arable land)	74	136	646
Population density, rural (people/sq. km of arable land)	277	355	524

Forests and biodiversity

Forest area (% of land area)	24.2	26.5	24.8
Annual deforestation (% change, 1990–2005)	1.7	0.6	0.5
Nationally protected areas (% of total land area)	5.6	8.7	7.7
Mammal species, total known	249		
Mammal species, threatened	15		
Bird species, total known	729		
Bird species, threatened	8		
GEF benefits index for biodiversity (0–100)	2.0		

Energy

GDP per unit of energy use (2000 PPP $/kg oil equiv)	5.0	2.8	4.2
Energy use per capita (kg oil equiv)	400	681	501
Energy from combustible renewables & waste (% of tot.)	66.6	57.4	48.9
Energy imports, net (% of energy use)	29	−59	−4
Electric power consumption per capita (kWh)	248	513	358
Electricity generated by coal (% of total)	..	68.0	46.3

Emissions and pollution

CO_2 emissions per unit of GDP (kg/2000 PPP $ of GDP)	0.2	0.4	0.4
CO_2 emissions per capita (metric tons)	0.4	0.7	0.8
Particulate matter (urban-pop.-weighted avg., μg/cu. m)	42	73	89
Passenger cars (per 1,000 people)	..	..	6

Water and sanitation

Internal freshwater resources per capita (cu. m)	1,399	5,353	3,456
Freshwater withdrawal			
Total (% of internal resources)	3.2	3.1	15.5
Agriculture (% of total freshwater withdrawal)	66	87	88
Access to improved water source (% of total population)	79	58	75
Rural (% of rural population)	68	45	69
Urban (% of urban population)	93	82	89
Access to improved sanitation (% of total population)	58	36	36
Rural (% of rural population)	46	26	24
Urban (% of urban population)	74	55	61

Environment and health

ARI prevalence (% of children under age 5)	..		
Diarrhea prevalence (% of children under age 5)	17.9		
Under-five mortality rate (per 1,000 live births)	112	168	122

National accounting aggregates, 2004

Gross savings (% of GNI)	28.1	17.1	22.7
Consumption of fixed capital (% of GNI)	8.7	10.9	9.2
Education expenditure (% of GNI)	2.8	3.9	3.4
Energy depletion (% of GNI)	0.1	9.8	6.7
Mineral depletion (% of GNI)	0.2	0.4	0.4
Net forest depletion (% of GNI)	2.3	0.6	0.7
CO_2 damage (% of GNI)	0.5	0.7	1.1
Particulate emission damage (% of GNI)	0.3	0.5	0.8
Adjusted net savings (% of GNI)	18.8	−1.9	7.3

Greece

Environmental strategy/action plan prepared in ..

	Country data	Group data High income
Population (millions)	11.1	1,004
Urban population (% of total)	61.1	78.5
GDP ($ billions)	205.2	32,900
GNI per capita, *World Bank Atlas* method ($)	16,730	32,112

Agriculture

Land area (1,000 sq. km)	129	33,018
Agricultural land (% of land area)	65	38
Irrigated land (% of cropland)	37.9	11.9
Fertilizer consumption (100 grams/ha of arable land)	1,491	1,205
Population density, rural (people/sq. km of arable land)	160	331

Forests and biodiversity

Forest area (% of land area)	29.1	29.3
Annual deforestation (% change, 1990–2005)	−0.9	−0.1
Nationally protected areas (% of total land area)	3.6	..
Mammal species, total known	118	
Mammal species, threatened	11	
Bird species, total known	412	
Bird species, threatened	14	
GEF benefits index for biodiversity (0–100)	3.0	

Energy

GDP per unit of energy use (2000 PPP $/kg oil equiv)	7.3	5.2
Energy use per capita (kg oil equiv)	2,709	5,410
Energy from combustible renewables & waste (% of tot.)	3.3	3.0
Energy imports, net (% of energy use)	67	19
Electric power consumption per capita (kWh)	5,041	9,503
Electricity generated by coal (% of total)	60.7	38.2

Emissions and pollution

CO_2 emissions per unit of GDP (kg/2000 PPP $ of GDP)	0.5	0.5
CO_2 emissions per capita (metric tons)	8.5	12.8
Particulate matter (urban-pop.-weighted avg., µg/cu. m)	48	29
Passenger cars (per 1,000 people)	331	433

Water and sanitation

Internal freshwater resources per capita (cu. m)	5,246	9,703
Freshwater withdrawal		
Total (% of internal resources)	13.4	10.4
Agriculture (% of total freshwater withdrawal)	80	42
Access to improved water source (% of total population)	..	99
Rural (% of rural population)	..	98
Urban (% of urban population)	..	100
Access to improved sanitation (% of total population)	..	..
Rural (% of rural population)	..	..
Urban (% of urban population)	..	..

Environment and health

ARI prevalence (% of children under age 5)	..	
Diarrhea prevalence (% of children under age 5)	..	
Under-five mortality rate (per 1,000 live births)	5	7

National accounting aggregates, 2004

Gross savings (% of GNI)	17.7	19.4
Consumption of fixed capital (% of GNI)	8.7	13.2
Education expenditure (% of GNI)	3.1	4.6
Energy depletion (% of GNI)	0.0	1.4
Mineral depletion (% of GNI)	0.0	0.0
Net forest depletion (% of GNI)	0.0	0.0
CO_2 damage (% of GNI)	0.3	0.3
Particulate emission damage (% of GNI)	1.0	0.4
Adjusted net savings (% of GNI)	10.8	8.7

Greenland

Environmental strategy/action plan prepared in ..

	Country data	Group data — High income
Population (millions)	0.1	1,004
Urban population (% of total)	82.7	78.5
GDP ($ billions)	..	32,900
GNI per capita, *World Bank Atlas* method ($)	..	32,112

Agriculture

Land area (1,000 sq km)	410	33,018
Agricultural land (% of land area)	1	38
Irrigated land (% of cropland)	..	11.9
Fertilizer consumption (100 grams/ha of arable land)	..	1,205
Population density, rural (people/sq. km of arable land)	..	331

Forests and biodiversity

Forest area (% of land area)	..	29.3
Annual deforestation (% change, 1990–2005)	..	–0.1
Nationally protected areas (% of total land area)	..	..
Mammal species, total known	33	
Mammal species, threatened	7	
Bird species, total known	133	
Bird species, threatened	0	
GEF benefits index for biodiversity (0–100)	1.4	

Energy

GDP per unit of energy use (2000 PPP $/kg oil equiv)	..	5.2
Energy use per capita (kg oil equiv)	..	5,410
Energy from combustible renewables & waste (% of tot.)	..	3.0
Energy imports, net (% of energy use)	..	19
Electric power consumption per capita (kWh)	..	9,503
Electricity generated by coal (% of total)	..	38.2

Emissions and pollution

CO_2 emissions per unit of GDP (kg/2000 PPP $ of GDP)	..	0.5
CO_2 emissions per capita (metric tons)	10.0	12.8
Particulate matter (urban-pop.-weighted avg., µg/cu. m)	..	29
Passenger cars (per 1,000 people)	..	433

Water and sanitation

Internal freshwater resources per capita (cu. m)	..	9,703
Freshwater withdrawal		
Total (% of internal resources)	..	10.4
Agriculture (% of total freshwater withdrawal)	..	42
Access to improved water source (% of total population)	..	99
Rural (% of rural population)	..	98
Urban (% of urban population)	..	100
Access to improved sanitation (% of total population)	..	..
Rural (% of rural population)	..	..
Urban (% of urban population)	..	..

Environment and health

ARI prevalence (% of children under age 5)	..	
Diarrhea prevalence (% of children under age 5)	..	
Under-five mortality rate (per 1,000 live births)	..	7

National accounting aggregates, 2004

Gross savings (% of GNI)	..	19.4
Consumption of fixed capital (% of GNI)	..	13.2
Education expenditure (% of GNI)	..	4.6
Energy depletion (% of GNI)	..	1.4
Mineral depletion (% of GNI)	..	0.0
Net forest depletion (% of GNI)	..	0.0
CO_2 damage (% of GNI)	..	0.3
Particulate emission damage (% of GNI)	..	0.4
Adjusted net savings (% of GNI)	..	8.7

Grenada

Environmental strategy/action plan prepared in ..

	Country data	Latin America & Caribbean	Upper middle income
		Group data	
Population (millions)	0.1	546	576
Urban population (% of total)	41.5	77.1	72.3
GDP ($ billions)	0.4	2,022	2,992
GNI per capita, *World Bank Atlas* method ($)	3,750	3,576	4,769
Agriculture			
Land area (1,000 sq. km)	0	20,057	28,983
Agricultural land (% of land area)	38	36	26
Irrigated land (% of cropland)	..	11.4	8.7
Fertilizer consumption (100 grams/ha of arable land)	..	923	469
Population density, rural (people/sq. km of arable land)	3,101	212	131
Forests and biodiversity			
Forest area (% of land area)	11.8	45.6	37.3
Annual deforestation (% change, 1990–2005)	0.0	0.4	0.1
Nationally protected areas (% of total land area)	..	11.1	..
Mammal species, total known	33		
Mammal species, threatened	1		
Bird species, total known	148		
Bird species, threatened	2		
GEF benefits index for biodiversity (0–100)	0.6		
Energy			
GDP per unit of energy use (2000 PPP $/kg oil equiv)	..	6.2	3.5
Energy use per capita (kg oil equiv)	..	1,148	2,574
Energy from combustible renewables & waste (% of tot.)	..	15.0	3.9
Energy imports, net (% of energy use)	..	–40	–51
Electric power consumption per capita (kWh)	..	1,615	3,378
Electricity generated by coal (% of total)	..	5.4	31.0
Emissions and pollution			
CO_2 emissions per unit of GDP (kg/2000 PPP $ of GDP)	0.3	0.3	0.7
CO_2 emissions per capita (metric tons)	2.2	2.4	6.2
Particulate matter (urban-pop.-weighted avg., µg/cu. m)	49	43	40
Passenger cars (per 1,000 people)	..	108	143
Water and sanitation			
Internal freshwater resources per capita (cu. m)	..	24,619	14,190
Freshwater withdrawal			
Total (% of internal resources)	..	2.0	3.8
Agriculture (% of total freshwater withdrawal)	..	71	53
Access to improved water source (% of total population)	95	89	93
Rural (% of rural population)	93	69	82
Urban (% of urban population)	97	96	97
Access to improved sanitation (% of total population)	97	75	81
Rural (% of rural population)	97	44	61
Urban (% of urban population)	96	84	91
Environment and health			
ARI prevalence (% of children under age 5)	..		
Diarrhea prevalence (% of children under age 5)	..		
Under-five mortality rate (per 1,000 live births)	21	31	28
National accounting aggregates, 2004			
Gross savings (% of GNI)	..	22.7	23.1
Consumption of fixed capital (% of GNI)	13.4	12.1	11.5
Education expenditure (% of GNI)	4.9	4.4	4.5
Energy depletion (% of GNI)	0.0	7.2	11.2
Mineral depletion (% of GNI)	0.0	1.1	0.6
Net forest depletion (% of GNI)	..	0.0	0.0
CO_2 damage (% of GNI)	0.4	0.5	0.9
Particulate emission damage (% of GNI)	..	0.6	0.7
Adjusted net savings (% of GNI)	..	5.6	2.6

Guam

Environmental strategy/action plan prepared in ..

	Country data	Group data: High income
Population (millions)	0.2	1,004
Urban population (% of total)	93.8	78.5
GDP ($ billions)	..	32,900
GNI per capita, *World Bank Atlas* method ($)	..	32,112
Agriculture		
Land area (1,000 sq. km)	1	33,018
Agricultural land (% of land area)	36	38
Irrigated land (% of cropland)	..	11.9
Fertilizer consumption (100 grams/ha of arable land)	..	1,205
Population density, rural (people/sq. km of arable land)	518	331
Forests and biodiversity		
Forest area (% of land area)	47.3	29.3
Annual deforestation (% change, 1990–2005)	0.0	–0.1
Nationally protected areas (% of total land area)	..	..
Mammal species, total known	10	
Mammal species, threatened	2	
Bird species, total known	61	
Bird species, threatened	6	
GEF benefits index for biodiversity (0–100)	0.6	
Energy		
GDP per unit of energy use (2000 PPP $/kg oil equiv)	..	5.2
Energy use per capita (kg oil equiv)	..	5,410
Energy from combustible renewables & waste (% of tot.)	..	3.0
Energy imports, net (% of energy use)	..	19
Electric power consumption per capita (kWh)	..	9,503
Electricity generated by coal (% of total)	..	38.2
Emissions and pollution		
CO_2 emissions per unit of GDP (kg/2000 PPP $ of GDP)	..	0.5
CO_2 emissions per capita (metric tons)	25.4	12.8
Particulate matter (urban-pop.-weighted avg., µg/cu. m)	..	29
Passenger cars (per 1,000 people)	..	433
Water and sanitation		
Internal freshwater resources per capita (cu. m)	..	9,703
Freshwater withdrawal		
Total (% of internal resources)	..	10.4
Agriculture (% of total freshwater withdrawal)	..	42
Access to improved water source (% of total population)	100	99
Rural (% of rural population)	100	98
Urban (% of urban population)	100	100
Access to improved sanitation (% of total population)	99	..
Rural (% of rural population)	98	..
Urban (% of urban population)	99	..
Environment and health		
ARI prevalence (% of children under age 5)	..	
Diarrhea prevalence (% of children under age 5)	..	
Under-five mortality rate (per 1,000 live births)	..	7
National accounting aggregates, 2004		
Gross savings (% of GNI)	..	19.4
Consumption of fixed capital (% of GNI)	..	13.2
Education expenditure (% of GNI)	..	4.6
Energy depletion (% of GNI)	..	1.4
Mineral depletion (% of GNI)	..	0.0
Net forest depletion (% of GNI)	..	0.0
CO_2 damage (% of GNI)	..	0.3
Particulate emission damage (% of GNI)	..	0.4
Adjusted net savings (% of GNI)	..	8.7

Guatemala

Environmental strategy/action plan prepared in **1994**

	Country data	Group data Latin America & Caribbean	Group data Lower middle income
Population (millions)	12.3	546	2,442
Urban population (% of total)	46.8	77.1	48.7
GDP ($ billions)	27.5	2,022	4,165
GNI per capita, *World Bank Atlas* method ($)	2,190	3,576	1,686
Agriculture			
Land area (1,000 sq. km)	108	20,057	38,470
Agricultural land (% of land area)	43	36	43
Irrigated land (% of cropland)	6.3	11.4	23.1
Fertilizer consumption (100 grams/ha of arable land)	1,307	923	1,530
Population density, rural (people/sq. km of arable land)	447	212	523
Forests and biodiversity			
Forest area (% of land area)	36.3	45.6	30.7
Annual deforestation (% change, 1990–2005)	1.1	0.4	0.1
Nationally protected areas (% of total land area)	20.0	11.1	7.7
Mammal species, total known	193		
Mammal species, threatened	7		
Bird species, total known	684		
Bird species, threatened	10		
GEF benefits index for biodiversity (0–100)	8.9		
Energy			
GDP per unit of energy use (2000 PPP $/kg oil equiv)	6.5	6.2	4.6
Energy use per capita (kg oil equiv)	608	1,148	1,090
Energy from combustible renewables & waste (% of tot.)	53.3	15.0	14.6
Energy imports, net (% of energy use)	25	−40	−14
Electric power consumption per capita (kWh)	396	1,615	1,329
Electricity generated by coal (% of total)	14.5	5.4	49.4
Emissions and pollution			
CO_2 emissions per unit of GDP (kg/2000 PPP $ of GDP)	0.2	0.3	0.5
CO_2 emissions per capita (metric tons)	0.9	2.4	2.6
Particulate matter (urban-pop.-weighted avg., µg/cu. m)	76	43	70
Passenger cars (per 1,000 people)	52	108	29
Water and sanitation			
Internal freshwater resources per capita (cu. m)	8,882	24,619	7,295
Freshwater withdrawal			
Total (% of internal resources)	1.8	2.0	7.7
Agriculture (% of total freshwater withdrawal)	80	71	75
Access to improved water source (% of total population)	95	89	81
Rural (% of rural population)	92	69	70
Urban (% of urban population)	99	96	93
Access to improved sanitation (% of total population)	61	75	57
Rural (% of rural population)	52	44	39
Urban (% of urban population)	72	84	78
Environment and health			
ARI prevalence (% of children under age 5)	..		
Diarrhea prevalence (% of children under age 5)	13.3		
Under-five mortality rate (per 1,000 live births)	45	31	40
National accounting aggregates, 2004			
Gross savings (% of GNI)	13.4	22.7	32.1
Consumption of fixed capital (% of GNI)	11.1	12.1	10.8
Education expenditure (% of GNI)	1.6	4.4	2.9
Energy depletion (% of GNI)	1.2	7.2	6.5
Mineral depletion (% of GNI)	0.0	1.1	0.5
Net forest depletion (% of GNI)	0.9	0.0	0.0
CO_2 damage (% of GNI)	0.3	0.5	1.1
Particulate emission damage (% of GNI)	0.4	0.6	1.0
Adjusted net savings (% of GNI)	1.2	5.6	15.1

Guinea

Environmental strategy/action plan prepared in **1994**

	Country data	Group data Sub-Saharan Africa	Low income
Population (millions)	9.2	726	2,343
Urban population (% of total)	35.7	36.4	30.6
GDP ($ billions)	3.9	523	1,239
GNI per capita, *World Bank Atlas* method ($)	410	601	507
Agriculture			
Land area (1,000 sq. km)	246	23,596	29,192
Agricultural land (% of land area)	51	44	45
Irrigated land (% of cropland)	5.4	3.6	23.9
Fertilizer consumption (100 grams/ha of arable land)	30	136	646
Population density, rural (people/sq. km of arable land)	533	355	524
Forests and biodiversity			
Forest area (% of land area)	27.4	26.5	24.8
Annual deforestation (% change, 1990–2005)	0.6	0.6	0.5
Nationally protected areas (% of total land area)	0.7	8.7	7.7
Mammal species, total known	215		
Mammal species, threatened	18		
Bird species, total known	640		
Bird species, threatened	10		
GEF benefits index for biodiversity (0–100)	2.6		
Energy			
GDP per unit of energy use (2000 PPP $/kg oil equiv)	..	2.8	4.2
Energy use per capita (kg oil equiv)	..	681	501
Energy from combustible renewables & waste (% of tot.)	..	57.4	48.9
Energy imports, net (% of energy use)	..	−59	−4
Electric power consumption per capita (kWh)	..	513	358
Electricity generated by coal (% of total)	..	68.0	46.3
Emissions and pollution			
CO_2 emissions per unit of GDP (kg/2000 PPP $ of GDP)	0.1	0.4	0.4
CO_2 emissions per capita (metric tons)	0.1	0.7	0.8
Particulate matter (urban-pop.-weighted avg., μg/cu. m)	63	73	89
Passenger cars (per 1,000 people)	..	..	6
Water and sanitation			
Internal freshwater resources per capita (cu. m)	24,561	5,353	3,456
Freshwater withdrawal			
Total (% of internal resources)	0.7	3.1	15.5
Agriculture (% of total freshwater withdrawal)	90	87	88
Access to improved water source (% of total population)	51	58	75
Rural (% of rural population)	38	45	69
Urban (% of urban population)	78	82	89
Access to improved sanitation (% of total population)	13	36	36
Rural (% of rural population)	6	26	24
Urban (% of urban population)	25	55	61
Environment and health			
ARI prevalence (% of children under age 5)	15.0		
Diarrhea prevalence (% of children under age 5)	21.2		
Under-five mortality rate (per 1,000 live births)	155	168	122
National accounting aggregates, 2004			
Gross savings (% of GNI)	8.0	17.1	22.7
Consumption of fixed capital (% of GNI)	8.8	10.9	9.2
Education expenditure (% of GNI)	2.0	3.9	3.4
Energy depletion (% of GNI)	0.0	9.8	6.7
Mineral depletion (% of GNI)	1.9	0.4	0.4
Net forest depletion (% of GNI)	1.8	0.6	0.7
CO_2 damage (% of GNI)	0.2	0.7	1.1
Particulate emission damage (% of GNI)	0.8	0.5	0.8
Adjusted net savings (% of GNI)	−3.5	−1.9	7.3

Guinea-Bissau

Environmental strategy/action plan prepared in **1993**

	Country data	Sub-Saharan Africa	Low income
		Group data	
Population (millions)	1.5	726	2,343
Urban population (% of total)	34.8	36.4	30.6
GDP ($ billions)	0.3	523	1,239
GNI per capita, *World Bank Atlas* method ($)	160	601	507
Agriculture			
Land area (1,000 sq. km)	28	23,596	29,192
Agricultural land (% of land area)	58	44	45
Irrigated land (% of cropland)	4.5	3.6	23.9
Fertilizer consumption (100 grams/ha of arable land)	80	136	646
Population density, rural (people/sq. km of arable land)	329	355	524
Forests and biodiversity			
Forest area (% of land area)	73.7	26.5	24.8
Annual deforestation (% change, 1990–2005)	0.4	0.6	0.5
Nationally protected areas (% of total land area)	..	8.7	7.7
Mammal species, total known	101		
Mammal species, threatened	5		
Bird species, total known	459		
Bird species, threatened	1		
GEF benefits index for biodiversity (0–100)	0.7		
Energy			
GDP per unit of energy use (2000 PPP $/kg oil equiv)	..	2.8	4.2
Energy use per capita (kg oil equiv)	..	681	501
Energy from combustible renewables & waste (% of tot.)	..	57.4	48.9
Energy imports, net (% of energy use)	..	−59	−4
Electric power consumption per capita (kWh)	..	513	358
Electricity generated by coal (% of total)	..	68.0	46.3
Emissions and pollution			
CO_2 emissions per unit of GDP (kg/2000 PPP $ of GDP)	0.2	0.4	0.4
CO_2 emissions per capita (metric tons)	0.2	0.7	0.8
Particulate matter (urban-pop.-weighted avg., µg/cu. m)	84	73	89
Passenger cars (per 1,000 people)	..	..	6
Water and sanitation			
Internal freshwater resources per capita (cu. m)	10,392	5,353	3,456
Freshwater withdrawal			
Total (% of internal resources)	1.1	3.1	15.5
Agriculture (% of total freshwater withdrawal)	82	87	88
Access to improved water source (% of total population)	59	58	75
Rural (% of rural population)	49	45	69
Urban (% of urban population)	79	82	89
Access to improved sanitation (% of total population)	34	36	36
Rural (% of rural population)	23	26	24
Urban (% of urban population)	57	55	61
Environment and health			
ARI prevalence (% of children under age 5)	10.1		
Diarrhea prevalence (% of children under age 5)	31.5		
Under-five mortality rate (per 1,000 live births)	203	168	122
National accounting aggregates, 2004			
Gross savings (% of GNI)	8.8	17.1	22.7
Consumption of fixed capital (% of GNI)	7.9	10.9	9.2
Education expenditure (% of GNI)	..	3.9	3.4
Energy depletion (% of GNI)	0.0	9.8	6.7
Mineral depletion (% of GNI)	0.0	0.4	0.4
Net forest depletion (% of GNI)	0.0	0.6	0.7
CO_2 damage (% of GNI)	0.6	0.7	1.1
Particulate emission damage (% of GNI)	1.0	0.5	0.8
Adjusted net savings (% of GNI)	..	−1.9	7.3

Guyana

Environmental strategy/action plan prepared in ..

	Country data	Group data Latin America & Caribbean	Lower middle income
Population (millions)	0.8	546	2,442
Urban population (% of total)	38.0	77.1	48.7
GDP ($ billions)	0.8	2,022	4,165
GNI per capita, World Bank Atlas method ($)	1,020	3,576	1,686
Agriculture			
Land area (1,000 sq. km)	197	20,057	38,470
Agricultural land (% of land area)	9	36	43
Irrigated land (% of cropland)	29.4	11.4	23.1
Fertilizer consumption (100 grams/ha of arable land)	372	923	1,530
Population density, rural (people/sq. km of arable land)	97	212	523
Forests and biodiversity			
Forest area (% of land area)	76.7	45.6	30.7
Annual deforestation (% change, 1990–2005)	0.0	0.4	0.1
Nationally protected areas (% of total land area)	0.3	11.1	7.7
Mammal species, total known	237		
Mammal species, threatened	13		
Bird species, total known	786		
Bird species, threatened	3		
GEF benefits index for biodiversity (0–100)	3.2		
Energy			
GDP per unit of energy use (2000 PPP $/kg oil equiv)	..	6.2	4.6
Energy use per capita (kg oil equiv)	..	1,148	1,090
Energy from combustible renewables & waste (% of tot.)	..	15.0	14.6
Energy imports, net (% of energy use)	..	–40	–14
Electric power consumption per capita (kWh)	..	1,615	1,329
Electricity generated by coal (% of total)	..	5.4	49.4
Emissions and pollution			
CO_2 emissions per unit of GDP (kg/2000 PPP $ of GDP)	0.5	0.3	0.5
CO_2 emissions per capita (metric tons)	2.2	2.4	2.6
Particulate matter (urban-pop.-weighted avg., µg/cu. m)	13	43	70
Passenger cars (per 1,000 people)	..	108	29
Water and sanitation			
Internal freshwater resources per capita (cu. m)	321,234	24,619	7,295
Freshwater withdrawal			
Total (% of internal resources)	0.7	2.0	7.7
Agriculture (% of total freshwater withdrawal)	98	71	75
Access to improved water source (% of total population)	83	89	81
Rural (% of rural population)	83	69	70
Urban (% of urban population)	83	96	93
Access to improved sanitation (% of total population)	70	75	57
Rural (% of rural population)	60	44	39
Urban (% of urban population)	86	84	78
Environment and health			
ARI prevalence (% of children under age 5)	..		
Diarrhea prevalence (% of children under age 5)	..		
Under-five mortality rate (per 1,000 live births)	64	31	40
National accounting aggregates, 2004			
Gross savings (% of GNI)	20.9	22.7	32.1
Consumption of fixed capital (% of GNI)	10.4	12.1	10.8
Education expenditure (% of GNI)	7.7	4.4	2.9
Energy depletion (% of GNI)	0.0	7.2	6.5
Mineral depletion (% of GNI)	6.5	1.1	0.5
Net forest depletion (% of GNI)	0.0	0.0	0.0
CO_2 damage (% of GNI)	1.4	0.5	1.1
Particulate emission damage (% of GNI)	..	0.6	1.0
Adjusted net savings (% of GNI)	10.3	5.6	15.1

Haiti

Environmental strategy/action plan prepared in **1999**

	Country data	Group data Latin America & Caribbean	Low income
Population (millions)	8.4	546	2,343
Urban population (% of total)	38.1	77.1	30.6
GDP ($ billions)	3.5	2,022	1,239
GNI per capita, *World Bank Atlas* method ($)	400	3,576	507
Agriculture			
Land area (1,000 sq. km)	28	20,057	29,192
Agricultural land (% of land area)	58	36	45
Irrigated land (% of cropland)	8.4	11.4	23.9
Fertilizer consumption (100 grams/ha of arable land)	179	923	646
Population density, rural (people/sq. km of arable land)	664	212	524
Forests and biodiversity			
Forest area (% of land area)	3.8	45.6	24.8
Annual deforestation (% change, 1990–2005)	0.6	0.4	0.5
Nationally protected areas (% of total land area)	0.4	11.1	7.7
Mammal species, total known	41		
Mammal species, threatened	4		
Bird species, total known	271		
Bird species, threatened	15		
GEF benefits index for biodiversity (0–100)	5.8		
Energy			
GDP per unit of energy use (2000 PPP $/kg oil equiv)	6.4	6.2	4.2
Energy use per capita (kg oil equiv)	270	1,148	501
Energy from combustible renewables & waste (% of tot.)	73.8	15.0	48.9
Energy imports, net (% of energy use)	25	–40	–4
Electric power consumption per capita (kWh)	31	1,615	358
Electricity generated by coal (% of total)	..	5.4	46.3
Emissions and pollution			
CO_2 emissions per unit of GDP (kg/2000 PPP $ of GDP)	0.1	0.3	0.4
CO_2 emissions per capita (metric tons)	0.2	2.4	0.8
Particulate matter (urban-pop.-weighted avg., µg/cu. m)	47	43	89
Passenger cars (per 1,000 people)	..	108	6
Water and sanitation			
Internal freshwater resources per capita (cu. m)	1,548	24,619	3,456
Freshwater withdrawal			
Total (% of internal resources)	7.6	2.0	15.5
Agriculture (% of total freshwater withdrawal)	94	71	88
Access to improved water source (% of total population)	71	89	75
Rural (% of rural population)	59	69	69
Urban (% of urban population)	91	96	89
Access to improved sanitation (% of total population)	34	75	36
Rural (% of rural population)	23	44	24
Urban (% of urban population)	52	84	61
Environment and health			
ARI prevalence (% of children under age 5)	31.2		
Diarrhea prevalence (% of children under age 5)	25.7		
Under-five mortality rate (per 1,000 live births)	117	31	122
National accounting aggregates, 2004			
Gross savings (% of GNI)	20.1	22.7	22.7
Consumption of fixed capital (% of GNI)	8.5	12.1	9.2
Education expenditure (% of GNI)	1.5	4.4	3.4
Energy depletion (% of GNI)	0.0	7.2	6.7
Mineral depletion (% of GNI)	0.0	1.1	0.4
Net forest depletion (% of GNI)	1.0	0.0	0.7
CO_2 damage (% of GNI)	0.3	0.5	1.1
Particulate emission damage (% of GNI)	0.3	0.6	0.8
Adjusted net savings (% of GNI)	11.5	5.6	7.3

Honduras

Environmental strategy/action plan prepared in **1993**

	Country data	Group data Latin America & Caribbean	Lower middle income
Population (millions)	7.0	546	2,442
Urban population (% of total)	46.0	77.1	48.7
GDP ($ billions)	7.4	2,022	4,165
GNI per capita, *World Bank Atlas* method ($)	1,040	3,576	1,686

Agriculture
Land area (1,000 sq. km)	112	20,057	38,470
Agricultural land (% of land area)	26	36	43
Irrigated land (% of cropland)	5.6	11.4	23.1
Fertilizer consumption (100 grams/ha of arable land)	470	923	1,530
Population density, rural (people/sq. km of arable land)	351	212	523

Forests and biodiversity
Forest area (% of land area)	41.5	45.6	30.7
Annual deforestation (% change, 1990–2005)	2.5	0.4	0.1
Nationally protected areas (% of total land area)	6.4	11.1	7.7
Mammal species, total known	201		
Mammal species, threatened	10		
Bird species, total known	699		
Bird species, threatened	6		
GEF benefits index for biodiversity (0–100)	7.9		

Energy
GDP per unit of energy use (2000 PPP $/kg oil equiv)	4.9	6.2	4.6
Energy use per capita (kg oil equiv)	522	1,148	1,090
Energy from combustible renewables & waste (% of tot.)	40.9	15.0	14.6
Energy imports, net (% of energy use)	54	−40	−14
Electric power consumption per capita (kWh)	556	1,615	1,329
Electricity generated by coal (% of total)	..	5.4	49.4

Emissions and pollution
CO_2 emissions per unit of GDP (kg/2000 PPP $ of GDP)	0.3	0.3	0.5
CO_2 emissions per capita (metric tons)	0.9	2.4	2.6
Particulate matter (urban-pop.-weighted avg., μg/cu. m)	46	43	70
Passenger cars (per 1,000 people)	52	108	29

Water and sanitation
Internal freshwater resources per capita (cu. m)	13,610	24,619	7,295
Freshwater withdrawal			
Total (% of internal resources)	0.9	2.0	7.7
Agriculture (% of total freshwater withdrawal)	80	71	75
Access to improved water source (% of total population)	90	89	81
Rural (% of rural population)	82	69	70
Urban (% of urban population)	99	96	93
Access to improved sanitation (% of total population)	68	75	57
Rural (% of rural population)	52	44	39
Urban (% of urban population)	89	84	78

Environment and health
ARI prevalence (% of children under age 5)	..		
Diarrhea prevalence (% of children under age 5)	..		
Under-five mortality rate (per 1,000 live births)	41	31	40

National accounting aggregates, 2004
Gross savings (% of GNI)	..	22.7	32.1
Consumption of fixed capital (% of GNI)	10.3	12.1	10.8
Education expenciture (% of GNI)	3.5	4.4	2.9
Energy depletion (% of GNI)	0.0	7.2	6.5
Mineral depletion (% of GNI)	0.2	1.1	0.5
Net forest depletion (% of GNI)	0.0	0.0	0.0
CO_2 damage (% of GNI)	0.6	0.5	1.1
Particulate emission damage (% of GNI)	0.3	0.6	1.0
Adjusted net savings (% of GNI)	..	5.6	15.1

Hong Kong, China

Environmental strategy/action plan prepared in ..

	Country data	Group data High income
Population (millions)	6.9	1,004
Urban population (% of total)	100.0	78.5
GDP ($ billions)	163.0	32,900
GNI per capita, *World Bank Atlas* method ($)	26,660	32,112

Agriculture		
Land area (1,000 sq. km)	..	33,018
Agricultural land (% of land area)	..	38
Irrigated land (% of cropland)	..	11.9
Fertilizer consumption (100 grams/ha of arable land)	..	1,205
Population density, rural (people/sq. km of arable land)	..	331

Forests and biodiversity		
Forest area (% of land area)	..	29.3
Annual deforestation (% change, 1990–2005)	..	–0.1
Nationally protected areas (% of total land area)	..	..
Mammal species, total known	57	
Mammal species, threatened	1	
Bird species, total known	306	
Bird species, threatened	20	
GEF benefits index for biodiversity (0–100)	..	

Energy		
GDP per unit of energy use (2000 PPP $/kg oil equiv)	10.9	5.2
Energy use per capita (kg oil equiv)	2,428	5,410
Energy from combustible renewables & waste (% of tot.)	0.3	3.0
Energy imports, net (% of energy use)	100	19
Electric power consumption per capita (kWh)	5,653	9,503
Electricity generated by coal (% of total)	77.7	38.2

Emissions and pollution		
CO_2 emissions per unit of GDP (kg/2000 PPP $ of GDP)	0.2	0.5
CO_2 emissions per capita (metric tons)	5.2	12.8
Particulate matter (urban-pop.-weighted avg., µg/cu. m)	38	29
Passenger cars (per 1,000 people)	59	433

Water and sanitation		
Internal freshwater resources per capita (cu. m)	..	9,703
Freshwater withdrawal		
Total (% of internal resources)	..	10.4
Agriculture (% of total freshwater withdrawal)	..	42
Access to improved water source (% of total population)	..	99
Rural (% of rural population)	..	98
Urban (% of urban population)	..	100
Access to improved sanitation (% of total population)	..	..
Rural (% of rural population)	..	..
Urban (% of urban population)	..	..

Environment and health		
ARI prevalence (% of children under age 5)	..	
Diarrhea prevalence (% of children under age 5)	..	
Under-five mortality rate (per 1,000 live births)	..	7

National accounting aggregates, 2004		
Gross savings (% of GNI)	31.7	19.4
Consumption of fixed capital (% of GNI)	13.8	13.2
Education expenditure (% of GNI)	3.7	4.6
Energy depletion (% of GNI)	0.0	1.4
Mineral depletion (% of GNI)	0.0	0.0
Net forest depletion (% of GNI)	0.0	0.0
CO_2 damage (% of GNI)	0.2	0.3
Particulate emission damage (% of GNI)	..	0.4
Adjusted net savings (% of GNI)	21.5	8.7

Hungary

Environmental strategy/action plan prepared in **1995**

	Country data	Europe & Central Asia	Upper middle income
		Group data	
Population (millions)	10.1	472	576
Urban population (% of total)	65.5	63.6	72.3
GDP ($ billions)	100.7	1,770	2,992
GNI per capita, *World Bank Atlas* method ($)	8,370	3,295	4,769
Agriculture			
Land area (1,000 sq. km)	92	23,371	28,983
Agricultural land (% of land area)	64	29	26
Irrigated land (% of cropland)	4.8	11.1	8.7
Fertilizer consumption (100 grams/ha of arable land)	1,087	347	469
Population density, rural (people/sq. km of arable land)	77	126	131
Forests and biodiversity			
Forest area (% of land area)	21.5	38.3	37.3
Annual deforestation (% change, 1990–2005)	–0.6	0.0	0.1
Nationally protected areas (% of total land area)	7.0	6.9	..
Mammal species, total known	88		
Mammal species, threatened	7		
Bird species, total known	367		
Bird species, threatened	9		
GEF benefits index for biodiversity (0–100)	0.2		
Energy			
GDP per unit of energy use (2000 PPP $/kg oil equiv)	5.6	2.7	3.5
Energy use per capita (kg oil equiv)	2,600	2,794	2,574
Energy from combustible renewables & waste (% of tot.)	3.1	2.4	3.9
Energy imports, net (% of energy use)	60	–26	–51
Electric power consumption per capita (kWh)	3,637	3,531	3,378
Electricity generated by coal (% of total)	27.1	29.8	31.0
Emissions and pollution			
CO_2 emissions per unit of GDP (kg/2000 PPP $ of GDP)	0.4	1.0	0.7
CO_2 emissions per capita (metric tons)	5.6	6.7	6.2
Particulate matter (urban-pop.-weighted avg., µg/cu. m)	22	35	40
Passenger cars (per 1,000 people)	259	142	143
Water and sanitation			
Internal freshwater resources per capita (cu. m)	594	11,123	14,190
Freshwater withdrawal			
Total (% of internal resources)	127.3	7.5	3.8
Agriculture (% of total freshwater withdrawal)	32	59	53
Access to improved water source (% of total population)	99	91	93
Rural (% of rural population)	98	80	82
Urban (% of urban population)	100	98	97
Access to improved sanitation (% of total population)	95	82	81
Rural (% of rural population)	85	63	61
Urban (% of urban population)	100	93	91
Environment and health			
ARI prevalence (% of children under age 5)	..		
Diarrhea prevalence (% of children under age 5)	..		
Under-five mortality rate (per 1,000 live births)	8	34	28
National accounting aggregates, 2004			
Gross savings (% of GNI)	15.4	23.4	23.1
Consumption of fixed capital (% of GNI)	13.8	10.7	11.5
Education expenditure (% of GNI)	5.2	4.1	4.5
Energy depletion (% of GNI)	0.5	12.0	11.2
Mineral depletion (% of GNI)	0.0	0.3	0.6
Net forest depletion (% of GNI)	0.0	0.0	0.0
CO_2 damage (% of GNI)	0.4	1.4	0.9
Particulate emission damage (% of GNI)	0.3	0.7	0.7
Adjusted net savings (% of GNI)	5.7	2.3	2.6

Iceland

Environmental strategy/action plan prepared in ..

	Country data	Group data High income
Population (millions)	0.3	1,004
Urban population (% of total)	92.9	78.5
GDP ($ billions)	12.2	32,900
GNI per capita, *World Bank Atlas* method ($)	37,920	32,112

Agriculture		
Land area (1,000 sq. km)	100	33,018
Agricultural land (% of land area)	23	38
Irrigated land (% of cropland)	..	11.9
Fertilizer consumption (100 grams/ha of arable land)	25,554	1,205
Population density, rural (people/sq. km of arable land)	298	331

Forests and biodiversity		
Forest area (% of land area)	0.5	29.3
Annual deforestation (% change, 1990–2005)	−5.6	−0.1
Nationally protected areas (% of total land area)	9.8	..
Mammal species, total known	33	
Mammal species, threatened	7	
Bird species, total known	305	
Bird species, threatened	0	
GEF benefits index for biodiversity (0–100)	1.0	

Energy		
GDP per unit of energy use (2000 PPP $/kg oil equiv)	2.5	5.2
Energy use per capita (kg oil equiv)	11,694	5,410
Energy from combustible renewables & waste (% of tot.)	0.1	3.0
Energy imports, net (% of energy use)	27	19
Electric power consumption per capita (kWh)	27,577	9,503
Electricity generated by coal (% of total)	..	38.2

Emissions and pollution		
CO_2 emissions per unit of GDP (kg/2000 PPP $ of GDP)	0.3	0.5
CO_2 emissions per capita (metric tons)	7.7	12.8
Particulate matter (urban-pop.-weighted avg., µg/cu. m)	20	29
Passenger cars per 1,000 people	562	433

Water and sanitation		
Internal freshwater resources per capita (cu. m)	582,000	9,703
Freshwater withdrawal		
Total (% of internal resources)	..	10.4
Agriculture (% of total freshwater withdrawal)	6	42
Access to improved water source (% of total population)	100	99
Rural (% of rural population)	100	98
Urban (% of urban population)	100	100
Access to improved sanitation (% of total population)	..	..
Rural (% of rural population)	..	..
Urban (% of urban population)	..	..

Environment and health		
ARI prevalence (% of children under age 5)	..	
Diarrhea prevalence (% of children under age 5)	..	
Under-five mortality rate (per 1,000 live births)	3	7

National accounting aggregates, 2004		
Gross savings (% of GNI)	13.7	19.4
Consumption of fixed capital (% of GNI)	12.6	13.2
Education expenditure (% of GNI)	7.0	4.6
Energy depletion (% of GNI)	0.0	1.4
Mineral depletion (% of GNI)	0.0	0.0
Net forest depletion (% of GNI)	0.0	0.0
CO_2 damage (% of GNI)	0.1	0.3
Particulate emission damage (% of GNI)	0.1	0.4
Adjusted net savings (% of GNI)	7.8	8.7

India

Environmental strategy/action plan prepared in **1993**

	Country data	Group data	
		South Asia	Low income
Population (millions)	1,079.7	1,447	2,343
Urban population (% of total)	28.5	28.3	30.6
GDP ($ billions)	691.2	880	1,239
GNI per capita, *World Bank Atlas* method ($)	620	594	507
Agriculture			
Land area (1,000 sq. km)	2,973	4,781	29,192
Agricultural land (% of land area)	61	54	45
Irrigated land (% of cropland)	32.9	39.6	23.9
Fertilizer consumption (100 grams/ha of arable land)	1,008	1,040	646
Population density, rural (people/sq. km of arable land)	475	586	524
Forests and biodiversity			
Forest area (% of land area)	22.8	16.8	24.8
Annual deforestation (% change, 1990–2005)	–0.4	–0.2	0.5
Nationally protected areas (% of total land area)	5.2	4.8	7.7
Mammal species, total known	422		
Mammal species, threatened	85		
Bird species, total known	1,180		
Bird species, threatened	79		
GEF benefits index for biodiversity (0–100)	43.9		
Energy			
GDP per unit of energy use (2000 PPP $/kg oil equiv)	5.3	5.3	4.2
Energy use per capita (kg oil equiv)	520	474	501
Energy from combustible renewables & waste (% of tot.)	38.2	38.8	48.9
Energy imports, net (% of energy use)	18	19	–4
Electric power consumption per capita (kWh)	435	394	358
Electricity generated by coal (% of total)	68.3	58.2	46.3
Emissions and pollution			
CO_2 emissions per unit of GDP (kg/2000 PPP $ of GDP)	0.5	0.4	0.4
CO_2 emissions per capita (metric tons)	1.2	1.0	0.8
Particulate matter (urban-pop.-weighted avg., µg/cu. m)	84	99	89
Passenger cars (per 1,000 people)	6	6	6
Water and sanitation			
Internal freshwater resources per capita (cu. m)	1,167	1,255	3,456
Freshwater withdrawal			
Total (% of internal resources)	51.2	51.8	15.5
Agriculture (% of total freshwater withdrawal)	86	90	88
Access to improved water source (% of total population)	86	84	75
Rural (% of rural population)	82	80	69
Urban (% of urban population)	96	94	89
Access to improved sanitation (% of total population)	30	35	36
Rural (% of rural population)	18	23	24
Urban (% of urban population)	58	64	61
Environment and health			
ARI prevalence (% of children under age 5)	..		
Diarrhea prevalence (% of children under age 5)	19.2		
Under-five mortality rate (per 1,000 live births)	85	92	122
National accounting aggregates, 2004			
Gross savings (% of GNI)	23.0	23.6	22.7
Consumption of fixed capital (% of GNI)	9.3	9.1	9.2
Education expenditure (% of GNI)	4.0	3.6	3.4
Energy depletion (% of GNI)	2.5	2.7	6.7
Mineral depletion (% of GNI)	0.4	0.3	0.4
Net forest depletion (% of GNI)	0.7	0.7	0.7
CO_2 damage (% of GNI)	1.3	1.2	1.1
Particulate emission damage (% of GNI)	0.8	0.8	0.8
Adjusted net savings (% of GNI)	12.0	12.4	7.3

Indonesia

Environmental strategy/action plan prepared in **1993**

	Country data	Group data East Asia & Pacific	Group data Lower middle income
Population (millions)	217.6	1,870	2,442
Urban population (% of total)	46.7	40.6	48.7
GDP ($ billions)	257.6	2,651	4,165
GNI per capita, *World Bank Atlas* method ($)	1,140	1,416	1,686
Agriculture			
Land area (1,000 sq. km)	1,812	15,885	38,470
Agricultural land (% of land area)	25	51	43
Irrigated land (% of cropland)	13.1	..	23.1
Fertilizer consumption (100 grams/ha of arable land)	1,460	2,296	1,530
Population density, rural (people/sq. km of arable land)	557	559	523
Forests and biodiversity			
Forest area (% of land area)	48.8	28.4	30.7
Annual deforestation (% change, 1990–2005)	1.6	−0.2	0.1
Nationally protected areas (% of total land area)	20.6	..	7.7
Mammal species, total known	667		
Mammal species, threatened	146		
Bird species, total known	1,604		
Bird species, threatened	121		
GEF benefits index for biodiversity (0–100)	90.0		
Energy			
GDP per unit of energy use (2000 PPP $/kg oil equiv)	4.3	4.6	4.6
Energy use per capita (kg oil equiv)	753	1,007	1,090
Energy from combustible renewables & waste (% of tot.)	26.8	17.7	14.6
Energy imports, net (% of energy use)	−55	−2	−14
Electric power consumption per capita (kWh)	440	1,184	1,329
Electricity generated by coal (% of total)	41.1	69.4	49.4
Emissions and pollution			
CO_2 emissions per unit of GDP (kg/2000 PPP $ of GDP)	0.4	0.5	0.5
CO_2 emissions per capita (metric tons)	1.4	2.4	2.6
Particulate matter (urban-pop.-weighted avg., µg/cu. m)	114	80	70
Passenger cars (per 1,000 people)	..	12	29
Water and sanitation			
Internal freshwater resources per capita (cu. m)	13,043	5,062	7,295
Freshwater withdrawal			
Total (% of internal resources)	2.9	10.2	7.7
Agriculture (% of total freshwater withdrawal)	91	74	75
Access to improved water source (% of total population)	78	78	81
Rural (% of rural population)	69	69	70
Urban (% of urban population)	89	92	93
Access to improved sanitation (% of total population)	52	49	57
Rural (% of rural population)	38	35	39
Urban (% of urban population)	71	72	78
Environment and health			
ARI prevalence (% of children under age 5)	..		
Diarrhea prevalence (% of children under age 5)	..		
Under-five mortality rate (per 1,000 live births)	38	37	40
National accounting aggregates, 2004			
Gross savings (% of GNI)	24.6	39.1	32.1
Consumption of fixed capital (% of GNI)	10.4	10.5	10.8
Education expenditure (% of GNI)	1.1	2.3	2.9
Energy depletion (% of GNI)	9.4	4.1	6.5
Mineral depletion (% of GNI)	1.6	0.4	0.5
Net forest depletion (% of GNI)	0.0	0.0	0.0
CO_2 damage (% of GNI)	0.7	1.2	1.1
Particulate emission damage (% of GNI)	0.9	1.2	1.0
Adjusted net savings (% of GNI)	2.6	23.9	15.1

Iran, Islamic Rep.

Environmental strategy/action plan prepared in ..

	Country data	Group data Middle East & North Africa	Lower middle income
Population (millions)	67.0	300	2,442
Urban population (% of total)	67.3	56.3	48.7
GDP ($ billions)	163.4	547	4,165
GNI per capita, World Bank Atlas method ($)	2,320	1,972	1,686
Agriculture			
Land area (1,000 sq. km)	1,636	8,955	38,470
Agricultural land (% of land area)	38	23	43
Irrigated land (% of cropland)	41.9	32.5	23.1
Fertilizer consumption (100 grams/ha of arable land)	860	842	1,530
Population density, rural (people/sq. km of arable land)	138	670	523
Forests and biodiversity			
Forest area (% of land area)	6.8	2.4	30.7
Annual deforestation (% change, 1990–2005)	0.0	–0.5	0.1
Nationally protected areas (% of total land area)	4.8	4.2	7.7
Mammal species, total known	158		
Mammal species, threatened	21		
Bird species, total known	498		
Bird species, threatened	18		
GEF benefits index for biodiversity (0–100)	7.9		
Energy			
GDP per unit of energy use (2000 PPP $/kg oil equiv)	3.2	4.2	4.6
Energy use per capita (kg oil equiv)	2,055	1,144	1,090
Energy from combustible renewables & waste (% of tot.)	0.6	1.3	14.6
Energy imports, net (% of energy use)	–95	–129	–14
Electric power consumption per capita (kWh)	1,916	1,212	1,329
Electricity generated by coal (% of total)	..	3.0	49.4
Emissions and pollution			
CO_2 emissions per unit of GDP (kg/2000 PPP $ of GDP)	1.0	0.7	0.5
CO_2 emissions per capita (metric tons)	5.5	3.2	2.6
Particulate matter (urban-pop.-weighted avg., µg/cu. m)	68	90	70
Passenger cars (per 1,000 people)	..	..	29
Water and sanitation			
Internal freshwater resources per capita (cu. m)	1,918	761	7,295
Freshwater withdrawal			
Total (% of internal resources)	56.7	105.0	7.7
Agriculture (% of total freshwater withdrawal)	91	89	75
Access to improved water source (% of total population)	93	88	81
Rural (% of rural population)	83	79	70
Urban (% of urban population)	98	95	93
Access to improved sanitation (% of total population)	84	75	57
Rural (% of rural population)	78	56	39
Urban (% of urban population)	86	89	78
Environment and health			
ARI prevalence (% of children under age 5)	..		
Diarrhea prevalence (% of children under age 5)	..		
Under-five mortality rate (per 1,000 live births)	38	55	40
National accounting aggregates, 2004			
Gross savings (% of GNI)	39.7	30.0	32.1
Consumption of fixed capital (% of GNI)	11.0	11.2	10.8
Education expenditure (% of GNI)	4.4	4.5	2.9
Energy depletion (% of GNI)	36.0	27.3	6.5
Mineral depletion (% of GNI)	0.2	0.1	0.5
Net forest depletion (% of GNI)	0.0	0.1	0.0
CO_2 damage (% of GNI)	1.7	1.2	1.1
Particulate emission damage (% of GNI)	0.9	0.9	1.0
Adjusted net savings (% of GNI)	–5.6	–6.2	15.1

Iraq

Environmental strategy/action plan prepared in ..

	Country data	Middle East & North Africa	Lower middle income
		Group data	
Population (millions)	28.1	300	2,442
Urban population (% of total)	67.1	56.3	48.7
GDP ($ billions)	12.6	547	4,165
GNI per capita, *World Bank Atlas* method ($)	..	1,972	1,686
Agriculture			
Land area (1,000 sq. km)	437	8,955	38,470
Agricultural land (% of land area)	23	23	43
Irrigated land (% of cropland)	58.6	32.5	23.1
Fertilizer consumption (100 grams/ha of arable land)	1,111	842	1,530
Population density, rural (people/sq. km of arable land)	156	670	523
Forests and biodiversity			
Forest area (% of land area)	1.9	2.4	30.7
Annual deforestation (% change, 1990–2005)	–0.1	–0.5	0.1
Nationally protected areas (% of total land area)	0.0	4.2	7.7
Mammal species, total known	102		
Mammal species, threatened	9		
Bird species, total known	396		
Bird species, threatened	18		
GEF benefits index for biodiversity (0–100)	1.7		
Energy			
GDP per unit of energy use (2000 PPP $/kg oil equiv)	..	4.2	4.6
Energy use per capita (kg oil equiv)	943	1,144	1,090
Energy from combustible renewables & waste (% of tot.)	0.1	1.3	14.6
Energy imports, net (% of energy use)	–166	–129	–14
Electric power consumption per capita (kWh)	977	1,212	1,329
Electricity generated by coal (% of total)	..	3.0	49.4
Emissions and pollution			
CO_2 emissions per unit of GDP (kg/2000 PPP $ of GDP)	..	0.7	0.5
CO_2 emissions per capita (metric tons)	3.0	3.2	2.6
Particulate matter (urban-pop.-weighted avg., µg/cu. m)	167	90	70
Passenger cars (per 1,000 people)	..	..	29
Water and sanitation			
Internal freshwater resources per capita (cu. m)	1,255	761	7,295
Freshwater withdrawal			
Total (% of internal resources)	121.3	105.0	7.7
Agriculture (% of total freshwater withdrawal)	92	89	75
Access to improved water source (% of total population)	81	88	81
Rural (% of rural population)	50	79	70
Urban (% of urban population)	97	95	93
Access to improved sanitation (% of total population)	80	75	57
Rural (% of rural population)	48	56	39
Urban (% of urban population)	95	89	78
Environment and health			
ARI prevalence (% of children under age 5)	..		
Diarrhea prevalence (% of children under age 5)	..		
Under-five mortality rate (per 1,000 live births)	125	55	40
National accounting aggregates, 2004			
Gross savings (% of GNI)	..	30.0	32.1
Consumption of fixed capital (% of GNI)	..	11.2	10.8
Education expenditure (% of GNI)	..	4.5	2.9
Energy depletion (% of GNI)	..	27.3	6.5
Mineral depletion (% of GNI)	..	0.1	0.5
Net forest depletion (% of GNI)	..	0.1	0.0
CO_2 damage (% of GNI)	..	1.2	1.1
Particulate emission damage (% of GNI)	2.7	0.9	1.0
Adjusted net savings (% of GNI)	..	–6.2	15.1

Ireland

Environmental strategy/action plan prepared in ..

	Country data	Group data — High income
Population (millions)	4.1	1,004
Urban population (% of total)	60.1	78.5
GDP ($ billions)	181.6	32,900
GNI per capita, *World Bank Atlas* method ($)	34,310	32,112
Agriculture		
Land area (1,000 sq. km)	69	33,018
Agricultural land (% of land area)	63	38
Irrigated land (% of cropland)	..	11.9
Fertilizer consumption (100 grams/ha of arable land)	5,236	1,205
Population density, rural (people/sq. km of arable land)	136	331
Forests and biodiversity		
Forest area (% of land area)	9.7	29.3
Annual deforestation (% change, 1990–2005)	–3.4	–0.1
Nationally protected areas (% of total land area)	1.7	..
Mammal species, total known	63	
Mammal species, threatened	4	
Bird species, total known	408	
Bird species, threatened	8	
GEF benefits index for biodiversity (0–100)	0.7	
Energy		
GDP per unit of energy use (2000 PPP $/kg oil equiv)	9.3	5.2
Energy use per capita (kg oil equiv)	3,777	5,410
Energy from combustible renewables & waste (% of tot.)	1.1	3.0
Energy imports, net (% of energy use)	87	19
Electric power consumption per capita (kWh)	6,098	9,503
Electricity generated by coal (% of total)	33.1	38.2
Emissions and pollution		
CO_2 emissions per unit of GDP (kg/2000 PPP $ of GDP)	0.4	0.5
CO_2 emissions per capita (metric tons)	11.0	12.8
Particulate matter (urban-pop.-weighted avg., µg/cu. m)	20	29
Passenger cars (per 1,000 people)	347	433
Water and sanitation		
Internal freshwater resources per capita (cu. m)	12,045	9,703
Freshwater withdrawal		
Total (% of internal resources)	2.3	10.4
Agriculture (% of total freshwater withdrawal)	0	42
Access to improved water source (% of total population)	..	99
Rural (% of rural population)	..	98
Urban (% of urban population)	100	100
Access to improved sanitation (% of total population)	..	..
Rural (% of rural population)	..	..
Urban (% of urban population)	..	..
Environment and health		
ARI prevalence (% of children under age 5)	..	
Diarrhea prevalence (% of children under age 5)	..	
Under-five mortality rate (per 1,000 live births)	6	7
National accounting aggregates, 2004		
Gross savings (% of GNI)	29.9	19.4
Consumption of fixed capital (% of GNI)	11.0	13.2
Education expenditure (% of GNI)	4.8	4.6
Energy depletion (% of GNI)	0.0	1.4
Mineral depletion (% of GNI)	0.0	0.0
Net forest depletion (% of GNI)	0.0	0.0
CO_2 damage (% of GNI)	0.2	0.3
Particulate emission damage (% of GNI)	0.1	0.4
Adjusted net savings (% of GNI)	23.3	8.7

Isle of Man

Environmental strategy/action plan prepared in ..

	Country data	Group data: High income
Population (millions)	..	1,004
Urban population (% of total)	..	78.5
GDP ($ billions)	2.3	32,900
GNI per capita, *World Bank Atlas* method ($)	..	32,112
Agriculture		
Land area (1,000 sq. km)	..	33,018
Agricultural land (% of land area)	..	38
Irrigated land (% of cropland)	..	11.9
Fertilizer consumption (100 grams/ha of arable land)	..	1,205
Population density, rural (people/sq. km of arable land)	..	331
Forests and biodiversity		
Forest area (% of land area)	..	29.3
Annual deforestation (% change, 1990–2005)	0.0	–0.1
Nationally protected areas (% of total land area)	..	..
Mammal species, total known	..	
Mammal species, threatened	..	
Bird species, total known	..	
Bird species, threatened	..	
GEF benefits index for biodiversity (0–100)	0.0	
Energy		
GDP per unit of energy use (2000 PPP $/kg oil equiv)	..	5.2
Energy use per capita (kg oil equiv)	..	5,410
Energy from combustible renewables & waste (% of tot.)	..	3.0
Energy imports, net (% of energy use)	..	19
Electric power consumption per capita (kWh)	..	9,503
Electricity generated by coal (% of total)	..	38.2
Emissions and pollution		
CO_2 emissions per unit of GDP (kg/2000 PPP $ of GDP)	..	0.5
CO_2 emissions per capita (metric tons)	..	12.8
Particulate matter (urban-pop.-weighted avg., µg/cu. m)	..	29
Passenger cars (per 1,000 people)	..	433
Water and sanitation		
Internal freshwater resources per capita (cu. m)	..	9,703
Freshwater withdrawal		
Total (% of internal resources)	..	10.4
Agriculture (% of total freshwater withdrawal)	..	42
Access to improved water source (% of total population)	..	99
Rural (% of rural population)	..	98
Urban (% of urban population)	..	100
Access to improved sanitation (% of total population)	..	..
Rural (% of rural population)	..	..
Urban (% of urban population)	..	..
Environment and health		
ARI prevalence (% of children under age 5)	..	
Diarrhea prevalence (% of children under age 5)	..	
Under-five mortality rate (per 1,000 live births)	..	7
National accounting aggregates, 2004		
Gross savings (% of GNI)	..	19.4
Consumption of fixed capital (% of GNI)	..	13.2
Education expenditure (% of GNI)	..	4.6
Energy depletion (% of GNI)	..	1.4
Mineral depletion (% of GNI)	..	0.0
Net forest depletion (% of GNI)	..	0.0
CO_2 damage (% of GNI)	..	0.3
Particulate emission damage (% of GNI)	..	0.4
Adjusted net savings (% of GNI)	..	8.7

Israel

Environmental strategy/action plan prepared in ..

	Country data	Group data High income
Population (millions)	6.8	1,004
Urban population (% of total)	91.7	78.5
GDP ($ billions)	116.9	32,900
GNI per capita, *World Bank Atlas* method ($)	17,360	32,112
Agriculture		
Land area (1,000 sq. km)	22	33,018
Agricultural land (% of land area)	26	38
Irrigated land (% cf cropland)	45.3	11.9
Fertilizer consumption (100 grams/ha of arable land)	2,384	1,205
Population density, rural (people/sq. km of arable land)	164	331
Forests and biodiversity		
Forest area (% of land area)	7.9	29.3
Annual deforestation (% change, 1990–2005)	–0.7	–0.1
Nationally protected areas (% of total land area)	15.0	..
Mammal species, total known	115	
Mammal species, threatened	13	
Bird species, total known	534	
Bird species, threatened	18	
GEF benefits index for biodiversity (0–100)	0.9	
Energy		
GDP per unit of energy use (2000 PPP $/kg oil equiv)	7.1	5.2
Energy use per capita (kg oil equiv)	3,086	5,410
Energy from combustible renewables & waste (% of tot.)	0.0	3.0
Energy imports, net (% of energy use)	96	19
Electric power consumption per capita (kWh)	6,599	9,503
Electricity generated by coal (% of total)	77.0	38.2
Emissions and pollution		
CO_2 emissions per unit of GDP (kg/2000 PPP $ of GDP)	0.4	0.5
CO_2 emissions per capita (metric tons)	10.6	12.8
Particulate matter (urban-pop.-weighted avg., µg/cu. m)	53	29
Passenger cars (per 1,000 people)	232	433
Water and sanitation		
Internal freshwater resources per capita (cu. m)	110	9,703
Freshwater withdrawal		
Total (% of internal resources)	273.3	10.4
Agriculture (% of total freshwater withdrawal)	62	42
Access to improved water source (% of total population)	100	99
Rural (% of rural population)	100	98
Urban (% of urban population)	100	100
Access to improved sanitation (% of total population)	..	..
Rural (% of rural population)	..	..
Urban (% of urban population)	100	..
Environment and health		
ARI prevalence (% of children under age 5)	..	
Diarrhea prevalence (% of children under age 5)	..	
Under-five mortality rate (per 1,000 live births)	6	7
National accounting aggregates, 2004		
Gross savings (% of GNI)	10.0	19.4
Consumption of fixed capital (% of GNI)	14.0	13.2
Education expenditure (% of GNI)	7.3	4.6
Energy depletion (% of GNI)	0.0	1.4
Mineral depletion (% of GNI)	0.0	0.0
Net forest depletion (% of GNI)	0.0	0.0
CO_2 damage (% of GNI)	0.4	0.3
Particulate emission damage (% of GNI)	1.2	0.4
Adjusted net savings (% of GNI)	1.6	8.7

Italy

Environmental strategy/action plan prepared in ..

	Country data	Group data High income
Population (millions)	57.6	1,004
Urban population (% of total)	67.5	78.5
GDP ($ billions)	1,677.8	32,900
GNI per capita, *World Bank Atlas* method ($)	26,280	32,112
Agriculture		
Land area (1,000 sq. km)	294	33,018
Agricultural land (% of land area)	51	38
Irrigated land (% of cropland)	25.7	11.9
Fertilizer consumption (100 grams/ha of arable land)	1,729	1,205
Population density, rural (people/sq. km of arable land)	236	331
Forests and biodiversity		
Forest area (% of land area)	33.9	29.3
Annual deforestation (% change, 1990–2005)	–1.3	–0.1
Nationally protected areas (% of total land area)	7.9	..
Mammal species, total known	132	
Mammal species, threatened	12	
Bird species, total known	478	
Bird species, threatened	15	
GEF benefits index for biodiversity (0–100)	4.4	
Energy		
GDP per unit of energy use (2000 PPP $/kg oil equiv)	8.2	5.2
Energy use per capita (kg oil equiv)	3,140	5,410
Energy from combustible renewables & waste (% of tot.)	1.7	3.0
Energy imports, net (% of energy use)	85	19
Electric power consumption per capita (kWh)	5,620	9,503
Electricity generated by coal (% of total)	15.6	38.2
Emissions and pollution		
CO_2 emissions per unit of GDP (kg/2000 PPP $ of GDP)	0.3	0.5
CO_2 emissions per capita (metric tons)	7.5	12.8
Particulate matter (urban-pop.-weighted avg., µg/cu. m)	33	29
Passenger cars (per 1,000 people)	545	433
Water and sanitation		
Internal freshwater resources per capita (cu. m)	3,170	9,703
Freshwater withdrawal		
Total (% of internal resources)	24.3	10.4
Agriculture (% of total freshwater withdrawal)	45	42
Access to improved water source (% of total population)	..	99
Rural (% of rural population)	..	98
Urban (% of urban population)	100	100
Access to improved sanitation (% of total population)	..	..
Rural (% of rural population)	..	..
Urban (% of urban population)	..	..
Environment and health		
ARI prevalence (% of children under age 5)	..	
Diarrhea prevalence (% of children under age 5)	..	
Under-five mortality rate (per 1,000 live births)	5	7
National accounting aggregates, 2004		
Gross savings (% of GNI)	19.5	19.4
Consumption of fixed capital (% of GNI)	13.9	13.2
Education expenditure (% of GNI)	4.5	4.6
Energy depletion (% of GNI)	0.1	1.4
Mineral depletion (% of GNI)	0.0	0.0
Net forest depletion (% of GNI)	0.0	0.0
CO_2 damage (% of GNI)	0.2	0.3
Particulate emission damage (% of GNI)	0.3	0.4
Adjusted net savings (% of GNI)	9.5	8.7

Jamaica

Environmental strategy/action plan prepared in **1994**

	Country data	Group data Latin America & Caribbean	Lower middle income
Population (millions)	2.6	546	2,442
Urban population (% of total)	52.2	77.1	48.7
GDP ($ billions)	8.9	2,022	4,165
GNI per capita, *World Bank Atlas* method ($)	3,300	3,576	1,686
Agriculture			
Land area (1,000 sq. km)	11	20,057	38,470
Agricultural land (% of land area)	47	36	43
Irrigated land (% of cropland)	8.8	11.4	23.1
Fertilizer consumption (100 grams/ha of arable land)	1,287	923	1,530
Population density, rural (people/sq. km of arable land)	723	212	523
Forests and biodiversity			
Forest area (% of land area)	31.3	45.6	30.7
Annual deforestation (% change, 1990–2005)	0.1	0.4	0.1
Nationally protected areas (% of total land area)	..	11.1	7.7
Mammal species, total known	35		
Mammal species, threatened	5		
Bird species, total known	298		
Bird species, threatened	12		
GEF benefits index for biodiversity (0–100)	4.9		
Energy			
GDP per unit of energy use (2000 PPP $/kg oil equiv)	2.5	6.2	4.6
Energy use per capita (kg oil equiv)	1,543	1,148	1,090
Energy from combustible renewables & waste (% of tot.)	11.3	15.0	14.6
Energy imports, net (% of energy use)	88	−40	−14
Electric power consumption per capita (kWh)	2,481	1,615	1,329
Electricity generated by coal (% of total)	..	5.4	49.4
Emissions and pollution			
CO_2 emissions per unit of GDP (kg/2000 PPP $ of GDP)	1.2	0.3	0.5
CO_2 emissions per capita (metric tons)	4.1	2.4	2.6
Particulate matter (urban-pop.-weighted avg., μg/cu. m)	43	43	70
Passenger cars (per 1,000 people)	..	108	29
Water and sanitation			
Internal freshwater resources per capita (cu. m)	3,556	24,619	7,295
Freshwater withdrawal			
Total (% of internal resources)	4.4	2.0	7.7
Agriculture (% of total freshwater withdrawal)	49	71	75
Access to improved water source (% of total population)	93	89	81
Rural (% of rural population)	87	69	70
Urban (% of urban population)	98	96	93
Access to improved sanitation (% of total population)	80	75	57
Rural (% of rural population)	68	44	39
Urban (% of urban population)	90	84	78
Environment and health			
ARI prevalence (% of children under age 5)	..		
Diarrhea prevalence (% of children under age 5)	..		
Under-five mortality rate (per 1,000 live births)	20	31	40
National accounting aggregates, 2004			
Gross savings (% of GNI)	26.6	22.7	32.1
Consumption of fixed capital (% of GNI)	12.1	12.1	10.8
Education expenditure (% of GNI)	5.0	4.4	2.9
Energy depletion (% of GNI)	0.0	7.2	6.5
Mineral depletion (% of GNI)	1.3	1.1	0.5
Net forest depletion (% of GNI)	0.0	0.0	0.0
CO_2 damage (% of GNI)	0.9	0.5	1.1
Particulate emission damage (% of GNI)	0.3	0.6	1.0
Adjusted net savings (% of GNI)	17.0	5.6	15.1

Japan

Environmental strategy/action plan prepared in ..

	Country data	Group data — High income
Population (millions)	127.8	1,004
Urban population (% of total)	65.6	78.5
GDP ($ billions)	4,622.8	32,900
GNI per capita, *World Bank Atlas* method ($)	37,050	32,112

Agriculture

Land area (1,000 sq. km)	365	33,018
Agricultural land (% of land area)	14	38
Irrigated land (% of cropland)	54.7	11.9
Fertilizer consumption (100 grams/ha of arable land)	2,906	1,205
Population density, rural (people/sq. km of arable land)	1,002	331

Forests and biodiversity

Forest area (% of land area)	68.2	29.3
Annual deforestation (% change, 1990–2005)	0.0	−0.1
Nationally protected areas (% of total land area)	6.8	..
Mammal species, total known	171	
Mammal species, threatened	37	
Bird species, total known	592	
Bird species, threatened	53	
GEF benefits index for biodiversity (0–100)	41.4	

Energy

GDP per unit of energy use (2000 PPP $/kg oil equiv)	6.5	5.2
Energy use per capita (kg oil equiv)	4,053	5,410
Energy from combustible renewables & waste (% of tot.)	1.3	3.0
Energy imports, net (% of energy use)	84	19
Electric power consumption per capita (kWh)	7,818	9,503
Electricity generated by coal (% of total)	28.2	38.2

Emissions and pollution

CO_2 emissions per unit of GDP (kg/2000 PPP $ of GDP)	0.4	0.5
CO_2 emissions per capita (metric tons)	9.4	12.8
Particulate matter (urban-pop.-weighted avg., µg/cu. m)	33	29
Passenger cars (per 1,000 people)	428	433

Water and sanitation

Internal freshwater resources per capita (cu. m)	3,366	9,703
Freshwater withdrawal		
Total (% of internal resources)	20.6	10.4
Agriculture (% of total freshwater withdrawal)	62	42
Access to improved water source (% of total population)	100	99
Rural (% of rural population)	100	98
Urban (% of urban population)	100	100
Access to improved sanitation (% of total population)	100	..
Rural (% of rural population)	100	..
Urban (% of urban population)	100	..

Environment and health

ARI prevalence (% of children under age 5)	..	
Diarrhea prevalence (% of children under age 5)	..	
Under-five mortality rate (per 1,000 live births)	4	7

National accounting aggregates, 2004

Gross savings (% of GNI)	26.3	19.4
Consumption of fixed capital (% of GNI)	14.4	13.2
Education expenditure (% of GNI)	3.1	4.6
Energy depletion (% of GNI)	0.0	1.4
Mineral depletion (% of GNI)	0.0	0.0
Net forest depletion (% of GNI)	0.0	0.0
CO_2 damage (% of GNI)	0.2	0.3
Particulate emission damage (% of GNI)	0.6	0.4
Adjusted net savings (% of GNI)	14.4	8.7

Jordan

Environmental strategy/action plan prepared in **1991**

	Country data	Middle East & North Africa	Lower middle income
		Group data	
Population (millions)	5.4	300	2,442
Urban population (% of total)	79.2	56.3	48.7
GDP ($ billions)	11.5	547	4,165
GNI per capita, *World Bank Atlas* method ($)	2,190	1,972	1,686
Agriculture			
Land area (1,000 sq. km)	88	8,955	38,470
Agricultural land (% of land area)	13	23	43
Irrigated land (% of cropland)	18.8	32.5	23.1
Fertilizer consumption (100 grams/ha of arable land)	1,136	842	1,530
Population density, rural (people/sq. km of arable land)	376	670	523
Forests and biodiversity			
Forest area (% of land area)	0.9	2.4	30.7
Annual deforestation (% change, 1990–2005)	0.0	−0.5	0.1
Nationally protected areas (% of total land area)	3.4	4.2	7.7
Mammal species, total known	93		
Mammal species, threatened	7		
Bird species, total known	397		
Bird species, threatened	14		
GEF benefits index for biodiversity (0–100)	0.3		
Energy			
GDP per unit of energy use (2000 PPP $/kg oil equiv)	4.0	4.2	4.6
Energy use per capita (kg oil equiv)	1,027	1,144	1,090
Energy from combustible renewables & waste (% of tot.)	0.1	1.3	14.6
Energy imports, net (% of energy use)	95	−129	−14
Electric power consumption per capita (kWh)	1,453	1,212	1,329
Electricity generated by coal (% of total)	..	3.0	49.4
Emissions and pollution			
CO_2 emissions per unit of GDP (kg/2000 PPP $ of GDP)	0.8	0.7	0.5
CO_2 emissions per capita (metric tons)	3.2	3.2	2.6
Particulate matter (urban-pop.-weighted avg., µg/cu. m)	69	90	70
Passenger cars (per 1,000 people)	..	..	29
Water and sanitation			
Internal freshwater resources per capita (cu. m)	125	761	7,295
Freshwater withdrawal			
Total (% of internal resources)	148.5	105.0	7.7
Agriculture (% of total freshwater withdrawal)	75	89	75
Access to improved water source (% of total population)	91	88	81
Rural (% of rural population)	91	79	70
Urban (% of urban population)	91	95	93
Access to improved sanitation (% of total population)	93	75	57
Rural (% of rural population)	85	56	39
Urban (% of urban population)	94	89	78
Environment and health			
ARI prevalence (% of children under age 5)	..		
Diarrhea prevalence (% of children under age 5)	..		
Under-five mortality rate (per 1,000 live births)	27	55	40
National accounting aggregates, 2004			
Gross savings (% of GNI)	21.0	30.0	32.1
Consumption of fixed capital (% of GNI)	10.7	11.2	10.8
Education expenditure (% of GNI)	5.6	4.5	2.9
Energy depletion (% of GNI)	0.3	27.3	6.5
Mineral depletion (% of GNI)	0.1	0.1	0.5
Net forest depletion (% of GNI)	0.0	0.1	0.0
CO_2 damage (% of GNI)	1.0	1.2	1.1
Particulate emission damage (% of GNI)	0.9	0.9	1.0
Adjusted net savings (% of GNI)	13.5	−6.2	15.1

Kazakhstan

Environmental strategy/action plan prepared in ..

	Country data	Europe & Central Asia	Lower middle income
		Group data	
Population (millions)	15.0	472	2,442
Urban population (% of total)	55.9	63.6	48.7
GDP ($ billions)	40.7	1,770	4,165
GNI per capita, *World Bank Atlas* method ($)	2,250	3,295	1,686
Agriculture			
Land area (1,000 sq. km)	2,700	23,371	38,470
Agricultural land (% of land area)	77	29	43
Irrigated land (% of cropland)	15.7	11.1	23.1
Fertilizer consumption (100 grams/ha of arable land)	29	347	1,530
Population density, rural (people/sq. km of arable land)	29	126	523
Forests and biodiversity			
Forest area (% of land area)	1.2	38.3	30.7
Annual deforestation (% change, 1990–2005)	0.2	0.0	0.1
Nationally protected areas (% of total land area)	2.7	6.9	7.7
Mammal species, total known	145		
Mammal species, threatened	15		
Bird species, total known	497		
Bird species, threatened	23		
GEF benefits index for biodiversity (0–100)	5.4		
Energy			
GDP per unit of energy use (2000 PPP $/kg oil equiv)	1.9	2.7	4.6
Energy use per capita (kg oil equiv)	3,342	2,794	1,090
Energy from combustible renewables & waste (% of tot.)	0.1	2.4	14.6
Energy imports, net (% of energy use)	–112	–26	–14
Electric power consumption per capita (kWh)	3,510	3,531	1,329
Electricity generated by coal (% of total)	69.9	29.8	49.4
Emissions and pollution			
CO_2 emissions per unit of GDP (kg/2000 PPP $ of GDP)	1.8	1.0	0.5
CO_2 emissions per capita (metric tons)	9.9	6.7	2.6
Particulate matter (urban-pop.-weighted avg., µg/cu. m)	25	35	70
Passenger cars (per 1,000 people)	71	142	29
Water and sanitation			
Internal freshwater resources per capita (cu. m)	5,030	11,123	7,295
Freshwater withdrawal			
Total (% of internal resources)	46.4	7.5	7.7
Agriculture (% of total freshwater withdrawal)	82	59	75
Access to improved water source (% of total population)	86	91	81
Rural (% of rural population)	72	80	70
Urban (% of urban population)	96	98	93
Access to improved sanitation (% of total population)	72	82	57
Rural (% of rural population)	52	63	39
Urban (% of urban population)	87	93	78
Environment and health			
ARI prevalence (% of children under age 5)	..		
Diarrhea prevalence (% of children under age 5)	13.4		
Under-five mortality rate (per 1,000 live births)	73	34	40
National accounting aggregates, 2004			
Gross savings (% of GNI)	27.0	23.4	32.1
Consumption of fixed capital (% of GNI)	12.0	10.7	10.8
Education expenditure (% of GNI)	4.4	4.1	2.9
Energy depletion (% of GNI)	39.9	12.0	6.5
Mineral depletion (% of GNI)	1.6	0.3	0.5
Net forest depletion (% of GNI)	0.0	0.0	0.0
CO_2 damage (% of GNI)	3.0	1.4	1.1
Particulate emission damage (% of GNI)	0.5	0.7	1.0
Adjusted net savings (% of GNI)	–25.5	2.3	15.1

Kenya

Environmental strategy/action plan prepared in **1994**

	Country data	Group data Sub-Saharan Africa	Low income
Population (millions)	33.5	726	2,343
Urban population (% of total)	40.5	36.4	30.6
GDP ($ billions)	16.1	523	1,239
GNI per capita, *World Bank Atlas* method ($)	480	601	507
Agriculture			
Land area (1,000 sq. km)	569	23,596	29,192
Agricultural land (% of land area)	47	44	45
Irrigated land (% of cropland)	2.0	3.6	23.9
Fertilizer consumption (100 grams/ha of arable land)	310	136	646
Population density, rural (people/sq. km of arable land)	427	355	524
Forests and biodiversity			
Forest area (% of land area)	6.2	26.5	24.8
Annual deforestation (% change, 1990–2005)	0.3	0.6	0.5
Nationally protected areas (% of total land area)	8.0	8.7	7.7
Mammal species, total known	407		
Mammal species, threatened	33		
Bird species, total known	1,103		
Bird species, threatened	28		
GEF benefits index for biodiversity (0–100)	9.9		
Energy			
GDP per unit of energy use (2000 PPP $/kg oil equiv)	2.1	2.8	4.2
Energy use per capita (kg oil equiv)	494	681	501
Energy from combustible renewables & waste (% of tot.)	77.5	57.4	48.9
Energy imports, net (% of energy use)	17	−59	−4
Electric power consumption per capita (kWh)	125	513	358
Electricity generated by coal (% of total)	..	68.0	46.3
Emissions and pollution			
CO_2 emissions per unit of GDP (kg/2000 PPP $ of GDP)	0.3	0.4	0.4
CO_2 emissions per capita (metric tons)	0.2	0.7	0.8
Particulate matter (urban-pop.-weighted avg., µg/cu. m)	38	73	89
Passenger cars (per 1,000 people)	8	..	6
Water and sanitation			
Internal freshwater resources per capita (cu. m)	619	5,353	3,456
Freshwater withdrawal			
Total (% of internal resources)	7.6	3.1	15.5
Agriculture (% of total freshwater withdrawal)	64	87	88
Access to improved water source (% of total population)	62	58	75
Rural (% of rural population)	46	45	69
Urban (% of urban population)	89	82	89
Access to improved sanitation (% of total population)	48	36	36
Rural (% of rural population)	43	26	24
Urban (% of urban population)	56	55	61
Environment and health			
ARI prevalence (% of children under age 5)	..		
Diarrhea prevalence (% of children under age 5)	17.1		
Under-five mortality rate (per 1,000 live births)	120	168	122
National accounting aggregates, 2004			
Gross savings (% of GNI)	13.7	17.1	22.7
Consumption of fixed capital (% of GNI)	9.0	10.9	9.2
Education expenditure (% of GNI)	6.6	3.9	3.4
Energy depletion (% of GNI)	0.0	9.8	6.7
Mineral depletion (% of GNI)	0.0	0.4	0.4
Net forest depletion (% of GNI)	0.2	0.6	0.7
CO_2 damage (% of GNI)	0.4	0.7	1.1
Particulate emission damage (% of GNI)	0.2	0.5	0.8
Adjusted net savings (% of GNI)	10.5	−1.9	7.3

Kiribati

Environmental strategy/action plan prepared in ..

	Country data	Group data East Asia & Pacific	Group data Lower middle income
Population (millions)	0.1	1,870	2,442
Urban population (% of total)	48.7	40.6	48.7
GDP ($ billions)	0.1	2,651	4,165
GNI per capita, *World Bank Atlas* method ($)	970	1,416	1,686

Agriculture

Land area (1,000 sq. km)	1	15,885	38,470
Agricultural land (% of land area)	51	51	43
Irrigated land (% of cropland)	..	..	23.1
Fertilizer consumption (100 grams/ha of arable land)	..	2,296	1,530
Population density, rural (people/sq. km of arable land)	2,540	559	523

Forests and biodiversity

Forest area (% of land area)	2.7	28.4	30.7
Annual deforestation (% change, 1990–2005)	0.0	−0.2	0.1
Nationally protected areas (% of total land area)	..	..	7.7
Mammal species, total known	1		
Mammal species, threatened	0		
Bird species, total known	50		
Bird species, threatened	5		
GEF benefits index for biodiversity (0–100)	1.6		

Energy

GDP per unit of energy use (2000 PPP $/kg oil equiv)	..	4.6	4.6
Energy use per capita (kg oil equiv)	..	1,007	1,090
Energy from combustible renewables & waste (% of tot.)	..	17.7	14.6
Energy imports, net (% of energy use)	..	−2	−14
Electric power consumption per capita (kWh)	..	1,184	1,329
Electricity generated by coal (% of total)	..	69.4	49.4

Emissions and pollution

CO_2 emissions per unit of GDP (kg/2000 PPP $ of GDP)	..	0.5	0.5
CO_2 emissions per capita (metric tons)	0.3	2.4	2.6
Particulate matter (urban-pop.-weighted avg., µg/cu. m)	..	80	70
Passenger cars (per 1,000 people)	..	12	29

Water and sanitation

Internal freshwater resources per capita (cu. m)	..	5,062	7,295
Freshwater withdrawal			
Total (% of internal resources)	..	10.2	7.7
Agriculture (% of total freshwater withdrawal)	..	74	75
Access to improved water source (% of total population)	64	78	81
Rural (% of rural population)	53	69	70
Urban (% of urban population)	77	92	93
Access to improved sanitation (% of total population)	39	49	57
Rural (% of rural population)	22	35	39
Urban (% of urban population)	59	72	78

Environment and health

ARI prevalence (% of children under age 5)	..		
Diarrhea prevalence (% of children under age 5)	..		
Under-five mortality rate (per 1,000 live births)	65	37	40

National accounting aggregates, 2004

Gross savings (% of GNI)	..	39.1	32.1
Consumption of fixed capital (% of GNI)	6.1	10.5	10.8
Education expenditure (% of GNI)	..	2.3	2.9
Energy depletion (% of GNI)	0.0	4.1	6.5
Mineral depletion (% of GNI)	0.0	0.4	0.5
Net forest depletion (% of GNI)	..	0.0	0.0
CO_2 damage (% of GNI)	0.2	1.2	1.1
Particulate emission damage (% of GNI)	..	1.2	1.0
Adjusted net savings (% of GNI)	..	23.9	15.1

Korea, Dem. Rep.

Environmental strategy/action plan prepared in ..

	Country data	East Asia & Pacific	Low income
		Group data	
Population (millions)	22.4	1,870	2,343
Urban population (% of total)	61.4	40.6	30.6
GDP ($ billions)	..	2,651	1,239
GNI per capita, *World Bank Atlas* method ($)	..	1,416	507
Agriculture			
Land area (1,000 sq. km)	120	15,885	29,192
Agricultural land (% of land area)	24	51	45
Irrigated land (% of cropland)	50.3	..	23.9
Fertilizer consumption (100 grams/ha of arable land)	986	2,296	646
Population density, rural (people/sq. km of arable land)	321	559	524
Forests and biodiversity			
Forest area (% of land area)	51.4	28.4	24.8
Annual deforestation (% change, 1990–2005)	1.6	–0.2	0.5
Nationally protected areas (% of total land area)	2.6	..	7.7
Mammal species, total known	105		
Mammal species, threatened	12		
Bird species, total known	369		
Bird species, threatened	22		
GEF benefits index for biodiversity (0–100)	0.7		
Energy			
GDP per unit of energy use (2000 PPP $/kg oil equiv)	..	4.6	4.2
Energy use per capita (kg oil equiv)	896	1,007	501
Energy from combustible renewables & waste (% of tot.)	5.1	17.7	48.9
Energy imports, net (% of energy use)	6	–2	–4
Electric power consumption per capita (kWh)	795	1,184	358
Electricity generated by coal (% of total)	39.4	69.4	46.3
Emissions and pollution			
CO_2 emissions per unit of GDP (kg/2000 PPP $ of GDP)	..	0.5	0.4
CO_2 emissions per capita (metric tons)	6.5	2.4	0.8
Particulate matter (urban-pop.-weighted avg., µg/cu. m)	88	80	89
Passenger cars (per 1,000 people)	..	12	6
Water and sanitation			
Internal freshwater resources per capita (cu. m)	2,993	5,062	3,456
Freshwater withdrawal			
Total (% of internal resources)	13.5	10.2	15.5
Agriculture (% of total freshwater withdrawal)	55	74	88
Access to improved water source (% of total population)	100	78	75
Rural (% of rural population)	100	69	69
Urban (% of urban population)	100	92	89
Access to improved sanitation (% of total population)	59	49	36
Rural (% of rural population)	60	35	24
Urban (% of urban population)	58	72	61
Environment and health			
ARI prevalence (% of children under age 5)	12.0		
Diarrhea prevalence (% of children under age 5)	..		
Under-five mortality rate (per 1,000 live births)	55	37	122
National accounting aggregates, 2004			
Gross savings (% of GNI)	..	39.1	22.7
Consumption of fixed capital (% of GNI)	..	10.5	9.2
Education expenditure (% of GNI)	..	2.3	3.4
Energy depletion (% of GNI)	..	4.1	6.7
Mineral depletion (% of GNI)	..	0.4	0.4
Net forest depletion (% of GNI)	..	0.0	0.7
CO_2 damage (% of GNI)	..	1.2	1.1
Particulate emission damage (% of GNI)	2.0	1.2	0.8
Adjusted net savings (% of GNI)	..	23.9	7.3

Korea, Rep.

Environmental strategy/action plan prepared in ..

	Country data	Group data: High income
Population (millions)	48.1	1,004
Urban population (% of total)	80.5	78.5
GDP ($ billions)	679.7	32,900
GNI per capita, *World Bank Atlas* method ($)	14,000	32,112

Agriculture

Land area (1,000 sq. km)	99	33,018
Agricultural land (% of land area)	19	38
Irrigated land (% of cropland)	47.6	11.9
Fertilizer consumption (100 grams/ha of arable land)	4,149	1,205
Population density, rural (people/sq. km of arable land)	572	331

Forests and biodiversity

Forest area (% of land area)	63.5	29.3
Annual deforestation (% change, 1990–2005)	0.1	–0.1
Nationally protected areas (% of total land area)	6.9	..
Mammal species, total known	89	
Mammal species, threatened	12	
Bird species, total known	423	
Bird species, threatened	34	
GEF benefits index for biodiversity (0–100)	1.8	

Energy

GDP per unit of energy use (2000 PPP $/kg oil equiv)	4.2	5.2
Energy use per capita (kg oil equiv)	4,291	5,410
Energy from combustible renewables & waste (% of tot.)	0.4	3.0
Energy imports, net (% of energy use)	82	19
Electric power consumption per capita (kWh)	7,018	9,503
Electricity generated by coal (% of total)	38.9	38.2

Emissions and pollution

CO_2 emissions per unit of GDP (kg/2000 PPP $ of GDP)	0.6	0.5
CO_2 emissions per capita (metric tons)	9.4	12.8
Particulate matter (urban-pop.-weighted avg., µg/cu. m)	43	29
Passenger cars (per 1,000 people)	204	433

Water and sanitation

Internal freshwater resources per capita (cu. m)	1,349	9,703
Freshwater withdrawal		
Total (% of internal resources)	28.7	10.4
Agriculture (% of total freshwater withdrawal)	48	42
Access to improved water source (% of total population)	92	99
Rural (% of rural population)	71	98
Urban (% of urban population)	97	100
Access to improved sanitation (% of total population)	..	..
Rural (% of rural population)	..	..
Urban (% of urban population)	..	..

Environment and health

ARI prevalence (% of children under age 5)	..	
Diarrhea prevalence (% of children under age 5)	..	
Under-five mortality rate (per 1,000 live births)	6	7

National accounting aggregates, 2004

Gross savings (% of GNI)	34.3	19.4
Consumption of fixed capital (% of GNI)	13.3	13.2
Education expenditure (% of GNI)	3.8	4.6
Energy depletion (% of GNI)	0.0	1.4
Mineral depletion (% of GNI)	0.0	0.0
Net forest depletion (% of GNI)	0.0	0.0
CO_2 damage (% of GNI)	0.5	0.3
Particulate emission damage (% of GNI)	1.3	0.4
Adjusted net savings (% of GNI)	22.9	8.7

Kuwait

Environmental strategy/action plan prepared in ..

	Country data	Group data High income
Population (millions)	2.5	1,004
Urban population (% of total)	96.3	78.5
GDP ($ billions)	55.7	32,900
GNI per capita, *World Bank Atlas* method ($)	22,470	32,112

Agriculture		
Land area (1,000 sq. km)	18	33,018
Agricultural land (% of land area)	9	38
Irrigated land (% of cropland)	72.2	11.9
Fertilizer consumption (100 grams/ha of arable land)	700	1,205
Population density, rural (people/sq. km of arable land)	601	331

Forests and biodiversity		
Forest area (% of land area)	0.3	29.3
Annual deforestation (% change, 1990–2005)	−6.7	−0.1
Nationally protected areas (% of total land area)	1.5	..
Mammal species, total known	23	
Mammal species, threatened	1	
Bird species, total known	358	
Bird species, threatened	12	
GEF benefits index for biodiversity (0–100)	0.1	

Energy		
GDP per unit of energy use (2000 PPP $/kg oil equiv)	1.8	5.2
Energy use per capita (kg oil equiv)	9,566	5,410
Energy from combustible renewables & waste (% of tot.)	..	3.0
Energy imports, net (% of energy use)	−427	19
Electric power consumption per capita (kWh)	14,808	9,503
Electricity generated by coal (% of total)	..	38.2

Emissions and pollution		
CO_2 emissions per unit of GDP (kg/2000 PPP $ of GDP)	1.5	0.5
CO_2 emissions per capita (metric tons)	25.6	12.8
Particulate matter (urban-pop.-weighted avg., µg/cu. m)	129	29
Passenger cars (per 1,000 people)	..	433

Water and sanitation		
Internal freshwater resources per capita (cu. m)	0	9,703
Freshwater withdrawal		
Total (% of internal resources)	..	10.4
Agriculture (% of total freshwater withdrawal)	52	42
Access to improved water source (% of total population)	..	99
Rural (% of rural population)	..	98
Urban (% of urban population)	..	100
Access to improved sanitation (% of total population)	..	..
Rural (% of rural population)	..	..
Urban (% of urban population)	..	..

Environment and health		
ARI prevalence (% of children under age 5)	..	
Diarrhea prevalence (% of children under age 5)	..	
Under-five mortality rate (per 1,000 live births)	12	7

National accounting aggregates, 2004		
Gross savings (% of GNI)	47.2	19.4
Consumption of fixed capital (% of GNI)	12.6	13.2
Education expenditure (% of GNI)	5.0	4.6
Energy depletion (% of GNI)	46.8	1.4
Mineral depletion (% of GNI)	0.0	0.0
Net forest depletion (% of GNI)	0.0	0.0
CO_2 damage (% of GNI)	0.7	0.3
Particulate emission damage (% of GNI)	2.7	0.4
Adjusted net savings (% of GNI)	−10.5	8.7

Kyrgyz Republic

Environmental strategy/action plan prepared in **1995**

	Country data	Group data Europe & Central Asia	Low income
Population (millions)	5.1	472	2,343
Urban population (% of total)	33.9	63.6	30.6
GDP ($ billions)	2.2	1,770	1,239
GNI per capita, *World Bank Atlas* method ($)	400	3,295	507
Agriculture			
Land area (1,000 sq. km)	192	23,371	29,192
Agricultural land (% of land area)	56	29	45
Irrigated land (% of cropland)	78.5	11.1	23.9
Fertilizer consumption (100 grams/ha of arable land)	211	347	646
Population density, rural (people/sq. km of arable land)	254	126	524
Forests and biodiversity			
Forest area (% of land area)	4.5	38.3	24.8
Annual deforestation (% change, 1990–2005)	–0.3	0.0	0.5
Nationally protected areas (% of total land area)	15.0	6.9	7.7
Mammal species, total known	58		
Mammal species, threatened	6		
Bird species, total known	207		
Bird species, threatened	4		
GEF benefits index for biodiversity (0–100)	1.2		
Energy			
GDP per unit of energy use (2000 PPP $/kg oil equiv)	3.2	2.7	4.2
Energy use per capita (kg oil equiv)	528	2,794	501
Energy from combustible renewables & waste (% of tot.)	0.2	2.4	48.9
Energy imports, net (% of energy use)	49	–26	–4
Electric power consumption per capita (kWh)	1,647	3,531	358
Electricity generated by coal (% of total)	3.6	29.8	46.3
Emissions and pollution			
CO_2 emissions per unit of GDP (kg/2000 PPP $ of GDP)	0.6	1.0	0.4
CO_2 emissions per capita (metric tons)	1.0	6.7	0.8
Particulate matter (urban-pop.-weighted avg., µg/cu. m)	36	35	89
Passenger cars (per 1,000 people)	38	142	6
Water and sanitation			
Internal freshwater resources per capita (cu. m)	9,121	11,123	3,456
Freshwater withdrawal			
Total (% of internal resources)	21.7	7.5	15.5
Agriculture (% of total freshwater withdrawal)	94	59	88
Access to improved water source (% of total population)	76	91	75
Rural (% of rural population)	66	80	69
Urban (% of urban population)	98	98	89
Access to improved sanitation (% of total population)	60	82	36
Rural (% of rural population)	51	63	24
Urban (% of urban population)	75	93	61
Environment and health			
ARI prevalence (% of children under age 5)	..		
Diarrhea prevalence (% of children under age 5)	..		
Under-five mortality rate (per 1,000 live births)	68	34	122
National accounting aggregates, 2004			
Gross savings (% of GNI)	9.8	23.4	22.7
Consumption of fixed capital (% of GNI)	9.1	10.7	9.2
Education expenditure (% of GNI)	4.4	4.1	3.4
Energy depletion (% of GNI)	1.0	12.0	6.7
Mineral depletion (% of GNI)	0.0	0.3	0.4
Net forest depletion (% of GNI)	0.0	0.0	0.7
CO_2 damage (% of GNI)	1.6	1.4	1.1
Particulate emission damage (% of GNI)	0.2	0.7	0.8
Adjusted net savings (% of GNI)	2.2	2.3	7.3

Lao PDR

Environmental strategy/action plan prepared in **1995**

	Country data	Group data East Asia & Pacific	Low income
Population (millions)	5.8	1,870	2,343
Urban population (% of total)	21.2	40.6	30.6
GDP ($ billions)	2.5	2,651	1,239
GNI per capita, *World Bank Atlas* method ($)	390	1,416	507
Agriculture			
Land area (1,000 sq. km)	231	15,885	29,192
Agricultural land (% of land area)	8	51	45
Irrigated land (% of cropland)	17.0	..	23.9
Fertilizer consumption (100 grams/ha of arable land)	76	2,296	646
Population density, rural (people/sq. km of arable land)	473	559	524
Forests and biodiversity			
Forest area (% of land area)	69.9	28.4	24.8
Annual deforestation (% change, 1990–2005)	0.5	–0.2	0.5
Nationally protected areas (% of total land area)	3.0	..	7.7
Mammal species, total known	215		
Mammal species, threatened	30		
Bird species, total known	704		
Bird species, threatened	21		
GEF benefits index for biodiversity (0–100)	5.4		
Energy			
GDP per unit of energy use (2000 PPP $/kg oil equiv)	..	4.6	4.2
Energy use per capita (kg oil equiv)	..	1,007	501
Energy from combustible renewables & waste (% of tot.)	..	17.7	48.9
Energy imports, net (% of energy use)	..	–2	–4
Electric power consumption per capita (kWh)	..	1,184	358
Electricity generated by coal (% of total)	..	69.4	46.3
Emissions and pollution			
CO_2 emissions per unit of GDP (kg/2000 PPP $ of GDP)	0.1	0.5	0.4
CO_2 emissions per capita (metric tons)	0.2	2.4	0.8
Particulate matter (urban-pop.-weighted avg., µg/cu. m)	25	80	89
Passenger cars (per 1,000 people)	..	12	6
Water and sanitation			
Internal freshwater resources per capita (cu. m)	32,878	5,062	3,456
Freshwater withdrawal			
Total (% of internal resources)	1.6	10.2	15.5
Agriculture (% of total freshwater withdrawal)	90	74	88
Access to improved water source (% of total population)	43	78	75
Rural (% of rural population)	38	69	69
Urban (% of urban population)	66	92	89
Access to improved sanitation (% of total population)	24	49	36
Rural (% of rural population)	14	35	24
Urban (% of urban population)	61	72	61
Environment and health			
ARI prevalence (% of children under age 5)	1.0		
Diarrhea prevalence (% of children under age 5)	6.2		
Under-five mortality rate (per 1,000 live births)	83	37	122
National accounting aggregates, 2004			
Gross savings (% of GNI)	10.7	39.1	22.7
Consumption of fixed capital (% of GNI)	9.1	10.5	9.2
Education expenditure (% of GNI)	1.3	2.3	3.4
Energy depletion (% of GNI)	0.0	4.1	6.7
Mineral depletion (% of GNI)	0.0	0.4	0.4
Net forest depletion (% of GNI)	0.0	0.0	0.7
CO_2 damage (% of GNI)	0.4	1.2	1.1
Particulate emission damage (% of GNI)	0.1	1.2	0.8
Adjusted net savings (% of GNI)	2.5	23.9	7.3

Latvia

Environmental strategy/action plan prepared in ..

	Country data	Group data	
		Europe & Central Asia	Upper middle income
Population (millions)	2.3	472	576
Urban population (% of total)	66.1	63.6	72.3
GDP ($ billions)	13.6	1,770	2,992
GNI per capita, *World Bank Atlas* method ($)	5,580	3,295	4,769
Agriculture			
Land area (1,000 sq. km)	62	23,371	28,983
Agricultural land (% of land area)	40	29	26
Irrigated land (% of cropland)	1.1	11.1	8.7
Fertilizer consumption (100 grams/ha of arable land)	273	347	469
Population density, rural (people/sq. km of arable land)	43	126	131
Forests and biodiversity			
Forest area (% of land area)	47.4	38.3	37.3
Annual deforestation (% change, 1990–2005)	−0.4	0.0	0.1
Nationally protected areas (% of total land area)	13.4	6.9	..
Mammal species, total known	68		
Mammal species, threatened	4		
Bird species, total known	325		
Bird species, threatened	8		
GEF benefits index for biodiversity (0–100)	0.0		
Energy			
GDP per unit of energy use (2000 PPP $/kg oil equiv)	5.3	2.7	3.5
Energy use per capita (kg oil equiv)	1,881	2,794	2,574
Energy from combustible renewables & waste (% of tot.)	28.9	2.4	3.9
Energy imports, net (% of energy use)	55	−26	−51
Electric power consumption per capita (kWh)	2,456	3,531	3,378
Electricity generated by coal (% of total)	0.6	29.8	31.0
Emissions and pollution			
CO_2 emissions per unit of GDP (kg/2000 PPP $ of GDP)	0.3	1.0	0.7
CO_2 emissions per capita (metric tons)	2.7	6.7	6.2
Particulate matter (urban-pop.-weighted avg., μg/cu. m)	17	35	40
Passenger cars (per 1,000 people)	265	142	143
Water and sanitation			
Internal freshwater resources per capita (cu. m)	7,238	11,123	14,190
Freshwater withdrawal			
Total (% of internal resources)	1.8	7.5	3.8
Agriculture (% of total freshwater withdrawal)	13	59	53
Access to improved water source (% of total population)	..	91	93
Rural (% of rural population)	..	80	82
Urban (% of urban population)	..	98	97
Access to improved sanitation (% of total population)	..	82	81
Rural (% of rural population)	..	63	61
Urban (% of urban population)	..	93	91
Environment and health			
ARI prevalence (% of children under age 5)	..		
Diarrhea prevalence (% of children under age 5)	..		
Under-five mortality rate (per 1,000 live births)	12	34	28
National accounting aggregates, 2004			
Gross savings (% of GNI)	18.0	23.4	23.1
Consumption of fixed capital (% of GNI)	12.0	10.7	11.5
Education expenditure (% of GNI)	5.6	4.1	4.5
Energy depletion (% of GNI)	0.0	12.0	11.2
Mineral depletion (% of GNI)	0.0	0.3	0.6
Net forest depletion (% of GNI)	0.0	0.0	0.0
CO_2 damage (% of GNI)	0.4	1.4	0.9
Particulate emission damage (% of GNI)	0.1	0.7	0.7
Adjusted net savings (% of GNI)	11.2	2.3	2.6

Lebanon

Environmental strategy/action plan prepared in ..

	Country data	Middle East & North Africa	Upper middle income
		Group data	
Population (millions)	3.5	300	576
Urban population (% of total)	87.7	56.3	72.3
GDP ($ billions)	21.8	547	2,992
GNI per capita, *World Bank Atlas* method ($)	6,010	1,972	4,769
Agriculture			
Land area (1,000 sq. km)	10	8,955	28,983
Agricultural land (% of land area)	32	23	26
Irrigated land (% of cropland)	33.2	32.5	8.7
Fertilizer consumption (100 grams/ha of arable land)	2,319	842	469
Population density, rural (people/sq. km of arable land)	259	670	131
Forests and biodiversity			
Forest area (% of land area)	13.3	2.4	37.3
Annual deforestation (% change, 1990–2005)	–0.8	–0.5	0.1
Nationally protected areas (% of total land area)	0.5	4.2	..
Mammal species, total known	70		
Mammal species, threatened	5		
Bird species, total known	377		
Bird species, threatened	10		
GEF benefits index for biodiversity (0–100)	0.2		
Energy			
GDP per unit of energy use (2000 PPP $/kg oil equiv)	3.0	4.2	3.5
Energy use per capita (kg oil equiv)	1,700	1,144	2,574
Energy from combustible renewables & waste (% of tot.)	2.1	1.3	3.9
Energy imports, net (% of energy use)	96	–129	–51
Electric power consumption per capita (kWh)	2,558	1,212	3,378
Electricity generated by coal (% of total)	..	3.0	31.0
Emissions and pollution			
CO_2 emissions per unit of GDP (kg/2000 PPP $ of GDP)	1.1	0.7	0.7
CO_2 emissions per capita (metric tons)	4.7	3.2	6.2
Particulate matter (urban-pop.-weighted avg., µg/cu. m)	43	90	40
Passenger cars (per 1,000 people)	..	..	143
Water and sanitation			
Internal freshwater resources per capita (cu. m)	1,356	761	14,190
Freshwater withdrawal			
Total (% of internal resources)	28.8	105.0	3.8
Agriculture (% of total freshwater withdrawal)	67	89	53
Access to improved water source (% of total population)	100	88	93
Rural (% of rural population)	100	79	82
Urban (% of urban population)	100	95	97
Access to improved sanitation (% of total population)	98	75	81
Rural (% of rural population)	87	56	61
Urban (% of urban population)	100	89	91
Environment and health			
ARI prevalence (% of children under age 5)	3.5		
Diarrhea prevalence (% of children under age 5)	19.3		
Under-five mortality rate (per 1,000 live births)	31	55	28
National accounting aggregates, 2004			
Gross savings (% of GNI)	2.4	30.0	23.1
Consumption of fixed capital (% of GNI)	12.9	11.2	11.5
Education expenditure (% of GNI)	2.6	4.5	4.5
Energy depletion (% of GNI)	0.0	27.3	11.2
Mineral depletion (% of GNI)	0.0	0.1	0.6
Net forest depletion (% of GNI)	0.0	0.1	0.0
CO_2 damage (% of GNI)	0.6	1.2	0.9
Particulate emission damage (% of GNI)	0.9	0.9	0.7
Adjusted net savings (% of GNI)	–9.3	–6.2	2.6

Lesotho

Environmental strategy/action plan prepared in **1989**

	Country data	Group data Sub-Saharan Africa	Low income
Population (millions)	1.8	726	2,343
Urban population (% of total)	18.1	36.4	30.6
GDP ($ billions)	1.3	523	1,239
GNI per capita, *World Bank Atlas* method ($)	730	601	507
Agriculture			
Land area (1,000 sq. km)	30	23,596	29,192
Agricultural land (% of land area)	77	44	45
Irrigated land (% of cropland)	0.9	3.6	23.9
Fertilizer consumption (100 grams/ha of arable land)	342	136	646
Population density, rural (people/sq. km of arable land)	447	355	524
Forests and biodiversity			
Forest area (% of land area)	0.3	26.5	24.8
Annual deforestation (% change, 1990–2005)	–4.0	0.6	0.5
Nationally protected areas (% of total land area)	0.2	8.7	7.7
Mammal species, total known	59		
Mammal species, threatened	3		
Bird species, total known	311		
Bird species, threatened	7		
GEF benefits index for biodiversity (0–100)	0.3		
Energy			
GDP per unit of energy use (2000 PPP $/kg oil equiv)	..	2.8	4.2
Energy use per capita (kg oil equiv)	..	681	501
Energy from combustible renewables & waste (% of tot.)	..	57.4	48.9
Energy imports, net (% of energy use)	..	–59	–4
Electric power consumption per capita (kWh)	..	513	358
Electricity generated by coal (% of total)	..	68.0	46.3
Emissions and pollution			
CO_2 emissions per unit of GDP (kg/2000 PPP $ of GDP)	..	0.4	0.4
CO_2 emissions per capita (metric tons)	..	0.7	0.8
Particulate matter (urban-pop.-weighted avg., µg/cu. m)	94	73	89
Passenger cars (per 1,000 people)	..	..	6
Water and sanitation			
Internal freshwater resources per capita (cu. m)	2,909	5,353	3,456
Freshwater withdrawal			
Total (% of internal resources)	1.0	3.1	15.5
Agriculture (% of total freshwater withdrawal)	20	87	88
Access to improved water source (% of total population)	76	58	75
Rural (% of rural population)	74	45	69
Urban (% of urban population)	88	82	89
Access to improved sanitation (% of total population)	37	36	36
Rural (% of rural population)	32	26	24
Urban (% of urban population)	61	55	61
Environment and health			
ARI prevalence (% of children under age 5)	..		
Diarrhea prevalence (% of children under age 5)	..		
Under-five mortality rate (per 1,000 live births)	112	168	122
National accounting aggregates, 2004			
Gross savings (% of GNI)	27.7	17.1	22.7
Consumption of fixed capital (% of GNI)	7.6	10.9	9.2
Education expenditure (% of GNI)	6.7	3.9	3.4
Energy depletion (% of GNI)	0.0	9.8	6.7
Mineral depletion (% of GNI)	0.0	0.4	0.4
Net forest depletion (% of GNI)	1.5	0.6	0.7
CO_2 damage (% of GNI)	0.0	0.7	1.1
Particulate emission damage (% of GNI)	0.9	0.5	0.8
Adjusted net savings (% of GNI)	20.2	–1.9	7.3

Liberia

Environmental strategy/action plan prepared in ..

	Country data	Group data Sub-Saharan Africa	Low Income
Population (millions)	3.2	726	2,343
Urban population (% of total)	47.3	36.4	30.6
GDP ($ billions)	0.5	523	1,239
GNI per capita, *World Bank Atlas* method ($)	120	601	507

Agriculture
Land area (1,000 sq. km)	96	23,596	29,192
Agricultural land (% of land area)	27	44	45
Irrigated land (% of cropland)	0.5	3.6	23.9
Fertilizer consumption (100 grams/ha of arable land)	0	136	646
Population density, rural (people/sq. km of arable land)	450	355	524

Forests and biodiversity
Forest area (% of land area)	32.7	26.5	24.8
Annual deforestation (% change, 1990–2005)	1.5	0.6	0.5
Nationally protected areas (% of total land area)	1.7	8.7	7.7
Mammal species, total known	183		
Mammal species, threatened	20		
Bird species, total known	576		
Bird species, threatened	11		
GEF benefits index for biodiversity (0–100)	2.9		

Energy
GDP per unit of energy use (2000 PPP $/kg oil equiv)	..	2.8	4.2
Energy use per capita (kg oil equiv)	..	681	501
Energy from combustible renewables & waste (% of tot.)	..	57.4	48.9
Energy imports, net (% of energy use)	..	−59	−4
Electric power consumption per capita (kWh)	..	513	358
Electricity generated by coal (% of total)	..	68.0	46.3

Emissions and pollution
CO_2 emissions per unit of GDP (kg/2000 PPP $ of GDP)	..	0.4	0.4
CO_2 emissions per capita (metric tons)	0.1	0.7	0.8
Particulate matter (urban-pop.-weighted avg., µg/cu. m)	39	73	89
Passenger cars (per 1,000 people)	..	..	6

Water and sanitation
Internal freshwater resources per capita (cu. m)	61,717	5,353	3,456
Freshwater withdrawal			
Total (% of internal resources)	0.1	3.1	15.5
Agriculture (% of total freshwater withdrawal)	55	87	88
Access to improved water source (% of total population)	62	58	75
Rural (% of rural population)	52	45	69
Urban (% of urban population)	72	82	89
Access to improved sanitation (% of total population)	26	36	36
Rural (% of rural population)	7	26	24
Urban (% of urban population)	49	55	61

Environment and health
ARI prevalence (% of children under age 5)	..		
Diarrhea prevalence (% of children under age 5)	..		
Under-five mortality rate (per 1,000 live births)	235	168	122

National accounting aggregates, 2004
Gross savings (% of GNI)	35.8	17.1	22.7
Consumption of fixed capital (% of GNI)	9.2	10.9	9.2
Education expenditure (% of GNI)	..	3.9	3.4
Energy depletion (% of GNI)	0.0	9.8	6.7
Mineral depletion (% of GNI)	0.0	0.4	0.4
Net forest depletion (% of GNI)	6.3	0.6	0.7
CO_2 damage (% of GNI)	0.5	0.7	1.1
Particulate emission damage (% of GNI)	0.2	0.5	0.8
Adjusted net savings (% of GNI)	..	−1.9	7.3

Libya

Environmental strategy/action plan prepared in ..

	Country data	Middle East & North Africa	Upper middle income
Population (millions)	5.7	300	576
Urban population (% of total)	86.6	56.3	72.3
GDP ($ billions)	29.1	547	2,992
GNI per capita, *World Bank Atlas* method ($)	4,400	1,972	4,769
Agriculture			
Land area (1,000 sq. km)	1,760	8,955	28,983
Agricultural land (% of land area)	9	23	26
Irrigated land (% of cropland)	21.9	32.5	8.7
Fertilizer consumption (100 grams/ha of arable land)	341	842	469
Population density, rural (people/sq. km of arable land)	43	670	131
Forests and biodiversity			
Forest area (% of land area)	0.1	2.4	37.3
Annual deforestation (% change, 1990–2005)	0.0	–0.5	0.1
Nationally protected areas (% of total land area)	0.1	4.2	..
Mammal species, total known	87		
Mammal species, threatened	5		
Bird species, total known	326		
Bird species, threatened	7		
GEF benefits index for biodiversity (0–100)	1.7		
Energy			
GDP per unit of energy use (2000 PPP $/kg oil equiv)	..	4.2	3.5
Energy use per capita (kg oil equiv)	3,191	1,144	2,574
Energy from combustible renewables & waste (% of tot.)	0.8	1.3	3.9
Energy imports, net (% of energy use)	–331	–129	–51
Electric power consumption per capita (kWh)	2,415	1,212	3,378
Electricity generated by coal (% of total)	..	3.0	31.0
Emissions and pollution			
CO_2 emissions per unit of GDP (kg/2000 PPP $ of GDP)	..	0.7	0.7
CO_2 emissions per capita (metric tons)	9.1	3.2	6.2
Particulate matter (urban-pop.-weighted avg., µg/cu. m)	121	90	40
Passenger cars (per 1,000 people)	..	..	143
Water and sanitation			
Internal freshwater resources per capita (cu. m)	105	761	14,190
Freshwater withdrawal			
Total (% of internal resources)	711.3	105.0	3.8
Agriculture (% of total freshwater withdrawal)	83	89	53
Access to improved water source (% of total population)	72	88	93
Rural (% of rural population)	68	79	82
Urban (% of urban population)	72	95	97
Access to improved sanitation (% of total population)	97	75	81
Rural (% of rural population)	96	56	61
Urban (% of urban population)	97	89	91
Environment and health			
ARI prevalence (% of children under age 5)	..		
Diarrhea prevalence (% of children under age 5)	..		
Under-five mortality rate (per 1,000 live births)	20	55	28
National accounting aggregates, 2004			
Gross savings (% of GNI)	..	30.0	23.1
Consumption of fixed capital (% of GNI)	12.6	11.2	11.5
Education expenditure (% of GNI)	..	4.5	4.5
Energy depletion (% of GNI)	60.7	27.3	11.2
Mineral depletion (% of GNI)	0.0	0.1	0.6
Net forest depletion (% of GNI)	0.0	0.1	0.0
CO_2 damage (% of GNI)	1.2	1.2	0.9
Particulate emission damage (% of GNI)	..	0.9	0.7
Adjusted net savings (% of GNI)	..	–6.2	2.6

Liechtenstein

Environmental strategy/action plan prepared in ..

	Country data	Group data — High Income
Population (millions)	0.0	1,004
Urban population (% of total)	21.7	78.5
GDP ($ billions)	..	32,900
GNI per capita, *World Bank Atlas* method ($)	..	32,112

Agriculture

Land area (1,000 sq. km)	0	33,018
Agricultural land (% of land area)	56	38
Irrigated land (% of cropland)	..	11.9
Fertilizer consumption (100 grams/ha of arable land)	..	1,205
Population density, rural (people/sq. km of arable land)	666	331

Forests and biodiversity

Forest area (% of land area)	43.8	29.3
Annual deforestation (% change, 1990–2005)	–1.1	–0.1
Nationally protected areas (% of total land area)	..	..
Mammal species, total known	56	
Mammal species, threatened	2	
Bird species, total known	241	
Bird species, threatened	1	
GEF benefits index for biodiversity (0–100)	0.0	

Energy

GDP per unit of energy use (2000 PPP $/kg oil equiv)	..	5.2
Energy use per capita (kg oil equiv)	..	5,410
Energy from combustible renewables & waste (% of tot.)	..	3.0
Energy imports, net (% of energy use)	..	19
Electric power consumption per capita (kWh)	..	9,503
Electricity generated by coal (% of total)	..	38.2

Emissions and pollution

CO_2 emissions per unit of GDP (kg/2000 PPP $ of GDP)	..	0.5
CO_2 emissions per capita (metric tons)	..	12.8
Particulate matter (urban-pop.-weighted avg., µg/cu. m)	62	29
Passenger cars (per 1,000 people)	..	433

Water and sanitation

Internal freshwater resources per capita (cu. m)	..	9,703
Freshwater withdrawal		
Total (% of internal resources)	..	10.4
Agriculture (% of total freshwater withdrawal)	..	42
Access to improved water source (% of total population)	..	99
Rural (% of rural population)	..	98
Urban (% of urban population)	..	100
Access to improved sanitation (% of total population)	..	..
Rural (% of rural population)	..	..
Urban (% of urban population)	..	..

Environment and health

ARI prevalence (% of children under age 5)	..	
Diarrhea prevalence (% of children under age 5)	..	
Under-five mortality rate (per 1,000 live births)	5	7

National accounting aggregates, 2004

Gross savings (% of GNI)	..	19.4
Consumption of fixed capital (% of GNI)	..	13.2
Education expenditure (% of GNI)	..	4.6
Energy depletion (% of GNI)	..	1.4
Mineral depletion (% of GNI)	..	0.0
Net forest depletion (% of GNI)	..	0.0
CO_2 damage (% of GNI)	..	0.3
Particulate emission damage (% of GNI)	..	0.4
Adjusted net savings (% of GNI)	..	8.7

Lithuania

Environmental strategy/action plan prepared in ..

	Country data	Europe & Central Asia	Upper middle income
		Group data	
Population (millions)	3.4	472	576
Urban population (% of total)	66.7	63.6	72.3
GDP ($ billions)	22.3	1,770	2,992
GNI per capita, *World Bank Atlas* method ($)	5,740	3,295	4,769
Agriculture			
Land area (1,000 sq. km)	63	23,371	28,983
Agricultural land (% of land area)	56	29	26
Irrigated land (% of cropland)	0.2	11.1	8.7
Fertilizer consumption (100 grams/ha of arable land)	662	347	469
Population density, rural (people/sq. km of arable land)	39	126	131
Forests and biodiversity			
Forest area (% of land area)	33.5	38.3	37.3
Annual deforestation (% change, 1990–2005)	−0.5	0.0	0.1
Nationally protected areas (% of total land area)	10.6	6.9	..
Mammal species, total known	71		
Mammal species, threatened	5		
Bird species, total known	227		
Bird species, threatened	4		
GEF benefits index for biodiversity (0–100)	0.0		
Energy			
GDP per unit of energy use (2000 PPP $/kg oil equiv)	4.3	2.7	3.5
Energy use per capita (kg oil equiv)	2,585	2,794	2,574
Energy from combustible renewables & waste (% of tot.)	7.6	2.4	3.9
Energy imports, net (% of energy use)	42	−26	−51
Electric power consumption per capita (kWh)	3,055	3,531	3,378
Electricity generated by coal (% of total)	..	29.8	31.0
Emissions and pollution			
CO_2 emissions per unit of GDP (kg/2000 PPP $ of GDP)	0.4	1.0	0.7
CO_2 emissions per capita (metric tons)	3.6	6.7	6.2
Particulate matter (urban-pop.-weighted avg., µg/cu. m)	22	35	40
Passenger cars (per 1,000 people)	340	142	143
Water and sanitation			
Internal freshwater resources per capita (cu. m)	4,529	11,123	14,190
Freshwater withdrawal			
Total (% of internal resources)	1.7	7.5	3.8
Agriculture (% of total freshwater withdrawal)	7	59	53
Access to improved water source (% of total population)	..	91	93
Rural (% of rural population)	..	80	82
Urban (% of urban population)	..	98	97
Access to improved sanitation (% of total population)	..	82	81
Rural (% of rural population)	..	63	61
Urban (% of urban population)	..	93	91
Environment and health			
ARI prevalence (% of children under age 5)	..		
Diarrhea prevalence (% of children under age 5)	..		
Under-five mortality rate (per 1,000 live births)	8	34	28
National accounting aggregates, 2004			
Gross savings (% of GNI)	15.3	23.4	23.1
Consumption of fixed capital (% of GNI)	12.8	10.7	11.5
Education expenditure (% of GNI)	5.7	4.1	4.5
Energy depletion (% of GNI)	0.5	12.0	11.2
Mineral depletion (% of GNI)	0.0	0.3	0.6
Net forest depletion (% of GNI)	0.3	0.0	0.0
CO_2 damage (% of GNI)	0.5	1.4	0.9
Particulate emission damage (% of GNI)	0.4	0.7	0.7
Adjusted net savings (% of GNI)	6.6	2.3	2.6

Luxembourg

Environmental strategy/action plan prepared in ..

	Country data	Group data High income
Population (millions)	0.5	1,004
Urban population (% of total)	92.1	78.5
GDP ($ billions)	31.9	32,900
GNI per capita, World Bank Atlas method ($)	56,380	32,112
Agriculture		
Land area (1,000 sq. km)	..	33,018
Agricultural land (% of land area)	..	38
Irrigated land (% of cropland)	..	11.9
Fertilizer consumption (100 grams/ha of arable land)	..	1,205
Population density, rural (people/sq. km of arable land)	..	331
Forests and biodiversity		
Forest area (% of land area)	..	29.3
Annual deforestation (% change, 1990–2005)	–0.1	–0.1
Nationally protected areas (% of total land area)	..	..
Mammal species, total known	66	
Mammal species, threatened	3	
Bird species, total known	284	
Bird species, threatened	3	
GEF benefits index for biodiversity (0–100)	0.0	
Energy		
GDP per unit of energy use (2000 PPP $/kg oil equiv)	6.5	5.2
Energy use per capita (kg oil equiv)	9,472	5,410
Energy from combustible renewables & waste (% of tot.)	1.2	3.0
Energy imports, net (% of energy use)	99	19
Electric power consumption per capita (kWh)	15,935	9,503
Electricity generated by coal (% of total)	..	38.2
Emissions and pollution		
CO_2 emissions per unit of GDP (kg/2000 PPP $ of GDP)	0.3	0.5
CO_2 emissions per capita (metric tons)	21.3	12.8
Particulate matter (urban-pop.-weighted avg., µg/cu. m)	17	29
Passenger cars (per 1,000 people)	633	433
Water and sanitation		
Internal freshwater resources per capita (cu. m)	2,206	9,703
Freshwater withdrawal		
Total (% of internal resources)	..	10.4
Agriculture (% of total freshwater withdrawal)	..	42
Access to improved water source (% of total population)	100	99
Rural (% of rural population)	100	98
Urban (% of urban population)	100	100
Access to improved sanitation (% of total population)	..	..
Rural (% of rural population)	..	..
Urban (% of urban population)	..	..
Environment and health		
ARI prevalence (% of children under age 5)	..	
Diarrhea prevalence (% of children under age 5)	..	
Under-five mortality rate (per 1,000 live births)	6	7
National accounting aggregates, 2004		
Gross savings (% of GNI)	33.1	19.4
Consumption of fixed capital (% of GNI)	17.6	13.2
Education expenditure (% of GNI)	3.7	4.6
Energy depletion (% of GNI)	0.0	1.4
Mineral depletion (% of GNI)	0.0	0.0
Net forest depletion (% of GNI)	0.0	0.0
CO_2 damage (% of GNI)	0.2	0.3
Particulate emission damage (% of GNI)	0.0	0.4
Adjusted net savings (% of GNI)	19.0	8.7

Macao, China

Environmental strategy/action plan prepared in ..

	Country data	Group data High income
Population (millions)	0.5	1,004
Urban population (% of total)	98.9	78.5
GDP ($ billions)	..	32,900
GNI per capita, *World Bank Atlas* method ($)	..	32,112

Agriculture		
Land area (1,000 sq. km)	..	33,018
Agricultural land (% of land area)	..	38
Irrigated land (% of cropland)	..	11.9
Fertilizer consumption (100 grams/ha of arable land)	..	1,205
Population density, rural (people/sq. km of arable land)	..	331

Forests and biodiversity		
Forest area (% of land area)	..	29.3
Annual deforestation (% change, 1990–2005)	..	–0.1
Nationally protected areas (% of total land area)	..	..
Mammal species, total known	4	
Mammal species, threatened	..	
Bird species, total known	56	
Bird species, threatened	2	
GEF benefits index for biodiversity (0–100)	..	

Energy		
GDP per unit of energy use (2000 PPP $/kg oil equiv)	..	5.2
Energy use per capita (kg oil equiv)	..	5,410
Energy from combustible renewables & waste (% of tot.)	..	3.0
Energy imports, net (% of energy use)	..	19
Electric power consumption per capita (kWh)	..	9,503
Electricity generated by coal (% of total)	..	38.2

Emissions and pollution		
CO_2 emissions per unit of GDP (kg/2000 PPP $ of GDP)	0.2	0.5
CO_2 emissions per capita (metric tons)	4.0	12.8
Particulate matter (urban-pop.-weighted avg., µg/cu. m)	102	29
Passenger cars (per 1,000 people)	121	433

Water and sanitation		
Internal freshwater resources per capita (cu. m)	..	9,703
Freshwater withdrawal		
Total (% of internal resources)	..	10.4
Agriculture (% of total freshwater withdrawal)	..	42
Access to improved water source (% of total population)	..	99
Rural (% of rural population)	..	98
Urban (% of urban population)	..	100
Access to improved sanitation (% of total population)	..	..
Rural (% of rural population)	..	..
Urban (% of urban population)	..	..

Environment and health		
ARI prevalence (% of children under age 5)	..	
Diarrhea prevalence (% of children under age 5)	..	
Under-five mortality rate (per 1,000 live births)	..	7

National accounting aggregates, 2004		
Gross savings (% of GNI)	..	19.4
Consumption of fixed capital (% of GNI)	..	13.2
Education expenditure (% of GNI)	..	4.6
Energy depletion (% of GNI)	..	1.4
Mineral depletion (% of GNI)	..	0.0
Net forest depletion (% of GNI)	..	0.0
CO_2 damage (% of GNI)	..	0.3
Particulate emission damage (% of GNI)	..	0.4
Adjusted net savings (% of GNI)	..	8.7

Macedonia, FYR

Environmental strategy/action plan prepared in ..

	Country data	Group data	
		Europe & Central Asia	Lower middle income
Population (millions)	2.0	472	2,442
Urban population (% of total)	59.6	63.6	48.7
GDP ($ billions)	5.4	1,770	4,165
GNI per capita, *World Bank Atlas* method ($)	2,420	3,295	1,686
Agriculture			
Land area (1,000 sq. km)	25	23,371	38,470
Agricultural land (% of land area)	49	29	43
Irrigated land (% of cropland)	9.0	11.1	23.1
Fertilizer consumption (100 grams/ha of arable land)	394	347	1,530
Population density, rural (people/sq. km of arable land)	145	126	523
Forests and biodiversity			
Forest area (% of land area)	35.6	38.3	30.7
Annual deforestation (% change, 1990–2005)	0.0	0.0	0.1
Nationally protected areas (% of total land area)	7.1	6.9	7.7
Mammal species, total known	89		
Mammal species, threatened	9		
Bird species, total known	291		
Bird species, threatened	9		
GEF benefits index for biodiversity (0–100)	0.2		
Energy			
GDP per unit of energy use (2000 PPP $/kg oil equiv)	..	2.7	4.6
Energy use per capita (kg oil equiv)	..	2,794	1,090
Energy from combustible renewables & waste (% of tot.)	..	2.4	14.6
Energy imports, net (% of energy use)	..	−26	−14
Electric power consumption per capita (kWh)	..	3,531	1,329
Electricity generated by coal (% of total)	..	29.8	49.4
Emissions and pollution			
CO_2 emissions per unit of GDP (kg/2000 PPP $ of GDP)	0.9	1.0	0.5
CO_2 emissions per capita (metric tons)	5.1	6.7	2.6
Particulate matter (urban-pop.-weighted avg., µg/cu. m)	29	35	70
Passenger cars (per 1,000 people)	..	142	29
Water and sanitation			
Internal freshwater resources per capita (cu. m)	2,659	11,123	7,295
Freshwater withdrawal			
Total (% of internal resources)	..	7.5	7.7
Agriculture (% of total freshwater withdrawal)	..	59	75
Access to improved water source (% of total population)	..	91	81
Rural (% of rural population)	..	80	70
Urban (% of urban population)	..	98	93
Access to improved sanitation (% of total population)	..	82	57
Rural (% of rural population)	..	63	39
Urban (% of urban population)	..	93	78
Environment and health			
ARI prevalence (% of children under age 5)	..		
Diarrhea prevalence (% of children under age 5)	..		
Under-five mortality rate (per 1,000 live births)	14	34	40
National accounting aggregates, 2004			
Gross savings (% of GNI)	15.2	23.4	32.1
Consumption of fixed capital (% of GNI)	11.2	10.7	10.8
Education expenditure (% of GNI)	4.9	4.1	2.9
Energy depletion (% of GNI)	0.0	12.0	6.5
Mineral depletion (% of GNI)	0.0	0.3	0.5
Net forest depletion (% of GNI)	0.2	0.0	0.0
CO_2 damage (% of GNI)	1.4	1.4	1.1
Particulate emission damage (% of GNI)	0.3	0.7	1.0
Adjusted net savings (% of GNI)	6.9	2.3	15.1

Madagascar

Environmental strategy/action plan prepared in **1988**

	Country data	Group data Sub-Saharan Africa	Group data Low Income
Population (millions)	18.1	726	2,343
Urban population (% of total)	26.8	36.4	30.6
GDP ($ billions)	4.4	523	1,239
GNI per capita, *World Bank Atlas* method ($)	290	601	507

Agriculture

Land area (1,000 sq. km)	582	23,596	29,192
Agricultural land (% of land area)	47	44	45
Irrigated land (% of cropland)	30.6	3.6	23.9
Fertilizer consumption (100 grams/ha of arable land)	31	136	646
Population density, rural (people/sq. km of arable land)	438	355	524

Forests and biodiversity

Forest area (% of land area)	22.1	26.5	24.8
Annual deforestation (% change, 1990–2005)	0.4	0.6	0.5
Nationally protected areas (% of total land area)	4.3	8.7	7.7
Mammal species, total known	165		
Mammal species, threatened	49		
Bird species, total known	262		
Bird species, threatened	34		
GEF benefits index for biodiversity (0–100)	31.4		

Energy

GDP per unit of energy use (2000 PPP $/kg oil equiv)	..	2.8	4.2
Energy use per capita (kg oil equiv)	..	681	501
Energy from combustible renewables & waste (% of tot.)	..	57.4	48.9
Energy imports, net (% of energy use)	..	−59	−4
Electric power consumption per capita (kWh)	..	513	358
Electricity generated by coal (% of total)	..	68.0	46.3

Emissions and pollution

CO_2 emissions per unit of GDP (kg/2000 PPP $ of GDP)	0.2	0.4	0.4
CO_2 emissions per capita (metric tons)	0.1	0.7	0.8
Particulate matter (urban-pop.-weighted avg., µg/cu. m)	51	73	89
Passenger cars (per 1,000 people)	..	..	6

Water and sanitation

Internal freshwater resources per capita (cu. m)	18,606	5,353	3,456
Freshwater withdrawal			
Total (% of internal resources)	4.4	3.1	15.5
Agriculture (% of total freshwater withdrawal)	96	87	88
Access to improved water source (% of total population)	45	58	75
Rural (% of rural population)	34	45	69
Urban (% of urban population)	75	82	89
Access to improved sanitation (% of total population)	33	36	36
Rural (% of rural population)	27	26	24
Urban (% of urban population)	49	55	61

Environment and health

ARI prevalence (% of children under age 5)	9.0		
Diarrhea prevalence (% of children under age 5)	12.8		
Under-five mortality rate (per 1,000 live births)	123	168	122

National accounting aggregates, 2004

Gross savings (% of GNI)	17.6	17.1	22.7
Consumption of fixed capital (% of GNI)	8.1	10.9	9.2
Education expenditure (% of GNI)	2.1	3.9	3.4
Energy depletion (% of GNI)	0.0	9.8	6.7
Mineral depletion (% of GNI)	0.0	0.4	0.4
Net forest depletion (% of GNI)	0.0	0.6	0.7
CO_2 damage (% of GNI)	0.4	0.7	1.1
Particulate emission damage (% of GNI)	0.3	0.5	0.8
Adjusted net savings (% of GNI)	10.8	−1.9	7.3

Malawi

Environmental strategy/action plan prepared in **1994**

	Country data	Group data Sub-Saharan Africa	Low income
Population (millions)	12.6	726	2,343
Urban population (% of total)	16.7	36.4	30.6
GDP ($ billions)	1.9	523	1,239
GNI per capita, *World Bank Atlas* method ($)	160	601	507
Agriculture			
Land area (1.000 sq. km)	94	23,596	29,192
Agricultural land (% of land area)	47	44	45
Irrigated land (% of cropland)	2.2	3.6	23.9
Fertilizer consumption (100 grams/ha of arable land)	839	136	646
Population density, rural (people/sq. km of arable land)	421	355	524
Forests and biodiversity			
Forest area (% of land area)	36.2	26.5	24.8
Annual deforestation (% change, 1990–2005)	0.8	0.6	0.5
Nationally protected areas (% of total land area)	11.2	8.7	7.7
Mammal species, total known	207		
Mammal species, threatened	7		
Bird species, total known	658		
Bird species, threatened	13		
GEF benefits index for biodiversity (0–100)	3.9		
Energy			
GDP per unit of energy use (2000 PPP $/kg oil equiv)	..	2.8	4.2
Energy use per capita (kg oil equiv)	..	681	501
Energy from combustible renewables & waste (% of tot.)	..	57.4	48.9
Energy imports, net (% of energy use)	..	−59	−4
Electric power consumption per capita (kWh)	..	513	358
Electricity generated by coal (% of total)	..	68.0	46.3
Emissions and pollution			
CO_2 emissions per unit of GDP (kg/2000 PPP $ of GDP)	0.1	0.4	0.4
CO_2 emissions per capita (metric tons)	0.1	0.7	0.8
Particulate matter (urban-pop.-weighted avg., µg/cu. m)	88	73	89
Passenger cars (per 1,000 people)	..	..	6
Water and sanitation			
Internal freshwater resources per capita (cu. m)	1,280	5,353	3,456
Freshwater withdrawal			
Total (% of internal resources)	6.3	3.1	15.5
Agriculture (% of total freshwater withdrawal)	80	87	88
Access to improved water source (% of total population)	67	58	75
Rural (% of rural population)	62	45	69
Urban (% of urban population)	96	82	89
Access to improved sanitation (% of total population)	46	36	36
Rural (% of rural population)	42	26	24
Urban (% of urban population)	66	55	61
Environment and health			
ARI prevalence (% of children under age 5)	41.6		
Diarrhea prevalence (% of children under age 5)	17.6		
Under-five mortality rate (per 1,000 live births)	175	168	122
National accounting aggregates, 2004			
Gross savings (% of GNI)	−7.9	17.1	22.7
Consumption of fixed capital (% of GNI)	7.5	10.9	9.2
Education expenditure (% of GNI)	5.0	3.9	3.4
Energy depletion (% of GNI)	0.0	9.8	6.7
Mineral depletion (% of GNI)	0.0	0.4	0.4
Net forest depletion (% of GNI)	2.1	0.6	0.7
CO_2 damage (% of GNI)	0.3	0.7	1.1
Particulate emission damage (% of GNI)	0.3	0.5	0.8
Adjusted net savings (% of GNI)	−13.1	−1.9	7.3

Malaysia

Environmental strategy/action plan prepared in **1991**

	Country data	Group data — East Asia & Pacific	Group data — Upper middle income
Population (millions)	24.9	1,870	576
Urban population (% of total)	64.4	40.6	72.3
GDP ($ billions)	118.3	2,651	2,992
GNI per capita, *World Bank Atlas* method ($)	4,520	1,416	4,769
Agriculture			
Land area (1,000 sq. km)	329	15,885	28,983
Agricultural land (% of land area)	24	51	26
Irrigated land (% of cropland)	4.8	..	8.7
Fertilizer consumption (100 grams/ha of arable land)	6,833	2,296	469
Population density, rural (people/sq. km of arable land)	492	559	131
Forests and biodiversity			
Forest area (% of land area)	63.6	28.4	37.3
Annual deforestation (% change, 1990–2005)	0.4	–0.2	0.1
Nationally protected areas (% of total land area)	5.7	..	..
Mammal species, total known	337		
Mammal species, threatened	50		
Bird species, total known	746		
Bird species, threatened	40		
GEF benefits index for biodiversity (0–100)	14.8		
Energy			
GDP per unit of energy use (2000 PPP $/kg oil equiv)	3.9	4.6	3.5
Energy use per capita (kg oil equiv)	2,318	1,007	2,574
Energy from combustible renewables & waste (% of tot.)	4.6	17.7	3.9
Energy imports, net (% of energy use)	–48	–2	–51
Electric power consumption per capita (kWh)	3,061	1,184	3,378
Electricity generated by coal (% of total)	14.4	69.4	31.0
Emissions and pollution			
CO_2 emissions per unit of GDP (kg/2000 PPP $ of GDP)	0.7	0.5	0.7
CO_2 emissions per capita (metric tons)	6.3	2.4	6.2
Particulate matter (urban-pop.-weighted avg., μg/cu. m)	28	80	40
Passenger cars (per 1,000 people)	209	12	143
Water and sanitation			
Internal freshwater resources per capita (cu. m)	23,298	5,062	14,190
Freshwater withdrawal			
Total (% of internal resources)	1.6	10.2	3.8
Agriculture (% of total freshwater withdrawal)	62	74	53
Access to improved water source (% of total population)	95	78	93
Rural (% of rural population)	94	69	82
Urban (% of urban population)	96	92	97
Access to improved sanitation (% of total population)	..	49	81
Rural (% of rural population)	98	35	61
Urban (% of urban population)	..	72	91
Environment and health			
ARI prevalence (% of children under age 5)	..		
Diarrhea prevalence (% of children under age 5)	..		
Under-five mortality rate (per 1,000 live births)	12	37	28
National accounting aggregates, 2004			
Gross savings (% of GNI)	37.3	39.1	23.1
Consumption of fixed capital (% of GNI)	12.6	10.5	11.5
Education expenditure (% of GNI)	5.1	2.3	4.5
Energy depletion (% of GNI)	14.1	4.1	11.2
Mineral depletion (% of GNI)	0.0	0.4	0.6
Net forest depletion (% of GNI)	0.0	0.0	0.0
CO_2 damage (% of GNI)	0.9	1.2	0.9
Particulate emission damage (% of GNI)	0.1	1.2	0.7
Adjusted net savings (% of GNI)	14.5	23.9	2.6

Maldives

Environmental strategy/action plan prepared in **1994**

	Country data	South Asia	Lower middle income
		Group data	
Population (millions)	0.3	1,447	2,442
Urban population (% of total)	29.3	28.3	48.7
GDP ($ billions)	0.8	880	4,165
GNI per capita, *World Bank Atlas* method ($)	2,410	594	1,686
Agriculture			
Land area (1,000 sq. km)	0	4,781	38,470
Agricultural land (% of land area)	47	54	43
Irrigated land (% of cropland)	..	39.6	23.1
Fertilizer consumption (100 grams/ha of arable land)	..	1,040	1,530
Population density, rural (people/sq. km of arable land)	5,576	586	523
Forests and biodiversity			
Forest area (% of land area)	3.3	16.8	30.7
Annual deforestation (% change, 1990–2005)	0.0	-0.2	0.1
Nationally protected areas (% of total land area)	..	4.8	7.7
Mammal species, total known	15		
Mammal species, threatened	0		
Bird species, total known	166		
Bird species, threatened	2		
GEF benefits index for biodiversity (0–100)	1.8		
Energy			
GDP per unit of energy use (2000 PPP $/kg oil equiv)	..	5.3	4.6
Energy use per capita (kg oil equiv)	..	474	1,090
Energy from combustible renewables & waste (% of tot.)	..	38.8	14.6
Energy imports, net (% of energy use)	..	19	-14
Electric power consumption per capita (kWh)	..	394	1,329
Electricity generated by coal (% of total)	..	58.2	49.4
Emissions and pollution			
CO_2 emissions per unit of GDP (kg/2000 PPP $ of GDP)	..	0.4	0.5
CO_2 emissions per capita (metric tons)	3.4	1.0	2.6
Particulate matter (urban-pop.-weighted avg., µg/cu. m)	54	99	70
Passenger cars (per 1,000 people)	..	6	29
Water and sanitation			
Internal freshwater resources per capita (cu. m)	93	1,255	7,295
Freshwater withdrawal			
Total (% of internal resources)	..	51.8	7.7
Agriculture (% of total freshwater withdrawal)	..	90	75
Access to improved water source (% of total population)	84	84	81
Rural (% of rural population)	78	80	70
Urban (% of urban population)	99	94	93
Access to improved sanitation (% of total population)	58	35	57
Rural (% of rural population)	42	23	39
Urban (% of urban population)	100	64	78
Environment and health			
ARI prevalence (% of children under age 5)	..		
Diarrhea prevalence (% of children under age 5)	..		
Under-five mortality rate (per 1,000 live births)	46	92	40
National accounting aggregates, 2004			
Gross savings (% of GNI)	37.7	23.6	32.1
Consumption of fixed capital (% of GNI)	11.5	9.1	10.8
Education expenditure (% of GNI)	3.0	3.6	2.9
Energy depletion (% of GNI)	0.0	2.7	6.5
Mineral depletion (% of GNI)	0.0	0.3	0.5
Net forest depletion (% of GNI)	0.0	0.7	0.0
CO_2 damage (% of GNI)	0.8	1.2	1.1
Particulate emission damage (% of GNI)	0.6	0.8	1.0
Adjusted net savings (% of GNI)	27.8	12.4	15.1

Mali

Environmental strategy/action plan prepared in ..

	Country data	Sub-Saharan Africa	Low income
		Group data	
Population (millions)	13.1	726	2,343
Urban population (% of total)	33.0	36.4	30.6
GDP ($ billions)	4.9	523	1,239
GNI per capita, *World Bank Atlas* method ($)	330	601	507
Agriculture			
Land area (1,000 sq. km)	1,220	23,596	29,192
Agricultural land (% of land area)	28	44	45
Irrigated land (% of cropland)	5.0	3.6	23.9
Fertilizer consumption (100 grams/ha of arable land)	90	136	646
Population density, rural (people/sq. km of arable land)	185	355	524
Forests and biodiversity			
Forest area (% of land area)	10.3	26.5	24.8
Annual deforestation (% change, 1990–2005)	0.7	0.6	0.5
Nationally protected areas (% of total land area)	3.7	8.7	7.7
Mammal species, total known	134		
Mammal species, threatened	12		
Bird species, total known	624		
Bird species, threatened	5		
GEF benefits index for biodiversity (0–100)	1.6		
Energy			
GDP per unit of energy use (2000 PPP $/kg oil equiv)	..	2.8	4.2
Energy use per capita (kg oil equiv)	..	681	501
Energy from combustible renewables & waste (% of tot.)	..	57.4	48.9
Energy imports, net (% of energy use)	..	−59	−4
Electric power consumption per capita (kWh)	..	513	358
Electricity generated by coal (% of total)	..	68.0	46.3
Emissions and pollution			
CO_2 emissions per unit of GDP (kg/2000 PPP $ of GDP)	0.1	0.4	0.4
CO_2 emissions per capita (metric tons)	0.0	0.7	0.8
Particulate matter (urban-pop.-weighted avg., µg/cu. m)	102	73	89
Passenger cars (per 1,000 people)	..	..	6
Water and sanitation			
Internal freshwater resources per capita (cu. m)	4,572	5,353	3,456
Freshwater withdrawal			
Total (% of internal resources)	10.9	3.1	15.5
Agriculture (% of total freshwater withdrawal)	90	87	88
Access to improved water source (% of total population)	48	58	75
Rural (% of rural population)	35	45	69
Urban (% of urban population)	76	82	89
Access to improved sanitation (% of total population)	45	36	36
Rural (% of rural population)	38	26	24
Urban (% of urban population)	59	55	61
Environment and health			
ARI prevalence (% of children under age 5)	..		
Diarrhea prevalence (% of children under age 5)	18.6		
Under-five mortality rate (per 1,000 live births)	219	168	122
National accounting aggregates, 2004			
Gross savings (% of GNI)	11.3	17.1	22.7
Consumption of fixed capital (% of GNI)	8.9	10.9	9.2
Education expenditure (% of GNI)	2.7	3.9	3.4
Energy depletion (% of GNI)	0.0	9.8	6.7
Mineral depletion (% of GNI)	0.0	0.4	0.4
Net forest depletion (% of GNI)	0.0	0.6	0.7
CO_2 damage (% of GNI)	0.1	0.7	1.1
Particulate emission damage (% of GNI)	0.6	0.5	0.8
Adjusted net savings (% of GNI)	4.4	−1.9	7.3

Malta

Environmental strategy/action plan prepared in ..

	Country data	Group data High income
Population (millions)	0.4	1,004
Urban population (% of total)	91.9	78.5
GDP ($ billions)	5.3	32,900
GNI per capita, *World Bank Atlas* method ($)	12,050	32,112
Agriculture		
Land area (1,000 sq. km)	0	33,018
Agricultural land (% of land area)	34	38
Irrigated land (% of cropland)	18.2	11.9
Fertilizer consumption (100 grams/ha of arable land)	778	1,205
Population density, rural (people/sq. km of arable land)	334	331
Forests and biodiversity		
Forest area (% of land area)	..	29.3
Annual deforestation (% change, 1990–2005)	..	–0.1
Nationally protected areas (% of total land area)	..	..
Mammal species, total known	34	
Mammal species, threatened	1	
Bird species, total known	357	
Bird species, threatened	10	
GEF benefits index for biodiversity (0–100)	0.1	
Energy		
GDP per unit of energy use (2000 PPP $/kg oil equiv)	7.7	5.2
Energy use per capita (kg oil equiv)	2,236	5,410
Energy from combustible renewables & waste (% of tot.)	..	3.0
Energy imports, net (% of energy use)	..	19
Electric power consumption per capita (kWh)	4,867	9,503
Electricity generated by coal (% of total)	..	38.2
Emissions and pollution		
CO_2 emissions per unit of GDP (kg/2000 PPP $ of GDP)	0.4	0.5
CO_2 emissions per capita (metric tons)	7.4	12.8
Particulate matter (urban-pop.-weighted avg., µg/cu. m)	..	29
Passenger cars (per 1,000 people)	505	433
Water and sanitation		
Internal freshwater resources per capita (cu. m)	126	9,703
Freshwater withdrawal		
Total (% of internal resources)	100.0	10.4
Agriculture (% of total freshwater withdrawal)	20	42
Access to improved water source (% of total population)	100	99
Rural (% of rural population)	100	98
Urban (% of urban population)	100	100
Access to improved sanitation (% of total population)	..	..
Rural (% of rural population)	..	..
Urban (% of urban population)	100	..
Environment and health		
ARI prevalence (% of children under age 5)	..	
Diarrhea prevalence (% of children under age 5)	..	
Under-five mortality rate (per 1,000 live births)	6	7
National accounting aggregates, 2004		
Gross savings (% of GNI)	12.6	19.4
Consumption of fixed capital (% of GNI)	13.5	13.2
Education expenditure (% of GNI)	4.4	4.6
Energy depletion (% of GNI)	0.0	1.4
Mineral depletion (% of GNI)	0.0	0.0
Net forest depletion (% of GNI)	..	0.0
CO_2 damage (% of GNI)	0.4	0.3
Particulate emission damage (% of GNI)	..	0.4
Adjusted net savings (% of GNI)	..	8.7

Marshall Islands

Environmental strategy/action plan prepared in ..

	Country data	East Asia & Pacific	Lower middle income
		Group data	
Population (millions)	0.1	1,870	2,442
Urban population (% of total)	66.6	40.6	48.7
GDP ($ billions)	0.1	2,651	4,165
GNI per capita, *World Bank Atlas* method ($)	2,320	1,416	1,686
Agriculture			
Land area (1,000 sq. km)	0	15,885	38,470
Agricultural land (% of land area)	78	51	43
Irrigated land (% of cropland)	..	..	23.1
Fertilizer consumption (100 grams/ha of arable land)	..	2,296	1,530
Population density, rural (people/sq. km of arable land)	992	559	523
Forests and biodiversity			
Forest area (% of land area)	..	28.4	30.7
Annual deforestation (% change, 1990–2005)	..	−0.2	0.1
Nationally protected areas (% of total land area)	..	..	7.7
Mammal species, total known	4		
Mammal species, threatened	1		
Bird species, total known	57		
Bird species, threatened	2		
GEF benefits index for biodiversity (0–100)	1.6		
Energy			
GDP per unit of energy use (2000 PPP $/kg oil equiv)	..	4.6	4.6
Energy use per capita (kg oil equiv)	..	1,007	1,090
Energy from combustible renewables & waste (% of tot.)	..	17.7	14.6
Energy imports, net (% of energy use)	..	−2	−14
Electric power consumption per capita (kWh)	..	1,184	1,329
Electricity generated by coal (% of total)	..	69.4	49.4
Emissions and pollution			
CO_2 emissions per unit of GDP (kg/2000 PPP $ of GDP)	..	0.5	0.5
CO_2 emissions per capita (metric tons)	..	2.4	2.6
Particulate matter (urban-pop.-weighted avg., μg/cu. m)	..	80	70
Passenger cars (per 1,000 people)	..	12	29
Water and sanitation			
Internal freshwater resources per capita (cu. m)	..	5,062	7,295
Freshwater withdrawal			
Total (% of internal resources)	..	10.2	7.7
Agriculture (% of total freshwater withdrawal)	..	74	75
Access to improved water source (% of total population)	85	78	81
Rural (% of rural population)	95	69	70
Urban (% of urban population)	80	92	93
Access to improved sanitation (% of total population)	82	49	57
Rural (% of rural population)	59	35	39
Urban (% of urban population)	93	72	78
Environment and health			
ARI prevalence (% of children under age 5)	..		
Diarrhea prevalence (% of children under age 5)	..		
Under-five mortality rate (per 1,000 live births)	59	37	40
National accounting aggregates, 2004			
Gross savings (% of GNI)	..	39.1	32.1
Consumption of fixed capital (% of GNI)	8.5	10.5	10.8
Education expenditure (% of GNI)	8.8	2.3	2.9
Energy depletion (% of GNI)	0.0	4.1	6.5
Mineral depletion (% of GNI)	0.0	0.4	0.5
Net forest depletion (% of GNI)	..	0.0	0.0
CO_2 damage (% of GNI)	0.0	1.2	1.1
Particulate emission damage (% of GNI)	..	1.2	1.0
Adjusted net savings (% of GNI)	..	23.9	15.1

Mauritania

Environmental strategy/action plan prepared in **1988**

	Country data	Group data Sub-Saharan Africa	Low income
Population (millions)	3.0	726	2,343
Urban population (% of total)	63.0	36.4	30.6
GDP ($ billions)	1.5	523	1,239
GNI per capita, *World Bank Atlas* method ($)	530	601	507
Agriculture			
Land area (1,000 sq. km)	1,025	23,596	29,192
Agricultural land (% of land area)	39	44	45
Irrigated land (% of cropland)	9.8	3.6	23.9
Fertilizer consumption (100 grams/ha of arable land)	59	136	646
Population density, rural (people/sq. km of arable land)	227	355	524
Forests and biodiversity			
Forest area (% of land area)	0.3	26.5	24.8
Annual deforestation (% change, 1990–2005)	2.4	0.6	0.5
Nationally protected areas (% of total land area)	1.7	8.7	7.7
Mammal species, total known	94		
Mammal species, threatened	7		
Bird species, total known	521		
Bird species, threatened	5		
GEF benefits index for biodiversity (0–100)	1.4		
Energy			
GDP per unit of energy use (2000 PPP $/kg oil equiv)	..	2.8	4.2
Energy use per capita (kg oil equiv)	..	681	501
Energy from combustible renewables & waste (% of tot.)	..	57.4	48.9
Energy imports, net (% of energy use)	..	−59	−4
Electric power consumption per capita (kWh)	..	513	358
Electricity generated by coal (% of total)	..	68.0	46.3
Emissions and pollution			
CO_2 emissions per unit of GDP (kg/2000 PPP $ of GDP)	0.7	0.4	0.4
CO_2 emissions per capita (metric tons)	1.1	0.7	0.8
Particulate matter (urban-pop.-weighted avg., μg/cu. m)	42	73	89
Passenger cars (per 1,000 people)	..	..	6
Water and sanitation			
Internal freshwater resources per capita (cu. m)	134	5,353	3,456
Freshwater withdrawal			
Total (% of internal resources)	425.0	3.1	15.5
Agriculture (% of total freshwater withdrawal)	88	87	88
Access to improved water source (% of total population)	56	58	75
Rural (% of rural population)	45	45	69
Urban (% of urban population)	63	82	89
Access to improved sanitation (% of total population)	42	36	36
Rural (% of rural population)	9	26	24
Urban (% of urban population)	64	55	61
Environment and health			
ARI prevalence (% of children under age 5)	31.1		
Diarrhea prevalence (% of children under age 5)	18.3		
Under-five mortality rate (per 1,000 live births)	125	168	122
National accounting aggregates, 2004			
Gross savings (% of GNI)	−6.3	17.1	22.7
Consumption of fixed capital (% of GNI)	8.5	10.9	9.2
Education expenditure (% of GNI)	3.2	3.9	3.4
Energy depletion (% of GNI)	0.0	9.8	6.7
Mineral depletion (% of GNI)	10.9	0.4	0.4
Net forest depletion (% of GNI)	0.7	0.6	0.7
CO_2 damage (% of GNI)	1.5	0.7	1.1
Particulate emission damage (% of GNI)	0.6	0.5	0.8
Adjusted net savings (% of GNI)	−25.3	−1.9	7.3

Mauritius

Environmental strategy/action plan prepared in **1990**

	Country data	Group data	
		Sub-Saharan Africa	Upper middle income
Population (millions)	1.2	726	576
Urban population (% of total)	43.6	36.4	72.3
GDP ($ billions)	6.0	523	2,992
GNI per capita, *World Bank Atlas* method ($)	4,640	601	4,769

Agriculture
Land area (1,000 sq. km)	2	23,596	28,983
Agricultural land (% of land area)	56	44	26
Irrigated land (% of cropland)	20.8	3.6	8.7
Fertilizer consumption (100 grams/ha of arable land)	2,500	136	469
Population density, rural (people/sq. km of arable land)	693	355	131

Forests and biodiversity
Forest area (% of land area)	18.2	26.5	37.3
Annual deforestation (% change, 1990–2005)	0.3	0.6	0.1
Nationally protected areas (% of total land area)	..	8.7	..
Mammal species, total known	14		
Mammal species, threatened	3		
Bird species, total known	137		
Bird species, threatened	13		
GEF benefits index for biodiversity (0–100)	4.2		

Energy
GDP per unit of energy use (2000 PPP $/kg oil equiv)	..	2.8	3.5
Energy use per capita (kg oil equiv)	..	681	2,574
Energy from combustible renewables & waste (% of tot.)	..	57.4	3.9
Energy imports, net (% of energy use)	..	−59	−51
Electric power consumption per capita (kWh)	..	513	3,378
Electricity generated by coal (% of total)	..	68.0	31.0

Emissions and pollution
CO_2 emissions per unit of GDP (kg/2000 PPP $ of GDP)	0.3	0.4	0.7
CO_2 emissions per capita (metric tons)	2.6	0.7	6.2
Particulate matter (urban-pop.-weighted avg., µg/cu. m)	47	73	40
Passenger cars (per 1,000 people)	84	..	143

Water and sanitation
Internal freshwater resources per capita (cu. m)	2,229	5,353	14,190
Freshwater withdrawal			
Total (% of internal resources)	22.2	3.1	3.8
Agriculture (% of total freshwater withdrawal)		87	53
Access to improved water source (% of total population)	100	58	93
Rural (% of rural population)	100	45	82
Urban (% of urban population)	100	82	97
Access to improved sanitation (% of total population)	99	36	81
Rural (% of rural population)	99	26	61
Urban (% of urban population)	100	55	91

Environment and health
ARI prevalence (% of children under age 5)	..		
Diarrhea prevalence (% of children under age 5)	..		
Under-five mortality rate (per 1,000 live births)	15	168	28

National accounting aggregates, 2004
Gross savings (% of GNI)	23.8	17.1	23.1
Consumption of fixed capital (% of GNI)	12.0	10.9	11.5
Education expenditure (% of GNI)	3.3	3.9	4.5
Energy depletion (% of GNI)	0.0	9.8	11.2
Mineral depletion (% of GNI)	0.0	0.4	0.6
Net forest depletion (% of GNI)	0.0	0.6	0.0
CO_2 damage (% of GNI)	0.4	0.7	0.9
Particulate emission damage (% of GNI)	..	0.5	0.7
Adjusted net savings (% of GNI)	14.8	−1.9	2.6

Mayotte

Environmental strategy/action plan prepared in **1988**

	Country data	Group data Sub-Saharan Africa	Group data Upper middle income
Population (millions)	0.2	726	576
Urban population (% of total)	..	36.4	72.3
GDP ($ billions)	..	523	2,992
GNI per capita, *World Bank Atlas* method ($)	..	601	4,769

Agriculture
Land area (1,000 sq. km)	..	23,596	28,983
Agricultural land (% of land area)	..	44	26
Irrigated land (% of cropland)	..	3.6	8.7
Fertilizer consumption (100 grams/ha of arable land)	..	136	469
Population density, rural (people/sq. km of arable land)	..	355	131

Forests and biodiversity
Forest area (% of land area)	..	26.5	37.3
Annual deforestation (% change, 1990–2005)	1.1	0.6	0.1
Nationally protected areas (% of total land area)	..	8.7	..
Mammal species, total known	..		
Mammal species, threatened	..		
Bird species, total known	..		
Bird species, threatened	..		
GEF benefits index for biodiversity (0–100)	0.3		

Energy
GDP per unit of energy use (2000 PPP $/kg oil equiv)	..	2.8	3.5
Energy use per capita (kg oil equiv)	..	681	2,574
Energy from combustible renewables & waste (% of tot.)	..	57.4	3.9
Energy imports, net (% of energy use)	..	−59	−51
Electric power consumption per capita (kWh)	..	513	3,378
Electricity generated by coal (% of total)	..	68.0	31.0

Emissions and pollution
CO_2 emissions per unit of GDP (kg/2000 PPP $ of GDP)	..	0.4	0.7
CO_2 emissions per capita (metric tons)	..	0.7	6.2
Particulate matter (urban-pop.-weighted avg., µg/cu. m)	..	73	40
Passenger cars (per 1,000 people)	..	..	143

Water and sanitation
Internal freshwater resources per capita (cu. m)	..	5,353	14,190
Freshwater withdrawal			
Total (% of internal resources)	..	3.1	3.8
Agriculture (% of total freshwater withdrawal)	..	87	53
Access to improved water source (% of total population)	..	58	93
Rural (% of rural population)	..	45	82
Urban (% of urban population)	..	82	97
Access to improved sanitation (% of total population)	..	36	81
Rural (% of rural population)	..	26	61
Urban (% of urban population)	..	55	91

Environment and health
ARI prevalence (% of children under age 5)	..		
Diarrhea prevalence (% of children under age 5)	..		
Under-five mortality rate (per 1,000 live births)	..	168	28

National accounting aggregates, 2004
Gross savings (% of GNI)	..	17.1	23.1
Consumption of fixed capital (% of GNI)	..	10.9	11.5
Education expenditure (% of GNI)	..	3.9	4.5
Energy depletion (% of GNI)	..	9.8	11.2
Mineral depletion (% of GNI)	..	0.4	0.6
Net forest depletion (% of GNI)	..	0.6	0.0
CO_2 damage (% of GNI)	..	0.7	0.9
Particulate emission damage (% of GNI)	..	0.5	0.7
Adjusted net savings (% of GNI)	..	−1.9	2.6

Mexico

Environmental strategy/action plan prepared in ..

	Country data	Latin America & Caribbean	Upper middle income
		Group data	
Population (millions)	103.8	546	576
Urban population (% of total)	75.8	77.1	72.3
GDP ($ billions)	676.5	2,022	2,992
GNI per capita, *World Bank Atlas* method ($)	6,790	3,576	4,769
Agriculture			
Land area (1,000 sq. km)	1,909	20,057	28,983
Agricultural land (% of land area)	56	36	26
Irrigated land (% of cropland)	23.2	11.4	8.7
Fertilizer consumption (100 grams/ha of arable land)	690	923	469
Population density, rural (people/sq. km of arable land)	101	212	131
Forests and biodiversity			
Forest area (% of land area)	33.7	45.6	37.3
Annual deforestation (% change, 1990–2005)	0.5	0.4	0.1
Nationally protected areas (% of total land area)	10.2	11.1	..
Mammal species, total known	544		
Mammal species, threatened	72		
Bird species, total known	1,026		
Bird species, threatened	57		
GEF benefits index for biodiversity (0–100)	75.8		
Energy			
GDP per unit of energy use (2000 PPP $/kg oil equiv)	5.6	6.2	3.5
Energy use per capita (kg oil equiv)	1,564	1,148	2,574
Energy from combustible renewables & waste (% of tot.)	5.1	15.0	3.9
Energy imports, net (% of energy use)	−52	−40	−51
Electric power consumption per capita (kWh)	1,801	1,615	3,378
Electricity generated by coal (% of total)	14.3	5.4	31.0
Emissions and pollution			
CO_2 emissions per unit of GDP (kg/2000 PPP $ of GDP)	0.4	0.3	0.7
CO_2 emissions per capita (metric tons)	3.8	2.4	6.2
Particulate matter (urban-pop.-weighted avg., μg/cu. m)	43	43	40
Passenger cars (per 1,000 people)	128	108	143
Water and sanitation			
Internal freshwater resources per capita (cu. m)	3,940	24,619	14,190
Freshwater withdrawal			
Total (% of internal resources)	19.1	2.0	3.8
Agriculture (% of total freshwater withdrawal)	77	71	53
Access to improved water source (% of total population)	91	89	93
Rural (% of rural population)	72	69	82
Urban (% of urban population)	97	96	97
Access to improved sanitation (% of total population)	77	75	81
Rural (% of rural population)	39	44	61
Urban (% of urban population)	90	84	91
Environment and health			
ARI prevalence (% of children under age 5)	..		
Diarrhea prevalence (% of children under age 5)	..		
Under-five mortality rate (per 1,000 live births)	28	31	28
National accounting aggregates, 2004			
Gross savings (% of GNI)	21.1	22.7	23.1
Consumption of fixed capital (% of GNI)	12.6	12.1	11.5
Education expenditure (% of GNI)	5.3	4.4	4.5
Energy depletion (% of GNI)	7.4	7.2	11.2
Mineral depletion (% of GNI)	0.1	1.1	0.6
Net forest depletion (% of GNI)	0.0	0.0	0.0
CO_2 damage (% of GNI)	0.4	0.5	0.9
Particulate emission damage (% of GNI)	0.6	0.6	0.7
Adjusted net savings (% of GNI)	5.3	5.6	2.6

Micronesia, Fed. Sts.

Environmental strategy/action plan prepared in ..

	Country data	Group data East Asia & Pacific	Group data Lower middle income
Population (millions)	0.1	1,870	2,442
Urban population (% of total)	29.7	40.6	48.7
GDP ($ billions)	0.2	2,651	4,165
GNI per capita, *World Bank Atlas* method ($)	2,300	1,416	1,686

Agriculture
Land area (1,000 sq. km)	1	15,885	38,470
Agricultural land (% of land area)	67	51	43
Irrigated land (% of cropland)	..	..	23.1
Fertilizer consumption (100 grams/ha of arable land)	..	2,296	1,530
Population density, rural (people/sq. km of arable land)	1,922	559	523

Forests and biodiversity
Forest area (% of land area)	90.0	28.4	30.7
Annual deforestation (% change, 1990–2005)	0.0	−0.2	0.1
Nationally protected areas (% of total land area)	..	..	7.7
Mammal species, total known	8		
Mammal species, threatened	..		
Bird species, total known	97		
Bird species, threatened	8		
GEF benefits index for biodiversity (0–100)	3.0		

Energy
GDP per unit of energy use (2000 PPP $/kg oil equiv)	..	4.6	4.6
Energy use per capita (kg oil equiv)	..	1,007	1,090
Energy from combustible renewables & waste (% of tot.)	..	17.7	14.6
Energy imports, net (% of energy use)	..	−2	−14
Electric power consumption per capita (kWh)	..	1,184	1,329
Electricity generated by coal (% of total)	..	69.4	49.4

Emissions and pollution
CO_2 emissions per unit of GDP (kg/2000 PPP $ of GDP)	..	0.5	0.5
CO_2 emissions per capita (metric tons)	..	2.4	2.6
Particulate matter (urban-pop.-weighted avg., μg/cu. m)	..	80	70
Passenger cars (per 1,000 people)	..	12	29

Water and sanitation
Internal freshwater resources per capita (cu. m)	..	5,062	7,295
Freshwater withdrawal			
Total (% of internal resources)	..	10.2	7.7
Agriculture (% of total freshwater withdrawal)	..	74	75
Access to improved water source (% of total population)	94	78	81
Rural (% of rural population)	94	69	70
Urban (% of urban population)	95	92	93
Access to improved sanitation (% of total population)	28	49	57
Rural (% of rural population)	14	35	39
Urban (% of urban population)	61	72	78

Environment and health
ARI prevalence (% of children under age 5)	..		
Diarrhea prevalence (% of children under age 5)	..		
Under-five mortality rate (per 1,000 live births)	23	37	40

National accounting aggregates, 2004
Gross savings (% of GNI)	..	39.1	32.1
Consumption of fixed capital (% of GNI)	10.2	10.5	10.8
Education expenditure (% of GNI)	..	2.3	2.9
Energy depletion (% of GNI)	0.0	4.1	6.5
Mineral depletion (% of GNI)	0.0	0.4	0.5
Net forest depletion (% of GNI)	..	0.0	0.0
CO_2 damage (% of GNI)	0.0	1.2	1.1
Particulate emission damage (% of GNI)	..	1.2	1.0
Adjusted net savings (% of GNI)	..	23.9	15.1

Moldova

Environmental strategy/action plan prepared in ..

	Country data	Group data Europe & Central Asia	Low income
Population (millions)	4.2	472	2,343
Urban population (% of total)	46.2	63.6	30.6
GDP ($ billions)	2.6	1,770	1,239
GNI per capita, *World Bank Atlas* method ($)	720	3,295	507
Agriculture			
Land area (1,000 sq. km)	33	23,371	29,192
Agricultural land (% of land area)	77	29	45
Irrigated land (% of cropland)	14.0	11.1	23.9
Fertilizer consumption (100 grams/ha of arable land)	55	347	646
Population density, rural (people/sq. km of arable land)	124	126	524
Forests and biodiversity			
Forest area (% of land area)	10.0	38.3	24.8
Annual deforestation (% change, 1990–2005)	–0.2	0.0	0.5
Nationally protected areas (% of total land area)	1.4	6.9	7.7
Mammal species, total known	50		
Mammal species, threatened	4		
Bird species, total known	203		
Bird species, threatened	8		
GEF benefits index for biodiversity (0–100)	0.0		
Energy			
GDP per unit of energy use (2000 PPP $/kg oil equiv)	1.9	2.7	4.2
Energy use per capita (kg oil equiv)	772	2,794	501
Energy from combustible renewables & waste (% of tot.)	1.8	2.4	48.9
Energy imports, net (% of energy use)	98	–26	–4
Electric power consumption per capita (kWh)	1,166	3,531	358
Electricity generated by coal (% of total)	5.4	29.8	46.3
Emissions and pollution			
CO_2 emissions per unit of GDP (kg/2000 PPP $ of GDP)	1.2	1.0	0.4
CO_2 emissions per capita (metric tons)	1.6	6.7	0.8
Particulate matter (urban-pop.-weighted avg., µg/cu. m)	41	35	89
Passenger cars (per 1,000 people)	52	142	6
Water and sanitation			
Internal freshwater resources per capita (cu. m)	237	11,123	3,456
Freshwater withdrawal			
Total (% of internal resources)	231.0	7.5	15.5
Agriculture (% of total freshwater withdrawal)	33	59	88
Access to improved water source (% of total population)	92	91	75
Rural (% of rural population)	88	80	69
Urban (% of urban population)	97	98	89
Access to improved sanitation (% of total population)	68	82	36
Rural (% of rural population)	52	63	24
Urban (% of urban population)	86	93	61
Environment and health			
ARI prevalence (% of children under age 5)	1.4		
Diarrhea prevalence (% of children under age 5)	4.2		
Under-five mortality rate (per 1,000 live births)	28	34	122
National accounting aggregates, 2004			
Gross savings (% of GNI)	18.8	23.4	22.7
Consumption of fixed capital (% of GNI)	8.2	10.7	9.2
Education expenditure (% of GNI)	6.9	4.1	3.4
Energy depletion (% of GNI)	0.0	12.0	6.7
Mineral depletion (% of GNI)	0.0	0.3	0.4
Net forest depletion (% of GNI)	0.0	0.0	0.7
CO_2 damage (% of GNI)	1.8	1.4	1.1
Particulate emission damage (% of GNI)	0.7	0.7	0.8
Adjusted net savings (% of GNI)	14.9	2.3	7.3

Monaco

Environmental strategy/action plan prepared in ..

	Country data	Group data High income
Population (millions)	0.0	1,004
Urban population (% of total)	100.0	78.5
GDP ($ billions)	..	32,900
GNI per capita, *World Bank Atlas* method ($)	..	32,112

Agriculture		
Land area (1,000 sq. km)	..	33,018
Agricultural land (% of land area)	..	38
Irrigated land (% of cropland)	..	11.9
Fertilizer consumption (100 grams/ha of arable land)	..	1,205
Population density, rural (people/sq. km of arable land)	..	331

Forests and biodiversity		
Forest area (% of land area)	..	29.3
Annual deforestation (% change, 1990–2005)	..	–0.1
Nationally protected areas (% of total land area)	..	..
Mammal species, total known	4	
Mammal species, threatened	0	
Bird species, total known	12	
Bird species, threatened	0	
GEF benefits index for biodiversity (0–100)	..	

Energy		
GDP per unit of energy use (2000 PPP $/kg oil equiv)	..	5.2
Energy use per capita (kg oil equiv)	..	5,410
Energy from combustible renewables & waste (% of tot.)	..	3.0
Energy imports, net (% of energy use)	..	19
Electric power consumption per capita (kWh)	..	9,503
Electricity generated by coal (% of total)	..	38.2

Emissions and pollution		
CO_2 emissions per unit of GDP (kg/2000 PPP $ of GDP)	..	0.5
CO_2 emissions per capita (metric tons)	..	12.8
Particulate matter (urban-pop.-weighted avg., µg/cu. m)	..	29
Passenger cars (per 1,000 people)	..	433

Water and sanitation		
Internal freshwater resources per capita (cu. m)	..	9,703
Freshwater withdrawal		
Total (% of internal resources)	..	10.4
Agriculture (% of total freshwater withdrawal)	..	42
Access to improved water source (% of total population)	..	99
Rural (% of rural population)	..	98
Urban (% of urban population)	100	100
Access to improved sanitation (% of total population)	..	..
Rural (% of rural population)	..	..
Urban (% of urban population)	100	..

Environment and health		
ARI prevalence (% of children under age 5)	..	
Diarrhea prevalence (% of children under age 5)	..	
Under-five mortality rate (per 1,000 live births)	5	7

National accounting aggregates, 2004		
Gross savings (% of GNI)	..	19.4
Consumption of fixed capital (% of GNI)	..	13.2
Education expenditure (% of GNI)	..	4.6
Energy depletion (% of GNI)	..	1.4
Mineral depletion (% of GNI)	..	0.0
Net forest depletion (% of GNI)	..	0.0
CO_2 damage (% of GNI)	..	0.3
Particulate emission damage (% of GNI)	..	0.4
Adjusted net savings (% of GNI)	..	8.7

Mongolia

Environmental strategy/action plan prepared in **1995**

	Country data	Group data — East Asia & Pacific	Group data — Low income
Population (millions)	2.5	1,870	2,343
Urban population (% of total)	56.9	40.6	30.6
GDP ($ billions)	1.6	2,651	1,239
GNI per capita, *World Bank Atlas* method ($)	600	1,416	507
Agriculture			
Land area (1,000 sq. km)	1,567	15,885	29,192
Agricultural land (% of land area)	83	51	45
Irrigated land (% of cropland)	7.0	..	23.9
Fertilizer consumption (100 grams/ha of arable land)	37	2,296	646
Population density, rural (people/sq. km of arable land)	89	559	524
Forests and biodiversity			
Forest area (% of land area)	6.5	28.4	24.8
Annual deforestation (% change, 1990–2005)	0.7	–0.2	0.5
Nationally protected areas (% of total land area)	11.5	..	7.7
Mammal species, total known	140		
Mammal species, threatened	13		
Bird species, total known	387		
Bird species, threatened	22		
GEF benefits index for biodiversity (0–100)	4.4		
Energy			
GDP per unit of energy use (2000 PPP $/kg oil equiv)	..	4.6	4.2
Energy use per capita (kg oil equiv)	..	1,007	501
Energy from combustible renewables & waste (% of tot.)	..	17.7	48.9
Energy imports, net (% of energy use)	..	–2	–4
Electric power consumption per capita (kWh)	..	1,184	358
Electricity generated by coal (% of total)	..	69.4	46.3
Emissions and pollution			
CO_2 emissions per unit of GDP (kg/2000 PPP $ of GDP)	1.9	0.5	0.4
CO_2 emissions per capita (metric tons)	3.4	2.4	0.8
Particulate matter (urban-pop.-weighted avg., µg/cu. m)	16	80	89
Passenger cars (per 1,000 people)	26	12	6
Water and sanitation			
Internal freshwater resources per capita (cu. m)	13,839	5,062	3,456
Freshwater withdrawal			
Total (% of internal resources)	1.3	10.2	15.5
Agriculture (% of total freshwater withdrawal)	52	74	88
Access to improved water source (% of total population)	62	78	75
Rural (% of rural population)	30	69	69
Urban (% of urban population)	87	92	89
Access to improved sanitation (% of total population)	59	49	36
Rural (% of rural population)	37	35	24
Urban (% of urban population)	75	72	61
Environment and health			
ARI prevalence (% of children under age 5)	2.3		
Diarrhea prevalence (% of children under age 5)	8.0		
Under-five mortality rate (per 1,000 live births)	52	37	122
National accounting aggregates, 2004			
Gross savings (% of GNI)	40.8	39.1	22.7
Consumption of fixed capital (% of GNI)	9.3	10.5	9.2
Education expenditure (% of GNI)	8.1	2.3	3.4
Energy depletion (% of GNI)	0.9	4.1	6.7
Mineral depletion (% of GNI)	8.4	0.4	0.4
Net forest depletion (% of GNI)	0.0	0.0	0.7
CO_2 damage (% of GNI)	3.8	1.2	1.1
Particulate emission damage (% of GNI)	0.0	1.2	0.8
Adjusted net savings (% of GNI)	26.6	23.9	7.3

Morocco

Environmental strategy/action plan prepared in ..

	Country data	Group data	
		Middle East & North Africa	Lower middle income
Population (millions)	29.8	300	2,442
Urban population (% of total)	58.1	56.3	48.7
GDP ($ billions)	50.0	547	4,165
GNI per capita, *World Bank Atlas* method ($)	1,570	1,972	1,686
Agriculture			
Land area (1,000 sq. km)	446	8,955	38,470
Agricultural land (% of land area)	68	23	43
Irrigated land (% of cropland)	15.4	32.5	23.1
Fertilizer consumption (100 grams/ha of arable land)	475	842	1,530
Population density, rural (people/sq. km of arable land)	145	670	523
Forests and biodiversity			
Forest area (% of land area)	9.8	2.4	30.7
Annual deforestation (% change, 1990–2005)	−0.1	−0.5	0.1
Nationally protected areas (% of total land area)	0.7	4.2	7.7
Mammal species, total known	129		
Mammal species, threatened	12		
Bird species, total known	430		
Bird species, threatened	13		
GEF benefits index for biodiversity (0–100)	4.0		
Energy			
GDP per unit of energy use (2000 PPP $/kg oil equiv)	10.2	4.2	4.6
Energy use per capita (kg oil equiv)	378	1,144	1,090
Energy from combustible renewables & waste (% of tot.)	4.1	1.3	14.6
Energy imports, net (% of energy use)	94	−129	−14
Electric power consumption per capita (kWh)	577	1,212	1,329
Electricity generated by coal (% of total)	67.7	3.0	49.4
Emissions and pollution			
CO_2 emissions per unit of GDP (kg/2000 PPP $ of GDP)	0.4	0.7	0.5
CO_2 emissions per capita (metric tons)	1.5	3.2	2.6
Particulate matter (urban-pop.-weighted avg., µg/cu. m)	27	90	70
Passenger cars (per 1,000 people)	45	..	29
Water and sanitation			
Internal freshwater resources per capita (cu. m)	972	761	7,295
Freshwater withdrawal			
Total (% of internal resources)	43.4	105.0	7.7
Agriculture (% of total freshwater withdrawal)	87	89	75
Access to improved water source (% of total population)	80	88	81
Rural (% of rural population)	56	79	70
Urban (% of urban population)	99	95	93
Access to improved sanitation (% of total population)	61	75	57
Rural (% of rural population)	31	56	39
Urban (% of urban population)	83	89	78
Environment and health			
ARI prevalence (% of children under age 5)	11.6		
Diarrhea prevalence (% of children under age 5)	..		
Under-five mortality rate (per 1,000 live births)	43	55	40
National accounting aggregates, 2004			
Gross savings (% of GNI)	28.0	30.0	32.1
Consumption of fixed capital (% of GNI)	10.7	11.2	10.8
Education expenditure (% of GNI)	6.1	4.5	2.9
Energy depletion (% of GNI)	0.0	27.3	6.5
Mineral depletion (% of GNI)	0.3	0.1	0.5
Net forest depletion (% of GNI)	0.0	0.1	0.0
CO_2 damage (% of GNI)	0.6	1.2	1.1
Particulate emission damage (% of GNI)	0.3	0.9	1.0
Adjusted net savings (% of GNI)	22.3	−6.2	15.1

Mozambique

Environmental strategy/action plan prepared in **1994**

	Country data	Group data Sub-Saharan Africa	Group data Low income
Population (millions)	19.4	726	2,343
Urban population (% of total)	36.8	36.4	30.6
GDP ($ billions)	6.1	523	1,239
GNI per capita, *World Bank Atlas* method ($)	270	601	507
Agriculture			
Land area (1,000 sq. km)	784	23,596	29,192
Agricultural land (% of land area)	62	44	45
Irrigated land (% of cropland)	2.6	3.6	23.9
Fertilizer consumption (100 grams/ha of arable land)	59	136	646
Population density, rural (people/sq. km of arable land)	282	355	524
Forests and biodiversity			
Forest area (% of land area)	24.6	26.5	24.8
Annual deforestation (% change, 1990–2005)	0.2	0.6	0.5
Nationally protected areas (% of total land area)	8.4	8.7	7.7
Mammal species, total known	228		
Mammal species, threatened	12		
Bird species, total known	685		
Bird species, threatened	23		
GEF benefits index for biodiversity (0–100)	8.2		
Energy			
GDP per unit of energy use (2000 PPP $/kg oil equiv)	2.5	2.8	4.2
Energy use per capita (kg oil equiv)	430	681	501
Energy from combustible renewables & waste (% of tot.)	86.1	57.4	48.9
Energy imports, net (% of energy use)	3	−59	−4
Electric power consumption per capita (kWh)	339	513	358
Electricity generated by coal (% of total)	..	68.0	46.3
Emissions and pollution			
CO_2 emissions per unit of GDP (kg/2000 PPP $ of GDP)	0.1	0.4	0.4
CO_2 emissions per capita (metric tons)	0.1	0.7	0.8
Particulate matter (urban-pop.-weighted avg., µg/cu. m)	44	73	89
Passenger cars (per 1,000 people)	..	..	6
Water and sanitation			
Internal freshwater resources per capita (cu. m)	5,164	5,353	3,456
Freshwater withdrawal			
Total (% of internal resources)	0.6	3.1	15.5
Agriculture (% of total freshwater withdrawal)	87	87	88
Access to improved water source (% of total population)	42	58	75
Rural (% of rural population)	24	45	69
Urban (% of urban population)	76	82	89
Access to improved sanitation (% of total population)	27	36	36
Rural (% of rural population)	14	26	24
Urban (% of urban population)	51	55	61
Environment and health			
ARI prevalence (% of children under age 5)	..		
Diarrhea prevalence (% of children under age 5)	..		
Under-five mortality rate (per 1,000 live births)	152	168	122
National accounting aggregates, 2004			
Gross savings (% of GNI)	6.6	17.1	22.7
Consumption of fixed capital (% of GNI)	8.8	10.9	9.2
Education expenditure (% of GNI)	1.8	3.9	3.4
Energy depletion (% of GNI)	0.0	9.8	6.7
Mineral depletion (% of GNI)	0.0	0.4	0.4
Net forest depletion (% of GNI)	0.0	0.6	0.7
CO_2 damage (% of GNI)	0.2	0.7	1.1
Particulate emission damage (% of GNI)	0.4	0.5	0.8
Adjusted net savings (% of GNI)	−1.0	−1.9	7.3

Myanmar

Environmental strategy/action plan prepared in ..

	Country data	East Asia & Pacific	Low income
		Group data	
Population (millions)	50.0	1,870	2,343
Urban population (% of total)	30.0	40.6	30.6
GDP ($ billions)	..	2,651	1,239
GNI per capita, *World Bank Atlas* method ($)	..	1,416	507
Agriculture			
Land area (1,000 sq. km)	658	15,885	29,192
Agricultural land (% of land area)	17	51	45
Irrigated land (% of cropland)	17.0	..	23.9
Fertilizer consumption (100 grams/ha of arable land)	134	2,296	646
Population density, rural (people/sq. km of arable land)	345	559	524
Forests and biodiversity			
Forest area (% of land area)	49.0	28.4	24.8
Annual deforestation (% change, 1990–2005)	1.2	–0.2	0.5
Nationally protected areas (% of total land area)	0.3	..	7.7
Mammal species, total known	288		
Mammal species, threatened	39		
Bird species, total known	1,047		
Bird species, threatened	41		
GEF benefits index for biodiversity (0–100)	10.6		
Energy			
GDP per unit of energy use (2000 PPP $/kg oil equiv)	..	4.6	4.2
Energy use per capita (kg oil equiv)	276	1,007	501
Energy from combustible renewables & waste (% of tot.)	73.5	17.7	48.9
Energy imports, net (% of energy use)	–34	–2	–4
Electric power consumption per capita (kWh)	101	1,184	358
Electricity generated by coal (% of total)	..	69.4	46.3
Emissions and pollution			
CO_2 emissions per unit of GDP (kg/2000 PPP $ of GDP)	..	0.5	0.4
CO_2 emissions per capita (metric tons)	0.2	2.4	0.8
Particulate matter (urban-pop.-weighted avg., µg/cu. m)	75	80	89
Passenger cars (per 1,000 people)	..	12	6
Water and sanitation			
Internal freshwater resources per capita (cu. m)	17,611	5,062	3,456
Freshwater withdrawal			
Total (% of internal resources)	3.8	10.2	15.5
Agriculture (% of total freshwater withdrawal)	98	74	88
Access to improved water source (% of total population)	80	78	75
Rural (% of rural population)	74	69	69
Urban (% of urban population)	95	92	89
Access to improved sanitation (% of total population)	73	49	36
Rural (% of rural population)	63	35	24
Urban (% of urban population)	96	72	61
Environment and health			
ARI prevalence (% of children under age 5)	2.0		
Diarrhea prevalence (% of children under age 5)	..		
Under-five mortality rate (per 1,000 live births)	106	37	122
National accounting aggregates, 2004			
Gross savings (% of GNI)	..	39.1	22.7
Consumption of fixed capital (% of GNI)	..	10.5	9.2
Education expenditure (% of GNI)	0.8	2.3	3.4
Energy depletion (% of GNI)	..	4.1	6.7
Mineral depletion (% of GNI)	..	0.4	0.4
Net forest depletion (% of GNI)	..	0.0	0.7
CO_2 damage (% of GNI)	..	1.2	1.1
Particulate emission damage (% of GNI)	0.6	1.2	0.8
Adjusted net savings (% of GNI)	..	23.9	7.3

Namibia

Environmental strategy/action plan prepared in **1992**

	Country data	Sub-Saharan Africa	Lower middle income
		Group data	
Population (millions)	2.0	726	2,442
Urban population (% of total)	33.0	36.4	48.7
GDP ($ billions)	5.7	523	4,165
GNI per capita, *World Bank Atlas* method ($)	2,380	601	1,686

Agriculture
Land area (1,000 sq. km)	823	23,596	38,470
Agricultural land (% of land area)	47	44	43
Irrigated land (% of cropland)	1.0	3.6	23.1
Fertilizer consumption (100 grams/ha of arable land)	4	136	1,530
Population density, rural (people/sq. km of arable land)	165	355	523

Forests and biodiversity
Forest area (% of land area)	9.3	26.5	30.7
Annual deforestation (% change, 1990–2005)	0.8	0.6	0.1
Nationally protected areas (% of total land area)	13.6	8.7	7.7
Mammal species, total known	192		
Mammal species, threatened	10		
Bird species, total known	619		
Bird species, threatened	18		
GEF benefits index for biodiversity (0–100)	5.9		

Energy
GDP per unit of energy use (2000 PPP $/kg oil equiv)	9.9	2.8	4.6
Energy use per capita (kg oil equiv)	635	681	1,090
Energy from combustible renewables & waste (% of tot.)	14.5	57.4	14.6
Energy imports, net (% of energy use)	76	−59	−14
Electric power consumption per capita (kWh)	1,277	513	1,329
Electricity generated by coal (% of total)	0.4	68.0	49.4

Emissions and pollution
CO_2 emissions per unit of GDP (kg/2000 PPP $ of GDP)	0.2	0.4	0.5
CO_2 emissions per capita (metric tons)	1.1	0.7	2.6
Particulate matter (urban-pop.-weighted avg., μg/cu. m)	50	73	70
Passenger cars (per 1,000 people)	42	..	29

Water and sanitation
Internal freshwater resources per capita (cu. m)	3,066	5,353	7,295
Freshwater withdrawal			
Total (% of internal resources)	4.9	3.1	7.7
Agriculture (% of total freshwater withdrawal)	71	87	75
Access to improved water source (% of total population)	80	58	81
Rural (% of rural population)	72	45	70
Urban (% of urban population)	98	82	93
Access to improved sanitation (% of total population)	30	36	57
Rural (% of rural population)	14	26	39
Urban (% of urban population)	66	55	78

Environment and health
ARI prevalence (% of children under age 5)	..		
Diarrhea prevalence (% of children under age 5)	..		
Under-five mortality rate (per 1,000 live births)	63	168	40

National accounting aggregates, 2004
Gross savings (% of GNI)	39.2	17.1	32.1
Consumption of fixed capital (% of GNI)	11.1	10.9	10.8
Education expenditure (% of GNI)	7.3	3.9	2.9
Energy depletion (% of GNI)	0.0	9.8	6.5
Mineral depletion (% of GNI)	0.6	0.4	0.5
Net forest depletion (% of GNI)	0.0	0.6	0.0
CO_2 damage (% of GNI)	0.3	0.7	1.1
Particulate emission damage (% of GNI)	0.2	0.5	1.0
Adjusted net savings (% of GNI)	34.3	−1.9	15.1

Nepal

Environmental strategy/action plan prepared in **1993**

	Country data	Group data South Asia	Low income
Population (millions)	26.6	1,447	2,343
Urban population (% of total)	15.4	28.3	30.6
GDP ($ billions)	6.7	880	1,239
GNI per capita, *World Bank Atlas* method ($)	250	594	507
Agriculture			
Land area (1,000 sq. km)	143	4,781	29,192
Agricultural land (% of land area)	30	54	45
Irrigated land (% of cropland)	47.0	39.6	23.9
Fertilizer consumption (100 grams/ha of arable land)	377	1,040	646
Population density, rural (people/sq. km of arable land)	937	586	524
Forests and biodiversity			
Forest area (% of land area)	25.4	16.8	24.8
Annual deforestation (% change, 1990–2005)	1.6	–0.2	0.5
Nationally protected areas (% of total land area)	8.9	4.8	7.7
Mammal species, total known	203		
Mammal species, threatened	29		
Bird species, total known	..		
Bird species, threatened	31		
GEF benefits index for biodiversity (0–100)	2.2		
Energy			
GDP per unit of energy use (2000 PPP $/kg oil equiv)	4.0	5.3	4.2
Energy use per capita (kg oil equiv)	336	474	501
Energy from combustible renewables & waste (% of tot.)	86.8	38.8	48.9
Energy imports, net (% of energy use)	11	19	–4
Electric power consumption per capita (kWh)	68	394	358
Electricity generated by coal (% of total)	..	58.2	46.3
Emissions and pollution			
CO_2 emissions per unit of GDP (kg/2000 PPP $ of GDP)	0.1	0.4	0.4
CO_2 emissions per capita (metric tons)	0.2	1.0	0.8
Particulate matter (urban-pop.-weighted avg., µg/cu. m)	43	99	89
Passenger cars (per 1,000 people)	..	6	6
Water and sanitation			
Internal freshwater resources per capita (cu. m)	7,454	1,255	3,456
Freshwater withdrawal			
Total (% of internal resources)	5.1	51.8	15.5
Agriculture (% of total freshwater withdrawal)	96	90	88
Access to improved water source (% of total population)	84	84	75
Rural (% of rural population)	82	80	69
Urban (% of urban population)	93	94	89
Access to improved sanitation (% of total population)	27	35	36
Rural (% of rural population)	20	23	24
Urban (% of urban population)	68	64	61
Environment and health			
ARI prevalence (% of children under age 5)	32.0		
Diarrhea prevalence (% of children under age 5)	..		
Under-five mortality rate (per 1,000 live births)	76	92	122
National accounting aggregates, 2004			
Gross savings (% of GNI)	26.9	23.6	22.7
Consumption of fixed capital (% of GNI)	8.1	9.1	9.2
Education expenditure (% of GNI)	2.6	3.6	3.4
Energy depletion (% of GNI)	0.0	2.7	6.7
Mineral depletion (% of GNI)	0.0	0.3	0.4
Net forest depletion (% of GNI)	2.8	0.7	0.7
CO_2 damage (% of GNI)	0.4	1.2	1.1
Particulate emission damage (% of GNI)	0.1	0.8	0.8
Adjusted net savings (% of GNI)	18.2	12.4	7.3

Netherlands

Environmental strategy/action plan prepared in **1994**

	Country data	Group data — High income
Population (millions)	16.3	1,004
Urban population (% of total)	66.3	78.5
GDP ($ billions)	579.0	32,900
GNI per capita, *World Bank Atlas* method ($)	32,130	32,112
Agriculture		
Land area (1,000 sq. km)	34	33,018
Agricultural land (% of land area)	57	38
Irrigated land (% of cropland)	59.9	11.9
Fertilizer consumption (100 grams/ha of arable land)	3,668	1,205
Population density, rural (people/sq. km of arable land)	608	331
Forests and biodiversity		
Forest area (% of land area)	10.8	29.3
Annual deforestation (% change, 1990–2005)	–0.4	–0.1
Nationally protected areas (% of total land area)	14.2	..
Mammal species, total known	95	
Mammal species, threatened	9	
Bird species, total known	444	
Bird species, threatened	11	
GEF benefits index for biodiversity (0–100)	0.1	
Energy		
GDP per unit of energy use (2000 PPP $/kg oil equiv)	5.8	5.2
Energy use per capita (kg oil equiv)	4,982	5,410
Energy from combustible renewables & waste (% of tot.)	2.4	3.0
Energy imports, net (% of energy use)	28	19
Electric power consumption per capita (kWh)	6,748	9,503
Electricity generated by coal (% of total)	28.4	38.2
Emissions and pollution		
CO_2 emissions per unit of GDP (kg/2000 PPP $ of GDP)	0.3	0.5
CO_2 emissions per capita (metric tons)	9.3	12.8
Particulate matter (urban-pop.-weighted avg., µg/cu. m)	40	29
Passenger cars (per 1,000 people)	383	433
Water and sanitation		
Internal freshwater resources per capita (cu. m)	676	9,703
Freshwater withdrawal		
Total (% of internal resources)	72.2	10.4
Agriculture (% of total freshwater withdrawal)	34	42
Access to improved water source (% of total population)	100	99
Rural (% of rural population)	99	98
Urban (% of urban population)	100	100
Access to improved sanitation (% of total population)	100	..
Rural (% of rural population)	100	..
Urban (% of urban population)	100	..
Environment and health		
ARI prevalence (% of children under age 5)	..	
Diarrhea prevalence (% of children under age 5)	..	
Under-five mortality rate (per 1,000 live births)	6	7
National accounting aggregates, 2004		
Gross savings (% of GNI)	23.6	19.4
Consumption of fixed capital (% of GNI)	16.0	13.2
Education expenditure (% of GNI)	4.9	4.6
Energy depletion (% of GNI)	1.0	1.4
Mineral depletion (% of GNI)	0.0	0.0
Net forest depletion (% of GNI)	0.0	0.0
CO_2 damage (% of GNI)	0.2	0.3
Particulate emission damage (% of GNI)	0.7	0.4
Adjusted net savings (% of GNI)	10.6	8.7

Netherlands Antilles

Environmental strategy/action plan prepared in ..

	Country data	Group data High income
Population (millions)	0.2	1,004
Urban population (% of total)	69.9	78.5
GDP ($ billions)	..	32,900
GNI per capita, *World Bank Atlas* method ($)	..	32,112

Agriculture
Land area (1,000 sq. km)	1	33,018
Agricultural land (% of land area)	10	38
Irrigated land (% of cropland)	..	11.9
Fertilizer consumption (100 grams/ha of arable land)	..	1,205
Population density, rural (people/sq. km of arable land)	676	331

Forests and biodiversity
Forest area (% of land area)	1.3	29.3
Annual deforestation (% change, 1990–2005)	0.0	–0.1
Nationally protected areas (% of total land area)	..	..
Mammal species, total known	41	
Mammal species, threatened	3	
Bird species, total known	259	
Bird species, threatened	4	
GEF benefits index for biodiversity (0–100)	0.2	

Energy
GDP per unit of energy use (2000 PPP $/kg oil equiv)	..	5.2
Energy use per capita (kg oil equiv)	9,210	5,410
Energy from combustible renewables & waste (% of tot.)	..	3.0
Energy imports, net (% of energy use)	..	19
Electric power consumption per capita (kWh)	5,251	9,503
Electricity generated by coal (% of total)	..	38.2

Emissions and pollution
CO_2 emissions per unit of GDP (kg/2000 PPP $ of GDP)	..	0.5
CO_2 emissions per capita (metric tons)	27.8	12.8
Particulate matter (urban-pop.-weighted avg., µg/cu. m)	30	29
Passenger cars (per 1,000 people)	303	433

Water and sanitation
Internal freshwater resources per capita (cu. m)	..	9,703
Freshwater withdrawal		
Total (% of internal resources)	..	10.4
Agriculture (% of total freshwater withdrawal)	..	42
Access to improved water source (% of total population)	..	99
Rural (% of rural population)	..	98
Urban (% of urban population)	..	100
Access to improved sanitation (% of total population)	..	..
Rural (% of rural population)	..	..
Urban (% of urban population)	..	..

Environment and health
ARI prevalence (% of children under age 5)	..	
Diarrhea prevalence (% of children under age 5)	..	
Under-five mortality rate (per 1,000 live births)	..	7

National accounting aggregates, 2004
Gross savings (% of GNI)	..	19.4
Consumption of fixed capital (% of GNI)	..	13.2
Education expenditure (% of GNI)	..	4.6
Energy depletion (% of GNI)	..	1.4
Mineral depletion (% of GNI)	..	0.0
Net forest depletion (% of GNI)	..	0.0
CO_2 damage (% of GNI)	..	0.3
Particulate emission damage (% of GNI)	..	0.4
Adjusted net savings (% of GNI)	..	8.7

New Caledonia

Environmental strategy/action plan prepared in ..

	Country data	Group data – High income
Population (millions)	0.2	1,004
Urban population (% of total)	61.5	78.5
GDP ($ billions)	..	32,900
GNI per capita, *World Bank Atlas* method ($)	..	32,112
Agriculture		
Land area (1,000 sq. km)	18	33,018
Agricultural land (% of land area)	14	38
Irrigated land (% of cropland)	100.0	11.9
Fertilizer consumption (100 grams/ha of arable land)	1,800	1,205
Population density, rural (people/sq. km of arable land)	1,457	331
Forests and biodiversity		
Forest area (% of land area)	39.2	29.3
Annual deforestation (% change, 1990–2005)	0.0	–0.1
Nationally protected areas (% of total land area)	..	..
Mammal species, total known	28	
Mammal species, threatened	6	
Bird species, total known	150	
Bird species, threatened	16	
GEF benefits index for biodiversity (0–100)	8.9	
Energy		
GDP per unit of energy use (2000 PPP $/kg oil equiv)	..	5.2
Energy use per capita (kg oil equiv)	..	5,410
Energy from combustible renewables & waste (% of tot.)	..	3.0
Energy imports, net (% of energy use)	..	19
Electric power consumption per capita (kWh)	..	9,503
Electricity generated by coal (% of total)	..	38.2
Emissions and pollution		
CO_2 emissions per unit of GDP (kg/2000 PPP $ of GDP)	0.4	0.5
CO_2 emissions per capita (metric tons)	8.2	12.8
Particulate matter (urban-pop.-weighted avg., µg/cu. m)	20	29
Passenger cars (per 1,000 people)	..	433
Water and sanitation		
Internal freshwater resources per capita (cu. m)	..	9,703
Freshwater withdrawal		
Total (% of internal resources)	..	10.4
Agriculture (% of total freshwater withdrawal)	..	42
Access to improved water source (% of total population)	..	99
Rural (% of rural population)	..	98
Urban (% of urban population)	..	100
Access to improved sanitation (% of total population)	..	..
Rural (% of rural population)	..	..
Urban (% of urban population)	..	..
Environment and health		
ARI prevalence (% of children under age 5)	..	
Diarrhea prevalence (% of children under age 5)	..	
Under-five mortality rate (per 1,000 live births)	..	7
National accounting aggregates, 2004		
Gross savings (% of GNI)	..	19.4
Consumption of fixed capital (% of GNI)	..	13.2
Education expenditure (% of GNI)	..	4.6
Energy depletion (% of GNI)	..	1.4
Mineral depletion (% of GNI)	..	0.0
Net forest depletion (% of GNI)	..	0.0
CO_2 damage (% of GNI)	..	0.3
Particulate emission damage (% of GNI)	..	0.4
Adjusted net savings (% of GNI)	..	8.7

New Zealand

Environmental strategy/action plan prepared in **1994**

	Country data	Group data — High income
Population (millions)	4.1	1,004
Urban population (% of total)	85.9	78.5
GDP ($ billions)	98.9	32,900
GNI per capita, *World Bank Atlas* method ($)	19,990	32,112
Agriculture		
Land area (1,000 sq. km)	268	33,018
Agricultural land (% of land area)	64	38
Irrigated land (% of cropland)	8.5	11.9
Fertilizer consumption (100 grams/ha of arable land)	5,686	1,205
Population density, rural (people/sq. km of arable land)	38	331
Forests and biodiversity		
Forest area (% of land area)	31.0	29.3
Annual deforestation (% change, 1990–2005)	–0.5	–0.1
Nationally protected areas (% of total land area)	29.6	..
Mammal species, total known	73	
Mammal species, threatened	8	
Bird species, total known	351	
Bird species, threatened	74	
GEF benefits index for biodiversity (0–100)	22.3	
Energy		
GDP per unit of energy use (2000 PPP $/kg oil equiv)	4.8	5.2
Energy use per capita (kg oil equiv)	4,333	5,410
Energy from combustible renewables & waste (% of tot.)	4.8	3.0
Energy imports, net (% of energy use)	24	19
Electric power consumption per capita (kWh)	8,896	9,503
Electricity generated by coal (% of total)	8.1	38.2
Emissions and pollution		
CO_2 emissions per unit of GDP (kg/2000 PPP $ of GDP)	0.4	0.5
CO_2 emissions per capita (metric tons)	8.6	12.8
Particulate matter (urban-pop.-weighted avg., μg/cu. m)	16	29
Passenger cars (per 1,000 people)	613	433
Water and sanitation		
Internal freshwater resources per capita (cu. m)	80,522	9,703
Freshwater withdrawal		
Total (% of internal resources)	0.6	10.4
Agriculture (% of total freshwater withdrawal)	42	42
Access to improved water source (% of total population)	..	99
Rural (% of rural population)	..	98
Urban (% of urban population)	100	100
Access to improved sanitation (% of total population)	..	..
Rural (% of rural population)	..	..
Urban (% of urban population)	..	..
Environment and health		
ARI prevalence (% of children under age 5)	..	
Diarrhea prevalence (% of children under age 5)	..	
Under-five mortality rate (per 1,000 live births)	7	7
National accounting aggregates, 2004		
Gross savings (% of GNI)	22.6	19.4
Consumption of fixed capital (% of GNI)	14.8	13.2
Education expenditure (% of GNI)	7.1	4.6
Energy depletion (% of GNI)	0.8	1.4
Mineral depletion (% of GNI)	0.1	0.0
Net forest depletion (% of GNI)	0.0	0.0
CO_2 damage (% of GNI)	0.3	0.3
Particulate emission damage (% of GNI)	0.0	0.4
Adjusted net savings (% of GNI)	13.7	8.7

Nicaragua

Environmental strategy/action plan prepared in **1994**

	Country data	Latin America & Caribbean	Low income
		Group data	
Population (millions)	5.4	546	2,343
Urban population (% of total)	57.7	77.1	30.6
GDP ($ billions)	4.6	2,022	1,239
GNI per capita, *World Bank Atlas* method ($)	830	3,576	507
Agriculture			
Land area (1,000 sq. km)	121	20,057	29,192
Agricultural land (% of land area)	57	36	45
Irrigated land (% of cropland)	2.8	11.4	23.9
Fertilizer consumption (100 grams/ha of arable land)	279	923	646
Population density, rural (people/sq. km of arable land)	117	212	524
Forests and biodiversity			
Forest area (% of land area)	42.7	45.6	24.8
Annual deforestation (% change, 1990–2005)	1.4	0.4	0.5
Nationally protected areas (% of total land area)	17.8	11.1	7.7
Mammal species, total known	181		
Mammal species, threatened	6		
Bird species, total known	632		
Bird species, threatened	8		
GEF benefits index for biodiversity (0–100)	3.6		
Energy			
GDP per unit of energy use (2000 PPP $/kg oil equiv)	5.5	6.2	4.2
Energy use per capita (kg oil equiv)	588	1,148	501
Energy from combustible renewables & waste (% of tot.)	49.9	15.0	48.9
Energy imports, net (% of energy use)	42	−40	−4
Electric power consumption per capita (kWh)	361	1,615	358
Electricity generated by coal (% of total)	..	5.4	46.3
Emissions and pollution			
CO_2 emissions per unit of GDP (kg/2000 PPP $ of GDP)	0.2	0.3	0.4
CO_2 emissions per capita (metric tons)	0.7	2.4	0.8
Particulate matter (urban-pop.-weighted avg., µg/cu. m)	32	43	89
Passenger cars (per 1,000 people)	16	108	6
Water and sanitation			
Internal freshwater resources per capita (cu. m)	35,293	24,619	3,456
Freshwater withdrawal			
Total (% of internal resources)	0.7	2.0	15.5
Agriculture (% of total freshwater withdrawal)	83	71	88
Access to improved water source (% of total population)	81	89	75
Rural (% of rural population)	65	69	69
Urban (% of urban population)	93	96	89
Access to improved sanitation (% of total population)	66	75	36
Rural (% of rural population)	51	44	24
Urban (% of urban population)	78	84	61
Environment and health			
ARI prevalence (% of children under age 5)	..		
Diarrhea prevalence (% of children under age 5)	14.0		
Under-five mortality rate (per 1,000 live births)	38	31	122
National accounting aggregates, 2004			
Gross savings (% of GNI)	10.8	22.7	22.7
Consumption of fixed capital (% of GNI)	10.1	12.1	9.2
Education expenditure (% of GNI)	2.9	4.4	3.4
Energy depletion (% of GNI)	0.0	7.2	6.7
Mineral depletion (% of GNI)	0.0	1.1	0.4
Net forest depletion (% of GNI)	1.0	0.0	0.7
CO_2 damage (% of GNI)	0.6	0.5	1.1
Particulate emission damage (% of GNI)	0.1	0.6	0.8
Adjusted net savings (% of GNI)	1.8	5.6	7.3

Niger

Environmental strategy/action plan prepared in ..

	Country data	Group data	
		Sub-Saharan Africa	Low income
Population (millions)	13.5	726	2,343
Urban population (% of total)	22.7	36.4	30.6
GDP ($ billions)	3.1	523	1,239
GNI per capita, *World Bank Atlas* method ($)	210	601	507
Agriculture			
Land area (1,000 sq. km)	1,267	23,596	29,192
Agricultural land (% of land area)	30	44	45
Irrigated land (% of cropland)	0.5	3.6	23.9
Fertilizer consumption (100 grams/ha of arable land)	3	136	646
Population density, rural (people/sq. km of arable land)	70	355	524
Forests and biodiversity			
Forest area (% of land area)	1.0	26.5	24.8
Annual deforestation (% change, 1990–2005)	2.3	0.6	0.5
Nationally protected areas (% of total land area)	7.7	8.7	7.7
Mammal species, total known	123		
Mammal species, threatened	10		
Bird species, total known	493		
Bird species, threatened	2		
GEF benefits index for biodiversity (0–100)	0.9		
Energy			
GDP per unit of energy use (2000 PPP $/kg oil equiv)	..	2.8	4.2
Energy use per capita (kg oil equiv)	..	681	501
Energy from combustible renewables & waste (% of tot.)	..	57.4	48.9
Energy imports, net (% of energy use)	..	−59	−4
Electric power consumption per capita (kWh)	..	513	358
Electricity generated by coal (% of total)	..	68.0	46.3
Emissions and pollution			
CO_2 emissions per unit of GDP (kg/2000 PPP $ of GDP)	0.1	0.4	0.4
CO_2 emissions per capita (metric tons)	0.1	0.7	0.8
Particulate matter (urban-pop.-weighted avg., μg/cu. m)	86	73	89
Passenger cars (per 1,000 people)	..	..	6
Water and sanitation			
Internal freshwater resources per capita (cu. m)	259	5,353	3,456
Freshwater withdrawal			
Total (% of internal resources)	62.3	3.1	15.5
Agriculture (% of total freshwater withdrawal)	95	87	88
Access to improved water source (% of total population)	46	58	75
Rural (% of rural population)	36	45	69
Urban (% of urban population)	80	82	89
Access to improved sanitation (% of total population)	12	36	36
Rural (% of rural population)	4	26	24
Urban (% of urban population)	43	55	61
Environment and health			
ARI prevalence (% of children under age 5)	11.8		
Diarrhea prevalence (% of children under age 5)	40.0		
Under-five mortality rate (per 1,000 live births)	259	168	122
National accounting aggregates, 2004			
Gross savings (% of GNI)	8.0	17.1	22.7
Consumption of fixed capital (% of GNI)	7.9	10.9	9.2
Education expenditure (% of GNI)	2.3	3.9	3.4
Energy depletion (% of GNI)	0.0	9.8	6.7
Mineral depletion (% of GNI)	0.0	0.4	0.4
Net forest depletion (% of GNI)	3.0	0.6	0.7
CO_2 damage (% of GNI)	0.3	0.7	1.1
Particulate emission damage (% of GNI)	0.5	0.5	0.8
Adjusted net savings (% of GNI)	−1.4	−1.9	7.3

Nigeria

Environmental strategy/action plan prepared in **1990**

	Country data	Group data Sub-Saharan Africa	Low income
Population (millions)	128.7	726	2,343
Urban population (% of total)	47.5	36.4	30.6
GDP ($ billions)	72.1	523	1,239
GNI per capita, *World Bank Atlas* method ($)	430	601	507
Agriculture			
Land area (1,000 sq. km)	911	23,596	29,192
Agricultural land (% of land area)	80	44	45
Irrigated land (% of cropland)	0.8	3.6	23.9
Fertilizer consumption (100 grams/ha of arable land)	55	136	646
Population density, rural (people/sq. km of arable land)	220	355	524
Forests and biodiversity			
Forest area (% of land area)	12.2	26.5	24.8
Annual deforestation (% change, 1990–2005)	2.4	0.6	0.5
Nationally protected areas (% of total land area)	3.3	8.7	7.7
Mammal species, total known	290		
Mammal species, threatened	25		
Bird species, total known	899		
Bird species, threatened	9		
GEF benefits index for biodiversity (0–100)	6.6		
Energy			
GDP per unit of energy use (2000 PPP $/kg oil equiv)	1.3	2.8	4.2
Energy use per capita (kg oil equiv)	777	681	501
Energy from combustible renewables & waste (% of tot.)	79.4	57.4	48.9
Energy imports, net (% of energy use)	–119	–59	–4
Electric power consumption per capita (kWh)	107	513	358
Electricity generated by coal (% of total)	..	68.0	46.3
Emissions and pollution			
CO_2 emissions per unit of GDP (kg/2000 PPP $ of GDP)	0.5	0.4	0.4
CO_2 emissions per capita (metric tons)	0.4	0.7	0.8
Particulate matter (urban-pop.-weighted avg., µg/cu. m)	95	73	89
Passenger cars (per 1,000 people)	..	..	6
Water and sanitation			
Internal freshwater resources per capita (cu. m)	1,717	5,353	3,456
Freshwater withdrawal			
Total (% of internal resources)	3.6	3.1	15.5
Agriculture (% of total freshwater withdrawal)	69	87	88
Access to improved water source (% of total population)	60	58	75
Rural (% of rural population)	49	45	69
Urban (% of urban population)	72	82	89
Access to improved sanitation (% of total population)	38	36	36
Rural (% of rural population)	30	26	24
Urban (% of urban population)	48	55	61
Environment and health			
ARI prevalence (% of children under age 5)	..		
Diarrhea prevalence (% of children under age 5)	15.3		
Under-five mortality rate (per 1,000 live births)	197	168	122
National accounting aggregates, 2004			
Gross savings (% of GNI)	32.6	17.1	22.7
Consumption of fixed capital (% of GNI)	10.9	10.9	9.2
Education expenditure (% of GNI)	0.9	3.9	3.4
Energy depletion (% of GNI)	49.1	9.8	6.7
Mineral depletion (% of GNI)	0.0	0.4	0.4
Net forest depletion (% of GNI)	0.1	0.6	0.7
CO_2 damage (% of GNI)	0.6	0.7	1.1
Particulate emission damage (% of GNI)	1.0	0.5	0.8
Adjusted net savings (% of GNI)	–28.2	–1.9	7.3

Northern Mariana Islands

Environmental strategy/action plan prepared in ..

	Country data	Group data East Asia & Pacific	Group data Upper middle income
Population (millions)	0.1	1,870	576
Urban population (% of total)	94.4	40.6	72.3
GDP ($ billions)	..	2,651	2,992
GNI per capita, World Bank Atlas method ($)	..	1,416	4,769

Agriculture

Land area (1,000 sq. km)	..	15,885	28,983
Agricultural land (% of land area)	..	51	26
Irrigated land (% of cropland)	..	..	8.7
Fertilizer consumption (100 grams/ha of arable land)	..	2,296	469
Population density, rural (people/sq. km of arable land)	..	559	131

Forests and biodiversity

Forest area (% of land area)	..	28.4	37.3
Annual deforestation (% change, 1990–2005)	0.4	−0.2	0.1
Nationally protected areas (% of total land area)	..	..	..
Mammal species, total known	6		
Mammal species, threatened	2		
Bird species, total known	93		
Bird species, threatened	13		
GEF benefits index for biodiversity (0–100)	1.7		

Energy

GDP per unit of energy use (2000 PPP $/kg oil equiv)	..	4.6	3.5
Energy use per capita (kg oil equiv)	..	1,007	2,574
Energy from combustible renewables & waste (% of tot.)	..	17.7	3.9
Energy imports, net (% of energy use)	..	−2	−51
Electric power consumption per capita (kWh)	..	1,184	3,378
Electricity generated by coal (% of total)	..	69.4	31.0

Emissions and pollution

CO_2 emissions per unit of GDP (kg/2000 PPP $ of GDP)	..	0.5	0.7
CO_2 emissions per capita (metric tons)	..	2.4	6.2
Particulate matter (urban-pop.-weighted avg., µg/cu. m)	..	80	40
Passenger cars (per 1,000 people)	..	12	143

Water and sanitation

Internal freshwater resources per capita (cu. m)	..	5,062	14,190
Freshwater withdrawal			
Total (% of internal resources)	..	10.2	3.8
Agriculture (% of total freshwater withdrawal)	..	74	53
Access to improved water source (% of total population)	98	78	93
Rural (% of rural population)	97	69	82
Urban (% of urban population)	98	92	97
Access to improved sanitation (% of total population)	94	49	81
Rural (% of rural population)	96	35	61
Urban (% of urban population)	94	72	91

Environment and health

ARI prevalence (% of children under age 5)	..		
Diarrhea prevalence (% of children under age 5)	..		
Under-five mortality rate (per 1,000 live births)	..	37	28

National accounting aggregates, 2004

Gross savings (% of GNI)	..	39.1	23.1
Consumption of fixed capital (% of GNI)	..	10.5	11.5
Education expenditure (% of GNI)	..	2.3	4.5
Energy depletion (% of GNI)	..	4.1	11.2
Mineral depletion (% of GNI)	..	0.4	0.6
Net forest depletion (% of GNI)	..	0.0	0.0
CO_2 damage (% of GNI)	..	1.2	0.9
Particulate emission damage (% of GNI)	..	1.2	0.7
Adjusted net savings (% of GNI)	..	23.9	2.6

Norway

Environmental strategy/action plan prepared in ..

	Country data	Group data High income
Population (millions)	4.6	1,004
Urban population (% of total)	79.5	78.5
GDP ($ billions)	250.1	32,900
GNI per capita, *World Bank Atlas* method ($)	51,810	32,112

Agriculture		
Land area (1,000 sq. km)	306	33,018
Agricultural land (% of land area)	3	38
Irrigated land (% of cropland)	..	11.9
Fertilizer consumption (100 grams/ha of arable land)	2,113	1,205
Population density, rural (people/sq. km of arable land)	112	331

Forests and biodiversity		
Forest area (% of land area)	30.7	29.3
Annual deforestation (% change, 1990–2005)	–0.2	–0.1
Nationally protected areas (% of total land area)	6.8	..
Mammal species, total known	83	
Mammal species, threatened	9	
Bird species, total known	442	
Bird species, threatened	6	
GEF benefits index for biodiversity (0–100)	1.6	

Energy		
GDP per unit of energy use (2000 PPP $/kg oil equiv)	6.8	5.2
Energy use per capita (kg oil equiv)	5,100	5,410
Energy from combustible renewables & waste (% of tot.)	6.5	3.0
Energy imports, net (% of energy use)	–899	19
Electric power consumption per capita (kWh)	23,169	9,503
Electricity generated by coal (% of total)	0.1	38.2

Emissions and pollution		
CO_2 emissions per unit of GDP (kg/2000 PPP $ of GDP)	0.3	0.5
CO_2 emissions per capita (metric tons)	13.9	12.8
Particulate matter (urban-pop.-weighted avg., µg/cu. m)	18	29
Passenger cars (per 1,000 people)	419	433

Water and sanitation		
Internal freshwater resources per capita (cu. m)	83,205	9,703
Freshwater withdrawal		
Total (% of internal resources)	0.6	10.4
Agriculture (% of total freshwater withdrawal)	11	42
Access to improved water source (% of total population)	100	99
Rural (% of rural population)	100	98
Urban (% of urban population)	100	100
Access to improved sanitation (% of total population)	..	..
Rural (% of rural population)	..	..
Urban (% of urban population)	..	..

Environment and health		
ARI prevalence (% of children under age 5)	..	
Diarrhea prevalence (% of children under age 5)	..	
Under-five mortality rate (per 1,000 live births)	4	7

National accounting aggregates, 2004		
Gross savings (% of GNI)	32.5	19.4
Consumption of fixed capital (% of GNI)	13.7	13.2
Education expenditure (% of GNI)	7.0	4.6
Energy depletion (% of GNI)	10.9	1.4
Mineral depletion (% of GNI)	0.0	0.0
Net forest depletion (% of GNI)	0.0	0.0
CO_2 damage (% of GNI)	0.1	0.3
Particulate emission damage (% of GNI)	0.1	0.4
Adjusted net savings (% of GNI)	14.8	8.7

Oman

Environmental strategy/action plan prepared in ..

	Country data	Middle East & North Africa	Upper middle income
		Group data	
Population (millions)	2.5	300	576
Urban population (% of total)	78.1	56.3	72.3
GDP ($ billions)	24.3	547	2,992
GNI per capita, *World Bank Atlas* method ($)	9,070	1,972	4,769
Agriculture			
Land area (1,000 sq. km)	310	8,955	28,983
Agricultural land (% of land area)	3	23	26
Irrigated land (% of cropland)	90.0	32.5	8.7
Fertilizer consumption (100 grams/ha of arable land)	3,219	842	469
Population density, rural (people/sq. km of arable land)	1,522	670	131
Forests and biodiversity			
Forest area (% of land area)	0.0	2.4	37.3
Annual deforestation (% change, 1990–2005)	0.0	–0.5	0.1
Nationally protected areas (% of total land area)	14.0	4.2	..
Mammal species, total known	74		
Mammal species, threatened	12		
Bird species, total known	483		
Bird species, threatened	14		
GEF benefits index for biodiversity (0–100)	4.4		
Energy			
GDP per unit of energy use (2000 PPP $/kg oil equiv)	2.8	4.2	3.5
Energy use per capita (kg oil equiv)	4,975	1,144	2,574
Energy from combustible renewables & waste (% of tot.)	..	1.3	3.9
Energy imports, net (% of energy use)	–379	–129	–51
Electric power consumption per capita (kWh)	3,505	1,212	3,378
Electricity generated by coal (% of total)	..	3.0	31.0
Emissions and pollution			
CO_2 emissions per unit of GDP (kg/2000 PPP $ of GDP)	0.8	0.7	0.7
CO_2 emissions per capita (metric tons)	12.1	3.2	6.2
Particulate matter (urban-pop.-weighted avg., µg/cu. m)	124	90	40
Passenger cars (per 1,000 people)	..	..	143
Water and sanitation			
Internal freshwater resources per capita (cu. m)	389	761	14,190
Freshwater withdrawal			
Total (% of internal resources)	138.1	105.0	3.8
Agriculture (% of total freshwater withdrawal)	90	89	53
Access to improved water source (% of total population)	79	88	93
Rural (% of rural population)	72	79	82
Urban (% of urban population)	81	95	97
Access to improved sanitation (% of total population)	89	75	81
Rural (% of rural population)	61	56	61
Urban (% of urban population)	97	89	91
Environment and health			
ARI prevalence (% of children under age 5)	..		
Diarrhea prevalence (% of children under age 5)	..		
Under-five mortality rate (per 1,000 live births)	13	55	28
National accounting aggregates, 2004			
Gross savings (% of GNI)	29.4	30.0	23.1
Consumption of fixed capital (% of GNI)	13.4	11.2	11.5
Education expenditure (% of GNI)	4.2	4.5	4.5
Energy depletion (% of GNI)	58.8	27.3	11.2
Mineral depletion (% of GNI)	0.0	0.1	0.6
Net forest depletion (% of GNI)	0.0	0.1	0.0
CO_2 damage (% of GNI)	0.8	1.2	0.9
Particulate emission damage (% of GNI)	1.1	0.9	0.7
Adjusted net savings (% of GNI)	–40.6	–6.2	2.6

Pakistan

Environmental strategy/action plan prepared in **1994**

	Country data	South Asia	Low income
		Group data	
Population (millions)	152.1	1,447	2,343
Urban population (% of total)	34.5	28.3	30.6
GDP ($ billions)	96.1	880	1,239
GNI per capita, *World Bank Atlas* method ($)	600	594	507
Agriculture			
Land area (1,000 sq. km)	771	4,781	29,192
Agricultural land (% of land area)	33	54	45
Irrigated land (% of cropland)	90.6	39.6	23.9
Fertilizer consumption (100 grams/ha of arable land)	1,371	1,040	646
Population density, rural (people/sq. km of arable land)	503	586	524
Forests and biodiversity			
Forest area (% of land area)	2.5	16.8	24.8
Annual deforestation (% change, 1990–2005)	1.6	–0.2	0.5
Nationally protected areas (% of total land area)	4.9	4.8	7.7
Mammal species, total known	195		
Mammal species, threatened	17		
Bird species, total known	625		
Bird species, threatened	30		
GEF benefits index for biodiversity (0–100)	5.1		
Energy			
GDP per unit of energy use (2000 PPP $/kg oil equiv)	4.2	5.3	4.2
Energy use per capita (kg oil equiv)	467	474	501
Energy from combustible renewables & waste (% of tot.)	37.3	38.8	48.9
Energy imports, net (% of energy use)	20	19	–4
Electric power consumption per capita (kWh)	408	394	358
Electricity generated by coal (% of total)	0.2	58.2	46.3
Emissions and pollution			
CO_2 emissions per unit of GDP (kg/2000 PPP $ of GDP)	0.4	0.4	0.4
CO_2 emissions per capita (metric tons)	0.7	1.0	0.8
Particulate matter (urban-pop.-weighted avg., μg/cu. m)	165	99	89
Passenger cars (per 1,000 people)	7	6	6
Water and sanitation			
Internal freshwater resources per capita (cu. m)	345	1,255	3,456
Freshwater withdrawal			
Total (% of internal resources)	323.3	51.8	15.5
Agriculture (% of total freshwater withdrawal)	96	90	88
Access to improved water source (% of total population)	90	84	75
Rural (% of rural population)	87	80	69
Urban (% of urban population)	95	94	89
Access to improved sanitation (% of total population)	54	35	36
Rural (% of rural population)	35	23	24
Urban (% of urban population)	92	64	61
Environment and health			
ARI prevalence (% of children under age 5)	..		
Diarrhea prevalence (% of children under age 5)	..		
Under-five mortality rate (per 1,000 live births)	101	92	122
National accounting aggregates, 2004			
Gross savings (% of GNI)	23.6	23.6	22.7
Consumption of fixed capital (% of GNI)	8.2	9.1	9.2
Education expenditure (% of GNI)	2.3	3.6	3.4
Energy depletion (% of GNI)	5.3	2.7	6.7
Mineral depletion (% of GNI)	0.0	0.3	0.4
Net forest depletion (% of GNI)	0.5	0.7	0.7
CO_2 damage (% of GNI)	0.8	1.2	1.1
Particulate emission damage (% of GNI)	1.4	0.8	0.8
Adjusted net savings (% of GNI)	9.7	12.4	7.3

Palau

Environmental strategy/action plan prepared in ..

	Country data	Group data East Asia & Pacific	Upper middle income
Population (millions)	0.0	1,870	576
Urban population (% of total)	68.5	40.6	72.3
GDP ($ billions)	0.1	2,651	2,992
GNI per capita, *World Bank Atlas* method ($)	6,870	1,416	4,769

Agriculture
Land area (1,000 sq. km)	..	15,885	28,983
Agricultural land (% of land area)	..	51	26
Irrigated land (% of cropland)	..	..	8.7
Fertilizer consumption (100 grams/ha of arable land)	..	2,296	469
Population density, rural (people/sq. km of arable land)	..	559	131

Forests and biodiversity
Forest area (% of land area)	..	28.4	37.3
Annual deforestation (% change, 1990–2005)	–0.4	–0.2	0.1
Nationally protected areas (% of total land area)	..	..	..
Mammal species, total known	8		
Mammal species, threatened	3		
Bird species, total known	112		
Bird species, threatened	2		
GEF benefits index for biodiversity (0–100)	1.5		

Energy
GDP per unit of energy use (2000 PPP $/kg oil equiv)	..	4.6	3.5
Energy use per capita (kg oil equiv)	..	1,007	2,574
Energy from combustible renewables & waste (% of tot.)	..	17.7	3.9
Energy imports, net (% of energy use)	..	–2	–51
Electric power consumption per capita (kWh)	..	1,184	3,378
Electricity generated by coal (% of total)	..	69.4	31.0

Emissions and pollution
CO_2 emissions per unit of GDP (kg/2000 PPP $ of GDP)	..	0.5	0.7
CO_2 emissions per capita (metric tons)	..	2.4	6.2
Particulate matter (urban-pop.-weighted avg., μg/cu. m)	..	80	40
Passenger cars per 1,000 people	..	12	143

Water and sanitation
Internal freshwater resources per capita (cu. m)	..	5,062	14,190
Freshwater withdrawal			
Total (% of internal resources)	..	10.2	3.8
Agriculture (% of total freshwater withdrawal)	..	74	53
Access to improved water source (% of total population)	84	78	93
Rural (% of rural population)	94	69	82
Urban (% of urban population)	79	92	97
Access to improved sanitation (% of total population)	83	49	81
Rural (% of rural population)	52	35	61
Urban (% of urban population)	96	72	91

Environment and health
ARI prevalence (% of children under age 5)	..		
Diarrhea prevalence (% of children under age 5)	..		
Under–five mortality rate (per 1,000 live births)	27	37	28

National accounting aggregates, 2004
Gross savings (% of GNI)	..	39.1	23.1
Consumption of fixed capital (% of GNI)	12.0	10.5	11.5
Education expenditure (% of GNI)	..	2.3	4.5
Energy depletion (% of GNI)	0.0	4.1	11.2
Mineral depletion (% of GNI)	0.0	0.4	0.6
Net forest depletion (% of GNI)	..	0.0	0.0
CO_2 damage (% of GNI)	1.3	1.2	0.9
Particulate emission damage (% of GNI)	..	1.2	0.7
Adjusted net savings (% of GNI)	..	23.9	2.6

Panama

Environmental strategy/action plan prepared in **1990**

	Country data	Latin America & Caribbean	Upper middle income
		Group data	
Population (millions)	3.2	546	576
Urban population (% of total)	57.5	77.1	72.3
GDP ($ billions)	13.7	2,022	2,992
GNI per capita, *World Bank Atlas* method ($)	4,210	3,576	4,769
Agriculture			
Land area (1,000 sq. km)	74	20,057	28,983
Agricultural land (% of land area)	30	36	26
Irrigated land (% of cropland)	6.2	11.4	8.7
Fertilizer consumption (100 grams/ha of arable land)	524	923	469
Population density, rural (people/sq. km of arable land)	244	212	131
Forests and biodiversity			
Forest area (% of land area)	57.7	45.6	37.3
Annual deforestation (% change, 1990–2005)	0.1	0.4	0.1
Nationally protected areas (% of total land area)	21.7	11.1	..
Mammal species, total known	241		
Mammal species, threatened	17		
Bird species, total known	904		
Bird species, threatened	20		
GEF benefits index for biodiversity (0–100)	11.7		
Energy			
GDP per unit of energy use (2000 PPP $/kg oil equiv)	7.6	6.2	3.5
Energy use per capita (kg oil equiv)	836	1,148	2,574
Energy from combustible renewables & waste (% of tot.)	17.1	15.0	3.9
Energy imports, net (% of energy use)	74	−40	−51
Electric power consumption per capita (kWh)	1,401	1,615	3,378
Electricity generated by coal (% of total)	..	5.4	31.0
Emissions and pollution			
CO_2 emissions per unit of GDP (kg/2000 PPP $ of GDP)	0.3	0.3	0.7
CO_2 emissions per capita (metric tons)	2.0	2.4	6.2
Particulate matter (urban-pop.-weighted avg., µg/cu. m)	58	43	40
Passenger cars (per 1,000 people)	76	108	143
Water and sanitation			
Internal freshwater resources per capita (cu. m)	46,426	24,619	14,190
Freshwater withdrawal			
Total (% of internal resources)	0.6	2.0	3.8
Agriculture (% of total freshwater withdrawal)	28	71	53
Access to improved water source (% of total population)	91	89	93
Rural (% of rural population)	79	69	82
Urban (% of urban population)	99	96	97
Access to improved sanitation (% of total population)	72	75	81
Rural (% of rural population)	51	44	61
Urban (% of urban population)	89	84	91
Environment and health			
ARI prevalence (% of children under age 5)	..		
Diarrhea prevalence (% of children under age 5)	..		
Under-five mortality rate (per 1,000 live births)	24	31	28
National accounting aggregates, 2004			
Gross savings (% of GNI)	13.8	22.7	23.1
Consumption of fixed capital (% of GNI)	12.8	12.1	11.5
Education expenditure (% of GNI)	4.4	4.4	4.5
Energy depletion (% of GNI)	0.0	7.2	11.2
Mineral depletion (% of GNI)	0.0	1.1	0.6
Net forest depletion (% of GNI)	0.0	0.0	0.0
CO_2 damage (% of GNI)	0.4	0.5	0.9
Particulate emission damage (% of GNI)	0.5	0.6	0.7
Adjusted net savings (% of GNI)	4.6	5.6	2.6

Papua New Guinea

Environmental strategy/action plan prepared in **1992**

	Country data	Group data — East Asia & Pacific	Low income
Population (millions)	5.8	1,870	2,343
Urban population (% of total)	13.2	40.6	30.6
GDP ($ billions)	3.9	2,651	1,239
GNI per capita, *World Bank Atlas* method ($)	560	1,416	507
Agriculture			
Land area (1,000 sq. km)	453	15,885	29,192
Agricultural land (% of land area)	2	51	45
Irrigated land (% of cropland)	..	..	23.9
Fertilizer consumption (100 grams/ha of arable land)	536	2,296	646
Population density, rural (people/sq. km of arable land)	2,181	559	524
Forests and biodiversity			
Forest area (% of land area)	65.0	28.4	24.8
Annual deforestation (% change, 1990–2005)	0.4	–0.2	0.5
Nationally protected areas (% of total land area)	2.3	..	7.7
Mammal species, total known	260		
Mammal species, threatened	58		
Bird species, total known	720		
Bird species, threatened	33		
GEF benefits index for biodiversity (0–100)	27.7		
Energy			
GDP per unit of energy use (2000 PPP $/kg oil equiv)	..	4.6	4.2
Energy use per capita (kg oil equiv)	..	1,007	501
Energy from combustible renewables & waste (% of tot.)	..	17.7	48.9
Energy imports, net (% of energy use)	..	–2	–4
Electric power consumption per capita (kWh)	..	1,184	358
Electricity generated by coal (% of total)	..	69.4	46.3
Emissions and pollution			
CO_2 emissions per unit of GDP (kg/2000 PPP $ of GDP)	0.2	0.5	0.4
CO_2 emissions per capita (metric tons)	0.4	2.4	0.8
Particulate matter (urban-pop.-weighted avg., µg/cu. m)	11	80	89
Passenger cars (per 1,000 people)	..	12	6
Water and sanitation			
Internal freshwater resources per capita (cu. m)	138,775	5,062	3,456
Freshwater withdrawal			
Total (% of internal resources)	0.0	10.2	15.5
Agriculture (% of total freshwater withdrawal)	..	74	88
Access to improved water source (% of total population)	39	78	75
Rural (% of rural population)	32	69	69
Urban (% of urban population)	88	92	89
Access to improved sanitation (% of total population)	45	49	36
Rural (% of rural population)	41	35	24
Urban (% of urban population)	67	72	61
Environment and health			
ARI prevalence (% of children under age 5)	..		
Diarrhea prevalence (% of children under age 5)	..		
Under-five mortality rate (per 1,000 live births)	93	37	122
National accounting aggregates, 2004			
Gross savings (% of GNI)	..	39.1	22.7
Consumption of fixed capital (% of GNI)	10.4	10.5	9.2
Education expenditure (% of GNI)	..	2.3	3.4
Energy depletion (% of GNI)	10.7	4.1	6.7
Mineral depletion (% of GNI)	25.1	0.4	0.4
Net forest depletion (% of GNI)	0.0	0.0	0.7
CO_2 damage (% of GNI)	0.5	1.2	1.1
Particulate emission damage (% of GNI)	..	1.2	0.8
Adjusted net savings (% of GNI)	..	23.9	7.3

Paraguay

Environmental strategy/action plan prepared in ..

	Country data	Group data Latin America & Caribbean	Group data Lower middle income
Population (millions)	6.0	546	2,442
Urban population (% of total)	57.9	77.1	48.7
GDP ($ billions)	7.3	2,022	4,165
GNI per capita, *World Bank Atlas* method ($)	1,140	3,576	1,686
Agriculture			
Land area (1,000 sq. km)	397	20,057	38,470
Agricultural land (% of land area)	63	36	43
Irrigated land (% of cropland)	2.1	11.4	23.1
Fertilizer consumption (100 grams/ha of arable land)	507	923	1,530
Population density, rural (people/sq. km of arable land)	83	212	523
Forests and biodiversity			
Forest area (% of land area)	46.5	45.6	30.7
Annual deforestation (% change, 1990–2005)	0.8	0.4	0.1
Nationally protected areas (% of total land area)	3.5	11.1	7.7
Mammal species, total known	168		
Mammal species, threatened	11		
Bird species, total known	696		
Bird species, threatened	27		
GEF benefits index for biodiversity (0–100)	3.3		
Energy			
GDP per unit of energy use (2000 PPP $/kg oil equiv)	6.4	6.2	4.6
Energy use per capita (kg oil equiv)	679	1,148	1,090
Energy from combustible renewables & waste (% of tot.)	54.4	15.0	14.6
Energy imports, net (% of energy use)	−66	−40	−14
Electric power consumption per capita (kWh)	801	1,615	1,329
Electricity generated by coal (% of total)	..	5.4	49.4
Emissions and pollution			
CO_2 emissions per unit of GDP (kg/2000 PPP $ of GDP)	0.1	0.3	0.5
CO_2 emissions per capita (metric tons)	0.7	2.4	2.6
Particulate matter (urban-pop.-weighted avg., µg/cu. m)	103	43	70
Passenger cars (per 1,000 people)	52	108	29
Water and sanitation			
Internal freshwater resources per capita (cu. m)	15,622	24,619	7,295
Freshwater withdrawal			
Total (% of internal resources)	0.5	2.0	7.7
Agriculture (% of total freshwater withdrawal)	71	71	75
Access to improved water source (% of total population)	83	89	81
Rural (% of rural population)	62	69	70
Urban (% of urban population)	100	96	93
Access to improved sanitation (% of total population)	78	75	57
Rural (% of rural population)	58	44	39
Urban (% of urban population)	94	84	78
Environment and health			
ARI prevalence (% of children under age 5)	..		
Diarrhea prevalence (% of children under age 5)	..		
Under-five mortality rate (per 1,000 live births)	24	31	40
National accounting aggregates, 2004			
Gross savings (% of GNI)	22.9	22.7	32.1
Consumption of fixed capital (% of GNI)	10.1	12.1	10.8
Education expenditure (% of GNI)	4.2	4.4	2.9
Energy depletion (% of GNI)	0.0	7.2	6.5
Mineral depletion (% of GNI)	0.0	1.1	0.5
Net forest depletion (% of GNI)	0.0	0.0	0.0
CO_2 damage (% of GNI)	0.4	0.5	1.1
Particulate emission damage (% of GNI)	0.7	0.6	1.0
Adjusted net savings (% of GNI)	16.0	5.6	15.1

Peru

Environmental strategy/action plan prepared in ..

	Country data	Latin America & Caribbean	Lower middle income
		Group data	
Population (millions)	27.6	546	2,442
Urban population (% of total)	74.2	77.1	48.7
GDP ($ billions)	68.6	2,022	4,165
GNI per capita, *World Bank Atlas* method ($)	2,360	3,576	1,686
Agriculture			
Land area (1,000 sq. km)	1,280	20,057	38,470
Agricultural land (% of land area)	17	36	43
Irrigated land (% of cropland)	27.8	11.4	23.1
Fertilizer consumption (100 grams/ha of arable land)	741	923	1,530
Population density, rural (people/sq. km of arable land)	192	212	523
Forests and biodiversity			
Forest area (% of land area)	53.7	45.6	30.7
Annual deforestation (% change, 1990–2005)	0.1	0.4	0.1
Nationally protected areas (% of total land area)	6.1	11.1	7.7
Mammal species, total known	441		
Mammal species, threatened	46		
Bird species, total known	1,781		
Bird species, threatened	94		
GEF benefits index for biodiversity (0–100)	36.3		
Energy			
GDP per unit of energy use (2000 PPP $/kg oil equiv)	11.3	6.2	4.6
Energy use per capita (kg oil equiv)	442	1,148	1,090
Energy from combustible renewables & waste (% of tot.)	18.7	15.0	14.6
Energy imports, net (% of energy use)	21	–40	–14
Electric power consumption per capita (kWh)	759	1,615	1,329
Electricity generated by coal (% of total)	3.3	5.4	49.4
Emissions and pollution			
CO_2 emissions per unit of GDP (kg/2000 PPP $ of GDP)	0.2	0.3	0.5
CO_2 emissions per capita (metric tons)	1.0	2.4	2.6
Particulate matter (urban-pop.-weighted avg., µg/cu. m)	68	43	70
Passenger cars per 1,000 people	29	108	29
Water and sanitation			
Internal freshwater resources per capita (cu. m)	58,631	24,619	7,295
Freshwater withdrawal			
Total (% of internal resources)	1.2	2.0	7.7
Agriculture (% of total freshwater withdrawal)	82	71	75
Access to improved water source (% of total population)	81	89	81
Rural (% of rural population)	66	69	70
Urban (% of urban population)	87	96	93
Access to improved sanitation (% of total population)	62	75	57
Rural (% of rural population)	33	44	39
Urban (% of urban population)	72	84	78
Environment and health			
ARI prevalence (% of children under age 5)	25.9		
Diarrhea prevalence (% of children under age 5)	15.4		
Under-five mortality rate (per 1,000 live births)	29	31	40
National accounting aggregates, 2004			
Gross savings (% of GNI)	19.2	22.7	32.1
Consumption of fixed capital (% of GNI)	11.7	12.1	10.8
Education expenditure (% of GNI)	2.9	4.4	2.9
Energy depletion (% of GNI)	1.5	7.2	6.5
Mineral depletion (% of GNI)	2.1	1.1	0.5
Net forest depletion (% of GNI)	0.0	0.0	0.0
CO_2 damage (% of GNI)	0.3	0.5	1.1
Particulate emission damage (% of GNI)	1.0	0.6	1.0
Adjusted net savings (% of GNI)	5.6	5.6	15.1

Philippines

Environmental strategy/action plan prepared in **1989**

	Country data	Group data — East Asia & Pacific	Group data — Lower middle income
Population (millions)	81.6	1,870	2,442
Urban population (% of total)	61.8	40.6	48.7
GDP ($ billions)	84.6	2,651	4,165
GNI per capita, *World Bank Atlas* method ($)	1,170	1,416	1,686
Agriculture			
Land area (1,000 sq. km)	298	15,885	38,470
Agricultural land (% of land area)	41	51	43
Irrigated land (% of cropland)	14.5	..	23.1
Fertilizer consumption (100 grams/ha of arable land)	1,268	2,296	1,530
Population density, rural (people/sq. km of arable land)	549	559	523
Forests and biodiversity			
Forest area (% of land area)	24.0	28.4	30.7
Annual deforestation (% change, 1990–2005)	2.2	–0.2	0.1
Nationally protected areas (% of total land area)	5.7	..	7.7
Mammal species, total known	222		
Mammal species, threatened	50		
Bird species, total known	590		
Bird species, threatened	70		
GEF benefits index for biodiversity (0–100)	33.7		
Energy			
GDP per unit of energy use (2000 PPP $/kg oil equiv)	7.8	4.6	4.6
Energy use per capita (kg oil equiv)	525	1,007	1,090
Energy from combustible renewables & waste (% of tot.)	24.5	17.7	14.6
Energy imports, net (% of energy use)	47	–2	–14
Electric power consumption per capita (kWh)	574	1,184	1,329
Electricity generated by coal (% of total)	27.5	69.4	49.4
Emissions and pollution			
CO_2 emissions per unit of GDP (kg/2000 PPP $ of GDP)	0.3	0.5	0.5
CO_2 emissions per capita (metric tons)	0.9	2.4	2.6
Particulate matter (urban-pop.-weighted avg., µg/cu. m)	34	80	70
Passenger cars (per 1,000 people)	9	12	29
Water and sanitation			
Internal freshwater resources per capita (cu. m)	5,869	5,062	7,295
Freshwater withdrawal			
Total (% of internal resources)	6.0	10.2	7.7
Agriculture (% of total freshwater withdrawal)	74	74	75
Access to improved water source (% of total population)	85	78	81
Rural (% of rural population)	77	69	70
Urban (% of urban population)	90	92	93
Access to improved sanitation (% of total population)	73	49	57
Rural (% of rural population)	61	35	39
Urban (% of urban population)	81	72	78
Environment and health			
ARI prevalence (% of children under age 5)	10.0		
Diarrhea prevalence (% of children under age 5)	7.4		
Under-five mortality rate (per 1,000 live births)	34	37	40
National accounting aggregates, 2004			
Gross savings (% of GNI)	34.1	39.1	32.1
Consumption of fixed capital (% of GNI)	9.2	10.5	10.8
Education expenditure (% of GNI)	2.8	2.3	2.9
Energy depletion (% of GNI)	0.3	4.1	6.5
Mineral depletion (% of GNI)	0.4	0.4	0.5
Net forest depletion (% of GNI)	0.2	0.0	0.0
CO_2 damage (% of GNI)	0.6	1.2	1.1
Particulate emission damage (% of GNI)	0.3	1.2	1.0
Adjusted net savings (% of GNI)	25.9	23.9	15.1

Poland

Environmental strategy/action plan prepared in **1993**

	Country data	Group data Europe & Central Asia	Group data Upper middle income
Population (millions)	38.2	472	576
Urban population (% of total)	62.0	63.6	72.3
GDP ($ billions)	242.3	1,770	2,992
GNI per capita, *World Bank Atlas* method ($)	6,100	3,295	4,769

Agriculture

Land area (1,000 sq. km)	306	23,371	28,983
Agricultural land (% of land area)	53	29	26
Irrigated land (% of cropland)	0.8	11.1	8.7
Fertilizer consumption (100 grams/ha of arable land)	1,162	347	469
Population density, rural (people/sq. km of arable land)	116	126	131

Forests and biodiversity

Forest area (% of land area)	30.0	38.3	37.3
Annual deforestation (% change, 1990–2005)	–0.2	0.0	0.1
Nationally protected areas (% of total land area)	12.3	6.9	..
Mammal species, total known	110		
Mammal species, threatened	12		
Bird species, total known	424		
Bird species, threatened	12		
GEF benefits index for biodiversity (0–100)	0.6		

Energy

GDP per unit of energy use (2000 PPP $/kg oil equiv)	4.6	2.7	3.5
Energy use per capita (kg oil equiv)	2,452	2,794	2,574
Energy from combustible renewables & waste (% of tot.)	5.6	2.4	3.9
Energy imports, net (% of energy use)	15	–26	–51
Electric power consumption per capita (kWh)	3,329	3,531	3,378
Electricity generated by coal (% of total)	95.1	29.8	31.0

Emissions and pollution

CO_2 emissions per unit of GDP (kg/2000 PPP $ of GDP)	0.7	1.0	0.7
CO_2 emissions per capita (metric tons)	7.7	6.7	6.2
Particulate matter (urban-pop.-weighted avg., µg/cu. m)	39	35	40
Passenger cars (per 1,000 people)	288	142	143

Water and sanitation

Internal freshwater resources per capita (cu. m)	1,404	11,123	14,190
Freshwater withdrawal			
Total (% of internal resources)	30.2	7.5	3.8
Agriculture (% of total freshwater withdrawal)	8	59	53
Access to improved water source (% of total population)	..	91	93
Rural (% of rural population)	..	80	82
Urban (% of urban population)	100	98	97
Access to improved sanitation (% of total population)	..	82	81
Rural (% of rural population)	..	63	61
Urban (% of urban population)	..	93	91

Environment and health

ARI prevalence (% of children under age 5)	..		
Diarrhea prevalence (% of children under age 5)	..		
Under-five mortality rate (per 1,000 live births)	8	34	28

National accounting aggregates, 2004

Gross savings (% of GNI)	18.9	23.4	23.1
Consumption of fixed capital (% of GNI)	12.6	10.7	11.5
Education expenditure (% of GNI)	5.3	4.1	4.5
Energy depletion (% of GNI)	0.5	12.0	11.2
Mineral depletion (% of GNI)	0.3	0.3	0.6
Net forest depletion (% of GNI)	0.1	0.0	0.0
CO_2 damage (% of GNI)	0.9	1.4	0.9
Particulate emission damage (% of GNI)	0.7	0.7	0.7
Adjusted net savings (% of GNI)	9.1	2.3	2.6

Portugal

Environmental strategy/action plan prepared in **1995**

	Country data	Group data High income
Population (millions)	10.5	1,004
Urban population (% of total)	55.1	78.5
GDP ($ billions)	167.7	32,900
GNI per capita, *World Bank Atlas* method ($)	14,220	32,112
Agriculture		
Land area (1,000 sq. km)	92	33,018
Agricultural land (% of land area)	41	38
Irrigated land (% of cropland)	28.1	11.9
Fertilizer consumption (100 grams/ha of arable land)	1,262	1,205
Population density, rural (people/sq. km of arable land)	298	331
Forests and biodiversity		
Forest area (% of land area)	41.3	29.3
Annual deforestation (% change, 1990–2005)	−1.5	−0.1
Nationally protected areas (% of total land area)	6.6	..
Mammal species, total known	105	
Mammal species, threatened	15	
Bird species, total known	501	
Bird species, threatened	15	
GEF benefits index for biodiversity (0–100)	3.8	
Energy		
GDP per unit of energy use (2000 PPP $/kg oil equiv)	7.2	5.2
Energy use per capita (kg oil equiv)	2,469	5,410
Energy from combustible renewables & waste (% of tot.)	11.0	3.0
Energy imports, net (% of energy use)	83	19
Electric power consumption per capita (kWh)	4,383	9,503
Electricity generated by coal (% of total)	31.2	38.2
Emissions and pollution		
CO_2 emissions per unit of GDP (kg/2000 PPP $ of GDP)	0.3	0.5
CO_2 emissions per capita (metric tons)	6.0	12.8
Particulate matter (urban-pop.-weighted avg., µg/cu. m)	31	29
Passenger cars (per 1,000 people)	429	433
Water and sanitation		
Internal freshwater resources per capita (cu. m)	3,618	9,703
Freshwater withdrawal		
Total (% of internal resources)	29.6	10.4
Agriculture (% of total freshwater withdrawal)	78	42
Access to improved water source (% of total population)	..	99
Rural (% of rural population)	..	98
Urban (% of urban population)	..	100
Access to improved sanitation (% of total population)	..	..
Rural (% of rural population)	..	..
Urban (% of urban population)	..	..
Environment and health		
ARI prevalence (% of children under age 5)	..	
Diarrhea prevalence (% of children under age 5)	..	
Under-five mortality rate (per 1,000 live births)	5	7
National accounting aggregates, 2004		
Gross savings (% of GNI)	15.6	19.4
Consumption of fixed capital (% of GNI)	18.2	13.2
Education expenditure (% of GNI)	5.7	4.6
Energy depletion (% of GNI)	0.0	1.4
Mineral depletion (% of GNI)	0.0	0.0
Net forest depletion (% of GNI)	0.0	0.0
CO_2 damage (% of GNI)	0.2	0.3
Particulate emission damage (% of GNI)	0.5	0.4
Adjusted net savings (% of GNI)	2.3	8.7

Puerto Rico

Environmental strategy/action plan prepared in ..

	Country data	Group data — High income
Population (millions)	3.9	1,004
Urban population (% of total)	96.9	78.5
GDP ($ billions)	..	32,900
GNI per capita, *World Bank Atlas* method ($)	..	32,112

Agriculture		
Land area (1,000 sq. km)	9	33,018
Agricultural land (% of land area)	25	38
Irrigated land (% of cropland)	48.2	11.9
Fertilizer consumption (100 grams/ha of arable land)	..	1,205
Population density, rural (people/sq. km of arable land)	432	331

Forests and biodiversity		
Forest area (% of land area)	46.0	29.3
Annual deforestation (% change, 1990–2005)	−0.1	−0.1
Nationally protected areas (% of total land area)	..	..
Mammal species, total known	38	
Mammal species, threatened	2	
Bird species, total known	310	
Bird species, threatened	12	
GEF benefits index for biodiversity (0–100)	3.8	

Energy		
GDP per unit of energy use (2000 PPP $/kg oil equiv)	..	5.2
Energy use per capita (kg oil equiv)	..	5,410
Energy from combustible renewables & waste (% of tot.)	..	3.0
Energy imports, net (% of energy use)	..	19
Electric power consumption per capita (kWh)	..	9,503
Electricity generated by coal (% of total)	..	38.2

Emissions and pollution		
CO_2 emissions per unit of GDP (kg/2000 PPP $ of GDP)	0.1	0.5
CO_2 emissions per capita (metric tons)	3.5	12.8
Particulate matter (urban-pop.-weighted avg., µg/cu. m)	62	29
Passenger cars (per 1,000 people)	..	433

Water and sanitation		
Internal freshwater resources per capita (cu. m)	1,823	9,703
Freshwater withdrawal		
Total (% of internal resources)	..	10.4
Agriculture (% of total freshwater withdrawal)	..	42
Access to improved water source (% of total population)	..	99
Rural (% of rural population)	..	98
Urban (% of urban population)	..	100
Access to improved sanitation (% of total population)	..	..
Rural (% of rural population)	..	..
Urban (% of urban population)	..	..

Environment and health		
ARI prevalence (% of children under age 5)	..	
Diarrhea prevalence (% of children under age 5)	..	
Under-five mortality rate (per 1,000 live births)	..	7

National accounting aggregates, 2004		
Gross savings (% of GNI)	..	19.4
Consumption of fixed capital (% of GNI)	..	13.2
Education expenditure (% of GNI)	..	4.6
Energy depletion (% of GNI)	..	1.4
Mineral depletion (% of GNI)	..	0.0
Net forest depletion (% of GNI)	..	0.0
CO_2 damage (% of GNI)	..	0.3
Particulate emission damage (% of GNI)	..	0.4
Adjusted net savings (% of GNI)	..	8.7

Qatar

Environmental strategy/action plan prepared in ..

	Country data	Group data High income
Population (millions)	0.8	1,004
Urban population (% of total)	92.2	78.5
GDP ($ billions)	20.4	32,900
GNI per capita, *World Bank Atlas* method ($)	..	32,112

Agriculture		
Land area (1,000 sq. km)	11	33,018
Agricultural land (% of land area)	6	38
Irrigated land (% of cropland)	61.9	11.9
Fertilizer consumption (100 grams/ha of arable land)	0	1,205
Population density, rural (people/sq. km of arable land)	326	331

Forests and biodiversity		
Forest area (% of land area)	..	29.3
Annual deforestation (% change, 1990–2005)	..	–0.1
Nationally protected areas (% of total land area)	..	..
Mammal species, total known	8	
Mammal species, threatened	0	
Bird species, total known	151	
Bird species, threatened	7	
GEF benefits index for biodiversity (0–100)	0.1	

Energy		
GDP per unit of energy use (2000 PPP $/kg oil equiv)	..	5.2
Energy use per capita (kg oil equiv)	20,726	5,410
Energy from combustible renewables & waste (% of tot.)	0.0	3.0
Energy imports, net (% of energy use)	–335	19
Electric power consumption per capita (kWh)	15,241	9,503
Electricity generated by coal (% of total)	..	38.2

Emissions and pollution		
CO_2 emissions per unit of GDP (kg/2000 PPP $ of GDP)	..	0.5
CO_2 emissions per capita (metric tons)	53.0	12.8
Particulate matter (urban-pop.-weighted avg., μg/cu. m)	57	29
Passenger cars (per 1,000 people)	377	433

Water and sanitation		
Internal freshwater resources per capita (cu. m)	66	9,703
Freshwater withdrawal		
Total (% of internal resources)	568.6	10.4
Agriculture (% of total freshwater withdrawal)	72	42
Access to improved water source (% of total population)	100	99
Rural (% of rural population)	100	98
Urban (% of urban population)	100	100
Access to improved sanitation (% of total population)	100	..
Rural (% of rural population)	100	..
Urban (% of urban population)	100	..

Environment and health		
ARI prevalence (% of children under age 5)	..	
Diarrhea prevalence (% of children under age 5)	8.8	
Under-five mortality rate (per 1,000 live births)	21	7

National accounting aggregates, 2004		
Gross savings (% of GNI)	..	19.4
Consumption of fixed capital (% of GNI)	..	13.2
Education expenditure (% of GNI)	..	4.6
Energy depletion (% of GNI)	..	1.4
Mineral depletion (% of GNI)	..	0.0
Net forest depletion (% of GNI)	..	0.0
CO_2 damage (% of GNI)	..	0.3
Particulate emission damage (% of GNI)	1.3	0.4
Adjusted net savings (% of GNI)	..	8.7

Romania

Environmental strategy/action plan prepared in **1995**

	Country data	Group data Europe & Central Asia	Group data Lower middle income
Population (millions)	21.7	472	2,442
Urban population (% of total)	54.7	63.6	48.7
GDP ($ billions)	73.2	1,770	4,165
GNI per capita, *World Bank Atlas* method ($)	2,960	3,295	1,686
Agriculture			
Land area (1,000 sq. km)	230	23,371	38,470
Agricultural land (% of land area)	64	29	43
Irrigated land (% of cropland)	31.2	11.1	23.1
Fertilizer consumption (100 grams/ha of arable land)	347	347	1,530
Population density, rural (people/sq. km of arable land)	105	126	523
Forests and biodiversity			
Forest area (% of land area)	27.7	38.3	30.7
Annual deforestation (% change, 1990–2005)	0.0	0.0	0.1
Nationally protected areas (% of total land area)	4.7	6.9	7.7
Mammal species, total known	101		
Mammal species, threatened	15		
Bird species, total known	365		
Bird species, threatened	13		
GEF benefits index for biodiversity (0–100)	..		
Energy			
GDP per unit of energy use (2000 PPP $/kg oil equiv)	4.0	2.7	4.6
Energy use per capita (kg oil equiv)	1,794	2,794	1,090
Energy from combustible renewables & waste (% of tot.)	7.5	2.4	14.6
Energy imports, net (% of energy use)	26	−26	−14
Electric power consumption per capita (kWh)	2,221	3,531	1,329
Electricity generated by coal (% of total)	42.9	29.8	49.4
Emissions and pollution			
CO_2 emissions per unit of GDP (kg/2000 PPP $ of GDP)	0.7	1.0	0.5
CO_2 emissions per capita (metric tons)	4.0	6.7	2.6
Particulate matter (urban-pop.-weighted avg., μg/cu. m)	20	35	70
Passenger cars (per 1,000 people)	144	142	29
Water and sanitation			
Internal freshwater resources per capita (cu. m)	1,951	11,123	7,295
Freshwater withdrawal			
Total (% of internal resources)	54.8	7.5	7.7
Agriculture (% of total freshwater withdrawal)	57	59	75
Access to improved water source (% of total population)	57	91	81
Rural (% of rural population)	16	80	70
Urban (% of urban population)	91	98	93
Access to improved sanitation (% of total population)	51	82	57
Rural (% of rural population)	10	63	39
Urban (% of urban population)	86	93	78
Environment and health			
ARI prevalence (% of children under age 5)	..		
Diarrhea prevalence (% of children under age 5)	..		
Under-five mortality rate (per 1,000 live births)	20	34	40
National accounting aggregates, 2004			
Gross savings (% of GNI)	18.2	23.4	32.1
Consumption of fixed capital (% of GNI)	11.7	10.7	10.8
Education expenditure (% of GNI)	3.2	4.1	2.9
Energy depletion (% of GNI)	3.3	12.0	6.5
Mineral depletion (% of GNI)	0.0	0.3	0.5
Net forest depletion (% of GNI)	0.0	0.0	0.0
CO_2 damage (% of GNI)	0.9	1.4	1.1
Particulate emission damage (% of GNI)	0.2	0.7	1.0
Adjusted net savings (% of GNI)	5.3	2.3	15.1

Russian Federation

Environmental strategy/action plan prepared in **1999**

	Country data	Group data Europe & Central Asia	Upper middle income
Population (millions)	143.8	472	576
Urban population (% of total)	73.3	63.6	72.3
GDP ($ billions)	581.4	1,770	2,992
GNI per capita, *World Bank Atlas* method ($)	3,400	3,295	4,769
Agriculture			
Land area (1,000 sq. km)	16,381	23,371	28,983
Agricultural land (% of land area)	13	29	26
Irrigated land (% of cropland)	3.7	11.1	8.7
Fertilizer consumption (100 grams/ha of arable land)	119	347	469
Population density, rural (people/sq. km of arable land)	32	126	131
Forests and biodiversity			
Forest area (% of land area)	49.4	38.3	37.3
Annual deforestation (% change, 1990–2005)	0.0	0.0	0.1
Nationally protected areas (% of total land area)	8.0	6.9	..
Mammal species, total known	296		
Mammal species, threatened	43		
Bird species, total known	645		
Bird species, threatened	47		
GEF benefits index for biodiversity (0–100)	37.1		
Energy			
GDP per unit of energy use (2000 PPP $/kg oil equiv)	1.9	2.7	3.5
Energy use per capita (kg oil equiv)	4,424	2,794	2,574
Energy from combustible renewables & waste (% of tot.)	1.0	2.4	3.9
Energy imports, net (% of energy use)	−73	−26	−51
Electric power consumption per capita (kWh)	5,480	3,531	3,378
Electricity generated by coal (% of total)	18.8	29.8	31.0
Emissions and pollution			
CO_2 emissions per unit of GDP (kg/2000 PPP $ of GDP)	1.4	1.0	0.7
CO_2 emissions per capita (metric tons)	9.8	6.7	6.2
Particulate matter (urban-pop.-weighted avg., µg/cu. m)	25	35	40
Passenger cars (per 1,000 people)	140	142	143
Water and sanitation			
Internal freshwater resources per capita (cu. m)	29,981	11,123	14,190
Freshwater withdrawal			
Total (% of internal resources)	1.8	7.5	3.8
Agriculture (% of total freshwater withdrawal)	18	59	53
Access to improved water source (% of total population)	96	91	93
Rural (% of rural population)	88	80	82
Urban (% of urban population)	99	98	97
Access to improved sanitation (% of total population)	87	82	81
Rural (% of rural population)	70	63	61
Urban (% of urban population)	93	93	91
Environment and health			
ARI prevalence (% of children under age 5)	..		
Diarrhea prevalence (% of children under age 5)	..		
Under-five mortality rate (per 1,000 live births)	21	34	28
National accounting aggregates, 2004			
Gross savings (% of GNI)	32.1	23.4	23.1
Consumption of fixed capital (% of GNI)	7.1	10.7	11.5
Education expenditure (% of GNI)	3.5	4.1	4.5
Energy depletion (% of GNI)	29.7	12.0	11.2
Mineral depletion (% of GNI)	0.6	0.3	0.6
Net forest depletion (% of GNI)	0.0	0.0	0.0
CO_2 damage (% of GNI)	2.0	1.4	0.9
Particulate emission damage (% of GNI)	0.6	0.7	0.7
Adjusted net savings (% of GNI)	−4.4	2.3	2.6

Rwanda

Environmental strategy/action plan prepared in **1991**

	Country data	Group data Sub-Saharan Africa	Low income
Population (millions)	8.9	726	2,343
Urban population (% of total)	20.1	36.4	30.6
GDP ($ billions)	1.8	523	1,239
GNI per capita, *World Bank Atlas* method ($)	210	601	507
Agriculture			
Land area (1,000 sq. km)	25	23,596	29,192
Agricultural land (% of land area)	78	44	45
Irrigated land (% of cropland)	0.6	3.6	23.9
Fertilizer consumption (100 grams/ha of arable land)	137	136	646
Population density, rural (people/sq. km of arable land)	595	355	524
Forests and biodiversity			
Forest area (% of land area)	19.5	26.5	24.8
Annual deforestation (% change, 1990–2005)	–3.4	0.6	0.5
Nationally protected areas (% of total land area)	6.2	8.7	7.7
Mammal species, total known	206		
Mammal species, threatened	13		
Bird species, total known	665		
Bird species, threatened	9		
GEF benefits index for biodiversity (0–100)	1.1		
Energy			
GDP per unit of energy use (2000 PPP $/kg oil equiv)	..	2.8	4.2
Energy use per capita (kg oil equiv)	..	681	501
Energy from combustible renewables & waste (% of tot.)	..	57.4	48.9
Energy imports, net (% of energy use)	..	–59	–4
Electric power consumption per capita (kWh)	..	513	358
Electricity generated by coal (% of total)	..	68.0	46.3
Emissions and pollution			
CO_2 emissions per unit of GDP (kg/2000 PPP $ of GDP)	0.1	0.4	0.4
CO_2 emissions per capita (metric tons)	0.1	0.7	0.8
Particulate matter (urban-pop.-weighted avg., µg/cu. m)	100	73	89
Passenger cars (per 1,000 people)	..	..	6
Water and sanitation			
Internal freshwater resources per capita (cu. m)	1,070	5,353	3,456
Freshwater withdrawal			
Total (% of internal resources)	1.6	3.1	15.5
Agriculture (% of total freshwater withdrawal)	68	87	88
Access to improved water source (% of total population)	73	58	75
Rural (% of rural population)	69	45	69
Urban (% of urban population)	92	82	89
Access to improved sanitation (% of total population)	41	36	36
Rural (% of rural population)	38	26	24
Urban (% of urban population)	56	55	61
Environment and health			
ARI prevalence (% of children under age 5)	30.2		
Diarrhea prevalence (% of children under age 5)	16.9		
Under-five mortality rate (per 1,000 live births)	203	168	122
National accounting aggregates, 2004			
Gross savings (% of GNI)	17.7	17.1	22.7
Consumption of fixed capital (% of GNI)	7.9	10.9	9.2
Education expenditure (% of GNI)	3.5	3.9	3.4
Energy depletion (% of GNI)	0.0	9.8	6.7
Mineral depletion (% of GNI)	0.0	0.4	0.4
Net forest depletion (% of GNI)	3.7	0.6	0.7
CO_2 damage (% of GNI)	0.2	0.7	1.1
Particulate emission damage (% of GNI)	0.2	0.5	0.8
Adjusted net savings (% of GNI)	9.1	–1.9	7.3

Samoa

Environmental strategy/action plan prepared in ..

	Country data	Group data East Asia & Pacific	Group data Lower middle income
Population (millions)	0.2	1,870	2,442
Urban population (% of total)	22.4	40.6	48.7
GDP ($ billions)	0.4	2,651	4,165
GNI per capita, *World Bank Atlas* method ($)	1,840	1,416	1,686
Agriculture			
Land area (1,000 sq. km)	3	15,885	38,470
Agricultural land (% of land area)	46	51	43
Irrigated land (% of cropland)	..	..	23.1
Fertilizer consumption (100 grams/ha of arable land)	583	2,296	1,530
Population density, rural (people/sq. km of arable land)	236	559	523
Forests and biodiversity			
Forest area (% of land area)	60.4	28.4	30.7
Annual deforestation (% change, 1990–2005)	–2.1	–0.2	0.1
Nationally protected areas (% of total land area)	..	..	7.7
Mammal species, total known	6		
Mammal species, threatened	3		
Bird species, total known	49		
Bird species, threatened	7		
GEF benefits index for biodiversity (0–100)	1.9		
Energy			
GDP per unit of energy use (2000 PPP $/kg oil equiv)	..	4.6	4.6
Energy use per capita (kg oil equiv)	..	1,007	1,090
Energy from combustible renewables & waste (% of tot.)	..	17.7	14.6
Energy imports, net (% of energy use)	..	–2	–14
Electric power consumption per capita (kWh)	..	1,184	1,329
Electricity generated by coal (% of total)	..	69.4	49.4
Emissions and pollution			
CO_2 emissions per unit of GDP (kg/2000 PPP $ of GDP)	0.2	0.5	0.5
CO_2 emissions per capita (metric tons)	0.8	2.4	2.6
Particulate matter (urban-pop.-weighted avg., µg/cu. m)	..	80	70
Passenger cars (per 1,000 people)	..	12	29
Water and sanitation			
Internal freshwater resources per capita (cu. m)	..	5,062	7,295
Freshwater withdrawal			
Total (% of internal resources)	..	10.2	7.7
Agriculture (% of total freshwater withdrawal)	..	74	75
Access to improved water source (% of total population)	88	78	81
Rural (% of rural population)	88	69	70
Urban (% of urban population)	91	92	93
Access to improved sanitation (% of total population)	100	49	57
Rural (% of rural population)	100	35	39
Urban (% of urban population)	100	72	78
Environment and health			
ARI prevalence (% of children under age 5)	..		
Diarrhea prevalence (% of children under age 5)	..		
Under-five mortality rate (per 1,000 live births)	30	37	40
National accounting aggregates, 2004			
Gross savings (% of GNI)	..	39.1	32.1
Consumption of fixed capital (% of GNI)	10.8	10.5	10.8
Education expenditure (% of GNI)	4.0	2.3	2.9
Energy depletion (% of GNI)	0.0	4.1	6.5
Mineral depletion (% of GNI)	0.0	0.4	0.5
Net forest depletion (% of GNI)	1.0	0.0	0.0
CO_2 damage (% of GNI)	0.3	1.2	1.1
Particulate emission damage (% of GNI)	..	1.2	1.0
Adjusted net savings (% of GNI)	..	23.9	15.1

San Marino

Environmental strategy/action plan prepared in ..

	Country data	Group data High income
Population (millions)	0.0	1,004
Urban population (% of total)	88.7	78.5
GDP ($ billions)	..	32,900
GNI per capita, *World Bank Atlas* method ($)	..	32,112
Agriculture		
Land area (1,000 sq. km)	0	33,018
Agricultural land (% of land area)	17	38
Irrigated land (% of cropland)	..	11.9
Fertilizer consumption (100 grams/ha of arable land)	..	1,205
Population density, rural (people/sq. km of arable land)	..	331
Forests and biodiversity		
Forest area (% of land area)	..	29.3
Annual deforestation (% change, 1990–2005)	..	–0.1
Nationally protected areas (% of total land area)	..	..
Mammal species, total known	3	
Mammal species, threatened	..	
Bird species, total known	6	
Bird species, threatened	..	
GEF benefits index for biodiversity (0–100)	..	
Energy		
GDP per unit of energy use (2000 PPP $/kg oil equiv)	..	5.2
Energy use per capita (kg oil equiv)	..	5,410
Energy from combustible renewables & waste (% of tot.)	..	3.0
Energy imports, net (% of energy use)	..	19
Electric power consumption per capita (kWh)	..	9,503
Electricity generated by coal (% of total)	..	38.2
Emissions and pollution		
CO_2 emissions per unit of GDP (kg/2000 PPP $ of GDP)	..	0.5
CO_2 emissions per capita (metric tons)	..	12.8
Particulate matter (urban-pop.-weighted avg., µg/cu. m)	19	29
Passenger cars (per 1,000 people)	..	433
Water and sanitation		
Internal freshwater resources per capita (cu. m)	..	9,703
Freshwater withdrawal		
Total (% of internal resources)	..	10.4
Agriculture (% of total freshwater withdrawal)	..	42
Access to improved water source (% of total population)	..	99
Rural (% of rural population)	..	98
Urban (% of urban population)	..	100
Access to improved sanitation (% of total population)	..	..
Rural (% of rural population)	..	..
Urban (% of urban population)	..	..
Environment and health		
ARI prevalence (% of children under age 5)	..	
Diarrhea prevalence (% of children under age 5)	..	
Under-five mortality rate (per 1,000 live births)	4	7
National accounting aggregates, 2004		
Gross savings (% of GNI)	..	19.4
Consumption of fixed capital (% of GNI)	..	13.2
Education expenditure (% of GNI)	..	4.6
Energy depletion (% of GNI)	..	1.4
Mineral depletion (% of GNI)	..	0.0
Net forest depletion (% of GNI)	..	0.0
CO_2 damage (% of GNI)	..	0.3
Particulate emission damage (% of GNI)	..	0.4
Adjusted net savings (% of GNI)	..	8.7

São Tomé and Principe

Environmental strategy/action plan prepared in ..

	Country data	Group data	
		Sub-Saharan Africa	Low Income
Population (millions)	0.2	726	2,343
Urban population (% of total)	37.9	36.4	30.6
GDP ($ billions)	0.1	523	1,239
GNI per capita, *World Bank Atlas* method ($)	390	601	507

Agriculture

Land area (1,000 sq. km)	1	23,596	29,192
Agricultural land (% of land area)	58	44	45
Irrigated land (% of cropland)	18.2	3.6	23.9
Fertilizer consumption (100 grams/ha of arable land)	..	136	646
Population density, rural (people/sq. km of arable land)	1,162	355	524

Forests and biodiversity

Forest area (% of land area)	28.1	26.5	24.8
Annual deforestation (% change, 1990–2005)	0.0	0.6	0.5
Nationally protected areas (% of total land area)	..	8.7	7.7
Mammal species, total known	14		
Mammal species, threatened	..		
Bird species, total known	112		
Bird species, threatened	..		
GEF benefits index for biodiversity (0–100)	3.0		

Energy

GDP per unit of energy use (2000 PPP $/kg oil equiv)	..	2.8	4.2
Energy use per capita (kg oil equiv)	..	681	501
Energy from combustible renewables & waste (% of tot.)	..	57.4	48.9
Energy imports, net (% of energy use)	..	−59	−4
Electric power consumption per capita (kWh)	..	513	358
Electricity generated by coal (% of total)	..	68.0	46.3

Emissions and pollution

CO_2 emissions per unit of GDP (kg/2000 PPP $ of GDP)	..	0.4	0.4
CO_2 emissions per capita (metric tons)	0.6	0.7	0.8
Particulate matter (urban-pop.-weighted avg., µg/cu. m)	76	73	89
Passenger cars (per 1,000 people)	..	..	6

Water and sanitation

Internal freshwater resources per capita (cu. m)	14,252	5,353	3,456
Freshwater withdrawal			
Total (% of internal resources)	..	3.1	15.5
Agriculture (% of total freshwater withdrawal)	..	87	88
Access to improved water source (% of total population)	79	58	75
Rural (% of rural population)	73	45	69
Urban (% of urban population)	89	82	89
Access to improved sanitation (% of total population)	24	36	36
Rural (% of rural population)	20	26	24
Urban (% of urban population)	32	55	61

Environment and health

ARI prevalence (% of children under age 5)	5.0		
Diarrhea prevalence (% of children under age 5)	..		
Under-five mortality rate (per 1,000 live births)	118	168	122

National accounting aggregates, 2004

Gross savings (% of GNI)	−23.0	17.1	22.7
Consumption of fixed capital (% of GNI)	9.1	10.9	9.2
Education expenditure (% of GNI)	..	3.9	3.4
Energy depletion (% of GNI)	0.0	9.8	6.7
Mineral depletion (% of GNI)	0.0	0.4	0.4
Net forest depletion (% of GNI)	0.0	0.6	0.7
CO_2 damage (% of GNI)	1.1	0.7	1.1
Particulate emission damage (% of GNI)	0.4	0.5	0.8
Adjusted net savings (% of GNI)	..	−1.9	7.3

Saudi Arabia

Environmental strategy/action plan prepared in ..

	Country data	Group data High income
Population (millions)	24.0	1,004
Urban population (% of total)	88.0	78.5
GDP ($ billions)	250.6	32,900
GNI per capita, *World Bank Atlas* method ($)	10,140	32,112
Agriculture		
Land area (1,000 sq. km)	2,150	33,018
Agricultural land (% of land area)	81	38
Irrigated land (% of cropland)	42.7	11.9
Fertilizer consumption (100 grams/ha of arable land)	1,059	1,205
Population density, rural (people/sq. km of arable land)	81	331
Forests and biodiversity		
Forest area (% of land area)	1.3	29.3
Annual deforestation (% change, 1990–2005)	0.0	–0.1
Nationally protected areas (% of total land area)	38.3	..
Mammal species, total known	94	
Mammal species, threatened	9	
Bird species, total known	433	
Bird species, threatened	17	
GEF benefits index for biodiversity (0–100)	3.4	
Energy		
GDP per unit of energy use (2000 PPP $/kg oil equiv)	2.2	5.2
Energy use per capita (kg oil equiv)	5,607	5,410
Energy from combustible renewables & waste (% of tot.)	0.0	3.0
Energy imports, net (% of energy use)	–308	19
Electric power consumption per capita (kWh)	6,259	9,503
Electricity generated by coal (% of total)	..	38.2
Emissions and pollution		
CO_2 emissions per unit of GDP (kg/2000 PPP $ of GDP)	1.1	0.5
CO_2 emissions per capita (metric tons)	15.0	12.8
Particulate matter (urban-pop.-weighted avg., µg/cu. m)	91	29
Passenger cars (per 1,000 people)	..	433
Water and sanitation		
Internal freshwater resources per capita (cu. m)	100	9,703
Freshwater withdrawal		
Total (% of internal resources)	721.7	10.4
Agriculture (% of total freshwater withdrawal)	89	42
Access to improved water source (% of total population)	..	99
Rural (% of rural population)	..	98
Urban (% of urban population)	97	100
Access to improved sanitation (% of total population)	..	..
Rural (% of rural population)	..	..
Urban (% of urban population)	100	..
Environment and health		
ARI prevalence (% of children under age 5)	..	
Diarrhea prevalence (% of children under age 5)	..	
Under-five mortality rate (per 1,000 live births)	27	7
National accounting aggregates, 2004		
Gross savings (% of GNI)	46.6	19.4
Consumption of fixed capital (% of GNI)	13.0	13.2
Education expenditure (% of GNI)	7.2	4.6
Energy depletion (% of GNI)	50.1	1.4
Mineral depletion (% of GNI)	0.0	0.0
Net forest depletion (% of GNI)	0.0	0.0
CO_2 damage (% of GNI)	0.9	0.3
Particulate emission damage (% of GNI)	1.0	0.4
Adjusted net savings (% of GNI)	–11.1	8.7

Senegal

Environmental strategy/action plan prepared in **1984**

	Country data	Group data Sub-Saharan Africa	Low Income
Population (millions)	11.4	726	2,343
Urban population (% of total)	50.3	36.4	30.6
GDP ($ billions)	7.8	523	1,239
GNI per capita, *World Bank Atlas* method ($)	630	601	507
Agriculture			
Land area (1,000 sq. km)	193	23,596	29,192
Agricultural land (% of land area)	42	44	45
Irrigated land (% of cropland)	4.8	3.6	23.9
Fertilizer consumption (100 grams/ha of arable land)	136	136	646
Population density, rural (people/sq. km of arable land)	228	355	524
Forests and biodiversity			
Forest area (% of land area)	45.0	26.5	24.8
Annual deforestation (% change, 1990–2005)	0.5	0.6	0.5
Nationally protected areas (% of total land area)	11.6	8.7	7.7
Mammal species, total known	191		
Mammal species, threatened	11		
Bird species, total known	612		
Bird species, threatened	5		
GEF benefits index for biodiversity (0–100)	1.3		
Energy			
GDP per unit of energy use (2000 PPP $/kg oil equiv)	5.2	2.8	4.2
Energy use per capita (kg oil equiv)	287	681	501
Energy from combustible renewables & waste (% of tot.)	53.0	57.4	48.9
Energy imports, net (% of energy use)	45	−59	−4
Electric power consumption per capita (kWh)	167	513	358
Electricity generated by coal (% of total)	..	68.0	46.3
Emissions and pollution			
CO_2 emissions per unit of GDP (kg/2000 PPP $ of GDP)	0.3	0.4	0.4
CO_2 emissions per capita (metric tons)	0.4	0.7	0.8
Particulate matter (urban-pop.-weighted avg., µg/cu. m)	93	73	89
Passenger cars (per 1,000 people)	11	..	6
Water and sanitation			
Internal freshwater resources per capita (cu. m)	2,266	5,353	3,456
Freshwater withdrawal			
Total (% of internal resources)	8.6	3.1	15.5
Agriculture (% of total freshwater withdrawal)	93	87	88
Access to improved water source (% of total population)	72	58	75
Rural (% of rural population)	54	45	69
Urban (% of urban population)	90	82	89
Access to improved sanitation (% of total population)	52	36	36
Rural (% of rural population)	34	26	24
Urban (% of urban population)	70	55	61
Environment and health			
ARI prevalence (% of children under age 5)	6.6		
Diarrhea prevalence (% of children under age 5)	..		
Under-five mortality rate (per 1,000 live births)	137	168	122
National accounting aggregates, 2004			
Gross savings (% of GNI)	17.2	17.1	22.7
Consumption of fixed capital (% of GNI)	9.6	10.9	9.2
Education expenditure (% of GNI)	3.4	3.9	3.4
Energy depletion (% of GNI)	0.0	9.8	6.7
Mineral depletion (% of GNI)	0.0	0.4	0.4
Net forest depletion (% of GNI)	0.2	0.6	0.7
CO_2 damage (% of GNI)	0.4	0.7	1.1
Particulate emission damage (% of GNI)	1.4	0.5	0.8
Adjusted net savings (% of GNI)	8.9	−1.9	7.3

Serbia and Montenegro

Environmental strategy/action plan prepared in ..

	Country data	Europe & Central Asia	Lower middle income
		Group data	
Population (millions)	8.1	472	2,442
Urban population (% of total)	52.2	63.6	48.7
GDP ($ billions)	24.0	1,770	4,165
GNI per capita, *World Bank Atlas* method ($)	2,680	3,295	1,686
Agriculture			
Land area (1,000 sq. km)	102	23,371	38,470
Agricultural land (% of land area)	55	29	43
Irrigated land (% of cropland)	0.9	11.1	23.1
Fertilizer consumption (100 grams/ha of arable land)	906	347	1,530
Population density, rural (people/sq. km of arable land)	115	126	523
Forests and biodiversity			
Forest area (% of land area)	26.4	38.3	30.7
Annual deforestation (% change, 1990–2005)	−0.4	0.0	0.1
Nationally protected areas (% of total land area)	..	6.9	7.7
Mammal species, total known	96		
Mammal species, threatened	10		
Bird species, total known	381		
Bird species, threatened	10		
GEF benefits index for biodiversity (0–100)	..		
Energy			
GDP per unit of energy use (2000 PPP $/kg oil equiv)	..	2.7	4.6
Energy use per capita (kg oil equiv)	1,991	2,794	1,090
Energy from combustible renewables & waste (% of tot.)	4.9	2.4	14.6
Energy imports, net (% of energy use)	29	−26	−14
Electric power consumption per capita (kWh)	3,975	3,531	1,329
Electricity generated by coal (% of total)	69.9	29.8	49.4
Emissions and pollution			
CO_2 emissions per unit of GDP (kg/2000 PPP $ of GDP)	..	1.0	0.5
CO_2 emissions per capita (metric tons)	..	6.7	2.6
Particulate matter (urban-pop.-weighted avg., µg/cu. m)	17	35	70
Passenger cars (per 1,000 people)	..	142	29
Water and sanitation			
Internal freshwater resources per capita (cu. m)	5,401	11,123	7,295
Freshwater withdrawal			
Total (% of internal resources)	..	7.5	7.7
Agriculture (% of total freshwater withdrawal)	..	59	75
Access to improved water source (% of total population)	93	91	81
Rural (% of rural population)	86	80	70
Urban (% of urban population)	99	98	93
Access to improved sanitation (% of total population)	87	82	57
Rural (% of rural population)	77	63	39
Urban (% of urban population)	97	93	78
Environment and health			
ARI prevalence (% of children under age 5)	2.7		
Diarrhea prevalence (% of children under age 5)	8.6		
Under-five mortality rate (per 1,000 live births)	15	34	40
National accounting aggregates, 2004			
Gross savings (% of GNI)	4.6	23.4	32.1
Consumption of fixed capital (% of GNI)	11.4	10.7	10.8
Education expenditure (% of GNI)	..	4.1	2.9
Energy depletion (% of GNI)	0.9	12.0	6.5
Mineral depletion (% of GNI)	0.0	0.3	0.5
Net forest depletion (% of GNI)	..	0.0	0.0
CO_2 damage (% of GNI)	0.3	1.4	1.1
Particulate emission damage (% of GNI)	0.1	0.7	1.0
Adjusted net savings (% of GNI)	..	2.3	15.1

Seychelles

Environmental strategy/action plan prepared in ..

	Country data	Group data Sub-Saharan Africa	Group data Upper middle income
Population (millions)	0.1	726	576
Urban population (% of total)	50.1	36.4	72.3
GDP ($ billions)	0.7	523	2,992
GNI per capita, *World Bank Atlas* method ($)	8,190	601	4,769

Agriculture
Land area (1,000 sq. km)	0	23,596	28,983
Agricultural land (% of land area)	15	44	26
Irrigated land (% of cropland)	..	3.6	8.7
Fertilizer consumption (100 grams/ha of arable land)	170	136	469
Population density, rural (people/sq. km of arable land)	4,138	355	131

Forests and biodiversity
Forest area (% of land area)	87.0	26.5	37.3
Annual deforestation (% change, 1990–2005)	0.0	0.6	0.1
Nationally protected areas (% of total land area)	..	8.7	..
Mammal species, total known	25		
Mammal species, threatened	3		
Bird species, total known	238		
Bird species, threatened	13		
GEF benefits index for biodiversity (0–100)	4.7		

Energy
GDP per unit of energy use (2000 PPP $/kg oil equiv)	..	2.8	3.5
Energy use per capita (kg oil equiv)	..	681	2,574
Energy from combustible renewables & waste (% of tot.)	..	57.4	3.9
Energy imports, net (% of energy use)	..	−59	−51
Electric power consumption per capita (kWh)	..	513	3,378
Electricity generated by coal (% of total)	..	68.0	31.0

Emissions and pollution
CO_2 emissions per unit of GDP (kg/2000 PPP $ of GDP)	0.4	0.4	0.7
CO_2 emissions per capita (metric tons)	6.4	0.7	6.2
Particulate matter (urban-pop.-weighted avg., µg/cu. m)	..	73	40
Passenger cars (per 1,000 people)	..	..	143

Water and sanitation
Internal freshwater resources per capita (cu. m)	..	5,353	14,190
Freshwater withdrawal			
Total (% of internal resources)	..	3.1	3.8
Agriculture (% of total freshwater withdrawal)	..	87	53
Access to improved water source (% of total population)	87	58	93
Rural (% of rural population)	75	45	82
Urban (% of urban population)	100	82	97
Access to improved sanitation (% of total population)	..	36	81
Rural (% of rural population)	100	26	61
Urban (% of urban population)	..	55	91

Environment and health
ARI prevalence (% of children under age 5)	..		
Diarrhea prevalence (% of children under age 5)	..		
Under-five mortality rate (per 1,000 live births)	14	168	28

National accounting aggregates, 2004
Gross savings (% of GNI)	5.2	17.1	23.1
Consumption of fixed capital (% of GNI)	13.3	10.9	11.5
Education expenditure (% of GNI)	5.3	3.9	4.5
Energy depletion (% of GNI)	0.0	9.8	11.2
Mineral depletion (% of GNI)	0.0	0.4	0.6
Net forest depletion (% of GNI)	0.0	0.6	0.0
CO_2 damage (% of GNI)	0.5	0.7	0.9
Particulate emission damage (% of GNI)	..	0.5	0.7
Adjusted net savings (% of GNI)	−3.4	−1.9	2.6

Sierra Leone

Environmental strategy/action plan prepared in **1994**

	Country data	Group data Sub-Saharan Africa	Group data Low income
Population (millions)	5.3	726	2,343
Urban population (% of total)	39.5	36.4	30.6
GDP ($ billions)	1.1	523	1,239
GNI per capita, *World Bank Atlas* method ($)	210	601	507
Agriculture			
Land area (1,000 sq. km)	72	23,596	29,192
Agricultural land (% of land area)	40	44	45
Irrigated land (% of cropland)	4.7	3.6	23.9
Fertilizer consumption (100 grams/ha of arable land)	6	136	646
Population density, rural (people/sq. km of arable land)	550	355	524
Forests and biodiversity			
Forest area (% of land area)	38.5	26.5	24.8
Annual deforestation (% change, 1990–2005)	0.6	0.6	0.5
Nationally protected areas (% of total land area)	2.1	8.7	7.7
Mammal species, total known	197		
Mammal species, threatened	12		
Bird species, total known	626		
Bird species, threatened	10		
GEF benefits index for biodiversity (0–100)	1.5		
Energy			
GDP per unit of energy use (2000 PPP $/kg oil equiv)	..	2.8	4.2
Energy use per capita (kg oil equiv)	..	681	501
Energy from combustible renewables & waste (% of tot.)	..	57.4	48.9
Energy imports, net (% of energy use)	..	−59	−4
Electric power consumption per capita (kWh)	..	513	358
Electricity generated by coal (% of total)	..	68.0	46.3
Emissions and pollution			
CO_2 emissions per unit of GDP (kg/2000 PPP $ of GDP)	0.3	0.4	0.4
CO_2 emissions per capita (metric tons)	0.1	0.7	0.8
Particulate matter (urban-pop.-weighted avg., μg/cu. m)	69	73	89
Passenger cars (per 1,000 people)	2	..	6
Water and sanitation			
Internal freshwater resources per capita (cu. m)	29,982	5,353	3,456
Freshwater withdrawal			
Total (% of internal resources)	0.2	3.1	15.5
Agriculture (% of total freshwater withdrawal)	92	87	88
Access to improved water source (% of total population)	57	58	75
Rural (% of rural population)	46	45	69
Urban (% of urban population)	75	82	89
Access to improved sanitation (% of total population)	39	36	36
Rural (% of rural population)	30	26	24
Urban (% of urban population)	53	55	61
Environment and health			
ARI prevalence (% of children under age 5)	8.7		
Diarrhea prevalence (% of children under age 5)	25.3		
Under-five mortality rate (per 1,000 live births)	283	168	122
National accounting aggregates, 2004			
Gross savings (% of GNI)	11.4	17.1	22.7
Consumption of fixed capital (% of GNI)	7.9	10.9	9.2
Education expenditure (% of GNI)	1.0	3.9	3.4
Energy depletion (% of GNI)	0.0	9.8	6.7
Mineral depletion (% of GNI)	0.0	0.4	0.4
Net forest depletion (% of GNI)	4.3	0.6	0.7
CO_2 damage (% of GNI)	0.4	0.7	1.1
Particulate emission damage (% of GNI)	0.6	0.5	0.8
Adjusted net savings (% of GNI)	−1.0	−1.9	7.3

Singapore

Environmental strategy/action plan prepared in **1993**

		Group data
	Country data	High income
Population (millions)	4.2	1,004
Urban population (% of total)	100.0	78.5
GDP ($ billions)	106.8	32,900
GNI per capita, *World Bank Atlas* method ($)	24,760	32,112

Agriculture

Land area (1,000 sq. km)	1	33,018
Agricultural land (% of land area)	3	38
Irrigated land (% of cropland)	..	11.9
Fertilizer consumption (100 grams/ha of arable land)	..	1,205
Population density, rural (people/sq. km of arable land)	0	331

Forests and biodiversity

Forest area (% of land area)	3.0	29.3
Annual deforestation (% change, 1990–2005)	0.0	–0.1
Nationally protected areas (% of total land area)	4.5	..
Mammal species, total known	73	
Mammal species, threatened	3	
Bird species, total known	400	
Bird species, threatened	10	
GEF benefits index for biodiversity (0–100)	0.1	

Energy

GDP per unit of energy use (2000 PPP $/kg oil equiv)	4.5	5.2
Energy use per capita (kg oil equiv)	5,359	5,410
Energy from combustible renewables & waste (% of tot.)	..	3.0
Energy imports, net (% of energy use)	99	19
Electric power consumption per capita (kWh)	7,977	9,503
Electricity generated by coal (% of total)	..	38.2

Emissions and pollution

CO_2 emissions per unit of GDP (kg/2000 PPP $ of GDP)	0.6	0.5
CO_2 emissions per capita (metric tons)	13.7	12.8
Particulate matter (urban-pop.-weighted avg., µg/cu. m)	48	29
Passenger cars (per 1,000 people)	97	433

Water and sanitation

Internal freshwater resources per capita (cu. m)	141	9,703
Freshwater withdrawal		
Total (% of internal resources)	..	10.4
Agriculture (% of total freshwater withdrawal)	..	42
Access to improved water source (% of total population)	..	99
Rural (% of rural population)	..	98
Urban (% of urban population)	100	100
Access to improved sanitation (% of total population)	..	..
Rural (% of rural population)	..	..
Urban (% of urban population)	100	..

Environment and health

ARI prevalence (% of children under age 5)	..	
Diarrhea prevalence (% of children under age 5)	..	
Under-five mortality rate (per 1,000 live births)	3	7

National accounting aggregates, 2004

Gross savings (% of GNI)	46.6	19.4
Consumption of fixed capital (% of GNI)	15.0	13.2
Education expenditure (% of GNI)	2.7	4.6
Energy depletion (% of GNI)	0.0	1.4
Mineral depletion (% of GNI)	0.0	0.0
Net forest depletion (% of GNI)	0.0	0.0
CO_2 damage (% of GNI)	0.4	0.3
Particulate emission damage (% of GNI)	0.9	0.4
Adjusted net savings (% of GNI)	33.0	8.7

Slovak Republic

Environmental strategy/action plan prepared in ..

	Country data	Group data Europe & Central Asia	Upper middle income
Population (millions)	5.4	472	576
Urban population (% of total)	57.7	63.6	72.3
GDP ($ billions)	41.1	1,770	2,992
GNI per capita, World Bank Atlas method ($)	6,480	3,295	4,769
Agriculture			
Land area (1,000 sq. km)	48	23,371	28,983
Agricultural land (% of land area)	..	29	26
Irrigated land (% of cropland)	..	11.1	8.7
Fertilizer consumption (100 grams/ha of arable land)	..	347	469
Population density, rural (people/sq. km of arable land)	..	126	131
Forests and biodiversity			
Forest area (% of land area)	..	38.3	37.3
Annual deforestation (% change, 1990–2005)	0.0	0.0	0.1
Nationally protected areas (% of total land area)	..	6.9	..
Mammal species, total known	87		
Mammal species, threatened	7		
Bird species, total known	332		
Bird species, threatened	11		
GEF benefits index for biodiversity (0–100)	0.1		
Energy			
GDP per unit of energy use (2000 PPP $/kg oil equiv)	3.7	2.7	3.5
Energy use per capita (kg oil equiv)	3,443	2,794	2,574
Energy from combustible renewables & waste (% of tot.)	1.9	2.4	3.9
Energy imports, net (% of energy use)	65	–26	–51
Electric power consumption per capita (kWh)	5,010	3,531	3,378
Electricity generated by coal (% of total)	20.6	29.8	31.0
Emissions and pollution			
CO_2 emissions per unit of GDP (kg/2000 PPP $ of GDP)	0.6	1.0	0.7
CO_2 emissions per capita (metric tons)	6.8	6.7	6.2
Particulate matter (urban-pop.-weighted avg., μg/cu. m)	20	35	40
Passenger cars (per 1,000 people)	247	142	143
Water and sanitation			
Internal freshwater resources per capita (cu. m)	2,341	11,123	14,190
Freshwater withdrawal			
Total (% of internal resources)	..	7.5	3.8
Agriculture (% of total freshwater withdrawal)	..	59	53
Access to improved water source (% of total population)	100	91	93
Rural (% of rural population)	100	80	82
Urban (% of urban population)	100	98	97
Access to improved sanitation (% of total population)	100	82	81
Rural (% of rural population)	100	63	61
Urban (% of urban population)	100	93	91
Environment and health			
ARI prevalence (% of children under age 5)	..		
Diarrhea prevalence (% of children under age 5)	..		
Under-five mortality rate (per 1,000 live births)	9	34	28
National accounting aggregates, 2004			
Gross savings (% of GNI)	23.4	23.4	23.1
Consumption of fixed capital (% of GNI)	21.8	10.7	11.5
Education expenditure (% of GNI)	4.2	4.1	4.5
Energy depletion (% of GNI)	0.1	12.0	11.2
Mineral depletion (% of GNI)	0.0	0.3	0.6
Net forest depletion (% of GNI)	0.4	0.0	0.0
CO_2 damage (% of GNI)	0.7	1.4	0.9
Particulate emission damage (% of GNI)	0.1	0.7	0.7
Adjusted net savings (% of GNI)	4.6	2.3	2.6

Slovenia

Environmental strategy/action plan prepared in **1994**

	Country data	Group data High income
Population (millions)	2.0	1,004
Urban population (% of total)	50.8	78.5
GDP ($ billions)	32.2	32,900
GNI per capita, *World Bank Atlas* method ($)	14,770	32,112
Agriculture		
Land area (1,000 sq. km)	20	33,018
Agricultural land (% of land area)	25	38
Irrigated land (% of cropland)	1.5	11.9
Fertilizer consumption (100 grams/ha of arable land)	4,160	1,205
Population density, rural (people/sq. km of arable land)	568	331
Forests and biodiversity		
Forest area (% of land area)	62.8	29.3
Annual deforestation (% change, 1990–2005)	–0.4	–0.1
Nationally protected areas (% of total land area)	6.0	..
Mammal species, total known	87	
Mammal species, threatened	7	
Bird species, total known	350	
Bird species, threatened	7	
GEF benefits index for biodiversity (0–100)	0.2	
Energy		
GDP per unit of energy use (2000 PPP $/kg oil equiv)	5.2	5.2
Energy use per capita (kg oil equiv)	3,518	5,410
Energy from combustible renewables & waste (% of tot.)	6.7	3.0
Energy imports, net (% of energy use)	53	19
Electric power consumption per capita (kWh)	6,817	9,503
Electricity generated by coal (% of total)	36.4	38.2
Emissions and pollution		
CO_2 emissions per unit of GDP (kg/2000 PPP $ of GDP)	0.4	0.5
CO_2 emissions per capita (metric tons)	7.7	12.8
Particulate matter (urban-pop.-weighted avg., µg/cu. m)	33	29
Passenger cars (per 1,000 people)	438	433
Water and sanitation		
Internal freshwater resources per capita (cu. m)	9,349	9,703
Freshwater withdrawal		
Total (% of internal resources)	..	10.4
Agriculture (% of total freshwater withdrawal)	..	42
Access to improved water source (% of total population)	..	99
Rural (% of rural population)	..	98
Urban (% of urban population)	..	100
Access to improved sanitation (% of total population)	..	..
Rural (% of rural population)	..	..
Urban (% of urban population)	..	..
Environment and health		
ARI prevalence (% of children under age 5)	..	
Diarrhea prevalence (% of children under age 5)	..	
Under-five mortality rate (per 1,000 live births)	4	7
National accounting aggregates, 2004		
Gross savings (% of GNI)	25.9	19.4
Consumption of fixed capital (% of GNI)	13.6	13.2
Education expenditure (% of GNI)	5.6	4.6
Energy depletion (% of GNI)	0.0	1.4
Mineral depletion (% of GNI)	0.0	0.0
Net forest depletion (% of GNI)	0.2	0.0
CO_2 damage (% of GNI)	0.3	0.3
Particulate emission damage (% of GNI)	0.2	0.4
Adjusted net savings (% of GNI)	17.2	8.7

Solomon Islands

Environmental strategy/action plan prepared in ..

	Country data	Group data — East Asia & Pacific	Low income
Population (millions)	0.5	1,870	2,343
Urban population (% of total)	16.8	40.6	30.6
GDP ($ billions)	0.3	2,651	1,239
GNI per capita, *World Bank Atlas* method ($)	560	1,416	507
Agriculture			
Land area (1,000 sq. km)	28	15,885	29,192
Agricultural land (% of land area)	4	51	45
Irrigated land (% of cropland)	..	..	23.9
Fertilizer consumption (100 grams/ha of arable land)	..	2,296	646
Population density, rural (people/sq. km of arable land)	2,105	559	524
Forests and biodiversity			
Forest area (% of land area)	77.6	28.4	24.8
Annual deforestation (% change, 1990–2005)	1.4	−0.2	0.5
Nationally protected areas (% of total land area)	0.3	..	7.7
Mammal species, total known	72		
Mammal species, threatened	20		
Bird species, total known	248		
Bird species, threatened	21		
GEF benefits index for biodiversity (0–100)	4.5		
Energy			
GDP per unit of energy use (2000 PPP $/kg oil equiv)	..	4.6	4.2
Energy use per capita (kg oil equiv)	..	1,007	501
Energy from combustible renewables & waste (% of tot.)	..	17.7	48.9
Energy imports, net (% of energy use)	..	−2	−4
Electric power consumption per capita (kWh)	..	1,184	358
Electricity generated by coal (% of total)	..	69.4	46.3
Emissions and pollution			
CO_2 emissions per unit of GDP (kg/2000 PPP $ of GDP)	0.2	0.5	0.4
CO_2 emissions per capita (metric tons)	0.4	2.4	0.8
Particulate matter (urban-pop.-weighted avg., µg/cu. m)	16	80	89
Passenger cars (per 1,000 people)	..	12	6
Water and sanitation			
Internal freshwater resources per capita (cu. m)	95,965	5,062	3,456
Freshwater withdrawal			
Total (% of internal resources)	..	10.2	15.5
Agriculture (% of total freshwater withdrawal)	..	74	88
Access to improved water source (% of total population)	70	78	75
Rural (% of rural population)	65	69	69
Urban (% of urban population)	94	92	89
Access to improved sanitation (% of total population)	31	49	36
Rural (% of rural population)	18	35	24
Urban (% of urban population)	98	72	61
Environment and health			
ARI prevalence (% of children under age 5)	..		
Diarrhea prevalence (% of children under age 5)	..		
Under-five mortality rate (per 1,000 live births)	56	37	122
National accounting aggregates, 2004			
Gross savings (% of GNI)	..	39.1	22.7
Consumption of fixed capital (% of GNI)	9.2	10.5	9.2
Education expenditure (% of GNI)	3.8	2.3	3.4
Energy depletion (% of GNI)	0.0	4.1	6.7
Mineral depletion (% of GNI)	0.0	0.4	0.4
Net forest depletion (% of GNI)	6.6	0.0	0.7
CO_2 damage (% of GNI)	0.4	1.2	1.1
Particulate emission damage (% of GNI)	0.0	1.2	0.8
Adjusted net savings (% of GNI)	..	23.9	7.3

Somalia

Environmental strategy/action plan prepared in ..

	Country data	Sub-Saharan Africa	Low income
		Group data	
Population (millions)	8.0	726	2,343
Urban population (% of total)	35.4	36.4	30.6
GDP ($ billions)	..	523	1,239
GNI per capita, *World Bank Atlas* method ($)	..	601	507
Agriculture			
Land area (1,000 sq. km)	627	23,596	29,192
Agricultural land (% of land area)	70	44	45
Irrigated land (% of cropland)	18.7	3.6	23.9
Fertilizer consumption (100 grams/ha of arable land)	5	136	646
Population density, rural (people/sq. km of arable land)	480	355	524
Forests and biodiversity			
Forest area (% of land area)	11.4	26.5	24.8
Annual deforestation (% change, 1990–2005)	0.9	0.6	0.5
Nationally protected areas (% of total land area)	0.8	8.7	7.7
Mammal species, total known	182		
Mammal species, threatened	15		
Bird species, total known	642		
Bird species, threatened	13		
GEF benefits index for biodiversity (0–100)	6.7		
Energy			
GDP per unit of energy use (2000 PPP $/kg oil equiv)	..	2.8	4.2
Energy use per capita (kg oil equiv)	..	681	501
Energy from combustible renewables & waste (% of tot.)	..	57.4	48.9
Energy imports, net (% of energy use)	..	−59	−4
Electric power consumption per capita (kWh)	..	513	358
Electricity generated by coal (% of total)	..	68.0	46.3
Emissions and pollution			
CO_2 emissions per unit of GDP (kg/2000 PPP $ of GDP)	..	0.4	0.4
CO_2 emissions per capita (metric tons)	..	0.7	0.8
Particulate matter (urban-pop.-weighted avg., µg/cu. m)	35	73	89
Passenger cars (per 1,000 people)	..	..	6
Water and sanitation			
Internal freshwater resources per capita (cu. m)	753	5,353	3,456
Freshwater withdrawal			
Total (% of internal resources)	54.8	3.1	15.5
Agriculture (% of total freshwater withdrawal)	100	87	88
Access to improved water source (% of total population)	29	58	75
Rural (% of rural population)	27	45	69
Urban (% of urban population)	32	82	89
Access to improved sanitation (% of total population)	25	36	36
Rural (% of rural population)	14	26	24
Urban (% of urban population)	47	55	61
Environment and health			
ARI prevalence (% of children under age 5)	..		
Diarrhea prevalence (% of children under age 5)	23.4		
Under-five mortality rate (per 1,000 live births)	225	168	122
National accounting aggregates, 2004			
Gross savings (% of GNI)	..	17.1	22.7
Consumption of fixed capital (% of GNI)	..	10.9	9.2
Education expenditure (% of GNI)	..	3.9	3.4
Energy depletion (% of GNI)	..	9.8	6.7
Mineral depletion (% of GNI)	..	0.4	0.4
Net forest depletion (% of GNI)	..	0.6	0.7
CO_2 damage (% of GNI)	..	0.7	1.1
Particulate emission damage (% of GNI)	0.2	0.5	0.8
Adjusted net savings (% of GNI)	..	−1.9	7.3

South Africa

Environmental strategy/action plan prepared in **1993**

	Country data	Sub-Saharan Africa	Upper middle income
		Group data	
Population (millions)	45.5	726	576
Urban population (% of total)	57.4	36.4	72.3
GDP ($ billions)	212.8	523	2,992
GNI per capita, *World Bank Atlas* method ($)	3,630	601	4,769
Agriculture			
Land area (1,000 sq. km)	1,214	23,596	28,983
Agricultural land (% of land area)	82	44	26
Irrigated land (% of cropland)	9.5	3.6	8.7
Fertilizer consumption (100 grams/ha of arable land)	654	136	469
Population density, rural (people/sq. km of arable land)	134	355	131
Forests and biodiversity			
Forest area (% of land area)	7.6	26.5	37.3
Annual deforestation (% change, 1990–2005)	0.0	0.6	0.1
Nationally protected areas (% of total land area)	5.5	8.7	..
Mammal species, total known	320		
Mammal species, threatened	29		
Bird species, total known	829		
Bird species, threatened	36		
GEF benefits index for biodiversity (0–100)	23.5		
Energy			
GDP per unit of energy use (2000 PPP $/kg oil equiv)	3.9	2.8	3.5
Energy use per capita (kg oil equiv)	2,587	681	2,574
Energy from combustible renewables & waste (% of tot.)	11.1	57.4	3.9
Energy imports, net (% of energy use)	–30	–59	–51
Electric power consumption per capita (kWh)	4,504	513	3,378
Electricity generated by coal (% of total)	93.5	68.0	31.0
Emissions and pollution			
CO_2 emissions per unit of GDP (kg/2000 PPP $ of GDP)	0.8	0.4	0.7
CO_2 emissions per capita (metric tons)	7.6	0.7	6.2
Particulate matter (urban-pop.-weighted avg., µg/cu. m)	24	73	40
Passenger cars (per 1,000 people)	92	..	143
Water and sanitation			
Internal freshwater resources per capita (cu. m)	984	5,353	14,190
Freshwater withdrawal			
Total (% of internal resources)	27.9	3.1	3.8
Agriculture (% of total freshwater withdrawal)	63	87	53
Access to improved water source (% of total population)	87	58	93
Rural (% of rural population)	73	45	82
Urban (% of urban population)	98	82	97
Access to improved sanitation (% of total population)	67	36	81
Rural (% of rural population)	44	26	61
Urban (% of urban population)	86	55	91
Environment and health			
ARI prevalence (% of children under age 5)	..		
Diarrhea prevalence (% of children under age 5)	13.2		
Under-five mortality rate (per 1,000 live births)	67	168	28
National accounting aggregates, 2004			
Gross savings (% of GNI)	14.7	17.1	23.1
Consumption of fixed capital (% of GNI)	12.1	10.9	11.5
Education expenditure (% of GNI)	5.3	3.9	4.5
Energy depletion (% of GNI)	0.0	9.8	11.2
Mineral depletion (% of GNI)	0.6	0.4	0.6
Net forest depletion (% of GNI)	0.3	0.6	0.0
CO_2 damage (% of GNI)	1.2	0.7	0.9
Particulate emission damage (% of GNI)	0.3	0.5	0.7
Adjusted net savings (% of GNI)	5.6	–1.9	2.6

Spain

Environmental strategy/action plan prepared in ..

	Country data	Group data High income
Population (millions)	42.7	1,004
Urban population (% of total)	76.6	78.5
GDP ($ billions)	1,039.9	32,900
GNI per capita, *World Bank Atlas* method ($)	21,530	32,112
Agriculture		
Land area (1,000 sq. km)	499	33,018
Agricultural land (% of land area)	60	38
Irrigated land (% of cropland)	20.2	11.9
Fertilizer consumption (100 grams/ha of arable land)	1,572	1,205
Population density, rural (people/sq. km of arable land)	72	331
Forests and biodiversity		
Forest area (% of land area)	35.9	29.3
Annual deforestation (% change, 1990–2005)	−2.2	−0.1
Nationally protected areas (% of total land area)	8.5	..
Mammal species, total known	132	
Mammal species, threatened	20	
Bird species, total known	515	
Bird species, threatened	20	
GEF benefits index for biodiversity (0–100)	6.6	
Energy		
GDP per unit of energy use (2000 PPP $/kg oil equiv)	7.0	5.2
Energy use per capita (kg oil equiv)	3,240	5,410
Energy from combustible renewables & waste (% of tot.)	3.5	3.0
Energy imports, net (% of energy use)	76	19
Electric power consumption per capita (kWh)	5,701	9,503
Electricity generated by coal (% of total)	29.5	38.2
Emissions and pollution		
CO_2 emissions per unit of GDP (kg/2000 PPP $ of GDP)	0.3	0.5
CO_2 emissions per capita (metric tons)	7.4	12.8
Particulate matter (urban-pop.-weighted avg., µg/cu. m)	40	29
Passenger cars (per 1,000 people)	458	433
Water and sanitation		
Internal freshwater resources per capita (cu. m)	2,605	9,703
Freshwater withdrawal		
Total (% of internal resources)	32.0	10.4
Agriculture (% of total freshwater withdrawal)	68	42
Access to improved water source (% of total population)	..	99
Rural (% of rural population)	..	98
Urban (% of urban population)	..	100
Access to improved sanitation (% of total population)	..	..
Rural (% of rural population)	..	..
Urban (% of urban population)	..	..
Environment and health		
ARI prevalence (% of children under age 5)	..	
Diarrhea prevalence (% of children under age 5)	..	
Under-five mortality rate (per 1,000 live births)	5	7
National accounting aggregates, 2004		
Gross savings (% of GNI)	23.4	19.4
Consumption of fixed capital (% of GNI)	14.5	13.2
Education expenditure (% of GNI)	4.1	4.6
Energy depletion (% of GNI)	0.0	1.4
Mineral depletion (% of GNI)	0.0	0.0
Net forest depletion (% of GNI)	0.0	0.0
CO_2 damage (% of GNI)	0.2	0.3
Particulate emission damage (% of GNI)	0.6	0.4
Adjusted net savings (% of GNI)	12.2	8.7

Sri Lanka

Environmental strategy/action plan prepared in **1994**

	Country data	South Asia	Lower middle income
		Group data	
Population (millions)	19.4	1,447	2,442
Urban population (% of total)	21.1	28.3	48.7
GDP ($ billions)	20.1	880	4,165
GNI per capita, *World Bank Atlas* method ($)	1,010	594	1,686
Agriculture			
Land area (1,000 sq. km)	65	4,781	38,470
Agricultural land (% of land area)	36	54	43
Irrigated land (% of cropland)	38.8	39.6	23.1
Fertilizer consumption (100 grams/ha of arable land)	3,103	1,040	1,530
Population density, rural (people/sq. km of arable land)	1,659	586	523
Forests and biodiversity			
Forest area (% of land area)	29.9	16.8	30.7
Annual deforestation (% change, 1990–2005)	1.2	–0.2	0.1
Nationally protected areas (% of total land area)	13.5	4.8	7.7
Mammal species, total known	123		
Mammal species, threatened	21		
Bird species, total known	381		
Bird species, threatened	16		
GEF benefits index for biodiversity (0–100)	6.6		
Energy			
GDP per unit of energy use (2000 PPP $/kg oil equiv)	8.8	5.3	4.6
Energy use per capita (kg oil equiv)	421	474	1,090
Energy from combustible renewables & waste (% of tot.)	49.5	38.8	14.6
Energy imports, net (% of energy use)	47	19	–14
Electric power consumption per capita (kWh)	325	394	1,329
Electricity generated by coal (% of total)	..	58.2	49.4
Emissions and pollution			
CO_2 emissions per unit of GDP (kg/2000 PPP $ of GDP)	0.1	0.4	0.5
CO_2 emissions per capita (metric tons)	0.5	1.0	2.6
Particulate matter (urban-pop.-weighted avg., μg/cu. m)	93	99	70
Passenger cars per 1,000 people	13	6	29
Water and sanitation			
Internal freshwater resources per capita (cu. m)	2,575	1,255	7,295
Freshwater withdrawal			
Total (% of internal resources)	25.2	51.8	7.7
Agriculture (% of total freshwater withdrawal)	95	90	75
Access to improved water source (% of total population)	78	84	81
Rural (% of rural population)	72	80	70
Urban (% of urban population)	99	94	93
Access to improved sanitation (% of total population)	91	35	57
Rural (% of rural population)	89	23	39
Urban (% of urban population)	98	64	78
Environment and health			
ARI prevalence (% of children under age 5)	..		
Diarrhea prevalence (% of children under age 5)	..		
Under-five mortality rate (per 1,000 live births)	14	92	40
National accounting aggregates, 2004			
Gross savings (% of GNI)	19.4	23.6	32.1
Consumption of fixed capital (% of GNI)	10.3	9.1	10.8
Education expenditure (% of GNI)	2.6	3.6	2.9
Energy depletion (% of GNI)	0.0	2.7	6.5
Mineral depletion (% of GNI)	0.0	0.3	0.5
Net forest depletion (% of GNI)	0.4	0.7	0.0
CO_2 damage (% of GNI)	0.4	1.2	1.1
Particulate emission damage (% of GNI)	0.5	0.8	1.0
Adjusted net savings (% of GNI)	10.4	12.4	15.1

St. Kitts and Nevis

Environmental strategy/action plan prepared in ..

	Country data	Latin America & Caribbean	Upper middle income
		Group data	
Population (millions)	0.0	546	576
Urban population (% of total)	32.0	77.1	72.3
GDP ($ billions)	0.4	2,022	2,992
GNI per capita, *World Bank Atlas* method ($)	6,980	3,576	4,769
Agriculture			
Land area (1,000 sq. km)	0	20,057	28,983
Agricultural land (% of land area)	28	36	26
Irrigated land (% of cropland)	..	11.4	8.7
Fertilizer consumption (100 grams/ha of arable land)	2,429	923	469
Population density, rural (people/sq. km of arable land)	452	212	131
Forests and biodiversity			
Forest area (% of land area)	13.9	45.6	37.3
Annual deforestation (% change, 1990–2005)	0.0	0.4	0.1
Nationally protected areas (% of total land area)	..	11.1	..
Mammal species, total known	7		
Mammal species, threatened	1		
Bird species, total known	132		
Bird species, threatened	2		
GEF benefits index for biodiversity (0–100)	0.1		
Energy			
GDP per unit of energy use (2000 PPP $/kg oil equiv)	..	6.2	3.5
Energy use per capita (kg oil equiv)	..	1,148	2,574
Energy from combustible renewables & waste (% of tot.)	..	15.0	3.9
Energy imports, net (% of energy use)	..	–40	–51
Electric power consumption per capita (kWh)	..	1,615	3,378
Electricity generated by coal (% of total)	..	5.4	31.0
Emissions and pollution			
CO_2 emissions per unit of GDP (kg/2000 PPP $ of GDP)	0.2	0.3	0.7
CO_2 emissions per capita (metric tons)	2.4	2.4	6.2
Particulate matter (urban-pop.-weighted avg., µg/cu. m)	33	43	40
Passenger cars (per 1,000 people)	..	108	143
Water and sanitation			
Internal freshwater resources per capita (cu. m)	511	24,619	14,190
Freshwater withdrawal			
Total (% of internal resources)	..	2.0	3.8
Agriculture (% of total freshwater withdrawal)	..	71	53
Access to improved water source (% of total population)	99	89	93
Rural (% of rural population)	99	69	82
Urban (% of urban population)	99	96	97
Access to improved sanitation (% of total population)	96	75	81
Rural (% of rural population)	96	44	61
Urban (% of urban population)	96	84	91
Environment and health			
ARI prevalence (% of children under age 5)	..		
Diarrhea prevalence (% of children under age 5)	..		
Under-five mortality rate (per 1,000 live births)	..	31	28
National accounting aggregates, 2004			
Gross savings (% of GNI)	..	22.7	23.1
Consumption of fixed capital (% of GNI)	14.5	12.1	11.5
Education expenditure (% of GNI)	3.7	4.4	4.5
Energy depletion (% of GNI)	0.0	7.2	11.2
Mineral depletion (% of GNI)	0.0	1.1	0.6
Net forest depletion (% of GNI)	..	0.0	0.0
CO_2 damage (% of GNI)	0.2	0.5	0.9
Particulate emission damage (% of GNI)	..	0.6	0.7
Adjusted net savings (% of GNI)	..	5.6	2.6

St. Lucia

Environmental strategy/action plan prepared in ..

	Country data	Group data Latin America & Caribbean	Upper middle income
Population (millions)	0.2	546	576
Urban population (% of total)	30.9	77.1	72.3
GDP ($ billions)	0.8	2,022	2,992
GNI per capita, *World Bank Atlas* method ($)	4,180	3,576	4,769
Agriculture			
Land area (1,000 sq. km)	1	20,057	28,983
Agricultural land (% of land area)	33	36	26
Irrigated land (% of cropland)	16.7	11.4	8.7
Fertilizer consumption (100 grams/ha of arable land)	3,358	923	469
Population density, rural (people/sq. km of arable land)	2,790	212	131
Forests and biodiversity			
Forest area (% of land area)	27.9	45.6	37.3
Annual deforestation (% change, 1990–2005)	0.0	0.4	0.1
Nationally protected areas (% of total land area)	..	11.1	..
Mammal species, total known	13		
Mammal species, threatened	2		
Bird species, total known	162		
Bird species, threatened	5		
GEF benefits index for biodiversity (0–100)	1.0		
Energy			
GDP per unit of energy use (2000 PPP $/kg oil equiv)	..	6.2	3.5
Energy use per capita (kg oil equiv)	..	1,148	2,574
Energy from combustible renewables & waste (% of tot.)	..	15.0	3.9
Energy imports, net (% of energy use)	..	–40	–51
Electric power consumption per capita (kWh)	..	1,615	3,378
Electricity generated by coal (% of total)	..	5.4	31.0
Emissions and pollution			
CO_2 emissions per unit of GDP (kg/2000 PPP $ of GDP)	0.4	0.3	0.7
CO_2 emissions per capita (metric tons)	2.4	2.4	6.2
Particulate matter (urban-pop.-weighted avg., µg/cu. m)	74	43	40
Passenger cars (per 1,000 people)	..	108	143
Water and sanitation			
Internal freshwater resources per capita (cu. m)	..	24,619	14,190
Freshwater withdrawal			
Total (% of internal resources)	..	2.0	3.8
Agriculture (% of total freshwater withdrawal)	0	71	53
Access to improved water source (% of total population)	98	89	93
Rural (% of rural population)	98	69	82
Urban (% of urban population)	98	96	97
Access to improved sanitation (% of total population)	89	75	81
Rural (% of rural population)	89	44	61
Urban (% of urban population)	89	84	91
Environment and health			
ARI prevalence (% of children under age 5)	..		
Diarrhea prevalence (% of children under age 5)	..		
Under-five mortality rate (per 1,000 live births)	14	31	28
National accounting aggregates, 2004			
Gross savings (% of GNI)	..	22.7	23.1
Consumption of fixed capital (% of GNI)	13.5	12.1	11.5
Education expenditure (% of GNI)	6.3	4.4	4.5
Energy depletion (% of GNI)	0.0	7.2	11.2
Mineral depletion (% of GNI)	0.0	1.1	0.6
Net forest depletion (% of GNI)	..	0.0	0.0
CO_2 damage (% of GNI)	0.3	0.5	0.9
Particulate emission damage (% of GNI)	1.0	0.6	0.7
Adjusted net savings (% of GNI)	..	5.6	2.6

St. Vincent & Grenadines

Environmental strategy/action plan prepared in ..

	Country data	Latin America & Caribbean	Upper middle income
Population (millions)	0.1	546	576
Urban population (% of total)	59.3	77.1	72.3
GDP ($ billions)	0.4	2,022	2,992
GNI per capita, *World Bank Atlas* method ($)	3,400	3,576	4,769
Agriculture			
Land area (1,000 sq. km)	0	20,057	28,983
Agricultural land (% of land area)	41	36	26
Irrigated land (% of cropland)	7.1	11.4	8.7
Fertilizer consumption (100 grams/ha of arable land)	3,047	923	469
Population density, rural (people/sq. km of arable land)	704	212	131
Forests and biodiversity			
Forest area (% of land area)	28.2	45.6	37.3
Annual deforestation (% change, 1990–2005)	–1.5	0.4	0.1
Nationally protected areas (% of total land area)	..	11.1	..
Mammal species, total known	32		
Mammal species, threatened	2		
Bird species, total known	153		
Bird species, threatened	2		
GEF benefits index for biodiversity (0–100)	1.1		
Energy			
GDP per unit of energy use (2000 PPP $/kg oil equiv)	..	6.2	3.5
Energy use per capita (kg oil equiv)	..	1,148	2,574
Energy from combustible renewables & waste (% of tot.)	..	15.0	3.9
Energy imports, net (% of energy use)	..	–40	–51
Electric power consumption per capita (kWh)	..	1,615	3,378
Electricity generated by coal (% of total)	..	5.4	31.0
Emissions and pollution			
CO_2 emissions per unit of GDP (kg/2000 PPP $ of GDP)	0.2	0.3	0.7
CO_2 emissions per capita (metric tons)	1.6	2.4	6.2
Particulate matter (urban-pop.-weighted avg., µg/cu. m)	56	43	40
Passenger cars (per 1,000 people)	96	108	143
Water and sanitation			
Internal freshwater resources per capita (cu. m)	..	24,619	14,190
Freshwater withdrawal			
Total (% of internal resources)	..	2.0	3.8
Agriculture (% of total freshwater withdrawal)	0	71	53
Access to improved water source (% of total population)	..	89	93
Rural (% of rural population)	93	69	82
Urban (% of urban population)	..	96	97
Access to improved sanitation (% of total population)	..	75	81
Rural (% of rural population)	96	44	61
Urban (% of urban population)	..	84	91
Environment and health			
ARI prevalence (% of children under age 5)	..		
Diarrhea prevalence (% of children under age 5)	..		
Under-five mortality rate (per 1,000 live births)	22	31	28
National accounting aggregates, 2004			
Gross savings (% of GNI)	12.0	22.7	23.1
Consumption of fixed capital (% of GNI)	12.2	12.1	11.5
Education expenditure (% of GNI)	9.8	4.4	4.5
Energy depletion (% of GNI)	0.0	7.2	11.2
Mineral depletion (% of GNI)	0.0	1.1	0.6
Net forest depletion (% of GNI)	0.0	0.0	0.0
CO_2 damage (% of GNI)	0.3	0.5	0.9
Particulate emission damage (% of GNI)	0.3	0.6	0.7
Adjusted net savings (% of GNI)	8.9	5.6	2.6

Sudan

Environmental strategy/action plan prepared in ..

	Country data	Sub-Saharan Africa	Low income
		Group data	
Population (millions)	35.5	726	2,343
Urban population (% of total)	39.9	36.4	30.6
GDP ($ billions)	21.1	523	1,239
GNI per capita, *World Bank Atlas* method ($)	530	601	507
Agriculture			
Land area (1,000 sq. km)	2,376	23,596	29,192
Agricultural land (% of land area)	57	44	45
Irrigated land (% of cropland)	10.7	3.6	23.9
Fertilizer consumption (100 grams/ha of arable land)	43	136	646
Population density, rural (people/sq. km of arable land)	125	355	524
Forests and biodiversity			
Forest area (% of land area)	28.4	26.5	24.8
Annual deforestation (% change, 1990–2005)	0.8	0.6	0.5
Nationally protected areas (% of total land area)	5.2	8.7	7.7
Mammal species, total known	302		
Mammal species, threatened	16		
Bird species, total known	952		
Bird species, threatened	10		
GEF benefits index for biodiversity (0–100)	5.5		
Energy			
GDP per unit of energy use (2000 PPP $/kg oil equiv)	3.7	2.8	4.2
Energy use per capita (kg oil equiv)	477	681	501
Energy from combustible renewables & waste (% of tot.)	80.6	57.4	48.9
Energy imports, net (% of energy use)	–62	–59	–4
Electric power consumption per capita (kWh)	81	513	358
Electricity generated by coal (% of total)	..	68.0	46.3
Emissions and pollution			
CO_2 emissions per unit of GDP (kg/2000 PPP $ of GDP)	0.1	0.4	0.4
CO_2 emissions per capita (metric tons)	0.3	0.7	0.8
Particulate matter (urban-pop.-weighted avg., μg/cu. m)	219	73	89
Passenger cars (per 1,000 people)	..	..	6
Water and sanitation			
Internal freshwater resources per capita (cu. m)	845	5,353	3,456
Freshwater withdrawal			
Total (% of internal resources)	124.4	3.1	15.5
Agriculture (% of total freshwater withdrawal)	97	87	88
Access to improved water source (% of total population)	69	58	75
Rural (% of rural population)	64	45	69
Urban (% of urban population)	78	82	89
Access to improved sanitation (% of total population)	34	36	36
Rural (% of rural population)	24	26	24
Urban (% of urban population)	50	55	61
Environment and health			
ARI prevalence (% of children under age 5)	..		
Diarrhea prevalence (% of children under age 5)	..		
Under-five mortality rate (per 1,000 live births)	91	168	122
National accounting aggregates, 2004			
Gross savings (% of GNI)	15.8	17.1	22.7
Consumption of fixed capital (% of GNI)	9.9	10.9	9.2
Education expenditure (% of GNI)	0.9	3.9	3.4
Energy depletion (% of GNI)	15.1	9.8	6.7
Mineral depletion (% of GNI)	0.0	0.4	0.4
Net forest depletion (% of GNI)	0.0	0.6	0.7
CO_2 damage (% of GNI)	0.3	0.7	1.1
Particulate emission damage (% of GNI)	0.8	0.5	0.8
Adjusted net savings (% of GNI)	–9.4	–1.9	7.3

Suriname

Environmental strategy/action plan prepared in ..

	Country data	Latin America & Caribbean	Lower middle income
		Group data	
Population (millions)	0.4	546	2,442
Urban population (% of total)	76.6	77.1	48.7
GDP ($ billions)	1.1	2,022	4,165
GNI per capita, *World Bank Atlas* method ($)	2,230	3,576	1,686
Agriculture			
Land area (1,000 sq. km)	156	20,057	38,470
Agricultural land (% of land area)	1	36	43
Irrigated land (% of cropland)	75.0	11.4	23.1
Fertilizer consumption (100 grams/ha of arable land)	982	923	1,530
Population density, rural (people/sq. km of arable land)	184	212	523
Forests and biodiversity			
Forest area (% of land area)	94.7	45.6	30.7
Annual deforestation (% change, 1990–2005)	0.0	0.4	0.1
Nationally protected areas (% of total land area)	4.9	11.1	7.7
Mammal species, total known	203		
Mammal species, threatened	12		
Bird species, total known	674		
Bird species, threatened	0		
GEF benefits index for biodiversity (0–100)	3.0		
Energy			
GDP per unit of energy use (2000 PPP $/kg oil equiv)	..	6.2	4.6
Energy use per capita (kg oil equiv)	..	1,148	1,090
Energy from combustible renewables & waste (% of tot.)	..	15.0	14.6
Energy imports, net (% of energy use)	..	–40	–14
Electric power consumption per capita (kWh)	..	1,615	1,329
Electricity generated by coal (% of total)	..	5.4	49.4
Emissions and pollution			
CO_2 emissions per unit of GDP (kg/2000 PPP $ of GDP)	..	0.3	0.5
CO_2 emissions per capita (metric tons)	5.1	2.4	2.6
Particulate matter (urban-pop.-weighted avg., µg/cu. m)	13	43	70
Passenger cars (per 1,000 people)	145	108	29
Water and sanitation			
Internal freshwater resources per capita (cu. m)	197,106	24,619	7,295
Freshwater withdrawal			
Total (% of internal resources)	0.8	2.0	7.7
Agriculture (% of total freshwater withdrawal)	93	71	75
Access to improved water source (% of total population)	92	89	81
Rural (% of rural population)	73	69	70
Urban (% of urban population)	98	96	93
Access to improved sanitation (% of total population)	93	75	57
Rural (% of rural population)	76	44	39
Urban (% of urban population)	99	84	78
Environment and health			
ARI prevalence (% of children under age 5)	4.0		
Diarrhea prevalence (% of children under age 5)	14.8		
Under-five mortality rate (per 1,000 live births)	39	31	40
National accounting aggregates, 2004			
Gross savings (% of GNI)	..	22.7	32.1
Consumption of fixed capital (% of GNI)	12.7	12.1	10.8
Education expenditure (% of GNI)	..	4.4	2.9
Energy depletion (% of GNI)	22.7	7.2	6.5
Mineral depletion (% of GNI)	1.1	1.1	0.5
Net forest depletion (% of GNI)	0.0	0.0	0.0
CO_2 damage (% of GNI)	1.7	0.5	1.1
Particulate emission damage (% of GNI)	..	0.6	1.0
Adjusted net savings (% of GNI)	..	5.6	15.1

Swaziland

Environmental strategy/action plan prepared in ..

	Country data	Group data Sub-Saharan Africa	Group data Lower middle income
Population (millions)	1.1	726	2,442
Urban population (% of total)	23.7	36.4	48.7
GDP ($ billions)	2.4	523	4,165
GNI per capita, *World Bank Atlas* method ($)	1,660	601	1,686
Agriculture			
Land area (1,000 sq. km)	17	23,596	38,470
Agricultural land (% of land area)	81	44	43
Irrigated land (% of cropland)	26.0	3.6	23.1
Fertilizer consumption (100 grams/ha of arable land)	393	136	1,530
Population density, rural (people/sq. km of arable land)	475	355	523
Forests and biodiversity			
Forest area (% of land area)	31.5	26.5	30.7
Annual deforestation (% change, 1990–2005)	–1.0	0.6	0.1
Nationally protected areas (% of total land area)	..	8.7	7.7
Mammal species, total known	124		
Mammal species, threatened	6		
Bird species, total known	490		
Bird species, threatened	6		
GEF benefits index for biodiversity (0–100)	0.1		
Energy			
GDP per unit of energy use (2000 PPP $/kg oil equiv)	..	2.8	4.6
Energy use per capita (kg oil equiv)	..	681	1,090
Energy from combustible renewables & waste (% of tot.)	..	57.4	14.6
Energy imports, net (% of energy use)	..	–59	–14
Electric power consumption per capita (kWh)	..	513	1,329
Electricity generated by coal (% of total)	..	68.0	49.4
Emissions and pollution			
CO_2 emissions per unit of GDP (kg/2000 PPP $ of GDP)	0.2	0.4	0.5
CO_2 emissions per capita (metric tons)	0.9	0.7	2.6
Particulate matter (urban-pop.-weighted avg., µg/cu. m)	71	73	70
Passenger cars (per 1,000 people)	39	..	29
Water and sanitation			
Internal freshwater resources per capita (cu. m)	2,357	5,353	7,295
Freshwater withdrawal			
Total (% of internal resources)	39.5	3.1	7.7
Agriculture (% of total freshwater withdrawal)	97	87	75
Access to improved water source (% of total population)	52	58	81
Rural (% of rural population)	42	45	70
Urban (% of urban population)	87	82	93
Access to improved sanitation (% of total population)	52	36	57
Rural (% of rural population)	44	26	39
Urban (% of urban population)	78	55	78
Environment and health			
ARI prevalence (% of children under age 5)	..		
Diarrhea prevalence (% of children under age 5)	..		
Under-five mortality rate (per 1,000 live births)	156	168	40
National accounting aggregates, 2004			
Gross savings (% of GNI)	16.8	17.1	32.1
Consumption of fixed capital (% of GNI)	11.0	10.9	10.8
Education expenditure (% of GNI)	5.5	3.9	2.9
Energy depletion (% of GNI)	0.0	9.8	6.5
Mineral depletion (% of GNI)	0.0	0.4	0.5
Net forest depletion (% of GNI)	0.0	0.6	0.0
CO_2 damage (% of GNI)	0.3	0.7	1.1
Particulate emission damage (% of GNI)	0.2	0.5	1.0
Adjusted net savings (% of GNI)	10.8	–1.9	15.1

Sweden

Environmental strategy/action plan prepared in ..

	Country data	Group data High income
Population (millions)	9.0	1,004
Urban population (% of total)	83.4	78.5
GDP ($ billions)	346.4	32,900
GNI per capita, *World Bank Atlas* method ($)	35,840	32,112

Agriculture

Land area (1,000 sq. km)	410	33,018
Agricultural land (% of land area)	8	38
Irrigated land (% of cropland)	4.3	11.9
Fertilizer consumption (100 grams/ha of arable land)	1,000	1,205
Population density, rural (people/sq. km of arable land)	56	331

Forests and biodiversity

Forest area (% of land area)	67.1	29.3
Annual deforestation (% change, 1990–2005)	0.0	–0.1
Nationally protected areas (% of total land area)	9.1	..
Mammal species, total known	85	
Mammal species, threatened	5	
Bird species, total known	457	
Bird species, threatened	9	
GEF benefits index for biodiversity (0–100)	0.3	

Energy

GDP per unit of energy use (2000 PPP $/kg oil equiv)	4.6	5.2
Energy use per capita (kg oil equiv)	5,754	5,410
Energy from combustible renewables & waste (% of tot.)	17.1	3.0
Energy imports, net (% of energy use)	39	19
Electric power consumption per capita (kWh)	15,403	9,503
Electricity generated by coal (% of total)	3.1	38.2

Emissions and pollution

CO_2 emissions per unit of GDP (kg/2000 PPP $ of GDP)	0.2	0.5
CO_2 emissions per capita (metric tons)	5.8	12.8
Particulate matter (urban-pop.-weighted avg., µg/cu. m)	14	29
Passenger cars (per 1,000 people)	453	433

Water and sanitation

Internal freshwater resources per capita (cu. m)	19,017	9,703
Freshwater withdrawal		
Total (% of internal resources)	1.7	10.4
Agriculture (% of total freshwater withdrawal)	9	42
Access to improved water source (% of total population)	100	99
Rural (% of rural population)	100	98
Urban (% of urban population)	100	100
Access to improved sanitation (% of total population)	100	..
Rural (% of rural population)	100	..
Urban (% of urban population)	100	..

Environment and health

ARI prevalence (% of children under age 5)	..	
Diarrhea prevalence (% of children under age 5)	..	
Under-five mortality rate (per 1,000 live births)	4	7

National accounting aggregates, 2004

Gross savings (% of GNI)	23.6	19.4
Consumption of fixed capital (% of GNI)	12.1	13.2
Education expenditure (% of GNI)	8.0	4.6
Energy depletion (% of GNI)	0.0	1.4
Mineral depletion (% of GNI)	0.1	0.0
Net forest depletion (% of GNI)	0.0	0.0
CO_2 damage (% of GNI)	0.1	0.3
Particulate emission damage (% of GNI)	0.0	0.4
Adjusted net savings (% of GNI)	19.4	8.7

Switzerland

Environmental strategy/action plan prepared in ..

	Country data	High income
		Group data
Population (millions)	7.4	1,004
Urban population (% of total)	67.5	78.5
GDP ($ billions)	357.5	32,900
GNI per capita, *World Bank Atlas* method ($)	49,600	32,112
Agriculture		
Land area (1,000 sq. km)	40	33,018
Agricultural land (% of land area)	38	38
Irrigated land (% of cropland)	5.8	11.9
Fertilizer consumption (100 grams/ha of arable land)	2,275	1,205
Population density, rural (people/sq. km of arable land)	582	331
Forests and biodiversity		
Forest area (% of land area)	30.5	29.3
Annual deforestation (% change, 1990–2005)	−0.4	−0.1
Nationally protected areas (% of total land area)	29.7	..
Mammal species, total known	93	
Mammal species, threatened	4	
Bird species, total known	382	
Bird species, threatened	8	
GEF benefits index for biodiversity (0–100)	0.2	
Energy		
GDP per unit of energy use (2000 PPP $/kg oil equiv)	8.1	5.2
Energy use per capita (kg oil equiv)	3,689	5,410
Energy from combustible renewables & waste (% of tot.)	6.2	3.0
Energy imports, net (% of energy use)	56	19
Electric power consumption per capita (kWh)	8,191	9,503
Electricity generated by coal (% of total)	..	38.2
Emissions and pollution		
CO_2 emissions per unit of GDP (kg/2000 PPP $ of GDP)	0.2	0.5
CO_2 emissions per capita (metric tons)	5.6	12.8
Particulate matter (urban-pop.-weighted avg., µg/cu. m)	27	29
Passenger cars (per 1,000 people)	508	433
Water and sanitation		
Internal freshwater resources per capita (cu. m)	5,467	9,703
Freshwater withdrawal		
Total (% of internal resources)	6.4	10.4
Agriculture (% of total freshwater withdrawal)	2	42
Access to improved water source (% of total population)	100	99
Rural (% of rural population)	100	98
Urban (% of urban population)	100	100
Access to improved sanitation (% of total population)	100	..
Rural (% of rural population)	100	..
Urban (% of urban population)	100	..
Environment and health		
ARI prevalence (% of children under age 5)	..	
Diarrhea prevalence (% of children under age 5)	..	
Under-five mortality rate (per 1,000 live births)	5	7
National accounting aggregates, 2004		
Gross savings (% of GNI)	..	19.4
Consumption of fixed capital (% of GNI)	13.9	13.2
Education expenditure (% of GNI)	5.0	4.6
Energy depletion (% of GNI)	0.0	1.4
Mineral depletion (% of GNI)	0.0	0.0
Net forest depletion (% of GNI)	0.0	0.0
CO_2 damage (% of GNI)	0.1	0.3
Particulate emission damage (% of GNI)	0.3	0.4
Adjusted net savings (% of GNI)	..	8.7

Syrian Arab Republic

Environmental strategy/action plan prepared in **1999**

	Country data	Group data Middle East & North Africa	Lower middle income
Population (millions)	18.6	300	2,442
Urban population (% of total)	50.2	56.3	48.7
GDP ($ billions)	24.0	547	4,165
GNI per capita, *World Bank Atlas* method ($)	1,230	1,972	1,686
Agriculture			
Land area (1,000 sq. km)	184	8,955	38,470
Agricultural land (% of land area)	75	23	43
Irrigated land (% of cropland)	24.6	32.5	23.1
Fertilizer consumption (100 grams/ha of arable land)	703	842	1,530
Population density, rural (people/sq. km of arable land)	197	670	523
Forests and biodiversity			
Forest area (% of land area)	2.5	2.4	30.7
Annual deforestation (% change, 1990–2005)	–1.6	–0.5	0.1
Nationally protected areas (% of total land area)	..	4.2	7.7
Mammal species, total known	82		
Mammal species, threatened	3		
Bird species, total known	350		
Bird species, threatened	11		
GEF benefits index for biodiversity (0–100)	0.9		
Energy			
GDP per unit of energy use (2000 PPP $/kg oil equiv)	3.4	4.2	4.6
Energy use per capita (kg oil equiv)	986	1,144	1,090
Energy from combustible renewables & waste (% of tot.)	0.0	1.3	14.6
Energy imports, net (% of energy use)	–90	–129	–14
Electric power consumption per capita (kWh)	1,243	1,212	1,329
Electricity generated by coal (% of total)	..	3.0	49.4
Emissions and pollution			
CO_2 emissions per unit of GDP (kg/2000 PPP $ of GDP)	0.9	0.7	0.5
CO_2 emissions per capita (metric tons)	2.8	3.2	2.6
Particulate matter (urban-pop.-weighted avg., µg/cu. m)	89	90	70
Passenger cars (per 1,000 people)	11	..	29
Water and sanitation			
Internal freshwater resources per capita (cu. m)	377	761	7,295
Freshwater withdrawal			
Total (% of internal resources)	285.0	105.0	7.7
Agriculture (% of total freshwater withdrawal)	95	89	75
Access to improved water source (% of total population)	79	88	81
Rural (% of rural population)	64	79	70
Urban (% of urban population)	94	95	93
Access to improved sanitation (% of total population)	77	75	57
Rural (% of rural population)	56	56	39
Urban (% of urban population)	97	89	78
Environment and health			
ARI prevalence (% of children under age 5)	..		
Diarrhea prevalence (% of children under age 5)	..		
Under-five mortality rate (per 1,000 live births)	16	55	40
National accounting aggregates, 2004			
Gross savings (% of GNI)	20.7	30.0	32.1
Consumption of fixed capital (% of GNI)	10.5	11.2	10.8
Education expenditure (% of GNI)	2.6	4.5	2.9
Energy depletion (% of GNI)	38.6	27.3	6.5
Mineral depletion (% of GNI)	0.1	0.1	0.5
Net forest depletion (% of GNI)	0.0	0.1	0.0
CO_2 damage (% of GNI)	1.5	1.2	1.1
Particulate emission damage (% of GNI)	1.0	0.9	1.0
Adjusted net savings (% of GNI)	–28.4	–6.2	15.1

Tajikistan

Environmental strategy/action plan prepared in ..

	Country data	Group data Europe & Central Asia	Low income
Population (millions)	6.4	472	2,343
Urban population (% of total)	24.5	63.6	30.6
GDP ($ billions)	2.1	1,770	1,239
GNI per capita, *World Bank Atlas* method ($)	280	3,295	507
Agriculture			
Land area (1,000 sq. km)	140	23,371	29,192
Agricultural land (% of land area)	30	29	45
Irrigated land (% of cropland)	68.3	11.1	23.9
Fertilizer consumption (100 grams/ha of arable land)	300	347	646
Population density, rural (people/sq. km of arable land)	514	126	524
Forests and biodiversity			
Forest area (% of land area)	2.9	38.3	24.8
Annual deforestation (% change, 1990–2005)	0.0	0.0	0.5
Nationally protected areas (% of total land area)	4.2	6.9	7.7
Mammal species, total known	76		
Mammal species, threatened	7		
Bird species, total known	351		
Bird species, threatened	9		
GEF benefits index for biodiversity (0–100)	0.7		
Energy			
GDP per unit of energy use (2000 PPP $/kg oil equiv)	2.1	2.7	4.2
Energy use per capita (kg oil equiv)	501	2,794	501
Energy from combustible renewables & waste (% of tot.)	..	2.4	48.9
Energy imports, net (% of energy use)	55	−26	−4
Electric power consumption per capita (kWh)	2,206	3,531	358
Electricity generated by coal (% of total)	..	29.8	46.3
Emissions and pollution			
CO_2 emissions per unit of GDP (kg/2000 PPP $ of GDP)	0.8	1.0	0.4
CO_2 emissions per capita (metric tons)	0.7	6.7	0.8
Particulate matter (urban-pop.-weighted avg., µg/cu. m)	57	35	89
Passenger cars (per 1,000 people)	..	142	6
Water and sanitation			
Internal freshwater resources per capita (cu. m)	10,311	11,123	3,456
Freshwater withdrawal			
Total (% of internal resources)	18.0	7.5	15.5
Agriculture (% of total freshwater withdrawal)	92	59	88
Access to improved water source (% of total population)	58	91	75
Rural (% of rural population)	47	80	69
Urban (% of urban population)	93	98	89
Access to improved sanitation (% of total population)	53	82	36
Rural (% of rural population)	47	63	24
Urban (% of urban population)	71	93	61
Environment and health			
ARI prevalence (% of children under age 5)	1.4		
Diarrhea prevalence (% of children under age 5)	20.8		
Under-five mortality rate (per 1,000 live births)	93	34	122
National accounting aggregates, 2004			
Gross savings (% of GNI)	5.7	23.4	22.7
Consumption of fixed capital (% of GNI)	8.7	10.7	9.2
Education expenditure (% of GNI)	2.8	4.1	3.4
Energy depletion (% of GNI)	0.4	12.0	6.7
Mineral depletion (% of GNI)	0.0	0.3	0.4
Net forest depletion (% of GNI)	0.0	0.0	0.7
CO_2 damage (% of GNI)	2.0	1.4	1.1
Particulate emission damage (% of GNI)	0.2	0.7	0.8
Adjusted net savings (% of GNI)	−2.8	2.3	7.3

Tanzania

Environmental strategy/action plan prepared in **1994**

	Country data	Group data	
		Sub-Saharan Africa	Low income
Population (millions)	37.6	726	2,343
Urban population (% of total)	36.5	36.4	30.6
GDP ($ billions)	10.9	523	1,239
GNI per capita, *World Bank Atlas* method ($)	320	601	507
Agriculture			
Land area (1,000 sq. km)	884	23,596	29,192
Agricultural land (% of land area)	54	44	45
Irrigated land (% of cropland)	3.6	3.6	23.9
Fertilizer consumption (100 grams/ha of arable land)	18	136	646
Population density, rural (people/sq. km of arable land)	596	355	524
Forests and biodiversity			
Forest area (% of land area)	39.9	26.5	24.8
Annual deforestation (% change, 1990–2005)	1.0	0.6	0.5
Nationally protected areas (% of total land area)	29.8	8.7	7.7
Mammal species, total known	375		
Mammal species, threatened	34		
Bird species, total known	1,056		
Bird species, threatened	37		
GEF benefits index for biodiversity (0–100)	15.1		
Energy			
GDP per unit of energy use (2000 PPP $/kg oil equiv)	1.3	2.8	4.2
Energy use per capita (kg oil equiv)	465	681	501
Energy from combustible renewables & waste (% of tot.)	92.0	57.4	48.9
Energy imports, net (% of energy use)	7	−59	−4
Electric power consumption per capita (kWh)	54	513	358
Electricity generated by coal (% of total)	2.7	68.0	46.3
Emissions and pollution			
CO_2 emissions per unit of GDP (kg/2000 PPP $ of GDP)	0.2	0.4	0.4
CO_2 emissions per capita (metric tons)	0.1	0.7	0.8
Particulate matter (urban-pop.-weighted avg., µg/cu. m)	38	73	89
Passenger cars (per 1,000 people)	..	..	6
Water and sanitation			
Internal freshwater resources per capita (cu. m)	2,232	5,353	3,456
Freshwater withdrawal			
Total (% of internal resources)	6.2	3.1	15.5
Agriculture (% of total freshwater withdrawal)	89	87	88
Access to improved water source (% of total population)	73	58	75
Rural (% of rural population)	62	45	69
Urban (% of urban population)	92	82	89
Access to improved sanitation (% of total population)	46	36	36
Rural (% of rural population)	41	26	24
Urban (% of urban population)	54	55	61
Environment and health			
ARI prevalence (% of children under age 5)	..		
Diarrhea prevalence (% of children under age 5)	12.4		
Under-five mortality rate (per 1,000 live births)	126	168	122
National accounting aggregates, 2004			
Gross savings (% of GNI)	8.5	17.1	22.7
Consumption of fixed capital (% of GNI)	8.2	10.9	9.2
Education expenditure (% of GNI)	2.4	3.9	3.4
Energy depletion (% of GNI)	0.0	9.8	6.7
Mineral depletion (% of GNI)	0.1	0.4	0.4
Net forest depletion (% of GNI)	0.0	0.6	0.7
CO_2 damage (% of GNI)	0.2	0.7	1.1
Particulate emission damage (% of GNI)	0.3	0.5	0.8
Adjusted net savings (% of GNI)	2.0	−1.9	7.3

Thailand

Environmental strategy/action plan prepared in ..

	Country data	East Asia & Pacific	Lower middle income
		Group data	
Population (millions)	63.7	1,870	2,442
Urban population (% of total)	32.2	40.6	48.7
GDP ($ billions)	161.7	2,651	4,165
GNI per capita, *World Bank Atlas* method ($)	2,490	1,416	1,686
Agriculture			
Land area (1,000 sq. km)	511	15,885	38,470
Agricultural land (% of land area)	36	51	43
Irrigated land (% of cropland)	28.2	..	23.1
Fertilizer consumption (100 grams/ha of arable land)	1,072	2,296	1,530
Population density, rural (people/sq. km of arable land)	304	559	523
Forests and biodiversity			
Forest area (% of land area)	28.4	28.4	30.7
Annual deforestation (% change, 1990–2005)	0.6	–0.2	0.1
Nationally protected areas (% of total land area)	13.9	..	7.7
Mammal species, total known	300		
Mammal species, threatened	36		
Bird species, total known	971		
Bird species, threatened	42		
GEF benefits index for biodiversity (0–100)	8.0		
Energy			
GDP per unit of energy use (2000 PPP $/kg oil equiv)	5.0	4.6	4.6
Energy use per capita (kg oil equiv)	1,406	1,007	1,090
Energy from combustible renewables & waste (% of tot.)	16.5	17.7	14.6
Energy imports, net (% of energy use)	46	–2	–14
Electric power consumption per capita (kWh)	1,752	1,184	1,329
Electricity generated by coal (% of total)	15.8	69.4	49.4
Emissions and pollution			
CO_2 emissions per unit of GDP (kg/2000 PPP $ of GDP)	0.5	0.5	0.5
CO_2 emissions per capita (metric tons)	3.7	2.4	2.6
Particulate matter (urban-pop.-weighted avg., µg/cu. m)	77	80	70
Passenger cars (per 1,000 people)	..	12	29
Water and sanitation			
Internal freshwater resources per capita (cu. m)	3,297	5,062	7,295
Freshwater withdrawal			
Total (% of internal resources)	41.5	10.2	7.7
Agriculture (% of total freshwater withdrawal)	95	74	75
Access to improved water source (% of total population)	85	78	81
Rural (% of rural population)	80	69	70
Urban (% of urban population)	95	92	93
Access to improved sanitation (% of total population)	99	49	57
Rural (% of rural population)	100	35	39
Urban (% of urban population)	97	72	78
Environment and health			
ARI prevalence (% of children under age 5)	..		
Diarrhea prevalence (% of children under age 5)	..		
Under-five mortality rate (per 1,000 live births)	21	37	40
National accounting aggregates, 2004			
Gross savings (% of GNI)	31.8	39.1	32.1
Consumption of fixed capital (% of GNI)	11.3	10.5	10.8
Education expenditure (% of GNI)	4.9	2.3	2.9
Energy depletion (% of GNI)	2.4	4.1	6.5
Mineral depletion (% of GNI)	0.0	0.4	0.5
Net forest depletion (% of GNI)	0.2	0.0	0.0
CO_2 damage (% of GNI)	1.0	1.2	1.1
Particulate emission damage (% of GNI)	0.6	1.2	1.0
Adjusted net savings (% of GNI)	21.2	23.9	15.1

Timor-Leste

Environmental strategy/action plan prepared in ..

	Country data	Group data East Asia & Pacific	Low income
Population (millions)	0.9	1,870	2,343
Urban population (% of total)	7.7	40.6	30.6
GDP ($ billions)	0.3	2,651	1,239
GNI per capita, World Bank Atlas method ($)	550	1,416	507
Agriculture			
Land area (1,000 sq. km)	15	15,885	29,192
Agricultural land (% of land area)	23	51	45
Irrigated land (% of cropland)	..	..	23.9
Fertilizer consumption (100 grams/ha of arable land)	..	2,296	646
Population density, rural (people/sq. km of arable land)	626	559	524
Forests and biodiversity			
Forest area (% of land area)	53.7	28.4	24.8
Annual deforestation (% change, 1990–2005)	1.2	–0.2	0.5
Nationally protected areas (% of total land area)	..	..	7.7
Mammal species, total known	..		
Mammal species, threatened	0		
Bird species, total known	1		
Bird species, threatened	7		
GEF benefits index for biodiversity (0–100)	..		
Energy			
GDP per unit of energy use (2000 PPP $/kg oil equiv)	..	4.6	4.2
Energy use per capita (kg oil equiv)	..	1,007	501
Energy from combustible renewables & waste (% of tot.)	..	17.7	48.9
Energy imports, net (% of energy use)	..	–2	–4
Electric power consumption per capita (kWh)	..	1,184	358
Electricity generated by coal (% of total)	..	69.4	46.3
Emissions and pollution			
CO_2 emissions per unit of GDP (kg/2000 PPP $ of GDP)	..	0.5	0.4
CO_2 emissions per capita (metric tons)	..	2.4	0.8
Particulate matter (urban-pop.-weighted avg., μg/cu. m)	..	80	89
Passenger cars (per 1,000 people)	..	12	6
Water and sanitation			
Internal freshwater resources per capita (cu. m)	..	5,062	3,456
Freshwater withdrawal			
Total (% of internal resources)	..	10.2	15.5
Agriculture (% of total freshwater withdrawal)	..	74	88
Access to improved water source (% of total population)	52	78	75
Rural (% of rural population)	51	69	69
Urban (% of urban population)	73	92	89
Access to improved sanitation (% of total population)	33	49	36
Rural (% of rural population)	30	35	24
Urban (% of urban population)	65	72	61
Environment and health			
ARI prevalence (% of children under age 5)	..		
Diarrhea prevalence (% of children under age 5)	..		
Under-five mortality rate (per 1,000 live births)	80	37	122
National accounting aggregates, 2004			
Gross savings (% of GNI)	..	39.1	22.7
Consumption of fixed capital (% of GNI)	..	10.5	9.2
Education expenditure (% of GNI)	..	2.3	3.4
Energy depletion (% of GNI)	..	4.1	6.7
Mineral depletion (% of GNI)	..	0.4	0.4
Net forest depletion (% of GNI)	..	0.0	0.7
CO_2 damage (% of GNI)	..	1.2	1.1
Particulate emission damage (% of GNI)	..	1.2	0.8
Adjusted net savings (% of GNI)	..	23.9	7.3

Togo

Environmental strategy/action plan prepared in **1991**

	Country data	Sub-Saharan Africa	Low Income
		Group data	
Population (millions)	6.0	726	2,343
Urban population (% of total)	35.8	36.4	30.6
GDP ($ billions)	2.1	523	1,239
GNI per capita, *World Bank Atlas* method ($)	310	601	507

Agriculture

Land area (1,000 sq. km)	54	23,596	29,192
Agricultural land (% of land area)	67	44	45
Irrigated land (% of cropland)	0.3	3.6	23.9
Fertilizer consumption (100 grams/ha of arable land)	68	136	646
Population density, rural (people/sq. km of arable land)	151	355	524

Forests and biodiversity

Forest area (% of land area)	7.1	26.5	24.8
Annual deforestation (% change, 1990–2005)	2.9	0.6	0.5
Nationally protected areas (% of total land area)	7.9	8.7	7.7
Mammal species, total known	175		
Mammal species, threatened	7		
Bird species, total known	565		
Bird species, threatened	2		
GEF benefits index for biodiversity (0–100)	0.4		

Energy

GDP per unit of energy use (2000 PPP $/kg oil equiv)	3.2	2.8	4.2
Energy use per capita (kg oil equiv)	445	681	501
Energy from combustible renewables & waste (% of tot.)	71.3	57.4	48.9
Energy imports, net (% of energy use)	28	−59	−4
Electric power consumption per capita (kWh)	94	513	358
Electricity generated by coal (% of total)	..	68.0	46.3

Emissions and pollution

CO_2 emissions per unit of GDP (kg/2000 PPP $ of GDP)	0.2	0.4	0.4
CO_2 emissions per capita (metric tons)	0.3	0.7	0.8
Particulate matter (urban-pop.-weighted avg., µg/cu. m)	45	73	89
Passenger cars (per 1,000 people)	..	..	6

Water and sanitation

Internal freshwater resources per capita (cu. m)	1,920	5,353	3,456
Freshwater withdrawal			
Total (% of internal resources)	1.5	3.1	15.5
Agriculture (% of total freshwater withdrawal)	45	87	88
Access to improved water source (% of total population)	51	58	75
Rural (% of rural population)	36	45	69
Urban (% of urban population)	80	82	89
Access to improved sanitation (% of total population)	34	36	36
Rural (% of rural population)	15	26	24
Urban (% of urban population)	71	55	61

Environment and health

ARI prevalence (% of children under age 5)	..		
Diarrhea prevalence (% of children under age 5)	31.1		
Under-five mortality rate (per 1,000 live births)	140	168	122

National accounting aggregates, 2004

Gross savings (% of GNI)	8.6	17.1	22.7
Consumption of fixed capital (% of GNI)	8.6	10.9	9.2
Education expenditure (% of GNI)	2.6	3.9	3.4
Energy depletion (% of GNI)	0.0	9.8	6.7
Mineral depletion (% of GNI)	0.1	0.4	0.4
Net forest depletion (% of GNI)	3.0	0.6	0.7
CO_2 damage (% of GNI)	0.6	0.7	1.1
Particulate emission damage (% of GNI)	0.3	0.5	0.8
Adjusted net savings (% of GNI)	−1.3	−1.9	7.3

Tonga

Environmental strategy/action plan prepared in ..

	Country data	East Asia & Pacific	Lower middle income
		Group data	
Population (millions)	0.1	1,870	2,442
Urban population (% of total)	33.8	40.6	48.7
GDP ($ billions)	0.2	2,651	4,165
GNI per capita, *World Bank Atlas* method ($)	1,860	1,416	1,686
Agriculture			
Land area (1,000 sq. km)	1	15,885	38,470
Agricultural land (% of land area)	42	51	43
Irrigated land (% of cropland)	..	..	23.1
Fertilizer consumption (100 grams/ha of arable land)	0	2,296	1,530
Population density, rural (people/sq. km of arable land)	450	559	523
Forests and biodiversity			
Forest area (% of land area)	5.6	28.4	30.7
Annual deforestation (% change, 1990–2005)	0.0	−0.2	0.1
Nationally protected areas (% of total land area)	..	..	7.7
Mammal species, total known	5		
Mammal species, threatened	2		
Bird species, total known	46		
Bird species, threatened	3		
GEF benefits index for biodiversity (0–100)	0.6		
Energy			
GDP per unit of energy use (2000 PPP $/kg oil equiv)	..	4.6	4.6
Energy use per capita (kg oil equiv)	..	1,007	1,090
Energy from combustible renewables & waste (% of tot.)	..	17.7	14.6
Energy imports, net (% of energy use)	..	−2	−14
Electric power consumption per capita (kWh)	..	1,184	1,329
Electricity generated by coal (% of total)	..	69.4	49.4
Emissions and pollution			
CO_2 emissions per unit of GDP (kg/2000 PPP $ of GDP)	0.2	0.5	0.5
CO_2 emissions per capita (metric tons)	1.0	2.4	2.6
Particulate matter (urban-pop.-weighted avg., µg/cu. m)	..	80	70
Passenger cars (per 1,000 people)	..	12	29
Water and sanitation			
Internal freshwater resources per capita (cu. m)	..	5,062	7,295
Freshwater withdrawal			
Total (% of internal resources)	..	10.2	7.7
Agriculture (% of total freshwater withdrawal)	..	74	75
Access to improved water source (% of total population)	100	78	81
Rural (% of rural population)	100	69	70
Urban (% of urban population)	100	92	93
Access to improved sanitation (% of total population)	97	49	57
Rural (% of rural population)	96	35	39
Urban (% of urban population)	98	72	78
Environment and health			
ARI prevalence (% of children under age 5)	..		
Diarrhea prevalence (% of children under age 5)	..		
Under-five mortality rate (per 1,000 live births)	25	37	40
National accounting aggregates, 2004			
Gross savings (% of GNI)	..	39.1	32.1
Consumption of fixed capital (% of GNI)	10.9	10.5	10.8
Education expenditure (% of GNI)	3.8	2.3	2.9
Energy depletion (% of GNI)	0.0	4.1	6.5
Mineral depletion (% of GNI)	0.0	0.4	0.5
Net forest depletion (% of GNI)	0.0	0.0	0.0
CO_2 damage (% of GNI)	0.4	1.2	1.1
Particulate emission damage (% of GNI)	..	1.2	1.0
Adjusted net savings (% of GNI)	..	23.9	15.1

Trinidad and Tobago

Environmental strategy/action plan prepared in ..

	Country data	Latin America & Caribbean	Upper middle income
		Group data	
Population (millions)	1.3	546	576
Urban population (% of total)	75.8	77.1	72.3
GDP ($ billions)	12.5	2,022	2,992
GNI per capita, *World Bank Atlas* method ($)	8,730	3,576	4,769
Agriculture			
Land area (1,000 sq. km)	5	20,057	28,983
Agricultural land (% of land area)	26	36	26
Irrigated land (% of cropland)	3.3	11.4	8.7
Fertilizer consumption (100 grams/ha of arable land)	434	923	469
Population density, rural (people/sq. km of arable land)	426	212	131
Forests and biodiversity			
Forest area (% of land area)	44.1	45.6	37.3
Annual deforestation (% change, 1990–2005)	0.3	0.4	0.1
Nationally protected areas (% of total land area)	6.0	11.1	..
Mammal species, total known	116		
Mammal species, threatened	1		
Bird species, total known	435		
Bird species, threatened	2		
GEF benefits index for biodiversity (0–100)	2.4		
Energy			
GDP per unit of energy use (2000 PPP $/kg oil equiv)	1.2	6.2	3.5
Energy use per capita (kg oil equiv)	8,553	1,148	2,574
Energy from combustible renewables & waste (% of tot.)	0.2	15.0	3.9
Energy imports, net (% of energy use)	−160	−40	−51
Electric power consumption per capita (kWh)	4,721	1,615	3,378
Electricity generated by coal (% of total)	..	5.4	31.0
Emissions and pollution			
CO_2 emissions per unit of GDP (kg/2000 PPP $ of GDP)	2.7	0.3	0.7
CO_2 emissions per capita (metric tons)	31.8	2.4	6.2
Particulate matter (urban-pop.-weighted avg., μg/cu. m)	22	43	40
Passenger cars per 1,000 people	..	108	143
Water and sanitation			
Internal freshwater resources per capita (cu. m)	2,951	24,619	14,190
Freshwater withdrawal			
Total (% of internal resources)	8.1	2.0	3.8
Agriculture (% of total freshwater withdrawal)	6	71	53
Access to improved water source (% of total population)	91	89	93
Rural (% of rural population)	88	69	82
Urban (% of urban population)	92	96	97
Access to improved sanitation (% of total population)	100	75	81
Rural (% of rural population)	100	44	61
Urban (% of urban population)	100	84	91
Environment and health			
ARI prevalence (% of children under age 5)	..		
Diarrhea prevalence (% of children under age 5)	..		
Under-five mortality rate (per 1,000 live births)	20	31	28
National accounting aggregates, 2004			
Gross savings (% of GNI)	28.5	22.7	23.1
Consumption of fixed capital (% of GNI)	12.3	12.1	11.5
Education expenditure (% of GNI)	4.0	4.4	4.5
Energy depletion (% of GNI)	46.2	7.2	11.2
Mineral depletion (% of GNI)	0.0	1.1	0.6
Net forest depletion (% of GNI)	0.0	0.0	0.0
CO_2 damage (% of GNI)	2.3	0.5	0.9
Particulate emission damage (% of GNI)	0.0	0.6	0.7
Adjusted net savings (% of GNI)	−28.3	5.6	2.6

Tunisia

Environmental strategy/action plan prepared in **1994**

	Country data	Middle East & North Africa	Lower middle income
		Group data	
Population (millions)	9.9	300	2,442
Urban population (% of total)	64.1	56.3	48.7
GDP ($ billions)	28.2	547	4,165
GNI per capita, *World Bank Atlas* method ($)	2,650	1,972	1,686
Agriculture			
Land area (1,000 sq. km)	155	8,955	38,470
Agricultural land (% of land area)	63	23	43
Irrigated land (% of cropland)	8.0	32.5	23.1
Fertilizer consumption (100 grams/ha of arable land)	368	842	1,530
Population density, rural (people/sq. km of arable land)	128	670	523
Forests and biodiversity			
Forest area (% of land area)	6.8	2.4	30.7
Annual deforestation (% change, 1990–2005)	–4.3	–0.5	0.1
Nationally protected areas (% of total land area)	0.3	4.2	7.7
Mammal species, total known	78		
Mammal species, threatened	10		
Bird species, total known	360		
Bird species, threatened	9		
GEF benefits index for biodiversity (0–100)	0.5		
Energy			
GDP per unit of energy use (2000 PPP $/kg oil equiv)	8.1	4.2	4.6
Energy use per capita (kg oil equiv)	837	1,144	1,090
Energy from combustible renewables & waste (% of tot.)	12.7	1.3	14.6
Energy imports, net (% of energy use)	22	–129	–14
Electric power consumption per capita (kWh)	1,118	1,212	1,329
Electricity generated by coal (% of total)	..	3.0	49.4
Emissions and pollution			
CO_2 emissions per unit of GDP (kg/2000 PPP $ of GDP)	0.3	0.7	0.5
CO_2 emissions per capita (metric tons)	2.3	3.2	2.6
Particulate matter (urban-pop.-weighted avg., µg/cu. m)	46	90	70
Passenger cars (per 1,000 people)	60	..	29
Water and sanitation			
Internal freshwater resources per capita (cu. m)	422	761	7,295
Freshwater withdrawal			
Total (% of internal resources)	62.9	105.0	7.7
Agriculture (% of total freshwater withdrawal)	82	89	75
Access to improved water source (% of total population)	82	88	81
Rural (% of rural population)	60	79	70
Urban (% of urban population)	94	95	93
Access to improved sanitation (% of total population)	80	75	57
Rural (% of rural population)	62	56	39
Urban (% of urban population)	90	89	78
Environment and health			
ARI prevalence (% of children under age 5)	..		
Diarrhea prevalence (% of children under age 5)	5.8		
Under-five mortality rate (per 1,000 live births)	25	55	40
National accounting aggregates, 2004			
Gross savings (% of GNI)	23.5	30.0	32.1
Consumption of fixed capital (% of GNI)	11.8	11.2	10.8
Education expenditure (% of GNI)	5.9	4.5	2.9
Energy depletion (% of GNI)	4.2	27.3	6.5
Mineral depletion (% of GNI)	0.2	0.1	0.5
Net forest depletion (% of GNI)	0.1	0.1	0.0
CO_2 damage (% of GNI)	0.6	1.2	1.1
Particulate emission damage (% of GNI)	0.4	0.9	1.0
Adjusted net savings (% of GNI)	12.1	–6.2	15.1

Turkey

Environmental strategy/action plan prepared in **1998**

	Country data	Europe & Central Asia	Upper middle Income
		Group data	
Population (millions)	71.7	472	576
Urban population (% of total)	66.8	63.6	72.3
GDP ($ billions)	302.8	1,770	2,992
GNI per capita, World Bank Atlas method ($)	3,750	3,295	4,769
Agriculture			
Land area (1,000 sq. km)	770	23,371	28,983
Agricultural land (% of land area)	51	29	26
Irrigated land (% of cropland)	20.0	11.1	8.7
Fertilizer consumption (100 grams/ha of arable land)	727	347	469
Population density, rural (people/sq. km of arable land)	102	126	131
Forests and biodiversity			
Forest area (% of land area)	13.2	38.3	37.3
Annual deforestation (% change, 1990–2005)	–0.3	0.0	0.1
Nationally protected areas (% of total land area)	1.6	6.9	..
Mammal species, total known	145		
Mammal species, threatened	15		
Bird species, total known	436		
Bird species, threatened	14		
GEF benefits index for biodiversity (0–100)	6.0		
Energy			
GDP per unit of energy use (2000 PPP $/kg oil equiv)	6.0	2.7	3.5
Energy use per capita (kg oil equiv)	1,117	2,794	2,574
Energy from combustible renewables & waste (% of tot.)	7.3	2.4	3.9
Energy imports, net (% of energy use)	70	–26	–51
Electric power consumption per capita (kWh)	1,656	3,531	3,378
Electricity generated by coal (% of total)	22.9	29.8	31.0
Emissions and pollution			
CO_2 emissions per unit of GDP (kg/2000 PPP $ of GDP)	0.5	1.0	0.7
CO_2 emissions per capita (metric tons)	3.0	6.7	6.2
Particulate matter (urban-pop.-weighted avg., µg/cu. m)	56	35	40
Passenger cars (per 1,000 people)	66	142	143
Water and sanitation			
Internal freshwater resources per capita (cu. m)	3,165	11,123	14,190
Freshwater withdrawal			
Total (% of internal resources)	16.5	7.5	3.8
Agriculture (% of total freshwater withdrawal)	74	59	53
Access to improved water source (% of total population)	93	91	93
Rural (% of rural population)	87	80	82
Urban (% of urban population)	96	98	97
Access to improved sanitation (% of total population)	83	82	81
Rural (% of rural population)	62	63	61
Urban (% of urban population)	94	93	91
Environment and health			
ARI prevalence (% of children under age 5)	29.0		
Diarrhea prevalence (% of children under age 5)	29.7		
Under-five mortality rate (per 1,000 live births)	32	34	28
National accounting aggregates, 2004			
Gross savings (% of GNI)	20.0	23.4	23.1
Consumption of fixed capital (% of GNI)	11.8	10.7	11.5
Education expenditure (% of GNI)	3.5	4.1	4.5
Energy depletion (% of GNI)	0.2	12.0	11.2
Mineral depletion (% of GNI)	0.0	0.3	0.6
Net forest depletion (% of GNI)	0.0	0.0	0.0
CO_2 damage (% of GNI)	0.5	1.4	0.9
Particulate emission damage (% of GNI)	1.4	0.7	0.7
Adjusted net savings (% of GNI)	9.4	2.3	2.6

Turkmenistan

Environmental strategy/action plan prepared in ..

	Country data	Group data	
		Europe & Central Asia	Lower middle income
Population (millions)	4.8	472	2,442
Urban population (% of total)	45.6	63.6	48.7
GDP ($ billions)	6.2	1,770	4,165
GNI per capita, *World Bank Atlas* method ($)	..	3,295	1,686

Agriculture
Land area (1,000 sq. km)	470	23,371	38,470
Agricultural land (% of land area)	70	29	43
Irrigated land (% of cropland)	79.4	11.1	23.1
Fertilizer consumption (100 grams/ha of arable land)	529	347	1,530
Population density, rural (people/sq. km of arable land)	117	126	523

Forests and biodiversity
Forest area (% of land area)	8.8	38.3	30.7
Annual deforestation (% change, 1990–2005)	0.0	0.0	0.1
Nationally protected areas (% of total land area)	4.2	6.9	7.7
Mammal species, total known	103		
Mammal species, threatened	12		
Bird species, total known	318		
Bird species, threatened	13		
GEF benefits index for biodiversity (0–100)	2.0		

Energy
GDP per unit of energy use (2000 PPP $/kg oil equiv)	..	2.7	4.6
Energy use per capita (kg oil equiv)	3,662	2,794	1,090
Energy from combustible renewables & waste (% of tot.)	..	2.4	14.6
Energy imports, net (% of energy use)	–240	–26	–14
Electric power consumption per capita (kWh)	1,750	3,531	1.329
Electricity generated by coal (% of total)	..	29.8	49.4

Emissions and pollution
CO_2 emissions per unit of GDP (kg/2000 PPP $ of GDP)	2.2	1.0	0.5
CO_2 emissions per capita (metric tons)	9.1	6.7	2.6
Particulate matter (urban-pop.-weighted avg., µg/cu. m)	73	35	70
Passenger cars (per 1,000 people)	..	142	29

Water and sanitation
Internal freshwater resources per capita (cu. m)	285	11,123	7,295
Freshwater withdrawal			
Total (% of internal resources)	1,812.5	7.5	7.7
Agriculture (% of total freshwater withdrawal)	98	59	75
Access to improved water source (% of total population)	71	91	81
Rural (% of rural population)	54	80	70
Urban (% of urban population)	93	98	93
Access to improved sanitation (% of total population)	62	82	57
Rural (% of rural population)	50	63	39
Urban (% of urban population)	77	93	78

Environment and health
ARI prevalence (% of children under age 5)	4.0		
Diarrhea prevalence (% of children under age 5)	3.2		
Under-five mortality rate (per 1,000 live births)	103	34	40

National accounting aggregates, 2004
Gross savings (% of GNI)	33.6	23.4	32.1
Consumption of fixed capital (% of GNI)	10.4	10.7	10.8
Education expenditure (% of GNI)	..	4.1	2.9
Energy depletion (% of GNI)	..	12.0	6.5
Mineral depletion (% of GNI)	0.0	0.3	0.5
Net forest depletion (% of GNI)	..	0.0	0.0
CO_2 damage (% of GNI)	4.0	1.4	1.1
Particulate emission damage (% of GNI)	0.6	0.7	1.0
Adjusted net savings (% of GNI)	..	2.3	15.1

Uganda

Environmental strategy/action plan prepared in **1994**

	Country data	Group data Sub-Saharan Africa	Group data Low income
Population (millions)	27.8	726	2,343
Urban population (% of total)	12.4	36.4	30.6
GDP ($ billions)	6.8	523	1,239
GNI per capita, *World Bank Atlas* method ($)	250	601	507
Agriculture			
Land area (1,000 sq. km)	197	23,596	29,192
Agricultural land (% of land area)	63	44	45
Irrigated land (% of cropland)	0.1	3.6	23.9
Fertilizer consumption (100 grams/ha of arable land)	18	136	646
Population density, rural (people/sq. km of arable land)	453	355	524
Forests and biodiversity			
Forest area (% of land area)	18.4	26.5	24.8
Annual deforestation (% change, 1990–2005)	1.8	0.6	0.5
Nationally protected areas (% of total land area)	24.6	8.7	7.7
Mammal species, total known	360		
Mammal species, threatened	29		
Bird species, total known	1,015		
Bird species, threatened	15		
GEF benefits index for biodiversity (0–100)	3.3		
Energy			
GDP per unit of energy use (2000 PPP $/kg oil equiv)	..	2.8	4.2
Energy use per capita (kg oil equiv)	..	681	501
Energy from combustible renewables & waste (% of tot.)	..	57.4	48.9
Energy imports, net (% of energy use)	..	−59	−4
Electric power consumption per capita (kWh)	..	513	358
Electricity generated by coal (% of total)	..	68.0	46.3
Emissions and pollution			
CO_2 emissions per unit of GDP (kg/2000 PPP $ of GDP)	0.1	0.4	0.4
CO_2 emissions per capita (metric tons)	0.1	0.7	0.8
Particulate matter (urban-pop.-weighted avg., μg/cu. m)	33	73	89
Passenger cars (per 1,000 people)	2	..	6
Water and sanitation			
Internal freshwater resources per capita (cu. m)	1,402	5,353	3,456
Freshwater withdrawal			
Total (% of internal resources)	0.8	3.1	15.5
Agriculture (% of total freshwater withdrawal)	40	87	88
Access to improved water source (% of total population)	56	58	75
Rural (% of rural population)	52	45	69
Urban (% of urban population)	87	82	89
Access to improved sanitation (% of total population)	41	36	36
Rural (% of rural population)	39	26	24
Urban (% of urban population)	53	55	61
Environment and health			
ARI prevalence (% of children under age 5)	22.0		
Diarrhea prevalence (% of children under age 5)	19.6		
Under-five mortality rate (per 1,000 live births)	138	168	122
National accounting aggregates, 2004			
Gross savings (% of GNI)	9.9	17.1	22.7
Consumption of fixed capital (% of GNI)	8.2	10.9	9.2
Education expenditure (% of GNI)	1.9	3.9	3.4
Energy depletion (% of GNI)	0.0	9.8	6.7
Mineral depletion (% of GNI)	0.0	0.4	0.4
Net forest depletion (% of GNI)	6.4	0.6	0.7
CO_2 damage (% of GNI)	0.2	0.7	1.1
Particulate emission damage (% of GNI)	0.0	0.5	0.8
Adjusted net savings (% of GNI)	−2.9	−1.9	7.3

Ukraine

Environmental strategy/action plan prepared in **1999**

	Country data	Group data Europe & Central Asia	Group data Lower middle income
Population (millions)	47.5	472	2,442
Urban population (% of total)	67.3	63.6	48.7
GDP ($ billions)	64.8	1,770	4,165
GNI per capita, *World Bank Atlas* method ($)	1,270	3,295	1,686
Agriculture			
Land area (1,000 sq. km)	579	23,371	38,470
Agricultural land (% of land area)	71	29	43
Irrigated land (% of cropland)	6.6	11.1	23.1
Fertilizer consumption (100 grams/ha of arable land)	181	347	1,530
Population density, rural (people/sq. km of arable land)	48	126	523
Forests and biodiversity			
Forest area (% of land area)	16.5	38.3	30.7
Annual deforestation (% change, 1990–2005)	−0.2	0.0	0.1
Nationally protected areas (% of total land area)	3.9	6.9	7.7
Mammal species, total known	120		
Mammal species, threatened	14		
Bird species, total known	325		
Bird species, threatened	13		
GEF benefits index for biodiversity (0–100)	0.4		
Energy			
GDP per unit of energy use (2000 PPP $/kg oil equiv)	1.9	2.7	4.6
Energy use per capita (kg oil equiv)	2,772	2,794	1,090
Energy from combustible renewables & waste (% of tot.)	0.2	2.4	14.6
Energy imports, net (% of energy use)	43	−26	−14
Electric power consumption per capita (kWh)	2,998	3,531	1,329
Electricity generated by coal (% of total)	18.3	29.8	49.4
Emissions and pollution			
CO_2 emissions per unit of GDP (kg/2000 PPP $ of GDP)	1.7	1.0	0.5
CO_2 emissions per capita (metric tons)	6.4	6.7	2.6
Particulate matter (urban-pop.-weighted avg., µg/cu. m)	29	35	70
Passenger cars (per 1,000 people)	111	142	29
Water and sanitation			
Internal freshwater resources per capita (cu. m)	1,119	11,123	7,295
Freshwater withdrawal			
Total (% of internal resources)	70.7	7.5	7.7
Agriculture (% of total freshwater withdrawal)	52	59	75
Access to improved water source (% of total population)	98	91	81
Rural (% of rural population)	94	80	70
Urban (% of urban population)	100	98	93
Access to improved sanitation (% of total population)	99	82	57
Rural (% of rural population)	97	63	39
Urban (% of urban population)	100	93	78
Environment and health			
ARI prevalence (% of children under age 5)	..		
Diarrhea prevalence (% of children under age 5)	..		
Under-five mortality rate (per 1,000 live births)	18	34	40
National accounting aggregates, 2004			
Gross savings (% of GNI)	29.9	23.4	32.1
Consumption of fixed capital (% of GNI)	10.4	10.7	10.8
Education expenditure (% of GNI)	4.4	4.1	2.9
Energy depletion (% of GNI)	5.7	12.0	6.5
Mineral depletion (% of GNI)	0.0	0.3	0.5
Net forest depletion (% of GNI)	0.0	0.0	0.0
CO_2 damage (% of GNI)	4.5	1.4	1.1
Particulate emission damage (% of GNI)	0.9	0.7	1.0
Adjusted net savings (% of GNI)	12.8	2.3	15.1

United Arab Emirates

Environmental strategy/action plan prepared in ..

	Country data	Group data — High income
Population (millions)	4.3	1,004
Urban population (% of total)	85.3	78.5
GDP ($ billions)	104.2	32,900
GNI per capita, *World Bank Atlas* method ($)	23,770	32,112
Agriculture		
Land area (1,000 sq. km)	84	33,018
Agricultural land (% of land area)	7	38
Irrigated land (% of cropland)	29.9	11.9
Fertilizer consumption (100 grams/ha of arable land)	4,667	1,205
Population density, rural (people/sq. km of arable land)	939	331
Forests and biodiversity		
Forest area (% of land area)	3.7	29.3
Annual deforestation (% change, 1990–2005)	–1.8	–0.1
Nationally protected areas (% of total land area)	0.0	..
Mammal species, total known	30	
Mammal species, threatened	5	
Bird species, total known	268	
Bird species, threatened	11	
GEF benefits index for biodiversity (0–100)	0.2	
Energy		
GDP per unit of energy use (2000 PPP $/kg oil equiv)	2.2	5.2
Energy use per capita (kg oil equiv)	9,707	5,410
Energy from combustible renewables & waste (% of tot.)	0.0	3.0
Energy imports, net (% of energy use)	–306	19
Electric power consumption per capita (kWh)	10,992	9,503
Electricity generated by coal (% of total)	..	38.2
Emissions and pollution		
CO_2 emissions per unit of GDP (kg/2000 PPP $ of GDP)	1.3	0.5
CO_2 emissions per capita (metric tons)	25.0	12.8
Particulate matter (urban-pop.-weighted avg., µg/cu. m)	109	29
Passenger cars (per 1,000 people)	..	433
Water and sanitation		
Internal freshwater resources per capita (cu. m)	35	9,703
Freshwater withdrawal		
Total (% of internal resources)	1,533.3	10.4
Agriculture (% of total freshwater withdrawal)	68	42
Access to improved water source (% of total population)	..	99
Rural (% of rural population)	..	98
Urban (% of urban population)	..	100
Access to improved sanitation (% of total population)	100	..
Rural (% of rural population)	100	..
Urban (% of urban population)	100	..
Environment and health		
ARI prevalence (% of children under age 5)	..	
Diarrhea prevalence (% of children under age 5)	..	
Under-five mortality rate (per 1,000 live births)	8	7
National accounting aggregates, 2004		
Gross savings (% of GNI)	39.2	19.4
Consumption of fixed capital (% of GNI)	14.1	13.2
Education expenditure (% of GNI)	..	4.6
Energy depletion (% of GNI)	29.2	1.4
Mineral depletion (% of GNI)	0.0	0.0
Net forest depletion (% of GNI)	..	0.0
CO_2 damage (% of GNI)	0.7	0.3
Particulate emission damage (% of GNI)	2.5	0.4
Adjusted net savings (% of GNI)	..	8.7

United Kingdom

Environmental strategy/action plan prepared in **1995**

	Country data	High income
		Group data
Population (millions)	59.9	1,004
Urban population (% of total)	89.2	78.5
GDP ($ billions)	2,124.4	32,900
GNI per capita, *World Bank Atlas* method ($)	33,630	32,112
Agriculture		
Land area (1,000 sq. km)	242	33,018
Agricultural land (% of land area)	70	38
Irrigated land (% of cropland)	3.0	11.9
Fertilizer consumption (100 grams/ha of arable land)	3,113	1,205
Population density, rural (people/sq. km of arable land)	115	331
Forests and biodiversity		
Forest area (% of land area)	11.8	29.3
Annual deforestation (% change, 1990–2005)	−0.6	−0.1
Nationally protected areas (% of total land area)	20.8	..
Mammal species, total known	103	
Mammal species, threatened	10	
Bird species, total known	557	
Bird species, threatened	10	
GEF benefits index for biodiversity (0–100)	2.1	
Energy		
GDP per unit of energy use (2000 PPP $/kg oil equiv)	7.1	5.2
Energy use per capita (kg oil equiv)	3,893	5,410
Energy from combustible renewables & waste (% of tot.)	1.2	3.0
Energy imports, net (% of energy use)	−6	19
Electric power consumption per capita (kWh)	6,209	9,503
Electricity generated by coal (% of total)	35.4	38.2
Emissions and pollution		
CO_2 emissions per unit of GDP (kg/2000 PPP $ of GDP)	0.4	0.5
CO_2 emissions per capita (metric tons)	9.2	12.8
Particulate matter (urban-pop.-weighted avg., µg/cu. m)	17	29
Passenger cars (per 1,000 people)	388	433
Water and sanitation		
Internal freshwater resources per capita (cu. m)	2,422	9,703
Freshwater withdrawal		
Total (% of internal resources)	6.6	10.4
Agriculture (% of total freshwater withdrawal)	3	42
Access to improved water source (% of total population)	..	99
Rural (% of rural population)	..	98
Urban (% of urban population)	100	100
Access to improved sanitation (% of total population)	..	..
Rural (% of rural population)	..	..
Urban (% of urban population)	..	..
Environment and health		
ARI prevalence (% of children under age 5)	..	
Diarrhea prevalence (% of children under age 5)	..	
Under-five mortality rate (per 1,000 live births)	6	7
National accounting aggregates, 2004		
Gross savings (% of GNI)	14.5	19.4
Consumption of fixed capital (% of GNI)	10.3	13.2
Education expenditure (% of GNI)	5.3	4.6
Energy depletion (% of GNI)	1.1	1.4
Mineral depletion (% of GNI)	0.0	0.0
Net forest depletion (% of GNI)	0.0	0.0
CO_2 damage (% of GNI)	0.2	0.3
Particulate emission damage (% of GNI)	0.1	0.4
Adjusted net savings (% of GNI)	8.1	8.7

United States

Environmental strategy/action plan prepared in **1995**

	Country data	High income
		Group data
Population (millions)	293.7	1,004
Urban population (% of total)	80.4	78.5
GDP ($ billions)	11,711.8	32,900
GNI per capita, *World Bank Atlas* method ($)	41,440	32,112

Agriculture
Land area (1,000 sq. km)	9,159	33,018
Agricultural land (% of land area)	45	38
Irrigated land (% of cropland)	12.8	11.9
Fertilizer consumption (100 grams/ha of arable land)	1,111	1,205
Population density, rural (people/sq. km of arable land)	33	331

Forests and biodiversity
Forest area (% of land area)	33.1	29.3
Annual deforestation (% change, 1990–2005)	–0.1	–0.1
Nationally protected areas (% of total land area)	25.9	..
Mammal species, total known	468	
Mammal species, threatened	40	
Bird species, total known	888	
Bird species, threatened	71	
GEF benefits index for biodiversity (0–100)	90.3	

Energy
GDP per unit of energy use (2000 PPP $/kg oil equiv)	4.5	5.2
Energy use per capita (kg oil equiv)	7,843	5,410
Energy from combustible renewables & waste (% of tot.)	3.0	3.0
Energy imports, net (% of energy use)	28	19
Electric power consumption per capita (kWh)	13,078	9,503
Electricity generated by coal (% of total)	51.4	38.2

Emissions and pollution
CO_2 emissions per unit of GDP (kg/2000 PPP $ of GDP)	0.6	0.5
CO_2 emissions per capita (metric tons)	20.2	12.8
Particulate matter (urban-pop.-weighted avg., µg/cu. m)	24	29
Passenger cars (per 1,000 people)	482	433

Water and sanitation
Internal freshwater resources per capita (cu. m)	9,535	9,703
Freshwater withdrawal		
Total (% of internal resources)	17.1	10.4
Agriculture (% of total freshwater withdrawal)	41	42
Access to improved water source (% of total population)	100	99
Rural (% of rural population)	100	98
Urban (% of urban population)	100	100
Access to improved sanitation (% of total population)	100	..
Rural (% of rural population)	100	..
Urban (% of urban population)	100	..

Environment and health
ARI prevalence (% of children under age 5)	..	
Diarrhea prevalence (% of children under age 5)	..	
Under-five mortality rate (per 1,000 live births)	8	7

National accounting aggregates, 2004
Gross savings (% of GNI)	13.4	19.4
Consumption of fixed capital (% of GNI)	12.2	13.2
Education expenditure (% of GNI)	4.8	4.6
Energy depletion (% of GNI)	1.3	1.4
Mineral depletion (% of GNI)	0.0	0.0
Net forest depletion (% of GNI)	0.0	0.0
CO_2 damage (% of GNI)	0.3	0.3
Particulate emission damage (% of GNI)	0.4	0.4
Adjusted net savings (% of GNI)	4.0	8.7

Uruguay

Environmental strategy/action plan prepared in ..

	Country data	Group data Latin America & Caribbean	Group data Upper middle income
Population (millions)	3.4	546	576
Urban population (% of total)	92.8	77.1	72.3
GDP ($ billions)	13.2	2,022	2,992
GNI per capita, *World Bank Atlas* method ($)	3,900	3,576	4,769
Agriculture			
Land area (1,000 sq. km)	175	20,057	28,983
Agricultural land (% of land area)	85	36	26
Irrigated land (% of cropland)	14.9	11.4	8.7
Fertilizer consumption (100 grams/ha of arable land)	941	923	469
Population density, rural (people/sq. km of arable land)	19	212	131
Forests and biodiversity			
Forest area (% of land area)	8.6	45.6	37.3
Annual deforestation (% change, 1990–2005)	-4.4	0.4	0.1
Nationally protected areas (% of total land area)	0.3	11.1	..
Mammal species, total known	118		
Mammal species, threatened	6		
Bird species, total known	414		
Bird species, threatened	24		
GEF benefits index for biodiversity (0–100)	1.4		
Energy			
GDP per unit of energy use (2000 PPP $/kg oil equiv)	10.5	6.2	3.5
Energy use per capita (kg oil equiv)	738	1,148	2,574
Energy from combustible renewables & waste (% of tot.)	17.0	15.0	3.9
Energy imports, net (% of energy use)	54	-40	-51
Electric power consumption per capita (kWh)	1,781	1,615	3,378
Electricity generated by coal (% of total)	..	5.4	31.0
Emissions and pollution			
CO_2 emissions per unit of GDP (kg/2000 PPP $ of GDP)	0.2	0.3	0.7
CO_2 emissions per capita (metric tons)	1.2	2.4	6.2
Particulate matter (urban-pop.-weighted avg., µg/cu. m)	154	43	40
Passenger cars (per 1,000 people)	..	108	143
Water and sanitation			
Internal freshwater resources per capita (cu. m)	17,154	24,619	14,190
Freshwater withdrawal			
Total (% of internal resources)	5.3	2.0	3.8
Agriculture (% of total freshwater withdrawal)	96	71	53
Access to improved water source (% of total population)	98	89	93
Rural (% of rural population)	93	69	82
Urban (% of urban population)	98	96	97
Access to improved sanitation (% of total population)	94	75	81
Rural (% of rural population)	85	44	61
Urban (% of urban population)	95	84	91
Environment and health			
ARI prevalence (% of children under age 5)	..		
Diarrhea prevalence (% of children under age 5)	..		
Under-five mortality rate (per 1,000 live births)	17	31	28
National accounting aggregates, 2004			
Gross savings (% of GNI)	12.0	22.7	23.1
Consumption of fixed capital (% of GNI)	12.2	12.1	11.5
Education expenditure (% of GNI)	2.6	4.4	4.5
Energy depletion (% of GNI)	0.0	7.2	11.2
Mineral depletion (% of GNI)	0.0	1.1	0.6
Net forest depletion (% of GNI)	0.3	0.0	0.0
CO_2 damage (% of GNI)	0.3	0.5	0.9
Particulate emission damage (% of GNI)	2.7	0.6	0.7
Adjusted net savings (% of GNI)	-0.8	5.6	2.6

Uzbekistan

Environmental strategy/action plan prepared in ..

	Country data	Group data Europe & Central Asia	Low income
Population (millions)	26.2	472	2,343
Urban population (% of total)	36.5	63.6	30.6
GDP ($ billions)	12.0	1,770	1,239
GNI per capita, *World Bank Atlas* method ($)	450	3,295	507
Agriculture			
Land area (1,000 sq. km)	425	23,371	29,192
Agricultural land (% of land area)	64	29	45
Irrigated land (% of cropland)	84.9	11.1	23.9
Fertilizer consumption (100 grams/ha of arable land)	1,602	347	646
Population density, rural (people/sq. km of arable land)	348	126	524
Forests and biodiversity			
Forest area (% of land area)	7.7	38.3	24.8
Annual deforestation (% change, 1990–2005)	−0.5	0.0	0.5
Nationally protected areas (% of total land area)	1.9	6.9	7.7
Mammal species, total known	91		
Mammal species, threatened	7		
Bird species, total known	343		
Bird species, threatened	16		
GEF benefits index for biodiversity (0–100)	1.2		
Energy			
GDP per unit of energy use (2000 PPP $/kg oil equiv)	0.8	2.7	4.2
Energy use per capita (kg oil equiv)	2,023	2,794	501
Energy from combustible renewables & waste (% of tot.)	..	2.4	48.9
Energy imports, net (% of energy use)	−7	−26	−4
Electric power consumption per capita (kWh)	1,741	3,531	358
Electricity generated by coal (% of total)	2.9	29.8	46.3
Emissions and pollution			
CO_2 emissions per unit of GDP (kg/2000 PPP $ of GDP)	3.2	1.0	0.4
CO_2 emissions per capita (metric tons)	4.8	6.7	0.8
Particulate matter (urban-pop.-weighted avg., µg/cu. m)	81	35	89
Passenger cars (per 1,000 people)	..	142	6
Water and sanitation			
Internal freshwater resources per capita (cu. m)	623	11,123	3,456
Freshwater withdrawal			
Total (% of internal resources)	357.0	7.5	15.5
Agriculture (% of total freshwater withdrawal)	93	59	88
Access to improved water source (% of total population)	89	91	75
Rural (% of rural population)	84	80	69
Urban (% of urban population)	97	98	89
Access to improved sanitation (% of total population)	57	82	36
Rural (% of rural population)	48	63	24
Urban (% of urban population)	73	93	61
Environment and health			
ARI prevalence (% of children under age 5)	..		
Diarrhea prevalence (% of children under age 5)	5.3		
Under-five mortality rate (per 1,000 live births)	69	34	122
National accounting aggregates, 2004			
Gross savings (% of GNI)	30.2	23.4	22.7
Consumption of fixed capital (% of GNI)	8.9	10.7	9.2
Education expenditure (% of GNI)	9.4	4.1	3.4
Energy depletion (% of GNI)	59.3	12.0	6.7
Mineral depletion (% of GNI)	0.0	0.3	0.4
Net forest depletion (% of GNI)	0.0	0.0	0.7
CO_2 damage (% of GNI)	7.6	1.4	1.1
Particulate emission damage (% of GNI)	0.7	0.7	0.8
Adjusted net savings (% of GNI)	−37.0	2.3	7.3

Vanuatu

Environmental strategy/action plan prepared in ..

	Country data	Group data East Asia & Pacific	Group data Lower middle income
Population (millions)	0.2	1,870	2,442
Urban population (% of total)	23.3	40.6	48.7
GDP ($ billions)	0.3	2,651	4,165
GNI per capita, *World Bank Atlas* method ($)	1,390	1,416	1,686

Agriculture

Land area (1,000 sq. km)	12	15,885	38,470
Agricultural land (% of land area)	12	51	43
Irrigated land (% of cropland)	..	..	23.1
Fertilizer consumption (100 grams/ha of arable land)	..	2,296	1,530
Population density, rural (people/sq. km of arable land)	784	559	523

Forests and biodiversity

Forest area (% of land area)	36.1	28.4	30.7
Annual deforestation (% change, 1990–2005)	0.0	–0.2	0.1
Nationally protected areas (% of total land area)	..	..	7.7
Mammal species, total known	22		
Mammal species, threatened	5		
Bird species, total known	108		
Bird species, threatened	7		
GEF benefits index for biodiversity (0–100)	2.2		

Energy

GDP per unit of energy use (2000 PPP $/kg oil equiv)	..	4.6	4.6
Energy use per capita (kg oil equiv)	..	1,007	1,090
Energy from combustible renewables & waste (% of tot.)	..	17.7	14.6
Energy imports, net (% of energy use)	..	–2	–14
Electric power consumption per capita (kWh)	..	1,184	1,329
Electricity generated by coal (% of total)	..	69.4	49.4

Emissions and pollution

CO_2 emissions per unit of GDP (kg/2000 PPP $ of GDP)	0.1	0.5	0.5
CO_2 emissions per capita (metric tons)	0.4	2.4	2.6
Particulate matter (urban-pop.-weighted avg., µg/cu. m)	10	80	70
Passenger cars (per 1,000 people)	..	12	29

Water and sanitation

Internal freshwater resources per capita (cu. m)	..	5,062	7,295
Freshwater withdrawal			
Total (% of internal resources)	..	10.2	7.7
Agriculture (% of total freshwater withdrawal)	..	74	75
Access to improved water source (% of total population)	60	78	81
Rural (% of rural population)	52	69	70
Urban (% of urban population)	85	92	93
Access to improved sanitation (% of total population)	50	49	57
Rural (% of rural population)	42	35	39
Urban (% of urban population)	78	72	78

Environment and health

ARI prevalence (% of children under age 5)	..		
Diarrhea prevalence (% of children under age 5)	..		
Under-five mortality rate (per 1,000 live births)	40	37	40

National accounting aggregates, 2004

Gross savings (% of GNI)	..	39.1	32.1
Consumption of fixed capital (% of GNI)	10.8	10.5	10.8
Education expenditure (% of GNI)	6.3	2.3	2.9
Energy depletion (% of GNI)	0.0	4.1	6.5
Mineral depletion (% of GNI)	0.0	0.4	0.5
Net forest depletion (% of GNI)	0.0	0.0	0.0
CO_2 damage (% of GNI)	0.2	1.2	1.1
Particulate emission damage (% of GNI)	..	1.2	1.0
Adjusted net savings (% of GNI)	..	23.9	15.1

Venezuela, RB

Environmental strategy/action plan prepared in ..

	Country data	Group data Latin America & Caribbean	Upper middle income
Population (millions)	26.1	546	576
Urban population (% of total)	87.9	77.1	72.3
GDP ($ billions)	110.1	2,022	2,992
GNI per capita, *World Bank Atlas* method ($)	4,030	3,576	4,769
Agriculture			
Land area (1,000 sq. km)	882	20,057	28,983
Agricultural land (% of land area)	25	36	26
Irrigated land (% of cropland)	16.9	11.4	8.7
Fertilizer consumption (100 grams/ha of arable land)	1,155	923	469
Population density, rural (people/sq. km of arable land)	122	212	131
Forests and biodiversity			
Forest area (% of land area)	54.1	45.6	37.3
Annual deforestation (% change, 1990–2005)	0.6	0.4	0.1
Nationally protected areas (% of total land area)	63.8	11.1	..
Mammal species, total known	353		
Mammal species, threatened	26		
Bird species, total known	1,392		
Bird species, threatened	25		
GEF benefits index for biodiversity (0–100)	26.8		
Energy			
GDP per unit of energy use (2000 PPP $/kg oil equiv)	2.3	6.2	3.5
Energy use per capita (kg oil equiv)	2,112	1,148	2,574
Energy from combustible renewables & waste (% of tot.)	1.0	15.0	3.9
Energy imports, net (% of energy use)	−231	−40	−51
Electric power consumption per capita (kWh)	2,664	1,615	3,378
Electricity generated by coal (% of total)	..	5.4	31.0
Emissions and pollution			
CO_2 emissions per unit of GDP (kg/2000 PPP $ of GDP)	1.2	0.3	0.7
CO_2 emissions per capita (metric tons)	4.3	2.4	6.2
Particulate matter (urban-pop.-weighted avg., µg/cu. m)	12	43	40
Passenger cars per 1,000 people)	..	108	143
Water and sanitation			
Internal freshwater resources per capita (cu. m)	27,652	24,619	14,190
Freshwater withdrawal			
Total (% of internal resources)	1.2	2.0	3.8
Agriculture (% of total freshwater withdrawal)	47	71	53
Access to improved water source (% of total population)	83	89	93
Rural (% of rural population)	70	69	82
Urban (% of urban population)	85	96	97
Access to improved sanitation (% of total population)	68	75	81
Rural (% of rural population)	48	44	61
Urban (% of urban population)	71	84	91
Environment and health			
ARI prevalence (% of children under age 5)	..		
Diarrhea prevalence (% of children under age 5)	..		
Under-five mortality rate (per 1,000 live births)	19	31	28
National accounting aggregates, 2004			
Gross savings (% of GNI)	35.2	22.7	23.1
Consumption of fixed capital (% of GNI)	12.2	12.1	11.5
Education expenditure (% of GNI)	4.4	4.4	4.5
Energy depletion (% of GNI)	34.7	7.2	11.2
Mineral depletion (% of GNI)	0.4	1.1	0.6
Net forest depletion (% of GNI)	0.0	0.0	0.0
CO_2 damage (% of GNI)	0.9	0.5	0.9
Particulate emission damage (% of GNI)	0.0	0.6	0.7
Adjusted net savings (% of GNI)	−8.6	5.6	2.6

Vietnam

Environmental strategy/action plan prepared in ..

	Country data	Group data East Asia & Pacific	Low income
Population (millions)	82.2	1,870	2,343
Urban population (% of total)	26.2	40.6	30.6
GDP ($ billions)	45.2	2,651	1,239
GNI per capita, *World Bank Atlas* method ($)	540	1,416	507
Agriculture			
Land area (1,000 sq. km)	325	15,885	29,192
Agricultural land (% of land area)	30	51	45
Irrigated land (% of cropland)	33.4	..	23.9
Fertilizer consumption (100 grams/ha of arable land)	2,993	2,296	646
Population density, rural (people/sq. km of arable land)	904	559	524
Forests and biodiversity			
Forest area (% of land area)	39.7	28.4	24.8
Annual deforestation (% change, 1990–2005)	–2.5	–0.2	0.5
Nationally protected areas (% of total land area)	3.7	..	7.7
Mammal species, total known	279		
Mammal species, threatened	41		
Bird species, total known	837		
Bird species, threatened	41		
GEF benefits index for biodiversity (0–100)	11.7		
Energy			
GDP per unit of energy use (2000 PPP $/kg oil equiv)	4.4	4.6	4.2
Energy use per capita (kg oil equiv)	544	1,007	501
Energy from combustible renewables & waste (% of tot.)	52.9	17.7	48.9
Energy imports, net (% of energy use)	–23	–2	–4
Electric power consumption per capita (kWh)	433	1,184	358
Electricity generated by coal (% of total)	17.7	69.4	46.3
Emissions and pollution			
CO_2 emissions per unit of GDP (kg/2000 PPP $ of GDP)	0.4	0.5	0.4
CO_2 emissions per capita (metric tons)	0.8	2.4	0.8
Particulate matter (urban-pop.-weighted avg., µg/cu. m)	66	80	89
Passenger cars (per 1,000 people)	..	12	6
Water and sanitation			
Internal freshwater resources per capita (cu. m)	4,461	5,062	3,456
Freshwater withdrawal			
Total (% of internal resources)	19.5	10.2	15.5
Agriculture (% of total freshwater withdrawal)	68	74	88
Access to improved water source (% of total population)	73	78	75
Rural (% of rural population)	67	69	69
Urban (% of urban population)	93	92	89
Access to improved sanitation (% of total population)	41	49	36
Rural (% of rural population)	26	35	24
Urban (% of urban population)	84	72	61
Environment and health			
ARI prevalence (% of children under age 5)	9.3		
Diarrhea prevalence (% of children under age 5)	11.3		
Under-five mortality rate (per 1,000 live births)	23	37	122
National accounting aggregates, 2004			
Gross savings (% of GNI)	32.7	39.1	22.7
Consumption of fixed capital (% of GNI)	9.2	10.5	9.2
Education expenditure (% of GNI)	2.8	2.3	3.4
Energy depletion (% of GNI)	9.5	4.1	6.7
Mineral depletion (% of GNI)	0.0	0.4	0.4
Net forest depletion (% of GNI)	0.6	0.0	0.7
CO_2 damage (% of GNI)	1.1	1.2	1.1
Particulate emission damage (% of GNI)	0.5	1.2	0.8
Adjusted net savings (% of GNI)	14.6	23.9	7.3

Virgin Islands (U.S.)

Environmental strategy/action plan prepared in ..

	Country data	Group data High income
Population (millions)	0.1	1,004
Urban population (% of total)	93.8	78.5
GDP ($ billions)	..	32,900
GNI per capita, *World Bank Atlas* method ($)	..	32,112

Agriculture
Land area (1,000 sq. km)	0	33,018
Agricultural land (% of land area)	17	38
Irrigated land (% of cropland)	..	11.9
Fertilizer consumption (100 grams/ha of arable land)	3,000	1,205
Population density, rural (people/sq. km of arable land)	362	331

Forests and biodiversity
Forest area (% of land area)	28.6	29.3
Annual deforestation (% change, 1990–2005)	1.1	–0.1
Nationally protected areas (% of total land area)	..	..
Mammal species, total known	11	
Mammal species, threatened	..	
Bird species, total known	223	
Bird species, threatened	..	
GEF benefits index for biodiversity (0–100)	0.3	

Energy
GDP per unit of energy use (2000 PPP $/kg oil equiv)	..	5.2
Energy use per capita (kg oil equiv)	..	5,410
Energy from combustible renewables & waste (% of tot.)	..	3.0
Energy imports, net (% of energy use)	..	19
Electric power consumption per capita (kWh)	..	9,503
Electricity generated by coal (% of total)	..	38.2

Emissions and pollution
CO_2 emissions per unit of GDP (kg/2000 PPP $ of GDP)	..	0.5
CO_2 emissions per capita (metric tons)	92.8	12.8
Particulate matter (urban-pop.-weighted avg., μg/cu. m)	43	29
Passenger cars (per 1,000 people)	..	433

Water and sanitation
Internal freshwater resources per capita (cu. m)	..	9,703
Freshwater withdrawal		
Total (% of internal resources)	..	10.4
Agriculture (% of total freshwater withdrawal)	..	42
Access to improved water source (% of total population)	..	99
Rural (% of rural population)	..	98
Urban (% of urban population)	..	100
Access to improved sanitation (% of total population)	..	..
Rural (% of rural population)	..	..
Urban (% of urban population)	..	..

Environment and health
ARI prevalence (% of children under age 5)	..	
Diarrhea prevalence (% of children under age 5)	..	
Under-five mortality rate (per 1,000 live births)	..	7

National accounting aggregates, 2004
Gross savings (% of GNI)	..	19.4
Consumption of fixed capital (% of GNI)	..	13.2
Education expenditure (% of GNI)	..	4.6
Energy depletion (% of GNI)	..	1.4
Mineral depletion (% of GNI)	..	0.0
Net forest depletion (% of GNI)	..	0.0
CO_2 damage (% of GNI)	..	0.3
Particulate emission damage (% of GNI)	..	0.4
Adjusted net savings (% of GNI)	..	8.7

West Bank and Gaza

Environmental strategy/action plan prepared in ..

	Country data	Group data Middle East & North Africa	Group data Lower middle income
Population (millions)	3.5	300	2,442
Urban population (% of total)	..	56.3	48.7
GDP ($ billions)	3.5	547	4,165
GNI per capita, *World Bank Atlas* method ($)	1,120	1,972	1,686
Agriculture			
Land area (1,000 sq. km)	..	8,955	38,470
Agricultural land (% of land area)	..	23	43
Irrigated land (% of cropland)	..	32.5	23.1
Fertilizer consumption (100 grams/ha of arable land)	..	842	1,530
Population density, rural (people/sq. km of arable land)	..	670	523
Forests and biodiversity			
Forest area (% of land area)	..	2.4	30.7
Annual deforestation (% change, 1990–2005)	..	–0.5	0.1
Nationally protected areas (% of total land area)	..	4.2	7.7
Mammal species, total known	..		
Mammal species, threatened	..		
Bird species, total known	..		
Bird species, threatened	..		
GEF benefits index for biodiversity (0–100)	..		
Energy			
GDP per unit of energy use (2000 PPP $/kg oil equiv)	..	4.2	4.6
Energy use per capita (kg oil equiv)	..	1,144	1,090
Energy from combustible renewables & waste (% of tot.)	..	1.3	14.6
Energy imports, net (% of energy use)	..	–129	–14
Electric power consumption per capita (kWh)	..	1,212	1,329
Electricity generated by coal (% of total)	..	3.0	49.4
Emissions and pollution			
CO_2 emissions per unit of GDP (kg/2000 PPP $ of GDP)	..	0.7	0.5
CO_2 emissions per capita (metric tons)	..	3.2	2.6
Particulate matter (urban-pop.-weighted avg., µg/cu. m)	..	90	70
Passenger cars (per 1,000 people)	..	..	29
Water and sanitation			
Internal freshwater resources per capita (cu. m)	13	761	7,295
Freshwater withdrawal			
Total (% of internal resources)	..	105.0	7.7
Agriculture (% of total freshwater withdrawal)	..	89	75
Access to improved water source (% of total population)	94	88	81
Rural (% of rural population)	86	79	70
Urban (% of urban population)	97	95	93
Access to improved sanitation (% of total population)	76	75	57
Rural (% of rural population)	70	56	39
Urban (% of urban population)	78	89	78
Environment and health			
ARI prevalence (% of children under age 5)	17.0		
Diarrhea prevalence (% of children under age 5)	..		
Under-five mortality rate (per 1,000 live births)	..	55	40
National accounting aggregates, 2004			
Gross savings (% of GNI)	..	30.0	32.1
Consumption of fixed capital (% of GNI)	..	11.2	10.8
Education expenditure (% of GNI)	..	4.5	2.9
Energy depletion (% of GNI)	..	27.3	6.5
Mineral depletion (% of GNI)	..	0.1	0.5
Net forest depletion (% of GNI)	..	0.1	0.0
CO_2 damage (% of GNI)	..	1.2	1.1
Particulate emission damage (% of GNI)	..	0.9	1.0
Adjusted net savings (% of GNI)	..	–6.2	15.1

Yemen, Rep.

Environmental strategy/action plan prepared in **1996**

	Country data	Middle East & North Africa	Low income
Group data			
Population (millions)	20.3	300	2,343
Urban population (% of total)	26.0	56.3	30.6
GDP ($ billions)	12.8	547	1,239
GNI per capita, *World Bank Atlas* method ($)	550	1,972	507
Agriculture			
Land area (1,000 sq. km)	528	8,955	29,192
Agricultural land (% of land area)	34	23	45
Irrigated land (% of cropland)	33.0	32.5	23.9
Fertilizer consumption (100 grams/ha of arable land)	75	842	646
Population density, rural (people/sq. km of arable land)	953	670	524
Forests and biodiversity			
Forest area (% of land area)	1.0	2.4	24.8
Annual deforestation (% change, 1990–2005)	0.0	−0.5	0.5
Nationally protected areas (% of total land area)	..	4.2	7.7
Mammal species, total known	74		
Mammal species, threatened	6		
Bird species, total known	385		
Bird species, threatened	14		
GEF benefits index for biodiversity (0–100)	3.4		
Energy			
GDP per unit of energy use (2000 PPP $/kg oil equiv)	2.8	4.2	4.2
Energy use per capita (kg oil equiv)	289	1,144	501
Energy from combustible renewables & waste (% of tot.)	1.4	1.3	48.9
Energy imports, net (% of energy use)	−284	−129	−4
Electric power consumption per capita (kWh)	158	1,212	358
Electricity generated by coal (% of total)	..	3.0	46.3
Emissions and pollution			
CO_2 emissions per unit of GDP (kg/2000 PPP $ of GDP)	0.6	0.7	0.4
CO_2 emissions per capita (metric tons)	0.7	3.2	0.8
Particulate matter (urban-pop.-weighted avg., µg/cu. m)	82	90	89
Passenger cars (per 1,000 people)	..	..	6
Water and sanitation			
Internal freshwater resources per capita (cu. m)	202	761	3,456
Freshwater withdrawal			
Total (% of internal resources)	161.7	105.0	15.5
Agriculture (% of total freshwater withdrawal)	95	89	88
Access to improved water source (% of total population)	69	88	75
Rural (% of rural population)	68	79	69
Urban (% of urban population)	74	95	89
Access to improved sanitation (% of total population)	30	75	36
Rural (% of rural population)	14	56	24
Urban (% of urban population)	76	89	61
Environment and health			
ARI prevalence (% of children under age 5)	24.0		
Diarrhea prevalence (% of children under age 5)	..		
Under-five mortality rate (per 1,000 live births)	111	55	122
National accounting aggregates, 2004			
Gross savings (% of GNI)	12.9	30.0	22.7
Consumption of fixed capital (% of GNI)	10.0	11.2	9.2
Education expenditure (% of GNI)	..	4.5	3.4
Energy depletion (% of GNI)	44.2	27.3	6.7
Mineral depletion (% of GNI)	0.0	0.1	0.4
Net forest depletion (% of GNI)	0.0	0.1	0.7
CO_2 damage (% of GNI)	0.7	1.2	1.1
Particulate emission damage (% of GNI)	0.5	0.9	0.8
Adjusted net savings (% of GNI)	..	−6.2	7.3

Zambia

Environmental strategy/action plan prepared in **1994**

	Country data	Group data Sub-Saharan Africa	Low income
Population (millions)	11.5	726	2,343
Urban population (% of total)	36.2	36.4	30.6
GDP ($ billions)	5.4	523	1,239
GNI per capita, *World Bank Atlas* method ($)	400	601	507
Agriculture			
Land area (1,000 sq. km)	743	23,596	29.192
Agricultural land (% of land area)	47	44	45
Irrigated land (% of cropland)	2.9	3.6	23.9
Fertilizer consumption (100 grams/ha of arable land)	124	136	646
Population density, rural (people/sq. km of arable land)	137	355	524
Forests and biodiversity			
Forest area (% of land area)	57.1	26.5	24.8
Annual deforestation (% change, 1990–2005)	0.9	0.6	0.5
Nationally protected areas (% of total land area)	31.9	8.7	7.7
Mammal species, total known	255		
Mammal species, threatened	11		
Bird species, total known	770		
Bird species, threatened	12		
GEF benefits index for biodiversity (0–100)	5.0		
Energy			
GDP per unit of energy use (2000 PPP $/kg oil equiv)	1.4	2.8	4.2
Energy use per capita (kg oil equiv)	592	681	501
Energy from combustible renewables & waste (% of tot.)	80.8	57.4	48.9
Energy imports, net (% of energy use)	5	−59	−4
Electric power consumption per capita (kWh)	576	513	358
Electricity generated by coal (% of total)	0.2	68.0	46.3
Emissions and pollution			
CO_2 emissions per unit of GDP (kg/2000 PPP $ of GDP)	0.2	0.4	0.4
CO_2 emissions per capita (metric tons)	0.2	0.7	0.8
Particulate matter (urban-pop.-weighted avg., μg/cu. m)	71	73	89
Passenger cars (per 1,000 people)	..	..	6
Water and sanitation			
Internal freshwater resources per capita (cu. m)	6,987	5,353	3,456
Freshwater withdrawal			
Total (% of internal resources)	2.2	3.1	15.5
Agriculture (% of total freshwater withdrawal)	76	87	88
Access to improved water source (% of total population)	55	58	75
Rural (% of rural population)	36	45	69
Urban (% of urban population)	90	82	89
Access to improved sanitation (% of total population)	45	36	36
Rural (% of rural population)	32	26	24
Urban (% of urban population)	68	55	61
Environment and health			
ARI prevalence (% of children under age 5)	43.1		
Diarrhea prevalence (% of children under age 5)	21.2		
Under-five mortality rate (per 1,000 live births)	182	168	122
National accounting aggregates, 2004			
Gross savings (% of GNI)	13.3	17.1	22.7
Consumption of fixed capital (% of GNI)	9.4	10.9	9.2
Education expenditure (% of GNI)	2.5	3.9	3.4
Energy depletion (% of GNI)	0.0	9.8	6.7
Mineral depletion (% of GNI)	3.7	0.4	0.4
Net forest depletion (% of GNI)	0.0	0.6	0.7
CO_2 damage (% of GNI)	0.3	0.7	1.1
Particulate emission damage (% of GNI)	1.0	0.5	0.8
Adjusted net savings (% of GNI)	1.4	−1.9	7.3

Zimbabwe

Environmental strategy/action plan prepared in **1987**

	Country data	Sub-Saharan Africa	Low income
		Group data	
Population (millions)	12.9	726	2,343
Urban population (% of total)	35.4	36.4	30.6
GDP ($ billions)	4.7	523	1,239
GNI per capita, *World Bank Atlas* method ($)	620	601	507
Agriculture			
Land area (1,000 sq. km)	387	23,596	29,192
Agricultural land (% of land area)	53	44	45
Irrigated land (% of cropland)	5.2	3.6	23.9
Fertilizer consumption (100 grams/ha of arable land)	342	136	646
Population density, rural (people/sq. km of arable land)	260	355	524
Forests and biodiversity			
Forest area (% of land area)	45.3	26.5	24.8
Annual deforestation (% change, 1990–2005)	1.4	0.6	0.5
Nationally protected areas (% of total land area)	12.1	8.7	7.7
Mammal species, total known	222		
Mammal species, threatened	8		
Bird species, total known	661		
Bird species, threatened	10		
GEF benefits index for biodiversity (0–100)	2.1		
Energy			
GDP per unit of energy use (2000 PPP $/kg oil equiv)	2.6	2.8	4.2
Energy use per capita (kg oil equiv)	752	681	501
Energy from combustible renewables & waste (% of tot.)	60.5	57.4	48.9
Energy imports, net (% of energy use)	12	−59	−4
Electric power consumption per capita (kWh)	819	513	358
Electricity generated by coal (% of total)	38.9	68.0	46.3
Emissions and pollution			
CO_2 emissions per unit of GDP (kg/2000 PPP $ of GDP)	0.5	0.4	0.4
CO_2 emissions per capita (metric tons)	1.0	0.7	0.8
Particulate matter (urban-pop.-weighted avg., µg/cu. m)	43	73	89
Passenger cars (per 1,000 people)	44	..	6
Water and sanitation			
Internal freshwater resources per capita (cu. m)	948	5,353	3,456
Freshwater withdrawal			
Total (% of internal resources)	34.3	3.1	15.5
Agriculture (% of total freshwater withdrawal)	79	87	88
Access to improved water source (% of total population)	83	58	75
Rural (% of rural population)	74	45	69
Urban (% of urban population)	100	82	89
Access to improved sanitation (% of total population)	57	36	36
Rural (% of rural population)	51	26	24
Urban (% of urban population)	69	55	61
Environment and health			
ARI prevalence (% of children under age 5)	..		
Diarrhea prevalence (% of children under age 5)	13.9		
Under-five mortality rate (per 1,000 live births)	129	168	122
National accounting aggregates, 2004			
Gross savings (% of GNI)	3.2	17.1	22.7
Consumption of fixed capital (% of GNI)	8.6	10.9	9.2
Education expenditure (% of GNI)	6.9	3.9	3.4
Energy depletion (% of GNI)	0.6	9.8	6.7
Mineral depletion (% of GNI)	1.3	0.4	0.4
Net forest depletion (% of GNI)	0.0	0.6	0.7
CO_2 damage (% of GNI)	1.6	0.7	1.1
Particulate emission damage (% of GNI)	0.4	0.5	0.8
Adjusted net savings (% of GNI)	−2.5	−1.9	7.3

Glossary

Access to an improved water source is the percentage of the population with reasonable access to an adequate amount of water from an improved source, such as a household connection, public standpipe, borehole, protected well or spring, or rainwater collection. Unimproved sources include vendors, tanker trucks, and unprotected wells and springs. Reasonable access to an adequate amount is defined as the availability of at least 20 liters a person a day from a source within 1 kilometer of the dwelling. (World Health Organization; data are for 2002)

Access to improved sanitation is the percentage of population with access to at least adequate excreta disposal facilities (private or shared, but not public) that can effectively prevent human, animal, and insect contact with excreta. Improved facilities range from simple but protected pit latrines to flush toilets with a sewerage connection. To be effective, facilities must be correctly constructed and properly maintained. (World Health Organization; data are for 2002)

Acute respiratory infection (ARI) prevalence refers to the percentage of children under age 5 with acute respiratory infection in the two weeks prior to the survey. (United Nations Children's Fund; data are for 1998–2004)

Adjusted net savings equal net savings plus education expenditures minus energy depletion, mineral depletion, net forest depletion, and particulate matter and carbon dioxide damage. (World Bank; data are for 2004)

Agricultural land refers to arable land, land under permanent crops, and permanent pastures. Arable land includes land defined by the Food and Agriculture Organization as land under temporary crops (double-cropped areas are counted once), temporary meadows for mowing or for pasture, land under market or kitchen gardens, and land temporarily fallow. Land abandoned as a result of shifting cultivation is excluded. Land under permanent crops is land cultivated with crops that occupy the land for long periods and need not be replanted after each harvest, such as cocoa, coffee, and rubber. This category includes land under flowering shrubs, fruit trees, nut trees, and vines, but excludes land under trees grown for wood or timber. Permanent pasture is land used for five or more years for forage, including natural and cultivated crops. (Food and Agriculture Organization; data are for 2003)

Annual deforestation refers to the permanent conversion of natural forest area to other uses, including shifting cultivation, permanent agriculture, ranching, settlements, and infrastructure development. Deforested areas do not include areas logged but intended for regeneration or areas degraded by fuelwood gathering, acid precipitation, or forest fires. Negative numbers indicate an increase in forest areas. (Food and Agriculture Organization; data are for 1990–2005)

Bird species, threatened, are the number of birds classified by the World Conservation Union as endangered, vulnerable, rare, indeterminate, out of danger, or insufficiently known. (World Conservation Monitoring Center and World Conservation Union; data are for 2004)

Bird species, total breeding, are listed for countries included within their breeding or wintering ranges. (World Conservation Monitoring Center and World Conservation Union; data are for 2004)

Carbon dioxide damage is estimated at $20 per ton of carbon (the unit damage in 1995 U.S. dollars) times the number of tons of carbon emitted. (World Bank estimates; data are for 2004)

Carbon dioxide emissions per capita are emissions stemming from the burning of fossil fuels and the manufacture of cement divided by population. They include carbon dioxide produced during consumption of solid, liquid, and gas fuels and gas flaring. (Carbon Dioxide Information Analysis Center; data are for 2002)

Carbon dioxide emissions per unit of GDP are carbon dioxide emissions in kilograms per unit of 2000 GDP in purchasing power parity (PPP) terms. PPP GDP is gross domestic product converted to international dollars using PPP rates. An international dollar has the same purchasing power over GDP as a U.S. dollar has in the United States. (Carbon Dioxide Information Analysis Center and World Bank; data are for 2002)

Consumption of fixed capital represents the replacement value of capital used up in the process of production. (United Nations; data are extrapolated from the most recent year available)

Diarrhea prevalence refers to the percentage of children under age five who had diarrhea in the two weeks prior to the survey. (United Nations Children's Fund; data are for 1998–2004)

Education expenditure refers to public current operating expenditures in education, including wages and salaries and excluding capital investments in buildings and equipment. (United Nations; data are extrapolated from the most recent year available)

Electric power consumption refers to the production of power plants and combined heat and power plants, minus transmission, distribution, and transformation losses and own use by heat and power plants plus imports minus exports. (International Energy Agency; data are for 2003)

Electricity generated by coal is coal as a percentage of total inputs to the generation of electricity. (International Energy Agency; data are for 2003)

Energy depletion is equal to the product of unit resource rents and the physical quantities of energy extracted. It covers crude oil, natural gas, and coal. (A wide range of data sources and estimation methods were used to arrive at resource depletion estimates and are described in World Bank, 2006, *Where Is the Wealth of Nations? Measuring Capital for the XXI Century*, Washington DC; data are for 2004)

Energy from combustible renewables and waste comprises solid biomass, liquid biomass, biogas, industrial waste, and municipal waste, measured as percentage of total energy use (International Energy Agency; data are for 2003)

Energy imports, net, are calculated as energy use less production, both measured in oil equivalents. A negative value indicates that the country is a net exporter. (Energy production and use from International Energy Agency; data are for 2003)

Energy use per capita refers to apparent consumption, which is equal to indigenous production plus imports and stock changes, minus exports and fuels supplied to ships and aircraft engaged in international transport. (International Energy Agency; data are for 2003)

Environmental strategies and action plans provide a comprehensive, cross-sectoral analysis of conservation and resource management issues to help integrate environmental concerns into the development process. They include national conservation strategies, national environmental action plans, national environmental management strategies, and national sustainable development strategies. The year shown for a country refers to the year in which a strategy or action plan was adopted. (World Resources Institute, International Institute for Environment and Development, World Conservation Union, and World Bank)

Fertilizer consumption measures the quantity of plant nutrients used per unit of arable land. Fertilizer products cover nitrogenous, potash, and phosphate fertilizers (including ground rock phosphate). The time reference for fertilizer consumption is the crop year (July through June). (Food and Agriculture Organization; data are for 2002)

Forest area is land under natural or planted stands of trees, whether productive or not. (Food and Agriculture Organization; data are for 2005)

Freshwater withdrawals, agriculture, are withdrawals for irrigation and livestock production as a percentage of total freshwater withdrawal. (World Resources Institute; data are for various years; for details see *World Development Indicators 2006, Primary Data Documentation*)

Freshwater withdrawals, total, refer to total water withdrawal, not counting evaporation losses from storage basins. Withdrawals also include water from desalination plants in countries where they are a significant source. Withdrawals can exceed 100 percent of internal renewable resources because river flows from other countries are not included, because extraction from nonrenewable aquifers or desalination plants is considerable, or because there is significant water reuse. (Food and Agriculture Organization and World Resources Institute; data are for various years; for details see *World Development Indicators 2006, Primary Data Documentation*)

GDP is gross domestic product and measures the total output of goods and services for final use occurring within the domestic territory of a given country, regardless of the allocation to domestic and foreign claims. GDP at purchaser values (market prices) is the sum of gross value added by all resident and nonresident producers in the economy plus any taxes and minus any subsidies not included in the value of the products. It is calculated without deductions for depreciation of fabricated assets or for depletion and degradation of natural resources. (World Bank, Organisation for Economic Co-operation and Development, and United Nations; data are for 2004)

GDP per unit of energy use is the 2000 GDP in purchasing power parity (PPP) terms per kilogram of oil equivalent of energy use. PPP GDP is gross domestic product converted to international dollars using PPP rates. An international dollar has the same purchasing power over GDP as a U.S. dollar has in the United States. (International Energy Agency and World Bank; data are for 2003)

GEF benefits index for biodiversity is a composite index of relative biodiversity potential for each country developed by the Global Environment Facility, based on the species represented in each country, their threat status, and the diversity of habitat types in each country. The index shown in the tables has been normalized so that values run from 0 (no biodiversity potential) to 100 (maximum biodiversity potential) (World Bank; estimates are for 2005)

GNI per capita is gross national income divided by midyear population. GNI is gross domestic product (GDP) plus net receipts of primary income (employee compensation and property income) from abroad. GDP is the sum of value added by all resident producers plus any product taxes (minus subsidies) not included in the valuation of output. GNI per capita is in current U.S. dollars, converted using the *World Bank Atlas* method (see *World Development Indicators 2006, Statistical Methods*). (World Bank, Organisation for Economic Co-operation and Development, and United Nations; data are for 2004)

Gross savings are the difference between gross national income and public and private consumption plus net current transfers. (World Bank, Organisation for Economic Co-operation and Development, and United Nations; data are for 2004)

Internal freshwater resources are internal renewable resources, which include flows of rivers and groundwater from rainfall in the country, but do not include river flows from other countries. Freshwater resources per capita are calculated using the World Bank's population estimates. (Food and Agriculture Organization and World Resources Institute; estimates are for 2004)

Irrigated land is area purposely provided with water, including land irrigated by controlled flooding. Cropland refers to arable land and land used for permanent crops. (Food and Agriculture Organization; data are for 2003)

Land area is a country's total land area, excluding area under inland water bodies, national claims to continental shelf, and exclusive economic zones. In most cases the definition of inland water bodies includes major rivers and lakes. (Food and Agriculture Organization; data are for 2003)

Mammal species, threatened, are the number of mammal species classified by the World Conservation Union as endangered, vulnerable, rare, indeterminate, out of danger, or insufficiently known. (World Conservation Monitoring Center and World Conservation Union; data are for 2004)

Mammal species, total known, exclude whales and porpoises. (World Conservation Monitoring Center and World Conservation Union; data are for 2004)

Mineral depletion is equal to the product of unit resource rents and the physical quantities of minerals extracted. It refers to bauxite, copper, iron, lead, nickel, phosphate, tin, gold, silver and zinc. (A wide range of data sources and estimation methods used to arrive at resource depletion estimates are described in World Bank, 2006, *Where Is the Wealth of Nations? Measuring Capital for the XXI Century*, Washington DC; data are for 2004)

Nationally protected areas are totally or partially protected areas of at least 1,000 hectares that are designated as national parks, natural monuments, nature reserves or wildlife sanctuaries, protected landscapes and seascapes, or scientific reserves. The indicator includes IUCN–protected area categories I–VI. (World Conservation Monitoring Center; data are tentative and for most recent years reported in 2004)

Net forest depletion is the product of unit resource rents and the excess of roundwood harvest over natural growth. If growth exceeds harvest, this figure is zero. (Food and Agriculture Organization and World Bank estimates of natural growth; data are for 2004)

Particulate emission damage is calculated as the willingness to pay to reduce the risk of illness and death attributable to particulate emissions. (World Bank estimates; data are for 2004)

Particulate matter is fine suspended particulates of less than 10 microns in diameter that are capable of penetrating deep into the respiratory tract and causing damage. It is the population-weighted average of all cities in the country with a population greater than 100,000. (World Bank estimates; data are for 2002)

Passenger cars refer to road motor vehicles, other than two-wheelers, intended for the carriage of passengers and designed to seat no more than nine people including the driver. (International Road Federation; data are for 2003)

Population includes all residents who are present regardless of legal status or citizenship except for refugees not permanently settled in the country of asylum, who are generally considered part of the population of their country of origin. The values shown are midyear estimates. (World Bank and United Nations; data are for 2004)

Population density, rural, is the rural population divided by the arable land area. Rural population is estimated as the difference between the total population and urban population. (See *urban population*; data are for 2004)

Under-five mortality rate is the probability that a newborn baby will die before reaching age 5, if subject to current age-specific mortality rates. (United Nations and United Nations Children's Fund; data are for 2004)

Urban population is the share of the midyear population living in areas defined as urban in each country. (United Nations; data are for 2004)